Unions, Parties, and Political Development

UNIONS, PARTIES, AND POLITICAL DEVELOPMENT

A Study of Mineworkers in Zambia

by Robert H. Bates

New Haven and London, Yale University Press

1971

Designed by John O. C. McCrillis
and set in Granjon type.
Printed in the United States of America by
The Colonial Press Inc., Clinton, Massachusetts.

Distributed in Great Britain, Europe, and Africa by
Yale University Press, Ltd., London; in Canada by
McGill-Queen's University Press, Montreal; in Mexico
by Centro Interamericano de Libros Académicos,
Mexico City; in Central and South America by Kaiman
& Polon, Inc., New York City; in Australasia by
Australia and New Zealand Book Co., Pty., Ltd.,
Artarmon, New South Wales; in India by UBS Publishers'
Distributors Pvt., Ltd., Delhi; in Japan by John
Weatherhill, Inc., Tokyo.

To Margaret

Contents

Charts

Acknowledgments

The research for this study was sponsored by the Foreign Area Fellowship Program of the Social Science Research Council and American Council of Learned Societies and by a grant to the Department of Political Science of the Massachusetts Institute of Technology from the National Science Foundation (Doctoral Dissertation Research in Political Science, Grant Number G.S. 1210). The research committee of the Division of Humanities and Social Sciences, California Institute of Technology, helped to defray the expenses of manuscript preparation.

Before proceeding to Zambia, I studied in the Department of Social Anthropology of Manchester University, and I owe a great debt to the members of the department. Their broad factual knowledge of the copperbelt, as well as their theoretical orientation toward tribe, class, and urban society in Zambia, accelerated my enculturation to the field situation and deeply influenced my interpretation of copperbelt society and politics. In particular, I wish to thank Professors Bruce Kapferer, Norman Long, and J. Clyde Mitchell.

I am also indebted to Professor Lionel Caplan, Mr. Michael Mann, and Mr. Grenson Lukwesa of the School of Oriental and African Studies of the University of London. Through Dr. Caplan, I was introduced to the field of social anthropology, and this was of great help to me. Mr. Mann, Mr. Lukwesa, and later Mr. Chishimba Katele of Manchester University, introduced me to the rigors and delights of Chibemba, the predominant language of the copperbelt. What modest linguistic skills I attained I owe to their patient efforts.

To persons in Zambia, I will remain a perpetual debtor. I can mention only a few of those to whom I owe particular thanks. The others may be assured that, while unmentioned, their assistance is not forgotten.

I wish to thank the staff of the National Archives of Zambia for their generous cooperation. I wish also to thank the University of Zambia and the Institute for Social Research for granting me the position of Research Affiliate while in Zambia. Professors William Tordoff and Richard Sklar of the Department of Political Science, and Professor Alastair Heron of the Institute for Social Research, were of the utmost assistance to me. I am indebted to Dr. Trevor Coombe and to all the Coombe family for their friendship and hospitality throughout the period of my research, and to Elena Berger, a friend and co-worker in the field.

The support of the copper mining industry for academic research in Zambia extended to my project as well. Dennis Etheredge of the Anglo-American Corporation, David Pownall of Rhokana Corporation, and Norrys Davis of the Copper Industry Service Bureau were of particular assistance to me; and company officials at all levels generously cooperated with this research.

I am grateful to the officials of the Head Office and Rhokana branch of the Mineworkers' Union of Zambia for their patience and good-humored assistance. They gave abundantly of their time in a period when there were many claimants to it.

I wish to express my gratitude to Mr. Misheck Nyondo, registrar of trade unions, and Mr. Emmanuel Kasonde, permanent secretary of the Ministry of Labour, for their cooperation with this project. To Mr. Nyondo, in particular, I owe special thanks for making me begin to understand what it means to be a trade unionist, a politician, and an African in modern Zambia.

My debt to the officials of the United National Independence Party is a great one. At a time of crisis in Zambia and in Southern Africa as a whole, they were still able to accommodate my research. My hope is that the information and interpretations of this study can assist them in attaining the goals of development and justice to which they aspire.

In particular, I wish to thank the members of the Central Committee of UNIP who permitted me to carry on my research even while unwilling officially to back it. I am specially indebted to the party officials of the Kitwe Region. While not promoting my research activities, they nonetheless extended their hospitality to me.

I wish also to thank the staff of the Mindolo Ecumenical Center, and the director, Mr. Grenville-Gray, and the assistant director, Mr. Jason Mvula, who extended Mindolo's facilities to me.

My thanks also go to Mr. Phillip Emanuel of the Afrika Studiecentrum, Leiden, Holland; Dr. Lars Clausen of the University of Münster; and Dr. David Mulford of White, Weld, & Co., London. The discussions I had with them during my return from the field helped to place my work in perspective.

I am deeply indebted to the following members of the Department of Political Science at the Massachusetts Institute of Technology: Professors Willard Johnson, Daniel Lerner, Lucian Pye, Robert Rotberg, and Myron Weiner, whose assistance extended from the time of preparation for this study to the time of its completion. I wish to express my gratitude for their advice and encouragement, as well as for their persistent and lucid criticism, though not all was accepted.

Professors Richard Sklar, Elliot Berg, Kenneth Frederick, and J. Clyde Mitchell read and extensively criticized the manuscript, helping me to avoid errors of fact and analysis.

Jo Anne Carroll, Judith Preckshot, Margaret Robison, Sarah Lee Harris, and especially Constance Viancour devoted many hours to typing and retyping this study; their patience, skill, and good humor are deeply appreciated. I am also grateful to Mrs. Nancy Pine for editing and correcting the manuscript.

Last, but foremost, I wish to thank Margaret Rouse Bates for her numerous contributions to this work, both as wife and scholar. I dedicate the book to her.

With so much help, clearly the faults in this work are my responsibility alone.

R. H. B.

Pasadena, California
January 1971

1 Labor and the Study of Development

Like most new nations of the world, Zambia aspires to rapid economic development. Zambia shares another major characteristic with many of its Third World partners: an economy based upon the production of a single major commodity—in this case, copper. Given the country's reliance on copper and its aspirations for rapid economic growth, the control of the behavior of the copper miners represents a crucial political task for Zambia's ambitious elite. This book will analyze the attempts of the government of Zambia to constrain the behavior of the African mineworkers in accord with its development objectives.

In seeking rapid development, the government of Zambia elaborates a labor policy that conflicts with many of the aspirations and demands of mine labor. Out of a regard for the national interest in rapid economic growth, the government asks the workers to restrain their wage demands, eschew strike action, work hard, and defer to the authority of their supervisors. To produce conformity with its policies, the government enlists the support of the two primary organizations that span the gap between the governing elite at the national level and the workers in the local mining communities: the Mineworkers' Union* and the United National Independence Party (UNIP), the governing party in Zambia.

Like many other nations, Zambia has been unable to reverse the private preoccupations of its workers. In explaining the low level of success achieved by the government's policies toward mine labor, this study focuses on the capacity of the union and

---

* This name, which I will use in referring to the union, is the common element to all the names it has taken throughout its history: the Northern Rhodesia African Mineworkers' Trade Union, the Northern Rhodesia African Mineworkers' Union, the Zambia Mineworkers' Union, and the Mineworkers' Union of Zambia.

party structures to regulate and control the behavior of their members in the mining industry. Since these structures have been charged with carrying out government labor policy, analyzing their characteristics can help to account for the degree to which public policy prevails over private interest in the African labor force.

One of the primary concerns in the study of labor and development is the content of labor policy. The work of Harbison, Kerr, Dunlop, and Myers represents perhaps the most concentrated effort to deal with this concern.[1] Drawing on case studies in India, Italy, Egypt, France, Russia, Japan, England, and other nations, the scholars find no single pattern of labor policy. Instead, they find that the kinds of labor policies adopted by different countries correspond to the kinds of elites which govern those countries. Defining five kinds of elites—middle class, colonial, dynastic, revolutionary, and nationalist—they assert, "Each of these elite groups has a strategy by which it seeks to order the surrounding society in a consistent fashion."[2] Policies toward labor are consistent with this central strategy.

The primary strategy of nationalist elites is to defend national sovereignty and attain rapid progress, and to achieve both through rapid industrialization. Falling within the category of nationalist elites and sharing its orientation toward labor, the government of Zambia seeks "rapid progress" and views the workers as economic "patriots." It seeks to "control" industrial conflict, utilize "nationalism" as an appeal for cooperation, and "replace" foreign workers with locals. Moreover, the government follows policies toward labor organizations which Harbison, Kerr, Dunlop, and Myers suggest are typical of nationalist elites, striving to consolidate "loyal" unions and give them advantages not shared by less cooperative labor organizations. The case of the Zambian copper miners thus falls within the class of cases that the authors designated as "nationalist industrializing," and contributes additional information about cases of this kind.[3]

While Harbison and his colleagues were predominantly concerned with accounting for variations in labor policies among industrializing nations, and their typology of elites represents an attempt to account for such differences,[4] they gave relatively little attention to explaining the levels of success achieved by the labor policies of these elites. This work, therefore, will move beyond these earlier efforts and focus on the crucial but nonetheless neglected question: what factors determine the degree to which the labor policies in the developing nations succeed or fail?

A second basic concern pervades the study of labor and development: the nature of trade unions in developing areas.[5] In studies of unions in newly independent nations, most scholars stress that government labor policy determines the characteristics of labor movements. Friedland, for example, notes the desire of new governments for rapid economic development and declares: "With the achievement of independence . . . a distinct shift in orientation can be noted, as unions voluntarily or not so voluntarily become *productionist*. More and more, unions are being converted into instruments for increasing the productivity and production of workers." [6] The case of Zambia adds to the studies of Friedland, Galenson, and others who examine the characteristics of postindependence trade unions,[7] for the government of Zambia also attempts to render the Mineworkers' Union an agency of economic development. Through the Trade Union Congress,* informal contacts with the Head Office of the union, and the lure of public office, the government seeks to induce the union into a productionist role. And through UNIP, the dominant political party, the governing elite has sought to control recruitment to posts within the union, and thus ensure the union's cooperation with its economic and political purposes. Since the Mineworkers' Union is so clearly and forcefully subject to the influence of the government, this examination of the union offers a valuable study of postindependence labor movements in the developing countries.

Here again, however, rather than merely adding further evi-

* This title will be employed to refer to the labor federation in Zambia. It represents a phrase common to the long series of names by which the federation has been known over the two decades of its existence.

dence to an ongoing research trend, the study seeks to move into an area relatively ignored by other works in the field. It does so by attempting to answer the questions: to what extent has the union fulfilled the role ascribed to it by the government in postindependence Zambia? And what appears to have determined its performance? [8]

The assignment of development tasks to the Mineworkers' Union in Zambia is, as I have suggested, typical of the actions of governments in many developing nations. As noted by Kilson, Wallerstein, Coleman, Rosberg, and others, the pattern is certainly a prevalent one in Africa, and finds its parallel in the assertion of central control over a wide range of interest groups and over the nationalist movement itself.[9] In the case of interest groups, "The relationship desired is one that ensures that the activities of such groups are congruent with and supportive of the modernization objectives of the regime." [10] In the case of the nationalist movement, the goal is to render it an effective instrument of governance and rule. Given their desire for a concerted effort to modernize, ruling elites seek to render the major political and economic structures in their nations means for controlling and regulating the conduct of the citizenry in conformity with public objectives.

Viewed from the perspective of development theory, the efforts of the postindependence regimes represent attempts to convert organizations which have traditionally functioned as "input structures" into "output structures." [11] The primary function of trade unions is to detect and articulate the demands of their members; and up to the point of independence, union leaders received the enthusiastic support of the aspiring political elite in the performance of this task. The primary function of the nationalist movement is to give voice to the grievances and aspirations of its members; and up to the time of independence, the political elite dedicated itself to furthering this objective. Once independence is obtained, however, the aspirant elite becomes the ruling elite; and rather than seeking power, the new leaders seek to utilize power to achieve the rapid modernization of their nation.

Particularly in the case of labor, this shift evokes a change in attitudes toward the expression of demands, since the demands of labor for better wages and conditions of service often run counter to the desires of the elites for rapid economic growth. The study of labor therefore gives great insight into one of the major political transformations in developing political systems: the recasting of structures that specialize in the articulation of demands into agencies for regulating and controlling the behavior of their members.

I will therefore use this study of labor policy in Zambia to assess the ability of the union and the party to forsake their traditional roles as input structures, articulating the demands of their members, in order to serve as output structures, governing the behavior of their members in conformity with public policy. It is best to state at the beginning the concept of the output process used here: the term refers to the flow of policy from the governing elite to the leadership of the major parapolitical groups in its environment and from the leadership of these groups to the rank and file. The term further implies that the policies, once disseminated, are enforced. There are thus three relevant dimensions to the concept of the output process: the *responsiveness* of the organization's leadership, the *transmission* of policies through the organization, and the *enforcement* of policies by the leadership. I will assess the performance of the union and party along these dimensions.

This study also offers an opportunity to examine the determinants of the capacity of developing political systems. The notion of capacity has two major referents: the ability of political systems to attain their objectives and their ability to intervene in and purposefully change their environments. In the case at hand, the two referents largely coincide, for a principal goal of the Zambian government is the regulation and transformation of its economy. In assessing and seeking to account for the success of the government, we will be examining the capacity of the Zambian political system and the determinants of its political capabilities.

Before beginning this inquiry, it is wise to register an important disclaimer. The study of labor and politics is fraught with value conflicts. On one side are those who support the minimal regulation of labor by government, view the role of unions as protecting and advancing the interests of workers, and concern themselves with the role of workers as consumers rather than as producers of national wealth. Ranged against these "free-laborites" are those who argue that government must regulate the behavior of workers to attain rapid development. These scholars regard workers as producers of the national product and unions as collaborators with governmental efforts to attain rapid rates of economic growth.[12]

I eschew entering this debate. My concern in this study is with the ability of governments to fulfill goals and to regulate the behavior of groups in order to realize objectives. As a result, government policies are adopted as the starting point of this analysis. The acceptance of the government's goals as given, and therefore seemingly as justified, is a by-product of its principal concern, and does not represent a basic value commitment.

2 The Party, the Union, and the Mining Industry

In the nineteenth century, the British South Africa Company (BSA), the company-cum-government that was the creation of Cecil John Rhodes, sent its representatives into Central Africa in quest of mineral deposits. Because of intertribal conflicts, Rhodes's agents were able to gain mineral rights in exchange for promises of military assistance and protection; in some instances, as with the Ngoni, they relied on conquest to gain the desired concessions. By 1899, the BSA had established a level of control that was sufficient to warrant official investiture with economic and governmental powers over much of the area that is currently Zambia.

The BSA at first found Northern Rhodesia, as the territory was then called, a disappointing venture; early prospecting failed to reveal profitable mineral deposits. As Gann, in his history of Northern Rhodesia, describes the company's reaction:

> As a commercial speculation Chartered Government proved a flop. . . . the ordinary investors, . . . more numerous than all the settlers in the two Rhodesias, had not as yet received a single dividend. Aid for an underdeveloped country was being supplied from the pockets of private lenders, and the lenders did not like it. Provided the Company received an adequate offer for its railway and mining interests as well as adequate compensation for its administrative deficits, the Directors were only too anxious to get rid of their unpopular and expensive commitments.[1]

Partially because of this reaction, in 1924, the BSA formally transferred responsibility for Northern Rhodesia to the government of Great Britain. Following the installation of British rule, two major issues dominated Northern Rhodesia's politics: What should be the relative power of the European settler community and the British government? And what should be the relationship between the settlers in Northern and Southern Rhodesia? The two issues were closely related, for they arose from a single source: the controversy over native policy. The settlers' representatives in the Legislative Council of Northern Rhodesia viewed amalgamation with Southern Rhodesia as a means of strengthening their power against the colonial administration and thereby asserting their interests over those of the African population.

Concerted pressure for settler self-government and amalgamation began after the publication in 1930 of the "Passfield Memorandum." The document contained the famed dictum that in East Africa "the interests of the African natives must be paramount, and that if, and when, those interests and the interests of the immigrant races should conflict, the former should prevail." [2] Seeing that their interests would occupy a secondary place in British colonial policy, the settlers' representatives in the Northern Rhodesian Legislative Council met with members of the Southern Rhodesian Parliament to explore ways and means of uniting in resistance to imperial rule. In 1933 they introduced a motion expressing the Legislative Council's approval of the principle of amalgamation with Southern Rhodesia. In 1936, the representatives from Northern and Southern Rhodesia again met and jointly resolved for early amalgamation with powers of complete self-government.[3] The height of the prewar campaign for amalgamation came with the appointment of the Bledisloe Commission by the government of Great Britain. While endorsing amalgamation in principle, the commission cited the divergence in native policies and the discrepancy in the status of Africans in Northern and Southern Rhodesia as major impediments to the federation of the two territories.[4]

The Rise of Nationalist Parties and the Triumph of UNIP

During World War II the issue of amalgamation gave way to problems of self-defense and mobilization, and after the war the issue reemerged with an entirely new dimension. The greater the efforts of the settlers to federate with Southern Rhodesia, the greater the efforts of the Africans to organize in resistance to the trend. Modern Zambian politics arose from this resistance to the postwar drive of the European settlers for federation with the South.

Following the war, settler representatives in the Legislative Council again introduced a resolution in support of amalgamation with Southern Rhodesia. While the motion failed, African political leaders nonetheless felt threatened by the initiative. As elsewhere in Africa, the African political leaders in Northern Rhodesia emerged from the leadership of indigenous welfare societies. The welfare societies were represented on the local councils in Northern Rhodesia, and the sentiments of the African leadership were registered in the council chambers. As noted by Rotberg, minutes of the councils reveal that "the members of the . . . councils constantly raised their voices in one . . . major refrain: we want no part, they said, of amalgamation with Southern Rhodesia in any form. Each of the councils voted yearly against amalgamation." [5] Partly in response to the postwar initiative of the European settlers, representatives of fourteen African welfare societies formed a Federation of Welfare Societies—the first national African political grouping.[6]

In 1948, Sir Stewart Gore-Browne, the settlers' representative nominated to give expression to the interests of blacks, supported a resolution in favor of "responsible Government" for Northern Rhodesia. As noted by Hall, "At that time the expression was synonymous with white rule on the Southern Rhodesia pattern." [7] In response, the Federation of Welfare Societies met in Lusaka. Condemning "responsible Government," "amalgamation," and "federation," the association resolved itself into the Northern Rhodesia African Congress.[8]

The Congress, later named the African National Congress (ANC), altered and modified its structure in response to further events in the European sphere of Northern Rhodesian politics. Thus, when in 1951 the British government accepted federation between Northern and Southern Rhodesia and thereby acceded to the political program of the settlers, Harry Nkumbula supplanted Godwin Lewanika as president of the Congress. At the time, Nkumbula represented the radical wing of the Congress and his accession to power committed it to more militant policies and tactics.[9]

During the era of the Federation of Rhodesia and Nyasaland (1953 to 1963), ANC initiated boycotts against local European businesses, protests against racial discrimination in public facilities, resistance to agricultural controls and reforms, and otherwise attempted to publicize and sustain political grievances against the Northern Rhodesian government. Throughout this period, Congress's central aim remained the withdrawal of Northern Rhodesia from the Federation. However, despite its commitment to a single, overriding objective, ANC split into two separate parties. Participating in the split was the leadership cadre that was to succeed in removing Northern Rhodesia from the Federation and leading it to independence as a sovereign black nation.

The immediate issue that gave rise to the split in ANC was Nkumbula's attempt to purge the Congress of dissident elements. The broader issue was Nkumbula's increasing accommodation with the colonial order, as reflected in his decision to participate in the 1959 Legislative Council elections and his apparently negligent conduct of negotiations with the colonial office. Whatever the real or apparent cause, in October 1958, Kaunda, Kapwepwe, Kamanga, and others quit ANC and formed the Zambia African National Congress (ZANC).

ZANC proved short-lived, for the leadership's spirited organization of the new party led to sporadic but intensive violence. The unrest, coinciding with declarations of emergency in Nyasaland and Southern Rhodesia in March 1959, provoked the detention of many of ZANC's leaders and an official ban on the party. Despite this setback, those leaders who had escaped detention preserved the lower units of ZANC intact and succeeded in reassembling them into a national-level party—the United National Independence Party (UNIP). Upon their release, the former leaders of ZANC assumed offices in UNIP comparable to their old positions.

The rise of UNIP to power in Zambia is directly related to the removal of Northern Rhodesia from the Federation and to the attainment of independence. Through a series of arduous negotiations, African political leaders attained constitutional reforms for Northern Rhodesia which enabled African political parties to exercise increased power within the territorial government. UNIP gained a majority of votes in the 1962 elections and coalesced at the national level with ANC to form the first African government in the history of the territory. It was this government, together with representatives of Nyasaland's African government, which succeeded in dismantling the Federation. In the elections of January 1964, UNIP won the overwhelming majority of seats in the National Assembly and formed a government on its own. This UNIP government brought Zambia to independence on 24 October 1964.[10]

In the postindependence period, UNIP continues to dominate the parliament and government of Zambia. Nonetheless, ANC remains a significant presence in certain areas of the country. In 1964, of the 65 African parliamentary seats, UNIP won 55, 24 of which were uncontested; ANC, 10; 10 seats were reserved for a largely European electorate. In 1968, UNIP won 81 of the 105 seats in an expanded parliament; ANC won 23. ANC has thus been largely eclipsed, and its strength has been largely confined to the Central and Southern Provinces. Nonetheless, it does remain active; and the switch of one major province—Barotse (now Western) Province—from UNIP to ANC in the 1968 election indicates its continued importance as a rallying point for dissident elements in Zambia.[11]

The origins of UNIP suggest several important attributes of the party. First, UNIP arose in protest to the domination of a racial minority. The objectives of racial equality and the enhancement of the status of Africans strongly influence both the content of the government's labor policy and the manner in which it is implemented. Secondly, a major reason for the opposition to federation in Northern Rhodesia was the manner in which the federal government allocated the wealth of the country; during the decade of federation, an estimated £70 million was taken from Northern Rhodesia, in excess of expenditures in the territory, and spent for the benefit of the European colony in the South.[12] In opposing federation, the nationalist movement sought to gain access to these funds and to direct them toward projects which would bring wealth and prosperity to the African population. This commitment to rapid development is another basic determinant of the content of the government's labor policy. Finally, the origins of UNIP underline the multiparty nature of the Zambian political system. Dissent can translate into active political opposition, strongly curtailing the use of coercion and promoting the use of persuasion and inducements in the implementation of the government's labor program.

The Structure of UNIP

As a full half of my analysis will focus on the use and limitations of UNIP as an agency of government policy, it is essential that its basic structure be understood.

At the time of my research, the party was governed by a central committee of eleven elected officers and four appointed trustees. Members of the Central Committee usually held ministerial positions in the government. Status positions in the party and governmental hierarchies were generally consistent, with the president and vice-president of the party holding comparable positions in the government. Members of the Central Committee were elected or confirmed in office by the rank and file at the party's General Conference. Delegates to the conference came from the branch level of the party. The Central Committee governed the party in collaboration with the National Council. The National Council recruited its members from the ranks of the party professionals below the level of the Central Committee. Representatives of labor, the civil service, and the armed forces often attended the meetings at the opening sessions of the National Council. In between meetings of the National Council, the

Central Committee governed through the party administration.
Below the Central Committee fell the ministers of state of the various provinces and their assistants. The ministers of state were charged with superintending both the party and governmental hierarchies in their province, and with regularizing relations between them. The assistant ministers performed the same functions for the major geographic units within the province. Both the minister of state and his assistants received their appointments directly from the president and received salaries at superscale levels from the government.

In January 1969, almost a year after the research for this project was completed, the elements of the party structure just described were radically altered. In a major effort at decentralization, the government has now posted a minister of full cabinet rank in each province; the cabinet minister, as he is called, governs through a provincial secretary, a minister of state, and a series of district governors. The last correspond to the assistant minister in the old administrative order. The blend of party and government remains in the new structure, for the cabinet minister is in charge of UNIP in his province and the district governors are party, not civil service, personnel. In an even more recent move, the Central Committee has been abolished, pending a major reorganization of the party.[13]

The regional secretary occupies the lowest rung of the party's national hierarchy; his position was not altered by the recent reforms. In the Western (now Copperbelt) Province, regional secretaries assume responsibility for subdivisions of the geographic domain of the assistant ministers. Their responsibilities extend solely to the party; while they can mediate relations with the government administration, regional secretaries occupy no position within its hierarchy. Moreover, they draw their salaries from the party and not from the government. The regional secretary thus constitutes a full-time party professional.

The regional secretary confronts the membership units of the party: the Main Body, Women's Brigade, and Youth League. Membership in the Women's Brigade is naturally restricted by sex, and the boundary between the Main Body and Youth League, at least formally, is one of age. For the purposes of this study we will concentrate almost entirely on the Main Body of the party, which organizes the adult male population.

UNIP's principal membership unit is the branch. Branches are geographically defined, being bounded by what the population regards as the natural geographic limits of their community. In the case of Kalela branch on the Rhokana Mine Township, the branch most closely scrutinized in this study, the boundary is the group of public facilities—shops, township offices, churches, and sports stadium—which divides Kalela residents from other members of the mine community. Each branch possesses an elected cabinet of eight members: chairman, secretary, treasurer, publicity secretary, and their assistants. All are part-time officials, performing their duties after work. The branch in turn breaks down into sections, which correspond to geographic subunits of the town. Thus Kalela has six sections, each of which constitutes eight to ten rows of houses. Each Main Body section also possesses a cabinet of eight officials. This structure exists in triplicate, with full sets of officers existing at each level for women and youths as well.

In Kitwe, the regional secretary confronts nearly thirty party branches. To simplify relations with the membership units, he deals with branch officials through the intermediary agency of two constituency cabinets. One constituency organizes ten branches and the other nineteen. Once again, each constituency cabinet possesses eight officials and all are part-time. Candidates are elected to constituency office by ballot among the branches falling within the area of the respective constituency.

The party organization that existed at the time of this study can best be summarized in terms of the accompanying diagram (chart 1). The criteria of selection is used to divide the party into national and local levels. As far down as the regional secretary, officials are selected by the national units of the party; below that, they are selected by ballot among the local members. The sole exception is the Central Committee which was elected by delegates drawn from the branch units of the party.

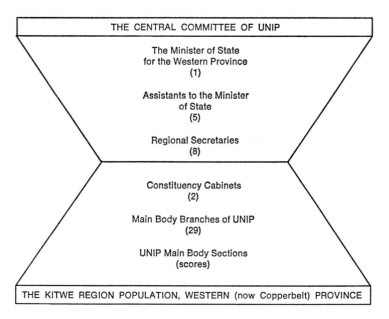

THE CENTRAL COMMITTEE OF UNIP

The Minister of State
for the Western Province
(1)

Assistants to the Minister
of State
(5)

Regional Secretaries
(8)

Constituency Cabinets
(2)

Main Body Branches of UNIP
(29)

UNIP Main Body Sections
(scores)

THE KITWE REGION POPULATION, WESTERN (now Copperbelt) PROVINCE

Chart 1. Structure of UNIP. Numbers in the top half of the diagram are for the Western Province; in the bottom half, they refer to the Kitwe Region.

The Development of Copper Mining

Copper has long been produced in Central Africa, with local tribesmen smelting and refining surface deposits and exporting "finished products." It was in the late nineteenth century, however, that Europeans began systematic explorations for mineral deposits. The initial impetus came from the BSA's decision to grant prospecting rights to smaller companies on the condition that they survey and develop claims which they discovered.[14] By 1910, a series of discoveries, several by the agents of these companies, completed the detection of the major mineral deposits in the territory.

Despite the linking of the Rhodesian and Congo railways in 1909, the mines in Northern Rhodesia languished. As Gann states:

On both sides of the border, in Northern Rhodesia as well as in the Belgian Congo, the early finds were of oxidized ores. But whereas in the Congo much of the ore averaged 15 per cent copper and some was as high as 25 per cent, in Northern Rhodesia the oxidized ores only averaged between 3 to 5 per cent of the red metal, and ores as rich as these were thrown on dumps as waste matter on the Belgian side of the border . . . the Northern Rhodesian fields remained the Cinderella.[15]

Several developments radically altered this state of affairs. Most important was the discovery that below the oxidized surface deposits lay rich and large deposits of sulphide ores. Since oxidized ores must be leached, whereas sulphide ores are amenable to treatment by much less expensive flotation methods, this discovery rendered the Northern Rhodesian mines far more profitable.[16]

The second major development was the organization of large-scale international financing for the mines. The prime movers were Alfred Chester Beatty of American Metal, a United States company, and Ernest Oppenheimer of Anglo-American, the famed South African firm. In 1914, representatives of American Metal and Anglo-American were drawn onto the board of Rhodesian Selection Trust (RST), a company with holdings in Bwana Mkubwa mine. Beatty was sufficiently impressed with the prospects for RST to secure American Metal's backing for the firm in 1927, thus enormously increasing the capital at its command. The next year, Oppenheimer organized Rhodesian Anglo-American, with holdings in Broken Hill and Nkana. Besides ensuring capital for these mining ventures, the formation of these companies facilitated the transfer of skilled technical and managerial personnel into Northern Rhodesia. By 1930, Bwana Mkubwa, Broken Hill, and Nchanga were being developed for Anglo-American, and Roan and Mufulira were being worked for Selection Trust.[17]

Copper production had no sooner begun, however, than the industry was affected by the depression. By the end of 1931, only Roan and Nkana were still in operation. Nonetheless, the industry revived rapidly in the late 1930s. The development of the automobile and the electrical industry, as well as rearmament, increased world demand for copper, and the shallow depths and high mineralization of Northern Rhodesia's mines yielded a cost advantage. In 1942, the Ministry of Supply in Great Britain signed bulk agreements with the copper companies for the duration of World War II. By the end of the war, Zambia was among the foremost producers of copper in the world. The outbreak of hostilities in Korea shortened the postwar slump in copper production, and a similar slump in the late 1950s gave way to a steady rise in copper prices by 1964.[18] The copper industry has prospered since independence. In 1969, Zambia moved past Chile to rank third among the world's copper producing nations; only the United States and the USSR surpassed her level of production.

During the period under consideration in this study, the mining industry was owned and operated by the same two groups of companies that had first developed the mines. Rhodesian Selection Trust, renamed Roan Selection Trust (RST), still drew the great bulk of its capital from the United States and Great Britain. RST also drew capital from the second group of companies, Anglo-American Corporation (AAC). AAC remained a South African firm, but was extensively financed by capital from the United States, Britain, and continental Europe. RST retained control of Roan, Mufulira, Chibuluma, Chambishi, and Kalengwa mines, while AAC controlled Rhokana, Nchanga, and Bancroft. Such was the corporate structure which dominated the copper industry at the time of this study.

In 1969, the government of Zambia puchased a controlling share in both companies, and now controls their boards of directors. The companies have been renamed: RST is now known as Roan Consolidated Mines Limited, and AAC as Nchanga Consolidated Copper Mines Limited. I discuss these changes more fully in chapter 10 and in the second appendix.

This background to the mining companies highlights several factors which will assume great importance in this study. The first is the size of the copper industry: it is immense, even on a world scale, and in Zambia it vastly overshadows other enterprises and dominates the nation's economy. A principal goal of the government is to harness this major industry so as to develop the rest of the country, and its policy toward mine labor is designed to fulfill this task.

The second is foreign ownership. During the period of this study the government of Zambia relied heavily on the copper industry for economic development, but it was also intensely suspicious of it. Not only were the companies foreign-owned; they were also dominated by foreign personnel. The top management, supervisory personnel, and a full 15 percent of the labor force were citizens of the former colonial power, Great Britain, or of Zambia's strongest international enemy, the Republic of South Africa.* The dominance of the industry by this foreign, racially distinct minority, has led to the patterns of racial conflict which both influence the content of government labor policies and significantly affect the success with which they are implemented.

The Rise of African Trade Unionism

While copper production began in the 1930s, it was not until the postwar period that local labor organized a formal association in defense of its interests. This association largely supplanted tribal modes of organizing and representing the interests of mineworkers. Even earlier, however, the African mineworkers had revealed a readiness to protest in defense of their economic interests. Thus, in 1935, the workers struck in support of wage demands; at Roan, six were killed and twenty-two wounded by the colonial police.[19] In 1940, the African miners again struck in support of a wage demand; at Rhokana the strikers rioted and the police shot and killed over fifty.[20]

As noted by Epstein in his 1958 work on the copperbelt town of Luanshya, the two prewar disturbances possessed an intriguing common element: the challenge to tribal forms of labor relations and the assertion of class-based interests.[21] The companies had

* Forty percent of the expatriate labor force in the mines at the end of 1965 were from South Africa. Richard L. Sklar, "Zambia's Response to UDI," *Mawazo* 1 (1968): 28.

maintained a system of labor relations based upon tribal elders. Each tribal group at the mines selected its elders; they represented the interests of the workers before the companies and communicated company policy to the workers themselves. Both in 1935 and 1940, however, the workers turned against this tribal form of organization. As Epstein notes, in the 1935 disturbances at Roan, "When the riot started, and a mob stormed the Compound Office, the Elders fled, and together with the compound police, sought safety within the Compound Office." [22] Similarly, in 1940, the tribal elders demanded wage increases of 25s. 6d. a ticket (one ticket equalled roughly thirty working days); however, the workers demanded an increase of 10s. a day and were furious with the relative timidity of their tribal leaders.

Equally as important as the rejection of the tribal representatives was the adoption of organizational forms which gave expression to the class interests of the mineworkers. Thus Epstein states that during the 1940 disturbances workers at Mufulira picked leaders from among their ranks to express their grievances; he views this committee as a leadership form appropriate to the class-based interests of the mineworkers. [23] Even more suggestive was the behavior of workers at Rhokana. In addition to selecting a leadership cadre to replace their tribal representatives, the workers created a form of organization that dramatized the solidarity of their commitment to their collective industrial interests. The strikers withdrew from the mine township and took up residence in the football grounds. They left a wide boundary between themselves and the nonstrikers in the townships, and they vigilantly controlled movements across that boundary. As noted by the district commissioner:

> The position seemed to be that the leaders of the strike, with those who willingly followed them and others who were unable to resist these stronger personalities who had emerged during the five days of the strike, were cut off to all intents and purposes from the ordinary normal life of the compound. . . .
> A man leaving the crowd had to cross a bare patch of

ground where he was clearly visible to everyone. This explained the cohesion of the mob.[24]

It was this isolated, organized, and cohesive group of strikers that vociferously articulated the interests of the mineworkers and ultimately rioted in support of their demands.

The transition from a structure of labor relations based upon ethnic principles to a structure based upon the interests of industrial workers took nearly a decade to accomplish. During the war years, the Labour Department experimented with Boss Boy and Works Committees as supplements to the tribal representatives.[25] After the war, the colonial office, following the recommendations of the Bevan Report, urged the formation of collective bargaining machinery for Africans and appointed a full-time Trade Union Labour Officer for the territory. This officer, Mr. W. M. Comrie, was to assist in the formation of African trade unions in Northern Rhodesia.[26]

Comrie gained an unexpectedly favorable reception. The colonial government and the mining companies had noted a growing interest in organizing the African labor force on the part of the leaders of the European Mine Workers' Union. Both feared the power of the union that would result should these efforts succeed. Moreover, the Labour Department was convinced that the European leaders only sought to frustrate the progress of the Africans by preventing the formation of an independent African union. The industrial and political powers in the territory, therefore, backed Comrie and resisted the efforts by the European leaders to frustrate Comrie's mission.[27]

Comrie found the African workers deeply interested in the idea of forming trade unions. The past history of the mineworkers had suggested their early commitment to class-based forms of association. Further events in Northern Rhodesia heightened their awareness of their economic interests. Thus, in 1948, the Dalgleish Commission investigated the prospects of African advancement in the mining industry. Another commission took testimony from African mineworkers as part of its investigation of the cost of living in Northern Rhodesia.[28] And, as we have seen, the companies and Labour Department had just initiated Works Committees on the mines. Lecturing before the Welfare Societies, Clerks' Associations, and Boss Boy Committees, Comrie helped to transform the workers' interest in trade unionism into organized action. In December 1947, the Nkana mineworkers formed a union branch. By March 1948, they had deposited £35 in a bank account, drafted a constitution and set of rules, and recruited 1,000 members. Moreover, they had dispatched a "good will" mission to other mines on the copperbelt.[29]

The president and secretary of the Nkana branch were Lawrence Katilungu and Simon Kaluwa. When the branches of the several mines combined to form an industry-wide union in May 1949, Katilungu, Kaluwa, and other members of the national executive committee negotiated a recognition agreement with the Chamber of Mines. The African Mineworkers' Union now became the official representative of African labor in the copper mining industry.

As noted by Epstein, with the formation of the union came the eclipse of the tribal element in the structure of labor relations. Quarrels between the leaders of the union and tribal representatives led to a referendum concerning the fate of tribal representation. With the strong urging of the union leaders, the mineworkers, in 1953, voted overwhelmingly to abolish the system: over 82 percent of the mines' African labor force voted against its retention.[30]

The new union made rapid progress. By 1956, it had increased average earnings by over 200 percent for its highly paid members and by 400 percent for miners at the bottom of the pay scale.[31] The union also became increasingly militant. In 1952, it sponsored a three-week strike. Three years later, it sponsored an eight-week strike. In August 1956, it initiated a series of strikes against the companies' recognition of a staff association. As a result of this last dispute, the colonial administration arrested and detained nearly all of its leaders. Following these detentions, the union slowly regained its position of power on the copperbelt; and following independence in Zambia, it regained the right to represent the staff grades in the mining industry. Despite its early reliance on the government's Trade Union Labour Officer, the union has thus proved itself a capable and singly independent defender of the interests of labor.

The Structure of the Union

The Mineworkers' Union has branches at all seven of the mines on the copperbelt, at Ndola Copper Refineries, and at the lead and zinc producing Broken Hill Development Company, 150 miles south of the copperbelt on the line of rail. Over 60 percent of the local mineworkers belong to the union; because of this, the union is entitled by law to subscriptions from all 40,000 local employees of the copper industry. With a membership in excess of 20,000 and an assured monthly income of £10,000, the Mineworkers' Union is by far the largest and wealthiest union in Zambia, and one of the largest and richest in Africa.

The union divides into national and local levels. The Head Office is the most prominent element of the national structure. It contains eight elected officials: the chairman, the president, the general secretary, the financial secretary, and their deputies. There are also three union trustees. Only the president, general secretary, deputy general secretary, and financial secretary work full-time as union officials. The remainder work part-time. In common usage, the term Head Office refers to these four elected officials who work as full-time unionists. This usage is justified, for it is they who handle the day-to-day work of the union and the bulk of the labor involved in conducting its industry-wide affairs. The chairman and his deputy simply preside over public functions; the deputy financial secretary stands in for the financial secretary when the latter is absent; and the trustees fulfill by their existence a legal requirement of British labor law.

The Head Office is situated at the center of nine branches and three subbranches. With but two exceptions, each branch corresponds to a copper mine. The sole exceptions are the locals at Ndola Copper Refineries, where Roan Selection Trust refines much of its copper ore, and at the Broken Hill Development Company, which mines lead and zinc. These are also the only two located off the copperbelt. In the discussions which follow we

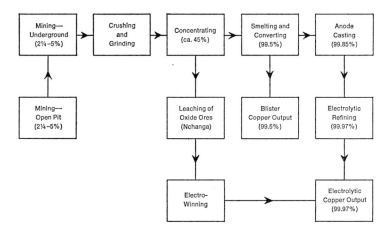

Chart 2. Flow of Copper Production. The boxes show the stages in production, with the percentage of copper at various stages.

will exclude them and concentrate on the four principal copper-belt branches of the Union: Nchanga, Rhokana, Roan Antelope, and Mufulira. These four branches organize 83 percent of the mine labor force on the copperbelt.[32]

The structure of the branches corresponds to the organization of the industrial plants whose workers they represent. Chart 2 depicts the stages associated with the production of copper. The flow of production groups into distinct but interdependent departments, each specializing either in the extraction of copper ore or the transformation of ore into high grade copper. The principal production departments are the underground department, which is subdivided into a number of shafts or open pits; the concentrator; the refinery; and the smelter. Each mine maintains a second series of departments which control, coordinate, or support the production departments. Members of this series include the administration, the mine store, and the engineering, laboratory, and personnel departments. Since historically the mines commenced large-scale production before any other industries or services had located in the copperbelt, the companies maintain a

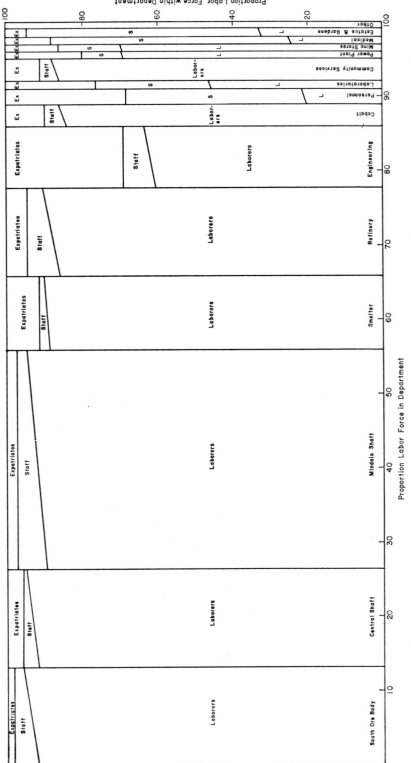

Chart 3. Proportion of Labor Force by Department, Rhokana Corporation, January 1, 1968. Note that "Staff" means African staff, throughout the chart. Abbreviations in the narrow columns are as follows: Ex = Expatriate; S = African staff; L = Laborers.

third series of departments which provide services that elsewhere would be furnished by independent agencies—the medical and community services departments, for example. The bar-graph (chart 3) represents along the horizontal axis the relative size of these departments at Rhokana Mine in terms of the relative proportion of the labor force located in each; South Ore Body (SOB), Central, and Mindolo are the three shafts which constitute the underground department at Rhokana Mine.

The Mineworkers' Union concentrates on representing the interests of the employees as industrial laborers. While this statement may at first appear absurdly obvious, it will acquire greater importance later in this analysis. What is relevant here is that, given this function, the union structures its branches so as to detect and handle grievances on the "shop floor," and therefore partially recapitulates in its structure the organization of the mine itself. Thus, the union maintains a network of shop stewards in each mine department. The authority of these stewards extends only to the department in which they work, and the number of stewards in any given department is a function of the relative size of the department in the mine. The branch committee constitutes the next level of the branch. Each member of the branch committee addresses himself to a distinct set of mine departments and oversees the work of the shop stewards within the departments for which he is responsible. Supervising the work of the shop stewards and the branch committee is the branch executive. The executive is composed of a branch chairman, secretary, and treasurer, and the deputies for each office (see chart 4).

The officials at the branch level work part-time. They receive no pay from the union, save in the form of compensation for expenses incurred on union business. The sole exception is the organizing secretary. As a professional unionist on full salary from the union, he maintains the records for the branch, recruits members, and attempts to ensure that the branch officers operate in conformity with the union's agreement.

The union branches negotiate with the personnel departments of their respective mines. As noted earlier, each mine belongs to one of two groups of companies. The two groups maintain the

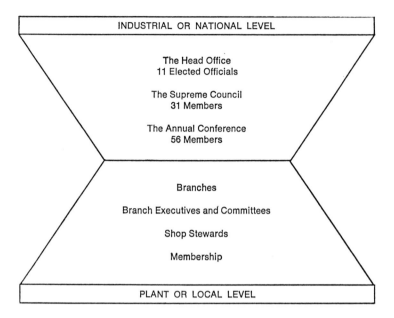

Chart 4. Structure of the Mineworkers' Union. For a discussion of the Supreme Council and Annual Conference, see chapter 6.

Copper Industry Service Bureau (CISB)—formerly called the Chamber of Mines—to handle labor relations on an industry-wide basis. While the branches confine their activities to the level of the individual companies, the Head Office represents the interests of all the industry's workers before CISB.

3 Government Labor Policy

There are two distinguishable elements in the Zambian government's labor policy: the first, a development labor policy; the second, a policy of social justice.

Development Labor Policy

It is difficult to overemphasize the level of the government's commitment to rapid economic development. To defend Zambia from hostile regimes to the east, west, and south; to consolidate political loyalty from competing sectional interests; to rally support for the governing party at the next election; and to "make up for the 10 years of criminal neglect most of the country . . . suffered" during the federal period [1]—all these political objectives lend urgency to the task of economic development, for all require the rapid creation of wealth.

The magnitude of this dedication is best demonstrated in terms of the growth rates which the government seeks to attain. In real terms, the rate of growth for the gross domestic product was to be 11 percent per annum over the seven-year period 1964–70. This overall growth rate was to result from increases of up to 198 percent in some sectors of the economy. As the most developed sector, the mines were expected to grow only 63 percent. But the government exhorted commerce to increase 117 percent; manufacturing, 146 percent; services, 147 percent; and construction, 198 percent. Rates of increase in the contributions of these sectors to the gross domestic product were thus to range from 9 percent to 28 percent per year. [2]

This commitment to rapid growth organized the government's plans and goals over a wide range of economic activities. It has undertaken major capital investment programs to create the necessary economic and social infrastructure. The Office of National Development and Planning (ONDP) allocated £30.2 million for roads; £5.0 million for railways, not including the planned railway to Tanzania; and £7.5 million for the creation

27

of airway facilities over the period 1964-70. ONDP earmarked a
further £22.4 million for two major hydroelectric schemes; a
third—an extension to the already existing Kariba power plant—
was to be financed from abroad.[3] In the field of human resources,
as well, the government was willing to make enormous efforts to
create the human basis for rapid economic development. Thus
enrolments in primary schools were to increase by over 30 percent between 1966 and 1970; in secondary schools, they were to
increase by nearly 300 percent; and at the university level, by
over 500 percent.[4]

In its drive for rapid development, the government is overwhelmingly reliant upon the copper industry. Statistics circulated
by the Copper Industry Service Bureau reveal that in 1960 the
industry produced 50 percent of Zambia's gross domestic product
and that in 1966 its portion was a full 41 percent. Copper mining
is almost the sole contributor to Zambia's foreign trade, producing
consistently in excess of 90 percent of the value of the country's
exports (table 1). In the face of these statistics, there can be no

TABLE 1

Copper Mining in the National Economy

(Millions of pounds)

Year	Net domestic product (£)	Copper's contribution to net domestic product		Value domestic exports f.o.b. (£)	Copper's contribution to exports	
		(£)	%		(£)	%
1960	195	98	50	129.9	121.7	93.7
1961	188	88	47	120.6	111.8	92.7
1962	184	86	47	120.7	110.9	91.9
1963	193	87	45	130.2	119.3	91.6
1964	226	108	48	163.4	151.1	92.4
1965	297	123	41	187.5	174.2	92.9
1966	370	152	41	236.0	225.0	95.3

Source: Copper Industry Service Bureau, *Copperbelt of Zambia Mining Industry Year Book, 1966* (Kitwe: CISB, 1967), p. 35.

TABLE 2
Monthly Earnings for Mine and Nonmine Labor
(Pounds)

Industry	1960	1961	1962	1963	1964	1965	1966
Agriculture	4.5	5.6	5.2	5.1	5.8	6.8	8.3
Construction	11.0	8.6	7.4	8.4	9.7	15.5	18.4
Retail	4.0	4.4	4.2	3.6	5.4	6.0	11.5
Transport	2.0	2.9	2.6	2.4	2.5	5.8	5.4
Mining	8.8	8.6	9.6	9.7	13.6	15.6	21.1

Source: Computed from Ministry of Labour, *Department of Labour Annual Report[s]*, *1961–66* (Lusaka: Government Printer, 1963–68).
Note: The assumptions are that all workers in the nonmining industries receive the highest recorded wage paid to local workers in that industry, and that all workers in the mining industry receive the lowest recorded wage paid to local workers. Expatriate workers were omitted in estimating the labor force strengths in each industrial sector.

wonder that the government refers to the industry as the "backbone of Zambia," or, more dramatically, as the "copper cow [that has been] milked for the benefit of the racialists in Rhodesia." [5]

The dominance of the copper industry is also revealed by statistics on wages. Figures from the Ministry of Labour reveal that the wages paid by the copper industry constitute an enormous share of the earnings of Zambian labor. To illustrate and dramatize the point, I have estimated the monthly income which workers in five industrial sectors would earn were they to be paid the highest existing reported wage in those industries. Then I compared their earnings with those of the mineworkers under the assumption that all the mineworkers were paid the lowest wage issued by the mining companies (table 2). Even on the basis of these assumptions, purposely selected to minimize interindustry disparities, the average monthly earnings for mine employees exceed those of the workers in other industrial sectors in almost every instance.[6]

Given the importance of copper in the economy and the vast disparity between the level of development of mining and other sectors, the government seeks to render the industry the sponsor of the development of the rest of the economy. It therefore attaches crucial importance to the companies' function of generating the revenues which can be employed by the government for the development of other sectors. The Office of National Development and Planning writes, "The capital investment available to Government for financing the First National Development Plan is determined almost entirely by revenue obtained from copper mining operations in Zambia." [7]

The government has delineated in quantitative terms the magnitude of its reliance on copper as a source of development funds (table 3). It committed itself to raising £524.8 million of the

TABLE 3

Planned Proportion of Recurrent Government Revenues from Copper
(Millions of pounds)

Source of revenues	1965–66	1966–67	1967–68	1968–69	1969–70	Total
1. Income tax						
a. Copper companies	26.5	32.2	31.3	32.6	34.3	131.4
b. Other companies and personal income	13.5	11.5	13.4	15.6	18.3	58.8
2. Customs and excise tax	12.4	13.4	15.2	17.5	19.8	65.9
3. Mineral royalties and export tax	41.2	58.2	43.3	45.0	47.4	193.9
4. Other	13.4	15.7	17.5	19.6	22.0	74.8
Total revenues	107.0	132.0	120.7	130.3	141.8	524.8
Proportion from copper[a]	63.3%	68.5%	61.8%	59.6%	57.6%	62.0%

Source: Republic of Zambia, Office of National Development and Planning, *First National Development Plan, 1966–70* (Lusaka: Office of National Development and Planning, July 1966), p. 14.

[a] Estimated by $\dfrac{1a + 3}{Total}$.

£620.8 million allotted for development activities over the four-year period 1966–70.[8] Of this £524.8 million, a full 62 percent was to be derived from tax revenues on copper production—revenues gained from an income tax on company earnings, an export tax on consignments of copper shipped abroad, and a royalty charged for the use of mineral rights.[9] The mines' proportion of the government's tax bill was to rise as high as 68.5 percent for a single given year, although it would decline to 57.6 percent over the four-year period. Clearly the copper mines are expected to be the single greatest financial contributor to Zambia's development effort.

The government's conception of its relationship with the mining industry goes beyond that of mere tax collection. It actively nurtures the companies' capacity to produce large and taxable profit margins. In the field of fiscal policy, the government altered its export tax—albeit, after much pressure from the industry—when it discovered that the tax disrupted the financial position of marginal mines, and it adjusted tax payments for mines temporarily running at a loss. In its program of capital investment, the government concentrated some of its largest efforts on projects designed to insure the orderly production and export of copper. With Rhodesia's unilateral declaration of independence in 1965, the mines' production capacity was threatened by the restriction placed upon fuel imports from southern Africa; the government responded by building a pipeline from the coast to Ndola and by constructing a refinery to process the imported fuels. The rebellion of Southern Rhodesia also compromised the mines' capacity to export copper; in order to insure continued exports, the government again responded—this time with large investments in a variety of projects. It allotted funds for the construction of a reliable road to the eastern coast, and purchased and maintained a fleet of lorries to transport copper to the ports of East Africa. It also helped to finance an air fleet for the export of copper, and sought international assistance for the construction of a railway to Tanzania.[10]

"Discipline" for Local Labor

Just as the government seeks to protect and enhance the revenue position of the mining industry through its fiscal and investment policies, so too does it assume the role of "patron" of mine revenues in its policy toward mine labor. The government aggregates many of its injunctions for mine labor under the slogan of "discipline." The slogan refers to three kinds of behavior: the on-the-job conduct of workers, their relationships with supervisors, and the manner in which they give expression to their grievances.

The government's concern with discipline is reflected in the tone of bemusement which characterizes a memo prepared by the Ministry of Labour: "The reasons why indiscipline prevails at plant level are very difficult to pinpoint. . . . Why can't Africans work properly unless they are supervised? What causes the telex-operator to go out without permission, leaving the tape heaped on the ground? . . . In short, why are not we Africans duty minded?" [11] The government's concern with "indiscipline . . . at plant level" translates directly into an advocacy of labor's responsibility to "work hard." The government states this forcefully in "A Code for Enhanced Productivity in Zambia"—a document on labor relations that was produced during discussions with company executives and labor leaders at Livingstone in April 1967.

> [High production] requires a personal commitment and the full acceptance by each individual of his responsibilities. In its simplest terms, higher productivity means that everyone must work harder and still harder. Any man, whatever his status, who does not work as hard as he is able to is guilty of causing low productivity.[12]

During the conference, the government obtained from the workers' representatives "A Pledge to the National Development Plan"; this pledge, which made explicit the relationship between hard work and the core value of economic growth, states in part:

> We, the workers, pledge that we will put the interests of

Zambia before our own interests, either as individuals or as members of trade unions; we will work hard to play our part in the National Development Plan; we will do a fair day's work on every working day and will strive to increase not only our own productivity but also the productivity of our fellow workers.[13]

In an exhortation directed specifically to the mineworkers, the president of Zambia, Dr. Kenneth Kaunda, again asked for hard work, and this time related the injunction directly to the necessity for the mines to sponsor the lagging sectors of the national economy.

If, countrymen, I can not move you on principles, I do not move you ideologically, morally, to hard work, then at least I can ask you if you do not want to work hard . . . [to] remember where we come from. The village. Your own mother is there. My own mother is there. . . . They are all there in the village. . . . If morally, ideologically, philosophically, I cannot move you to hard work, at least I can remind you now your own mother, your own aunt, your own uncle, your own father is there in the village, suffering. . . . What is your contribution? . . . What is your contribution? This is my question.[14]

There is evidence that the government is embarrassed by the vagueness of its injunction to work hard. Thus, at a meeting in Kitwe in 1967, when the vice-president was confronted by the question, "What do you mean by hard work?" he evidenced unaccustomed confusion and finally solicited another question. Nonetheless, government spokesmen continue to reiterate the slogan and to communicate it with deep fervor. It is my belief that the strength of their commitment to the symbol derives from their conception of the development process in Zambia. Only by hard work can labor enhance the financial position of the employing firms and thus make revenues available for national development. For the workers not to work hard, therefore, is tantamount to a rejection of their role in the development of the nation. As the minister of labor states:

> Strikes . . . are only one means whereby the economy and our future development can be sabotaged. A more subtle but equally effective "saboteur" is the person or group of persons who only put into their work the very minimum of effort necessary to avoid being discharged. . . . Zambia will only become great if, more than anything else, we all contribute our quota of hard and unremitting work.[15]

A second referent of discipline is obedience to supervisors. The government believes that in order for industries to achieve the most productive use of labor and thereby maximize their earnings, the authority of management must be safeguarded. Challenges to this authority, as represented by workers' refusal to obey orders, cannot be tolerated for fear of imperiling the government's economic goals. The government's concern with the insubordination of workers is revealed in numerous statements; for example, the minister of labor declares:

> We are anxious to see that responsible respect for supervisors is maintained in industry. My Ministry has, to be frank, been extremely disturbed by a number of reliable reports which have been received in recent months indicating that on all too many occasions, workers have deliberately flouted normal instructions from supervisors.[16]

Belief in the equation between insubordination and lowered output is illustrated in further remarks by the minister of labor, these made during an inquiry into the causes of low output on the copper mines: "Your Excellency, the most serious thing . . . is indiscipline. There are certain people who are supposed to carry out instructions when they are given instructions and some of these people are not prepared to carry out instructions."[17] In the report on discussions between management and labor in Livingstone in 1967, the government reiterated its belief in the relationship between insubordination and lowered output, and made clear the strength of its reaffirmation of managerial authority.

High levels of productivity are not possible without the enforcement of industrial discipline. The cornerstone of this is the relationship between the supervisor and his workers. . . . The responsible position of the supervisors must be recognised by all levels and he should be enabled to exercise his function without fear or favor from any source.[18]

A last quotation underlines the magnitude of the government's commitment to the authority of the supervisory ranks of industrial firms.

> Zambian workers are reluctant to obey lawful and reasonable orders. They either refuse to do what they are told or they do it grudgingly, reluctantly, and half-heartedly and with poor grace. . . . Zambia is not going to put up with this. . . .
> [The supervisors] are afraid of being unpopular. They are afraid of unpleasantness. If a supervisor is not prepared to supervise, then let him resign and make way for someone who will. Undisciplined and inefficient workers and lily-livered supervisors are not going to be allowed to impede Zambia's progress towards economic independence.[19]

When the government exhorts the mineworkers to discipline, it is also exhorting them to observe rules and procedures for the peaceful resolution of industrial disputes. Strikes can halt output more dramatically than slothful work; and their effects on the earnings of the copper mines can be more precisely measured. That the government perceives the relation between strikes and the attainment of their goal of rapid economic growth is clearly suggested in the minister of labor's claim that "the successful fulfillment of the [First National Development Plan] can not be achieved . . . without the maintenance of industrial peace."[20] It is also suggested by his reference to strikers as economic "saboteurs."[21] This view is further demonstrated in a speech by President Kaunda in which he relates the effects of strikes on the copper mines upon lagging sectors in the Zambian economy.

> Your Government has ever expressed its views over massive strikes and quite true [they] will cripple and ruin our future.

Who is going to gain? Who suffers? . . . Your Mother,
Father, Brother and the like at home will never forgive you
for having failed to get a local clinic, school, roads, etc.[22]

In conformity with the high valuation government places on
economic growth and its perception of the necessity of financing
such growth from mine profits, the government perceives strike
action as both threatening and dangerous. And as in the case
of other challenges to the financial position of the mines, the
government responds with policies designed to protect the
sources of their development revenues. While not outlawing
strikes per se, the government declares that "withdrawal of labour
must only be used in the last resort."[23] It has elicited public
pledges from workers' representatives that "when any dispute
arises of any nature, . . . the employees must follow the provisions of [their] disputes' procedure . . . rather than resorting to
unconstitutional . . . action."[24] It also gained a pledge from the
workers to "use all our efforts to maintain industrial peace."[25]
Moreover, the government has empowered the Congress of Trade
Unions to approve or not approve strike ballots and strikes by
member unions, including the Mineworkers' Union.[26] Vigorous
opposition to strike action thus constitutes a third element of
government labor policy.

While the slogan "discipline" refers to the elements of labor
policy just described, the slogan "productivity" refers to a fourth
major element of government policy toward the mineworkers: its
policy on mine wages. The policy can be briefly stated: The government supports workers' demands for wage increases only
insofar as the rate of these increases is matched by a comparable
rise in the levels of output per man.

Numerous statements by official spokesmen reveal the government's resolve to link wage increases with increases in productivity. At a conference of trade unionists, for example, the minister
of labor declared:

On this question of wages I have stated time and again that
wages must be related to productivity. . . . At the moment

our wages have gone appreciably higher whilst, on the other side, productivity has remained relatively low. . . .

Now we must have a pause . . . just a pause while we get our breath back.[27]

The government's fear of wage increases derives from its conviction that higher wages would threaten the attainment of key economic objectives. It fears that wage increases will lead to capital substitution for labor, with debilitating effects on the employment targets posited in the National Development Plan.[28] The government also fears inflation, with its effects on the real value of government salaries, the international position of Zambia's currency, and the encouragement of yet further wage demands. Equally as powerful as all these considerations, however, is the government's conception of how development takes place in Zambia. Wage rises in excess of productivity increases represent an expansion of the workers' share of corporate revenues— an expansion that must take place at the expense of the share of the government. Such increases are regarded by the government as threats to the taxable margin of corporate revenues and as encroachments by the workers upon the resources available for development purposes. The assistant labor commissioner, speaking for the minister of labor, articulates this interpretation. Positing an increase in wages, he declares:

The profits of the firm will remain the same or decline. Consequently, the firm will not expand. In fact, it may decline. . . . Government revenues from [the] Company Tax will also remain the same or decline. . . .

In the case of a fall in revenue some Government services or projects will have to be cut down.[29]

In a speech before trade unionists in Kitwe, the minister of labor made clear just how strongly the government views the expansion of the workers' share of corporate revenues as a threat to its capacity to transfer development funds to lagging sectors in the economy:

If we are to give way any further to demands for increases we would very likely place in jeopardy the programme of development on which we place our main hope for a better future for the mass of the nation, most of whom at present live in rural areas at far lower standards of life than the urban average earner.[30]

Thus the edict: "For the next few years . . . any substantial improvement in wages and other conditions must be balanced by corresponding improvements in productivity. . . . [Past] wage increases have resulted [in] a reasonable share of the national product for wage earners as a whole." [31]

The Policies of Social Justice

The uneven distribution of wealth along racial lines in Zambia gives rise to the second government labor policy: the pursuit of social justice. As the minister of labor states in a widely distributed pamphlet: "Zambia has more than her share of . . . anachronisms. The ones in which this ministry is directly involved are wages . . . [and] the differentials in wages between expatriates and local workers. . . . With regard to these . . . the Zambian nation started on the wrong foot." [32] The government has noted that racial disparities in wealth pervade every sector of the economy. The ministry of labor records that non-Africans earn four to five times as much as Africans in manufacturing and nine to ten times as much as Africans in agriculture.[33] In nonagricultural occupations, Africans earn an average yearly income of £198 while non-Africans earn an average yearly income of £1,700; the corresponding figures are £63 and £330 respectively in agriculture.[34] So too in the field of mining, where the government contends that non-Africans earn nearly eight times the average annual wage of African employees.[35]

To illustrate the racial basis for the distribution of wealth that figures so prominently in government statistics, we have plotted wage distributions for five industries from data presented in the 1966 annual report of the Ministry of Labour (chart 5). The distributions are disjunctive; in most cases the highest paid African

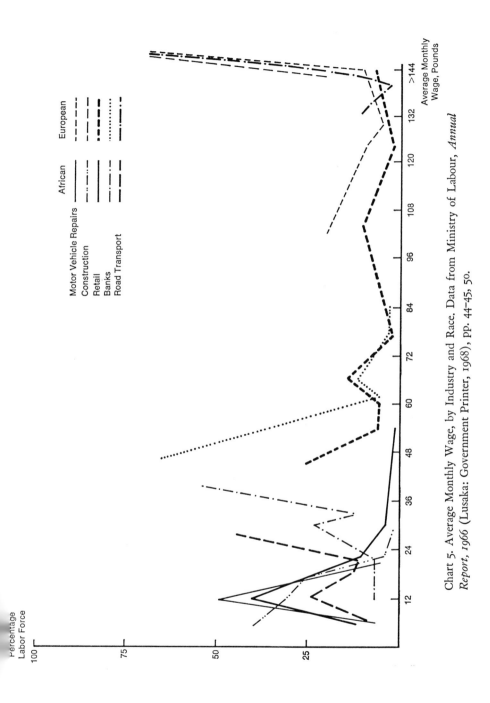

Chart 5. Average Monthly Wage, by Industry and Race. Data from Ministry of Labour, *Annual Report, 1966* (Lusaka: Government Printer, 1968), pp. 44–45, 50.

does not earn as much as the lowest paid European. Typical too is that European employees cluster at the highest wage levels and the African employees concentrate at the bottom end of the scale. Only in the cases of banking and retail trades do African earnings approximate those of European employees.

The government is determined to abolish these inequities, both in the Zambian economy as a whole and in the mining industry in particular. President Kaunda enunciated the slogan: "Political independence without matching economic independence is meaningless." [36] And with regard to the mining sector, the government states, "The long accumulation of economic inequities and racial injustices which is our inheritance must now be broken." [37] A later paragraph in the same document makes clear the scope of its plans: "We believe it absolutely imperative . . . that every vestige of racial discrimination be eradicated from the mining industry. This must run the entire gamut of industrial relations, from the right to use facilities to the level of wages paid." [38]

To achieve its objectives of racial equality the government elaborates several policies. The first is Zambianization. If the European possesses more wealth than the African, so the government reasons, it is largely because the Europeans occupy higher posts in industry. Racial disparities in the economy can therefore be reduced by compelling the mines to grant the workers' demands for more rapid and more pervasive advancement. President Kaunda states his commitment to localization in a public meeting on the copperbelt: "I want to see more Zambians grow up in every industry. I don't want to see people just beginning as personnel managers and ending there. I want to see them occupying exacting posts." [39] As he reaffirmed his position in a speech before the National Council of UNIP: "Now, as I have said before, we must open up the economic stream to Zambian participation." [40]

That the government is responding to the demands of the labor force is made clear in the president's statements before the Zambia Congress of Trade Unions.

> This process whereby Zambians are progressively taking over
> the executive, managerial and technical posts in our country,

is of the greatest possible importance. For if the process . . .
is not carried forward with significant speed, then we deny
legitimate opportunity to advance to many of our people
and will build up a feeling of frustration which will be a
danger to society.[41]

Training for Zambianization must be provided quickly, for so
strong are the demands that "time is not with us." [42] Responding
to the demands of the workers on the one hand, the government
seeks to evoke compliance from the companies on the other. It
created a Zambianization Committee to survey the possibilities
for advancement in the mines and to encourage the mines to
accelerate the training and promotion of local personnel. The
government also elicited a public statement from employers'
representatives that:

> We, the employers, pledge that we will Zambianize our
> undertakings as rapidly as possible and, to this end, will
> provide opportunities to our workers for industrial training.[43]

As the minister of labor assured trade union leaders, "You may
rest assured that no stone will be left unturned to bring about
rapid Zambianisation." [44]

The second area of government action is in the field of facilities
and perquisites. If access to monetary rewards is racially distributed on the mines, so too is access to superior housing, hospital care, and on-the-job facilities such as change houses and
shower rooms. In the field of housing, a government spokesman
noted: "To secure a good house with all modern facilities, you
must be a European. . . . To qualify for one of these objects
[picture of an African house] you must be an African and employed as a common worker on the mines." [45] A similar pattern
prevails in the mine hospitals:

> In the past, their [Anglo-American Corporation] racialism
> was unadulterated. If you were an African, you went to the
> African hospital, if European you went to a European hos-
> pital.
>
> [Now there will be] the "free" hospital which due to

economic circumstances will be catering for Africans only while Nkana will be "fee" paying catering for the privileged few.[46]

Economic circumstances insure that the "privileged few" will be principally Europeans. So too in facilities at the workpoints: Europeans, insofar as they possess the better jobs, possess as well superior access to better facilities. The supervisors' change house and the supervisors' level on the two-storied lift that transports miners down the shaft have both been used nearly exclusively by European miners.[47] The government's reaction to this situation is best summarized in its paper on the report of a commission of inquiry into the mining industry.

> [The Government] accepts that, in any industrial hierarchy, perquisites are in fact one form of remuneration and are likely to vary with status in the industry. Until Zambianisation has progressed much further, however, this conception as applied in the mining industry will be hedged with difficulties. . . . Government is convinced that the industry has been inexcusably lax in that it has permitted (possibly even encouraged) situations to develop which, to the local employees, can only be taken for racial discrimination. . . . We therefore feel that the companies must undertake whatever recasting is necessary to eliminate once and for all any existing racial discrimination, and to remove completely any chance of existing rules or restrictions being misunderstood by local employees, or misrepresented to them by racially minded expatriates. If disciplinary measures against the latter are necessary, they should be used.[48]

Wages are the last area in which the government seeks to overcome racial disparities. Until very recently, the mines maintained a dual-wage structure derived from their confrontation of two distinct labor markets—one expatriate and the other local. In the expatriate market, the companies must bid for skills in short supply; they must compete in a market in which wage levels are far in excess of those paid locally in Zambia; and they must offer an inducement to move to a relatively "backward" area, devoid of many of the amenities available in Europe and South Africa. By contrast, the companies face none of these conditions on the local labor market. The requisite skills for common labor are in abundant supply; mine wages easily compete with those offered by other local employers; and the amenities of the copperbelt exceed those to be found elsewhere in Zambia. This resulted in the dual-wage structure which the local workers naturally perceived as racially discriminatory. They agitated militantly against it. The government, in a major policy statement, revealed its sensitivity to the workers' demands:

> Wide differences in wages and other conditions exist . . . between expatriates and local employees. It was these latter differences . . . which were the immediate reason for the appointment of the Brown Commission of Inquiry in March of this year [1966]. Unrest over the glaring disparities in wages paid for similar work in the mining industry—disparities which were closely patterned on race—had led to a six-fold increase in the rate of industrial stoppages. . . . Clearly the Government had a duty to order an objective and searching inquiry into the causes of the situation.[49]

In the same statement, the government revealed its commitment to pressure the companies to respond to these demands. "We believe it absolutely imperative . . . that every vestige of racial discrimination be eradicated from the mining industry. This must run the entire gamut of industrial relations, from the right to use facilities to the level of wages paid." [50] It recommended that there be a "rate for the job" which would give equal pay for the same work irrespective of the origin of the employees. "Turning to wages, Government strongly supports the Commission's recommendation that present dual wage scales be replaced by a new basic scale payable without regard to the worker's origin." [51]

In May 1969 the companies and the Mineworkers' Union agreed to negotiate a single basic wage rate for Zambian and expatriate workers. However, an additional element would be added to the expatriates' wages. This "expatriate element" would induce skilled labor to come to Zambia and thus assist in the competition for skilled labor on the foreign market. As President Kaunda stated: "Now listen, Zambian policy is that there is going to be a basic wage for everybody, but there is going to be an expatriate allowance. Those who come from the outside for a few years will be given a little more but the basic wage is the same." [52] As part of its attempts to advance the relative standing of Africans in the economy, therefore, the government thus identified with the position of the African labor force in the area of wage demands and required an adjustment in the position of the mining companies.

Strategies for Implementing a Development Labor Policy

There exists a significant difference between the development and social justice streams of the government's labor policy. The development policy addresses the mine employees as industrial workers and emphasizes the restraint and containment of labor demands: workers are to resist laziness, to contain their opposition to supervisors, to dampen the militancy with which they express their grievances, and to limit their wage demands. By contrast, the social justice policy addresses itself to the mine employees as Africans and champions their demands: African workers are to advance their status in industry, to have greater access to superior facilities, and to achieve basic wages equal to those of their European counterparts.

There can be no doubt that the members of the political elite are deeply and genuinely dedicated to eradicating racial injustice; this has always been true in independent Zambia. But what is important at this point is that the existence of a social justice policy yields the government a means for attaining its development objectives. For the coexistence of the two policies enables the government to attempt to indulge the demands of the mineworkers as Africans while at the same time constraining their behavior as working men. Thus, for example, the government can assert that it supports all Africans "in seeing that they get a fair deal," while at the same time demanding that the workers "keep the wheels of industry turning." [53] By advocating the abolition of discriminatory facilities, the government can demand in return that the workers not "endanger the smooth and efficient workings of . . . industry." [54]

While the exchange is often implicit, it is also explicitly manifest in public statements by government officials. Thus the reaction of one official to a strike on the mines: "How can the miners do this to us when we have brought them the fruits of independence and fought for the dignity of Africans in the industry?" [55] And the minister of labor, after reviewing the government's programs for the advancement of African working men, comments:

> In the words of a king who reigned in Palestine about 3,000 years ago—"My father (read 'My step-father, the late, un-lamented colonial regime of unhappy memory') chastised you with whips but I will chastise you with scorpions. My step-father made your burdens heavy, but I will make them ten times heavier." Because the greater the privilege, the greater the responsibility. . . . In future there is not going to be quid (or *kwacha*)* without plenty of pro quo. I am not going to tolerate behavior from workers crying "Give, give" without them giving in return.[56]

Using the Mineworkers' Union

A second strategy for implementing the development labor policy is to place the burden of implementation on the workers' own representatives—the leaders of the Mineworkers' Union.

In the field of social justice, the main role of the union is to vigorously champion the demands of the African mineworkers. The union is asked, in effect, to pursue its traditional role as the defender of the interests of mine labor. The government's pro-nouncements can be quickly detailed.

In the field of Zambianization, the president announces: "It is the duty of the Union to fight for this. They must see that the people get proper training to grow up in all industries. This is one of the major function[s] of unions." [57] In another speech,

---

* *Kwacha* is the basic denomination in Zambia's currency. It equals roughly $1.40, or 10 shillings in predevaluation Sterling.

he emphasizes the reliance government places on the unions in this field.

> There is one thing that is certain, that if they [the Unions] wait for others to do the job for them, then it won't get done. This could mean that our programme of Zambianisation will be held back because there is no one to keep pushing the employers if they attempt to dodge their responsibility.[58]

Just as the union must take up the task of Zambianization, so too must it work for the abolition of discriminatory perquisites on the mines. As the assistant labor commissioner states:

> Here the Trade Union Movement . . . was born before the State. The exploitation that existed was based on the colour of a man. During [this] pre-independence period the Trade Union Movement was concerned not only with the protection of the interests of the workers but also with the liberation of the country from foreign dominance and [racial] exploitation. . . . Now this pattern . . . should continue.[59]

The union movement is thus to carry on the fight for the abolition of racial exploitation and European dominance that characterized the struggle for independence. The government paper on the Brown Commission of Inquiry corroborates the position of the assistant labor commissioner. After demanding the abolition of differential facilities, the government states its commitment to voluntary settlements in the mining industry and urges that its views form the basis for further negotiations in the mining industry.[60]

So too with its wage policy. The government concludes its endorsement of a single wage scale for the copper industry by stating, "Government feels strongly that negotiation between the parties concerned will be along these lines."[61] And President Kaunda, referring to the dual-wage structure, comments:

> I understand that some Africans that do the same job as Europeans on the mines get one-third and the Europeans get three hundred per cent. Now you say Government is

standing in your way. Where? How? It is not our fault, but the fault of the Unions. You are there to negotiate as a union. We don't rule you at all.[62]

There exists a similar pattern in government's development policy: it is the workers' own representatives who are to implement the government's program. Instead of emphasizing the union's role as a defender of the workers' interests, however, in the field of development policy, the government emphasizes the union's role as a defender of the interests of the nation. Rather than transmitting and fighting for the demands of its members, the union is to regulate their behavior in conformity with public policy. In short, the union is to deviate from its traditional role as an input structure, and to serve as an agency for implementing public policy.

Thus, the government urges the union leaders to communicate its image of the national economy and demonstrate to the workers their position within it. The government's frequent injunctions to the union leaders to "educate . . . your members to the importance of their jobs in the context of the country's over-all development" [63] give evidence of its concern. So too does the statement:

All our workers in the Republic must be advised strongly that before they take to strike action they must bear in mind the following important points:

. . . .

3. They must consider the effects of the strike on the industry and the interests it serves in the country;
4. They must consider the overall effects of the strike on the national economy as a whole.[64]

The government also elicits the assistance of the union in enforcing the specific tenets of its labor policies. The union is to help the government exhort the mineworkers to hard work.

I would say that . . . your [the trade unionists] main task for the foreseeable future . . . [is] to keep the wheels of

industry turning. . . . [You] should encourage each worker,
each citizen, and each participant in our national production
programme to contribute his best in terms of efficiency . . .
and production.[65]

You need to ruthlessly curb laziness, lethargy, workshy-
ness, absenteeism among your members.[66]

The union must also refuse to protect lazy workers. Thus, in the
case of a worker too lazy to come to work: "You must wash
your hands of him. . . . You are the champions and defenders of
the workers—when they are in the right. I repeat—when they are
in the right. If a worker is absent without permission and without
any good reason, he is not entitled to your sympathy." [67] The
union leaders must also help the government to preserve industrial
peace. In remarks before the Congress of Trade Unions, the
assistant commissioner of labor places the prevention of strikes
among the two most important tasks of the union: "Let me say
that, in my opinion, the role of the trade union movement in
. . . national development . . . is purely and simply the maintenance of industrial peace and an increase in productivity." [68]
The minister of labor goes so far as to suggest that a union
leader is no leader at all if he cannot prevent illegitimate strike
action:

> Why have you tolerated . . . wild cat strikes? Have you no
> control over your members? Have your members no respect
> for you? Do you have no influence with them? If this is so,
> you should not be where you are. If a leader cannot lead, he
> should resign, and make way for those who can and will
> lead.[69]

As the president states before the Governing Council of the
Zambian Congress of Trade Unions, the union should also assist
in curbing wage demands.

> This is the reality for Zambia that we cannot have big in-
> creases in wages. . . . Therefore it is of the greatest impor-
> tance that trade unions when considering claims for extra
> wages should have regard for the effect their actions may

have on the national interests. This is, of course, a great responsibility for the Unions to accept.[70]

In response to what he sees as an imbalance between labor costs and output per man, the assistant labor commissioner tells labor leaders, "I would rather [that you looked] upon the welfare of your members as a reward to be earned after a period of self-denial and greater effort."[71] And in his typically forceful manner, the minister of labor underscores this position: "You need to gear up your members to resist the temptation of always demanding and demanding for some more. You have to work to change them from consumptionist attitudes to productionist attitudes."[72]

The government thus seeks the active cooperation of the union leaders in implementing the tenets of its development labor policy. The union leaders are to realize that, "It is the patriotic duty of the unions to pursue constructive and responsible policies because it is these policies which will serve the people in their struggle for economic progress."[73]

Why the Union?

Particularly in the area of development policy, there is a strange disparity between the government's goals and the means it has chosen to realize them. The policy contains a fairly harsh series of injunctions for the mineworkers and obviously runs counter to their or any other workers' conceptions of their interests. Nonetheless, the means for implementing the policy remain highly voluntaristic. The policy is not forced upon the workers; rather, it is to be enforced by the representatives the workers themselves have chosen as their public spokesmen. Why should there be this inconsistency between the ends and means of the government's labor policy? The basic reason is the government's conviction that the union and mineworkers are immensely powerful.

In part, the government's conviction is based upon the observed power of the union to militantly champion the interests of its members. While I shall argue that this aspect of union power should not be confounded with its capacity to regulate the behavior of its members in a direction contrary to their interests, the distinction is a relatively subtle one, and the government has barely had time to grasp it.

In part, the government's conviction derives from the past experience of the political leaders with the leaders of the union. As will be discussed in chapter 7, during the nationalist struggle, the present leaders of Zambia attempted to impel the union to adopt and to champion their political objectives. The union leaders vigorously and successfully resisted their attempts to impose or exercise political controls. In the majority of their attempts to intervene in the union's affairs, the political leaders were soundly rebuffed. These experiences created a healthy regard on the part of the government for the ability of the union leaders to fight for and defend their independent positions.

The government's belief in the power of the union also stems from its acute awareness of the costs of a direct confrontation with the union or the mineworkers. The workers' proven capacity to paralyze the mining industry constitutes an extremely effective political sanction. In the event of a confrontation, given the police power at its command, there is no doubt that the government could destroy the union and install a more closely controlled set of union leaders; and eventually, the mineworkers would return to their jobs. The intervening period of chaos and disruption would be extremely costly to the government, however, as would the possibly permanent alienation of the political allegiance of the labor force.

All these calculations are made in the context of a competitive party system. While a single-party system effectively prevails on the copperbelt, and while UNIP clearly dominates in the nation as a whole, opposition parties continue to exist in Zambia, and in fact have gained strong backing in the Central, Southern, and Barotse (now Western) provinces. Moreover, while the opposition parties are extremely weak on the copperbelt, they are nonetheless present and they do receive some electoral support.[74] Given the presence of an opposition, the government must always recognize the possibility of the defection of the union or the copper miners to its opponents; and the government realizes that were this to happen, it would face a grave political crisis and indeed would be forced to maneuver for its very survival. The mineworkers' ability to sanction the government at the polls, in addition to their ability to sanction it through strikes, thus places a heavy premium on the use of persuasion and inducements.

The government's identification with the interests of the Africans in the mining community provides yet another reason for preferring pressure to force. As shown in its policies of social justice, the political leaders in Zambia have regarded the copper companies as foreign, European dominated, and racially biased institutions. As Africans, former workers, and former subjects in a colonial order underpinned by the mining industry, the political leaders strongly identify with the sense of grievance of the mines' labor force. Sharing much of their outlook toward the companies, the Zambian political elite finds it intensely distasteful to oppose the mineworkers and to appear to identify with the interests of management. As will be discussed in chapter 10, however, the recent nationalization of the mines removes this impediment to forceful government action and may mark the beginning of more direct intervention in the conduct of labor relations. If the workers demand higher wages from the companies, they now "push a wage claim against the people." [75]

The government has a last reason for working with the union leaders rather than coercing or bypassing them: it possesses a relatively satisfactory working relationship with the Head Office of the union. Since independence, the union leaders have sought to cooperate with the government in the sphere of labor policy. It is only recently that the government has realized that the cooperation of the Head Office is not enough to ensure the success of its program.

4 The Failure of Government Policy

Response of Union Leaders

Interviews with the seven members of the Head Office of the Mineworkers' Union convinced me that the national-level leaders of the union endorse the conception of the national economy that orders so much of the government's thinking on labor matters. The officers share the government's frame of reference; they think in national terms, viewing the mining industry in relation to other sectors of the economy and especially in relation to the government's economic objectives. These leaders frequently refer to Zambia as a "new" nation, and they regard the government's development goals as necessary for Zambia. They fully realize that they represent the labor force of the wealthiest sector of the economy; from this realization they derive a sense of responsibility for the economic well-being of Zambia as a whole. These patterns of thinking can be detected in the following statement of David Mwila, the current president of the union.

> The Union can not have the idea that its duty is to do something for the members alone. The duty of the Union is to a wider field, to develop the country as Zambia is. No, we can not have the same ideas as we had before independence; as a new nation, we must adopt a program that will benefit the country as a whole and not just our members. The country belongs to us; we will not let it down just because we are trade unionists.[1]

The financial secretary's remark that "our union of course is working with the Government to see that the Four Year Plan is well done in the country" suggests his acceptance of the government's development goals; and his contention that "with the Four Year Plan, we do not want the workers to frustrate it" indicates his willingness to use his position for output purposes, structuring labor's behavior so as to achieve the government's economic objectives.[2]

This acceptance of the government's conception of the economy facilitates the Head Office's endorsement of the specific tenets of the development labor policy. While Head Office leaders do not feel it appropriate to exhort their members to work hard, they do warn the rank and file of their unwillingness to protest management action against workers with poor work records. Thus the general secretary states that "loafers," "slip-shod workers," and others with poor reputations as mine employees cannot obtain full protection from the union. He explains that by fighting for these people, "the Union loses its reputation in the eyes of management and the Government; with weak cases like these the most we promise our members is that we will plead long service, his family, his children's education, loss of pension and so on. But we can't be tough." [3]

The Head Office also shares the government's concern with the preservation of supervisory authority in the mines. The best demonstration of this commitment came in 1967, when the Head Office incorporated the local mine supervisors into the union's field of jurisdiction. In order to win management's consent for this measure, the Head Office made plain its opposition to the use of the union as a weapon for blunting the authority of local supervisors. The Head Office assured the companies that it would protect the right of supervisors to maintain "essential services" during strikes, refuse to sponsor cases in retaliation against supervisors for disciplinary action they may have taken, forestall intimidation, and make clear to their supervisory members that they need not fear union action against them for any unpopular duties they may have to perform as part of their jobs.[4]

Agreement between the union and government extends to strike action as well. The Head Office fully realizes that the disruption of copper production injures the national economy. As the general secretary stated, "I have been a trade unionist for three-fourths of my life, and I have never seen a strike that didn't have the same consequences: the loss to the land and to the industry." [5] Supporting the merger of the Staff Association and the Mineworkers' Union, the general treasurer noted that many strikes had resulted from competition between the two organizations. He contended that "we must join together" and so "stop these strikes," for "there is the problem of the Four Year Plan." [6] In the Supreme Council meeting of 8 January 1963, four of the six Head Office officials spoke out against a series of strikes that were being led by branch officials; the basis of their criticism was that the strikes were "a bad thing . . . for our African government." [7]

While endorsing the discipline tenets of the government's labor policy, the Head Office is more equivocal in its support of the tenet that wages must increase only in proportion to increases in productivity. Both the general secretary and the president of the union fully agreed with the government's contention that wage demands must be "responsible" to prevent the disruption of the economy. But the union officials felt that the disparity between local and expatriate wage levels was fully as important as the relationship between productivity and wage increases in determining what could be viewed as a responsible wage demand. While the juxtaposition of the productivity and racial justice criteria characterizes government thought as well, it has been noted that after the 1964 and 1966 wage increases, the government felt that no further wage increases were necessary for the next few years.[8] The government appeared to feel that the wage increases had produced parity between the basic wages of local and expatriate employees; what disparities remained, the government seemed to regard as a legitimate "expatriate element." [9] The union leaders were less willing to accept that the 1964 and 1966 increases produced a single-wage scale in the mining industry. While they freely granted that the racial disparities in wages had been greatly reduced, they felt that significant disparities nonetheless remained which could only be reduced by further across-the-board raises in local wage rates.*

What is more impressive than the Head Office officials' dis-

---

* The negotiation of the single basic wage scale in May 1969 resulted in a modest rise in wages. See chapter 10.

agreement with the government's position on mine wages is the restraint they exhibit in their actual conduct on wage matters. The attitudes of the Head Office may be at variance with government policy, but their behavior largely supports the government's position. Thus, in 1965, the Head Office declared an official dispute over the companies' dual-wage structure, pitched its wage demands at a level designed to reduce the difference between local and expatriate wages, and prepared for strike action. Legal difficulties necessitated the postponement of a strike ballot, and during the period of this postponement, Rhodesia unilaterally declared its independence from Great Britain, thus plunging Zambia into a major economic crisis. Drastically reducing its wage claim, the Head Office quickly negotiated an agreement with the mining companies, and campaigned intensively among the mineworkers for restraint in formulating wage demands.[10] In so reacting to the Rhodesian crisis, the Head Office clearly restrained a large wage demand out of consideration for the well-being of the greater national economy. This pattern is also evident in their behavior in 1967. While the Head Office could have negotiated further wage increases, and had in fact placed the item on the negotiating agenda, they postponed the matter. Interviews revealed that the postponement stemmed from the Head Office's reluctance to take a position at variance with the government and fear of the consequences of so overt a breach with government policy. While not agreeing with government policy on wages, therefore, the Head Office does behave with delicacy and restraint in that area and in so doing conforms in its behavior with the current dictates of government policy.

Just as the Head Office largely cooperates with the government in the sphere of development labor policy, so too does it cooperate in implementing the policies of social justice. The best illustration of this cooperation is the union leaders' encouragement of Zambianization. When the government formed a Zambianization Committee to implement local advancement in the mines, the union assigned a full-time representative to the committee. He actively championed the views of local employees before the committee and cited cases where advancement was retarded by oversight or supposed design. Instances included the cases of qualified personnel who were passed over for promotion; opposition to the promotion and training of alien Africans; and suggestions that training be done by full-time training officers instead of by the very supervisors whom the locals were scheduled to replace.[11] The actions of the Head Office help to explain the success of this element of government labor policy. The Zambianization Committee has assured that only Zambians will receive promotion and training for supervisory posts.[12] Company training programs were increased to insure the Zambianization of two-thirds of the underground shift bosses by 1971 and the entire personnel department by the end of 1969. The companies agreed to modify their promotional routes accordingly.[13] And the committee is currently introducing similar adjustments for other surface departments.

Response of the Mineworkers

The Head Office thus accepts the basic premises of the government's development labor policy and most of the specific tenets as well. Insofar as the government seeks to develop an output orientation among the national leaders of the union, it has therefore been successful. But insofar as the government assumes that the support and collaboration of the union leaders will translate into support from the mass of the mineworkers, it appears to have erred. The available evidence forces me to conclude that the union leaders have failed to evoke the workers' support for the government's labor program.

The Discipline Tenets

It has been noted that the government seeks to instill the mineworkers with discipline: commitment to hard work, obedience to supervisors, and adherence to peaceful means of resolving disputes. Evidence indicates that rather than obtaining higher levels of discipline from the mass of the copper miners, the government has been confronted with less willingness to work hard, greater insubordination, and increased propensities to strike.

Data on miners' attitudes toward work unfortunately do not

exist. Two kinds of behavioral indicators are available, however: measures of offenses and of labor productivity in underground operations. Taking the frequency of absenteeism as a measure of the miners' willingness to work hard, the records of offenses from the central shaft and smelter at Rhokana Corporation indicate that there was a decline in the miners' commitment to work hard following independence. Corrected for alterations in the size of the labor force since 1964, the data in table 4 indicate an increase of 113 percent and 63 percent in the frequency of absenteeism in the central shaft and smelter respectively.[14,15]

While evidence from two departments in one mine is not impressive, the inferences are largely corroborated by data on the productivity of mine labor. The figures on productivity pertain solely to underground operations and are therefore perhaps the most valid that could be used. Productivity measures on the surface departments are influenced by the performance of other departments—specifically, by underground operations; for the efficiency of labor in surface operations depends on the capacity of the underground departments to supply regular inputs of copper ore. The productivity of underground labor is independent of other mine departments, however, for the underground

TABLE 4
Number of Offenses
(By year)

	1964	1965	1966	1967	Percentage increase 1964–67	
					Uncorrected	Corrected
Cases of absenteeism						
Central shaft	445	678	980	1,007	126	113
Smelter	228	289	418	401	76	63
Work strength on the mine	9,414	10,331	10,764	10,653	13	

Source: Rhokana Corporation, "Comments on Questions Arising from Productivity Seminar" (Photocopy, Author's Collection, 12 February, 1968)

Note: "Corrected" means adjusted for changes in mine labor strength.

department receives major inputs from no other sector of the mine. Moreover, the irregular fuel supplies that have hampered mine operations since the Rhodesian rebellion would affect measures of productivity in the surface departments to a greater degree than in underground operations. In fact, following the rebellion, the companies had to resort to stockpiling ore in order to adjust to the disparate pace of production in the surface and underground departments. Lastly, while technological innovations have recently been introduced in the surface departments— for example, electric furnaces have recently been installed—no such innovations have been made in the underground departments for which the productivity calculations are to be presented.[16] To a greater extent than would be true in other departments, therefore, measures of productivity in underground operations actually measure the performance of the labor force itself. By the same reasoning, for our purposes, the productivity calculations for underground labor furnish a measure superior to those based upon productivity estimates for the entire mine's labor force.[17]

Insofar as our measures reflect the willingness of labor to work hard, the data suggest a general decline in the miners' commitment to their jobs. Five categories of labor productivity registered significant decreases over the 1964–67 period at Rhokana Mine (table 5). The application of similar measures at Roan Antelope Mine (table 6) reveals even greater decreases in productivity over a five-year period. These data suggest that the inference drawn from the analysis of mineworker absenteeism is valid: the commitment of mine labor to working hard declined following independence in Zambia.[18]

The miners' readiness to disobey their supervisors increased markedly over this period. Penalty records again furnish evidence of the mineworkers' behavior. Utilizing the number of offenses of *failing to obey instructions* as an indicator of insubordination, the data in table 7 indicate that the frequency of insubordination increased by 525 percent in central shaft and by 769 percent at the smelter in Rhokana Mine since 1964. The corresponding figure for Roan Antelope, presented in table 8, shows an in-

TABLE 5
Productivity, Rhokana Mine

Measure	1964	1965	1966	1967	Percentage decrease 1964–67
Tons per man shift (mining)	3.98	3.66	2.83	3.19	19.92
Feet drilled per machine shift (roto)	96	89	94	80	16.67
Feet drilled per machine shift (perc)	108	105	92	92	14.81
Feet advanced per machine shift	7.83	5.42	4.87	5.22	33.33
Tons lashed per shift (Central and SOB shaft)	5.15	4.63	4.39	4.48	13.01

Source: Rhokana Corporation, "Comments on Questions Arising from Productivity Seminar" (Photocopy, Author's Collection, 12 February, 1968).
Note: "Roto" refers to rotary drilling, while "perc" refers to percussion drilling.

crease in these offenses in all departments of 53 percent. If instead we adopt the number of offenses for *refusing to obey instructions* as an index of insubordination, the rate of increase becomes 159 percent for central shaft and 377 percent for the smelter at Rhokana Mine. A third index of the miners' resistance to supervisory authority is the number of protests against super-

TABLE 6
Productivity, Roan Antelope Mine

Measure	1963	1964	1965	1966	1967	Percentage Decrease 1963–67
Tons per man shift (mining)	4.58	4.42	4.32	3.76	3.40	25.76
Feet drilled per machine shift	....	....	....	....	....	47.00
Tons broken per stoping shift	....	....	....	....	....	34.00

Source: Copper Industry Service Bureau, "Transcript, Productivity Seminar, Luanshya and Ndola" (Photocopy, Author's Collection, 6 January, 1968), p. 9.
Note: Yearly data on the last two indicators was missing on the original document.

TABLE 7
Offenses, Rhokana Mine
(By year)

Offenses reported	1964	1965	1966	1967	Percentage increase 1964–67	
					Uncorrected	Corrected
Failing to obey instructions						
Central shaft	60	74	121	383	538	525
Smelter	11	26	41	97	782	769
Refusing to obey instructions						
Central shaft	22	20	26	60	172	159
Smelter	29	52	44	142	390	377
Work strength on the mine	9,414	10,331	10,764	10,653	13	

Source: Rhokana Corporation, "Comments on Questions Arising from Productivity Seminar" (Photocopy, Author's Collection, 12 February, 1968).
Note: "Corrected" means adjusted for changes in mine labor strength.

visors lodged with the personnel departments. My own counts of these protests, presented in table 9, indicate that the frequency of complaints against supervisors rose dramatically at the time

TABLE 8
Offenses, Roan Antelope Mine
(By year)

Offenses reported	1964	1965	Percentage increase 1964–65	
			Uncorrected	Corrected
Failing to obey instructions	374	590	58	53
Work strength on the mine	7,412	7,766	5	

Source: Copper Industry Service Bureau, "Transcript, Productivity Seminar, Luanshya and Ndola" (Photocopy, Author's Collection, 6 January, 1968), p. 9.
Note: "Corrected" means adjusted for changes in mine labor strength.

TABLE 9
Protests against Supervisors

	1950-63	1964-68	Total
Number of protests against supervisors	39	44	83
Of all protests against supervisors (1950–68), percentage which fall in this period	47	53	100
Protests against supervisors as percentage of total demands	10	25	15
Total number demands made by mineworkers	396	177	573

of self-government; 53 percent of all protests submitted since the founding of the union have been made since self-government in Zambia.[19] By whatever index used, therefore, the data suggest that the workers accord a much lower level of respect to their supervisors than that advocated by government.

The Head Office, it must be noted, appears to have adhered to this tenet of government labor policy in deed as well as word. Employing the third index of obedience to supervision, it can be seen from table 10 that since self-government the Head Office has handled fewer protests against supervisors, despite the overall increase in supervisory disputes.

The third discipline tenet of government labor policy is the abnegation of strike action. Data on the incidence of strikes on the mines indicate that the frequency of this kind of indiscipline has risen since self-government in Zambia. We see in table 11 that not only has the absolute number of strikes increased, but also the proportion of grievances that result in strike action. Over half the strikes that have taken place since the creation of the Mineworkers' Union in 1949 have occurred since self-government in Zambia. Over this period, the Head Office has neither initiated nor supported a single strike action. While the Head Office endorses the discipline tenets of government policy, therefore, the policy once again fails to find support among the mass of the workers on the mines.

TABLE 10
Protests against Supervisors by Union Level

	1950-63	1964-68	Total
Protests acted on by branch alone			
Total number	32	41	73
Of total supervisory protests acted on by branches alone (1950-68), percentage falling in this period	44	56	100
Of all supervisory protests by union in this period, percentage acted on by branch alone	82	93	
Protests acted on by Head Office and branches together			
Total number	7	3	10
Of total supervisory protests acted on by both levels together (1950-68), percentage falling in this period	70	30	100
Of all supervisory protests by union in this period, percentage acted on by both levels together	18	7	
Total supervisory protests	39	44	83

Note: The Head Office never took up a protest against a supervisor on its own.

The Wage Tenet

The wage tenet follows a similar pattern. As shown in table 12, the average annual increase of the average annual earnings of African miners has been 14.7 percent since 1963; this represents an average annual increase of 9.4 percent in real terms.

TABLE 11
Strikes

	1950-63	1964-68
Grievances which result in strikes	75	86
Percentage of total grievances	19	49
Grievances not resulting in strikes	321	91
Percentage of total grievances	81	51
Total number grievances	396	177

TABLE 12
Changes in Average Annual Earnings of African Mineworkers

Year	Average annual earnings African mineworkers	Cost of living index, all items, low incomes, copperbelt
1960	£257	101.8
1961	258	101.7
1962	245	103.5
1963	279	102.3
1964	324	106.5
1965	358	113.5
1966	423	126.8
	Average annual change since 1963	
	+14.7%	+5.3%

Source: Earnings figures taken from the notebooks used to compile the Copper Industry Service Bureau, *Copperbelt of Zambia Mining Industry Year Book* [*various years*] (Kitwe: CISB, various years). The cost of living index is taken from the Central Statistical Office, *Monthly Digest of Statistics* 4, no. 1 (January–February 1968): 48.

In large part, these wage increases have resulted from large-scale protests by members against the moderate behavior of their leaders. Thus, when the Head Office agreed to the 1964 contract which preserved a vast disparity between local and expatriate wages, the members of the Union were infuriated by the conduct of their leaders. Reacting to the pressures of the rank and file, the Head Office improved the settlement through further negotiations; nevertheless the militant membership initiated a series of strikes which so severely disrupted the industry that the government intervened. It appointed a commission of inquiry (the Brown Commission) which recommended an immediate 22 percent increase in basic wage rates for all local employees. And the companies, regarding the increase as the price for industrial peace, immediately complied with the commission's recommendation.

While this sequence of events is the most dramatic instance of the members' rejection of moderate Head Office policies, data on the day-to-day occurrence of grievances provides further evidence of the failure to transmit the policy of wage restraint to the local level. Wage levels can rise for reasons other than the revision of basic rates of pay. Demands for job regrading and bonus increases constitute demands for higher pay. When these and other "hidden" wage demands are counted, it can be seen from table 13 that the frequency of these demands has increased

TABLE 13
Wage Demands

	1950–63	1964–68
Direct demands for wage increases	15	5
Percentage wage demands that are demands for increased basic wages	24	14
Of all demands for increased basic wages, percentage that fall in this period	75	25
Demands for "hidden" wage increases	47	30
Percentage wage demands that are demands for "hidden" wage increases	76	86
Of all demands for "hidden" wage increases, percentage that fall in this period	61	39
Total wage demands	62	35

by 10 percent since self-government in Zambia. And when the demands are classified by their origin, as in table 14, it can be

TABLE 14
Wage Demands by Union Level

	1950–63	1964–68
Number from branch	26	25
Percentage from branch	46	71
Number from Head Office	27	6
Percentage from Head Office	48	17
Number from joint action	3	4
Percentage from joint action	6	12
Total wage demands	56	35

Note: Disparity in totals between this and preceding table is due to the unassignability of some cases.

seen that despite the overall increase in wage demands, the Head Office has radically curtailed the frequency with which it requests increases in mine wages. In this, as in other areas of labor policy, despite cooperation from the Head Office, the government fails to evoke support for its policies from the mass of the mineworkers.

Current and Future Rates of Economic Growth

While the government has won cooperation with its development labor policy from the national-level officers of the union, it has thus failed to win the support of the mineworkers themselves. And while the government has made progress in the field of social justice, little cooperation with development policy has been forthcoming from the mine employees. Though it is impossible to trace out the consequences of the failure of each governmental injunction, it *is* possible to indicate the consequences of the failure to impose wage restraint. Using the behavior of wages as an indicator for the policy as a whole, we can assess the consequences of the failure of the government's labor policy.

Thus, over the four-year period 1963–66, the average annual rate of growth of the gross domestic product remained in the vicinity of 15 percent (table 15). Equally impressive was the rate

TABLE 15
Gross Domestic Product by Year
(Current prices, millions of pounds)

Year	GDP
1963	202.2
1964	234.8
1965	274.1
1966	322.6

Source: Ministry of Finance, *Economic Report*[s], *1964–67* (Lusaka: Government Printer, 1964–67).

of investment. In terms of actual capital formation, table 16 reveals a strong and concerted effort to invest in productive capabilities. On the basis of per capita income, allowing for inflation as well as for population increases, the rate of growth of the gross domestic product over this four-year period exceeded 10 percent per annum.[20]

In the short run, therefore, the failure of the government's labor policy appears not to have significantly damaged the growth of the national economy. The principal reason is that the effects of wage increases have been more than offset by other factors. Of these factors, the price of copper and the availability to government of new sources of revenues have been the most important.

Since 1964, the average yearly price of copper has climbed well beyond £350 per long ton; the previous five years, it remained at, or below, £250.[21] As seen in table 17, the result has been that the profits of the mining companies grew even in the face of an increased wages bill. Another reason for the persistence of high corporate profits is that wages represent a small proportion of the total costs of production. One study estimates the proportion to be 9.4 percent for the industry as a whole; 1967 figures for Rhokana corporation suggest a figure of 15 percent.[22] Given the disparity between the rate of increase in prices and wages, and the low percentage of production costs which wages represent,

TABLE 16
Gross Fixed Capital Formation
(Millions of pounds)

	1963	1964	1965	1966
Private enterprise	20.5	27.2	37.8	45.6
Public sector	12.4			
Government enterprise	....	2.2	6.5	11.1
Central government	....	6.9	13.4	28.2
Local government	....	1.8	2.5	1.7
Total gross fixed capital formation	32.9	38.1	60.2	86.6

Source: Ministry of Finance, *Economic Report[s]*, *1964–67* (Lusaka: Government Printer, 1964–67).

TABLE 17
Revenues and Taxation

Year	Profits before taxation (× 1,000)	Taxes paid (× 1,000)	London Metal Exchange, mean price, wire bars (per long ton)	Output in short tons (× 1,000)
1963	£40,393	£14,139	£234	635.0
1964	47,315	21,612	352	707.9
1965	52,153	21,825	469	654.8
1966	57,182	23,630	550	645.9
1967	50,617	19,905	418	679.3

Source: Figures for profits and taxation calculated from year-end accounts. The volume of output and copper price are taken from Copper Industry Service Bureau, *Copperbelt of Zambia Mining Industry Year Book 1968* (Kitwe: CISB, 1969).
Note: For Mufulira, Roan, Nchanga, and Rhokana only.

the mining industry has been able to prosper despite the failure of government policy. And as shown in table 17, they have also been able to produce great quantities of public revenues for development expenditures.

Secondly, at the time of independence, there was a vast increase in the sources of income available to government which could be invested in development projects. With the breakup of the Federation, customs duties reverted to Zambia; given the value of copper exports, these duties represented a major source of income. At the time of independence, the government took over the mineral royalties which had been paid to the B.S.A. Moreover, funds that had formerly been diverted to Southern Rhodesia now were returned to Zambia; their magnitude has been calculated at £10 million per year.[23] Lastly, the government, in 1966, took advantage of the high price of copper to create a new source of revenues. It levied an export tax, set at 40 percent of the amount by which the London Metal Exchange price of copper exceeded £300 per long ton. The result of all these factors was the creation in the immediate postindependence period of vast public revenues for development purposes—revenues which were capable of more than offsetting the immediate debilitating effects of wage increases. Thus, in the short run, Zambia's economy has grown rapidly, and there have been ample funds to insure its high rate of growth, despite the failure of the government's labor policy.

More significant, however, have been the long-run effects of the failure of government policy: the weakened capacity of Zambia to insure the continuation of this rate of growth in future periods. Wage rates in the mines form a reference point for wages in other industries. The inability of the government to restrain wages on the mines has resulted in increases throughout other economic sectors. Following the 22 percent increase in mine wages in 1966, the government found it necessary to increase the wages of teachers and civil servants. In November 1966, the commercial and wholesale traders increased their salaries. In May 1967, the Wages Council for hotels and catering services granted a pay raise to workers in those industries. At the same time, wages in building, civil engineering, and contracting rose by 33 percent. Later in 1967, agricultural workers and domestic servants were granted a 30 percent increase in minimum wages.[24] The dynamics of this phenomenon are revealed in the report of the government commission on the causes of teachers' strikes in the Western Province. "The grievances seem to have been exacerbated by comparisons with the salaries paid to miners [and] to teachers in the mine schools." [25] As Knight observes, in his study of Zambian wages:

> A widening of the existing gap between mining and other earnings caused discontent among workers in other sectors, so producing pressures on the government as an employer and on its Wages Board; and it influenced wage negotiations elsewhere in the economy.[26]

In terms of Zambia's potential for continued growth, one of the most significant consequences of the wage spread has been its effect upon inflation. We cannot argue that increased wages are the greatest single cause of inflation in Zambia. But we can argue that increased wages strengthen inflationary forces which already exist in the Zambian economy.

As we have noted, Zambia is in the midst of a rapid and concerted drive for economic development. Public investment has burgeoned in the postindependence period. The government has mounted an expansion in expenditure which, in the context of Zambia's history, is extraordinary for its rapidity and magnitude.

Development expenditures, given inelasticities in supply, tend to be inflationary. What makes the situation particularly severe in Zambia is the restriction of supply produced by Rhodesia's declaration of independence. During federation, locational advantages and the policies of the federal government encouraged the formation of secondary industries in Southern Rhodesia at the expense of the development of Northern Rhodesia. At independence, many of Zambia's basic commodities and essential supplies had to be shipped from Rhodesia. Moreover, many of the goods which were not imported directly from Rhodesia were imported through it. The vast majority of Zambia's imports— over 90 percent—were carried by Rhodesian Railways. Following Rhodesia's unilateral declaration of independence (UDI), Zambia and Rhodesia engaged in a bitter conflict over rail rates and traffic flows. The result was the disruption of rail traffic and the constriction of essential supplies for the Zambian economy; the rebellion brought a decrease of over 20 percent in the monthly tonnage of imports carried on Rhodesian Railways.[27] Exacerbating the problem were the vigorous efforts of the Zambian government to direct traffic away from the Southern routes toward Tanzania. The political merits of the policy were unarguable; however, the economic consequences were costly. Thus, not only were goods more scarce after UDI; even when they did become available from other sources, the diversion of trade had made them more expensive.

As a result of these factors, the inflationary potential in post-independence Zambia was great. This potential lent even greater importance to the control of wages. Contributing to the urgency of this task was the extremely low marginal propensity to save among Africans in Zambia. Fragmentary evidence suggests that increases in earnings do not tend to create higher levels of savings among Africans in Zambia; rather, they tend to feed increasing demand and thereby drive up prices.[28] Moreover, those Zambian industries whose cost structures contain the highest wage component face the least competition from foreign sources; as a result, they can pass the increased costs of labor on to the consumer in the form of increased prices.[29] Added to the factors noted above, these trends mean that the government's failure to control wage increases led to an increase of over 40 percent in average prices, as measured by the consumer price index.[30]

The most important victim of inflation, and the one most directly affected by rising wages, has been the government itself. Wages constitute over 50 percent of the recurrent expenditures in the public sector, and with the postindependence increase in rates of pay and other forms of recurrent costs, the government found the price of its development program rapidly increasing. Even with its expanding financial resources, the government was therefore compelled, in 1969, to reduce by over 20 percent its investment expenditures.[31] The government's development effort has thus fallen victim to the inflationary spiral, and with it, a significant portion of the investment in Zambia's future rate of growth.

Wage increases also threaten Zambia's capacity for future growth through their effect upon its balance of payments. Since independence, copper production and inflated copper prices have enabled Zambia to maintain a surplus external balance. However, as table 18 reveals, the surplus on current account is diminishing year by year, and a principal cause of this reduction is the rising purchase of foreign goods. Breaking down the goods category into consumer and producer goods (tables 19 and 20), we find that, in part, the decreased balance is "eufunctional" to Zambia's future growth, for it reflects the importation of goods necessary for an increased rate of production. However, the breakdown also reveals a major increase in the rate at which consumer goods have been imported since independence. The result is that Zambia's ability to import producers' goods is being undermined by the growth in imports of consumer items.

TABLE 18
Balance of Payments, Current Account
(Tens of thousands of Kwacha)

Category	1964 Export	1964 Import	1965 Export	1965 Import	1966 Export	1966 Import
Goods	33,030	14,290	35,712	20,892	43,136	24,914
Services	1,634	6,242	1,702	4,860	1,856	7,492
Investments	1,376	8,290	1,702	6,254	1,756	7,554
Transfers	2,156	1,816	2,382	2,728	1,250	2,204
Net surplus, current acct.	7,558		6,764		5,834	

Source: Republic of Zambia, *Monthly Digest of Statistics* 4, no. 1 (January–February 1968): 54.
Note: 1 *Kwacha* = 10 shillings sterling = approximately $1.40.

The single most important determinant of the rate of foreign consumer purchases is private income. Given the rate of increase of Zambia's wages, the increased inflow of consumer items is a natural result. Our calculations reveal that given a one-year

TABLE 19
Goods Category, Value of Imports
(Thousands of pounds)

Category	1964	1965	1966	1967[a]
1. Food	7,132	8,266	9,894	10,812
2. Beverages	1,445	1,402	1,513	944
3. Materials	1,581	1,833	2,295	2,364
4. Fuels, power	8,723	9,938	9,800	15,838
5. Oils, fats	394	647	1,315	1,668
6. Chemicals	8,160	10,076	9,622	9,380
7. Manufactures	17,222	24,875	27,559	32,096
8. Machinery	21,210	34,795	48,968	67,096
9. Miscellaneous manufactures	10,560	12,979	11,909	13,876
10. Miscellaneous	1,792	198	183	1,840

Source: Calculated from materials contained in Ministry of Finance, *Economic Report 1967* (Lusaka: Government Printer, 1967).
[a] Estimated.

TABLE 20
Goods Category Breakdown
(Thousands of pounds)

Category	1964	1965	1966	1967
Consumer (1, 2, 5, 7, 9)	36,753	48,169	52,190	59,396
Producer (3, 4, 6, 8)	39,674	56,642	70,685	94,678
Miscellaneous (10)	1,792	198	183	1,840

time lag, increases in mine wages correlate with increases in consumer imports with $r = .93$. The effect is both direct and indirect, the indirect component being the influence of mine wages upon wages in other sectors. Reinforcing both effects is the high income elasticity of the demand for imports; cross-sectional comparisons of African household budgets in Zambia reveal imports to be the form of expenditure most responsive to variations in income.[32] The ability of Zambia to maintain a favorable trade balance and its capacity to import the producers' goods necessary to preserve a rapid rate of growth are thus being undermined by the government's inability to contain increases in wages.

In the short run, therefore, Zambia's economy has flourished. But rising costs have already compelled a reduction in Zambia's public investments, and decreasing trade balances threaten to impair its ability to purchase capital goods from abroad without external borrowing. Both of these adverse trends are related to the failure of the government's labor policy. The present needs of labor have been met at the expense of future increased production.[33]

I have emphasized the effects of wage increases upon the factor of primary concern to this study: Zambia's rate of economic growth. There have been effects in other critical areas as well, however. For instance, while the wage-earning sector, which is primarily urban, increased its earnings by 32 percent in the period

1964–68, the peasant population, approximately 80 percent of the population of Zambia as a whole, increased its earnings by an estimated 3.4 percent. As President Kaunda has warned, the trend threatens to create two nations in Zambia and to generate a dangerously aggrieved rural sector.[34] Equally as important, rising wages have altered the relative prices of the factors of production in favor of capital equipment. The trend toward capital substitution is strong in Zambia, and the inevitable result is that the rate of job creation lags behind the rate of economic growth. Current estimates are that, of the 100,000 jobs that were to be produced under the First National Development Plan, only 60,000 will be available.[35] The clear implication is a rise in unemployment; and the disparity between the earnings of rural and city dwellers can only entice further unemployables into the urban sector. These consequences of increased wages are fully as important as their effects upon the rate of growth; and they too must be taken into account in assessing the significance of the failure of the government's labor policy.

5 The Union Divided: Response of the Union's Leadership

The Mineworkers' Union is charged by the government with the responsibility of countering and moderating the demands of the workers. The union's failure in this task results in large part from the existence of deep cleavages between its national officers and local branch officials. While the Head Office adheres to the government's formulation of the public interest, the local branch leaders conceive of their interests as being identical with those of the mineworkers. An examination of the government's campaign for the union's support of its development policies reveals important reasons for the disparate responses of the two union levels.

The Government's Campaign for Union Support

The government seeks to incorporate the Head Office into the sphere of the national political elite. Head Office officials receive recognition as leaders of national importance, and they are encouraged by government to maintain close connections with public officials at the national center.

Head Office officials are encouraged to feel that their counterpart in labor matters is the minister of labor in Lusaka, the national capital, and not his lower-level representatives on the copperbelt—the assistant commissioner of labor in Kitwe and the labor officers in each of the copperbelt towns. Thus, one union leader was asked how he finds out about government thinking on labor matters; he replied: "We don't sit down and think what the government is thinking about us. . . . We go to Lusaka to see the Minister; his Permanent Secretary tells him we are there and he says 'Oh! They are outside. Well, show them in.' According to our traditions, Mr. Bates, we cannot be allowed to go back. We sleep in Lusaka a day or two, and he will find time to fit us in." [1] That the Head Office leaders utilize the government's invitation for free interchange with the minister of labor is indicated by the frequency of the visits they made with him: four in the three-month period of April to June 1967. In political matters, the government encourages the national leaders of the union to communicate directly with the minister of state for the Western Province—a direct appointee of the president and the head of both the administration and ruling party in the copperbelt. Through him, the union leaders maintain further ties with the government at the ministerial level.

The government's attribution of national status is also revealed in the phenomenon of ministerial touring. Not only do the union leaders visit cabinet officials in Lusaka, but cabinet officials themselves also circulate freely throughout the copperbelt (table 21).

TABLE 21

Ministerial Tours of Kitwe

Official	Appearances		Appearances on labor matters		Days in Kitwe per month (average)		Days on labor matters per month (average)	
	May–July 1967	Jan.–May 1968	May–July 1967	Jan.–May 1968	May–July 1967	Jan.–May 1968	May–July 1967	Jan.–May 1968
President	3	4	0	2	3.7	4.0	0	2.0
Vice-President	4	2	2	1	5.3	2.5	2.7	0.8
Minister of Labour	3	7	3	5	1.7	9.3	1.7	7.3
Other cabinet officials	21	6	1	4	8.0	8.0	2.7	2.5

Over an eight-month period, I recorded no less than fifty such tours in Kitwe alone by officials of ministerial rank. The relative importance of local officials is clearly signified during these ministerial tours. The most important officials in any town are those who form the delegation to receive ministers and attend functions with the ministers during their stay. At the arrival of ministers in Kitwe—the site of the Head Office—the national leaders of the Mineworkers' Union form part of the reception line; very often they join the touring party as well.

The government thus ascribes national status to the union leaders, and maintains a high frequency of interchanges between national-level political officials and the members of the Head Office of the Mineworkers' Union. The creation of a feeling of national status encourages the union leaders to take on a national frame of reference when viewing governmental policies. And the frequent meetings between the Head Office officials and the government yield the union leaders a high degree of exposure to government thinking. These experiences are not shared by the branch officials, however. They do not travel to conferences with the minister of labor in Lusaka, nor would they feel entitled to do so. Branch officials do not communicate directly with the minister of state, but only with the lower levels of the party and governmental apparatus. Nor do branch officials greet ministers, save as part of the crowd of citizens that marks the arrival in town of leaders from Lusaka. The only occasions on which they would tour with ministers is when the ministers inspect their mine; even then, branch officials cede the place of precedence to the Head Office representatives. The difference between the Head Office and branch officials' conception of their status in the national political system, and between the degrees to which they are exposed to national-level politicians, thus helps to explain the differences between their reactions to government labor policy.

The government also involves the Head Office in a series of structures and institutions which specifically deal with labor matters. In this way, the government focuses the attention of the union leaders directly upon the content of its labor policy and encourages them to assume an output orientation toward their role as labor leaders.

THE CONGRESS OF TRADE UNIONS. One of the chief structures for the communication of government policies is the Zambian Congress of Trade Unions (ZCTU), created by legislative enactment in 1964. Formally, the congress is a powerful agency for the regulation of trade union affairs. The government empowered it to judge the validity of alterations in the constitutions of member unions and no member union can strike without first consulting the ZCTU. The government has ensured that all major unions will fall under the authority of the congress; for by government enactment, only unions which affiliate with the ZCTU can be authorized to levy union dues from all the employees of the industry which they represent.[2] Despite its extensive formal powers, however, the congress fails to regulate closely the affairs of member trade unions. During this study, we did not record a single instance in which the Congress exercised its right to review constitutional changes; and despite frequent pronouncements against strikes by member unions, the congress never reversed their strike decisions. The congress simply did not use the formal powers granted it by the government.

That the ZCTU has failed to assume the regulatory role which the government conceived for it does not mean that the congress is an insignificant organization. The ZCTU performs valuable services for the trade union movement in Zambia. Thus, when approached by plantation workers seeking to form a union, the ZCTU provided transport and funds for union organizers. They also furnished the Building and Woodworkers Union with knowledge of agreements negotiated in related trades, both in Zambia and abroad, thereby assisting it to negotiate new wage demands. And on numerous occasions during 1967 and 1968, the congress assisted union leaders in their efforts to persuade dissident members to abandon wildcat strikes.[3]

Even more important than the services the congress provides, however, is the role it plays in disseminating government policies to the leaders of organized labor. The ZCTU sponsors numerous occasions for cabinet-level officials to address labor leaders on government policy. When the congress was formed in 1965, the president addressed its initial session. Following the first election to the congress' Executive in 1967, the minister of labor addressed the delegates to the electoral conference. A few months later, the congress sponsored a four-day convention on the role of labor in national development; the vice-president, the minister of labor, and additional government and party officials addressed the delegates to the convention. And when, in 1968, the ZCTU sponsored a mammoth May Day rally in Kitwe, President Kaunda was the featured speaker in the program. Through the creation of the congress, therefore, the government has established an institution which focuses the attention of union leaders on government policy toward labor; and through their frequent attendance at congress functions, government officials have rendered it a means of exposing union leaders to the content of government labor policies.

Within the hierarchy of the Mineworkers' Union, there exist differential rates of participation in the activities of the Congress of Trade Unions. Only Head Office officials hold office in the ZCTU; no branch official of the union serves as an official of the congress.[4] Moreover, the delegation of the Mineworkers' Union to the conference of the ZCTU is composed overwhelmingly of national-level union officials: six of the eleven national-level officials are members of the delegation, whereas only four branch officials attend congress conventions on behalf of the Mineworkers' Union.[5] Through the operations of the congress, therefore, it is the attention of the Head Office leaders, and not the branch officials, that is focused on government policy; and it is largely the Head Office leaders who receive intensive instruction in the government's conception of the output role of labor organizations.

GOVERNMENT SEMINARS AND CONVENTIONS. The government also encourages the union to take part in the series of conventions and seminars that characterize the government's efforts to evoke support for the National Development Plan. Many of these seminars focus specifically on the role of labor in national development. Between January 1967 and January 1968, four such convocations were held, two in the form of national conventions and two in the form of courses for trade unionists. In all four of these meetings, the government structured the proceedings around presentations of national economic programs and discussions of the role labor should play in the national development effort. Thus, for example, at the national convention in Kitwe, January 1967, one committee dealt with "The Challenge of the Four Year Develop-ment Plan," another with "Productivity, Including Cooperatives, Agriculture, and Mines," and a third with "Labour Relations"; government ministers chaired all of the committees. The Living-stone Labour Conference, April 1967, was opened with a speech on government labor policy; officials of the ministry of labor pre-sided over all but one of the sessions of the conference. And at the two seminars, in August and November 1967, labor depart-ment officials delivered lectures on their view of the national economy and on the role of labor in economic development.

The government is convinced that by encouraging their partici-pation in these convocations, it can compel the union leaders to pay attention to its development policies and increase their ac-ceptance of the regulative role of trade unions and labor officials. As in the case of the ZCTU, however, the government appears to achieve its objectives for the Head Office of the union but not for the leadership at the branch level. Every representative of the Mineworkers' Union at the two national conventions came from the Head Office of the union. And only two branch officials attended either of the government seminars.[6]

Patterns of Union Exposure to the Demands of the Mineworkers

While the environment of the Head Office is characterized by the regular presence of government spokesmen seeking to contain the demands of mine labor, the environment of the local branch leadership is characterized by the continuous presence of ag-grieved and protesting mine employees. It is the branch leader-ship of the union that maintains immediate face-to-face contact with the mineworkers. As part-time union officials, branch leaders work with and among the people they represent. As one might expect, the branch level unionists thus receive greater exposure to the demands of mine labor than do the Head Office officials.

An analysis of data on labor relations at the four principal mines and the Copper Industry Service Bureau (CISB) provides quantitative corroboration of this argument. I recorded 427 cases at the branch level, 70 at the Head Office level, and 79 involving both levels over the period 1950–68. Moreover, the branch officials spent a much greater amount of time dealing with grievances than did their Head Office counterparts; the branches spent roughly 26,500 days in negotiations with the personnel departments of the local mines, whereas the Head Office spent on the order of 6,500 days with the group representatives at CISB.[7]

The Head Office and branch leaders differ not only in the magnitude of their exposure to the demands of mine employees, but also in the intensity of that exposure. Not all kinds of demands distribute equally between the Head Office and branch levels; some types of demands are handled more frequently by the branch than by the Head Office. Moreover, not all the demands are equal in their intensity. An index of the intensity of a demand is the probability that it will result in strike action. Applying this index, we find in table 22 that the most intense

TABLE 22
Issue Intensity, Local Level

	Issues leading to action by locals	
	Frequently	*Infrequently*
Issues resulting in strikes		
Frequently	4	0
Infrequently	3	4

Note: "Frequently" means more than 50% of the time; "infrequently" covers the remainder of cases.

demands are the ones which are the most likely to be lodged at the branch level of the union.

Conversely, as shown in table 23, four out of five of those issues with a high probability of leading to strikes are simply never handled by the Head Office at all. To a greater extent than the Head Office, therefore, the local branch leaders receive exposure to grievances which are intensely felt.

TABLE 23
Issue Intensity, Head Office

| | Head Office role | |
Issues resulting in strikes	*Present*	*Absent*
Frequently	1	4
Infrequently	6	0

Note: "Frequently" means more than 50% of the time; "infrequently" covers the remainder of cases.

Involvement in the Social Structure of the Mine

As members of the mining community, the branch leaders of the union are directly affected by the structure of that community and their attitudes toward labor relations are shaped by the same forces that affect the behavior of the other members. The total number of African workers in the mining community is 40,000; and, as shown in table 24, the four principal copper

TABLE 24
Local Employees, 1962–66

Year	Mufulira	Nchanga	Rhokana	Roan	Total
1962	8,857	6,118	8,861	7,668	31,504
1963	8,889	5,889	8,928	7,259	30,965
1964	8,991	6,506	9,413	7,407	32,317
1965	8,859	6,777	10,290	7,535	33,461
1966	8,547	8,357	10,891	7,805	35,600

Source: Compiled from notebooks used to prepare the Copper Industry Service Bureau, *Copperbelt of Zambia Mining Industry Year Book [various years]* (Kitwe: CISB, various years).

mines employ over 35,000 people. In the sections which follow, the discussion is largely confined to the largest of these mines, Rhokana, where my fieldwork was conducted.

SOCIAL STRATIFICATION IN THE MINES. The most striking characteristic of the social structure of the mines is the pattern of racial stratification. At the time of this study, there was a perfect correlation between race and income, for the mines' dual-wage structure ensured that Africans and Europeans did not receive the same rates of pay. The bar graph in chapter 2 (chart 3) illustrates this relationship. Distributing income along the vertical axis, the perfectly horizontal lines within each bar indicate that even the highest-paid African received less pay than the lowest-paid European employee working in the same department. A comparison of the mean income of the two racial groups suggests the degree of the disparity between their wages. As shown in table 25, the average annual income of a European employee

TABLE 25
The Dual-Wage Structure: Average Annual
Mining Wages
(By race)

Year	African	European	European wage as proportion of African wage
1962	£245	£2,102	858%
1963	279	2,065	740
1964	324	2,289	706
1965	358	2,282	637
1966	423	3,158	747

Source: From notebooks used to compile the Copper Industry Service Bureau, *Copperbelt of Zambia Mining Industry Year Book, 1962–66* (Kitwe: CISB, 1963–67).

was six to eight times greater than that of an African. While there is not enough information to compute a Lorenz curve or Gini index of inequality, we do know that while Europeans constituted only 13 percent of the labor force in 1966, they earned over half of the wages paid by the mining companies (table 26). Ranked according to the criterion of income, therefore, Africans and Europeans tend to form mutually exclusive strata.[8]

Another correlate with race is supervisory authority. The structure of supervision on the mines is near military in its

TABLE 26
African and European Earnings in All Copperbelt Mines, 1966

Earnings of the 41,815 African employees	£18,788,787
African earnings as percentage of all wages	48%
African employees as percentage of total labor force	87%
Earnings of the 6,309 European employees	£20,716,270
European earnings as percentage of all wages	52%
Eu:opean employees as percentage of total labor force	13%

Source: From notebooks used to prepare The Copper Industry Service Bureau, *Copperbelt of Zambia Mining Industry Year Book, 1966* (Kitwe: CISB, 1967).

clarity. Using the underground department at Rhokana Mine as an example, there is one mine superintendent; beneath the mine superintendent, there is an underground manager and at least one assistant for each shaft. Mine captains occupy the third rung in the ladder. Shift bosses fill the next slot, followed by section bosses. Below the section bosses fall the actual workers who constitute more than 90 percent of the labor force in the department. The racial distribution of authority is made clear in the figures for Mindolo Shaft at Rhokana Mine.[9] As table 27 reveals,

TABLE 27
Proportion of Locals at Various Levels in the Mindolo Shaft

	Expatriate	Local	Percentage local
Mine captain and above	18	0	0
Shift bosses and foremen	40	17	30
Section bosses	0	171	100
Below section bosses	0	2,000+	100

Source: Rhokana Corporation, Manpower Services Department, Monthly Report, 24 January 1968, Files, Manpower Services Department.

in 1968, Africans composed 100 percent of those to whom the companies extend no authority; insofar as Africans did penetrate into the supervisory ranks, they did so only on the lowest levels;[10] and even in the levels of supervision they attained, Africans formed a distinct minority.

A third criterion for stratification are the quasi-monetary rewards and benefits distributed by the mining companies. Here
again, such values distribute unequally among the racial groups.
For example, the Europeans' terms of service include fine, well-
spaced houses, sited in attractive townships; Africans, for the
most part, occupy smaller, lower-quality houses, sited in high or
middle density townships. European houses include appliances;
when "advanced" Africans move into these houses, the appliances
are removed.[11] At the time in which the data were collected,
European employees received a housing allowance of £8 per
month; African employees, despite the poorer quality of their
houses and their lower incomes, paid rent.[12] Europeans received
£200 to £300 annual education allowance for children attending
secondary schools outside of Zambia, but Africans received no
such educational allowances.[13] Lastly, Europeans received twenty-
five to fifty-five days leave per annum, whereas the maximum
permissible leave for African employees was but twenty-eight
days per year.[14] The pattern of disparities could be further extended, but the point is clear: the European employees received
better perquisites than did Africans. Although the correlation
between race and these indulgences largely results from Europeans holding better jobs on the mines and therefore, strictly
speaking, is spurious, what is significant for the behavior of the
workers is that the correlation does in fact exist.

Whatever criteria of stratification is applied, therefore, Europeans occupy the higher rankings. Moreover, the rankings are
consistent with one another; there is no instance of Europeans
ranking higher than Africans in wealth but lower in authority, for
example. These patterns make it immensely difficult for the government to implement its labor policy and for the union and
party to transmit it successfully. One obvious reason is that the
mineworkers and the government have conflicting evaluations of
the status of the miners. The government's frame of reference
is national; that of the mineworkers is local. And while the
workers are an economically privileged group within the government's frame of reference, they are disadvantaged within the
frame of reference which they themselves employ. The oppor-

tunities for misunderstanding and conflict thus abound. Because the government perceives the mineworkers as one of the wealthiest groups in the country, it feels justified in asking them to sacrifice for the sake of the less fortunate citizens in the other sectors of the national economy. But, because they perceive themselves in relation to the European miners, the mineworkers feel poverty stricken and they are unwilling to acknowledge this obligation. While at Rhokana, I repeatedly heard allusions to the wealth of the Europeans and statements like: "Mr. Bates, we are poverty stricken," "we are poor," "we are oppressed." The workers also feel that "we need more money," and they are therefore unwilling to make the sacrifices which the government asks of them.

The structure of the mining community thus gives ample reason for the workers to remain both privileged and militant, and we can understand why the richest group of workers in the nation should behave like one of the most aggrieved. Three other phenomena help to translate the pattern of stratification into militant industrial relations: social mobility, relative deprivation, and status inconsistency.

SOCIAL MOBILITY AND LABOR MILITANCY. Since the time of self-government in Zambia, a strong current of upward mobility has been introduced in the mining industry. In large part, this trend results from the government's commitment to a policy of racial justice. The trend has been accelerated by the efforts of the Zambianization Committee to implement that policy.[15]

Evidence for upward mobility is to be found in the reduction of European employees on the mines and the increase in the number of Africans filling jobs formerly held by Europeans. In 1963 Europeans constituted 17 percent of the labor force on the mines, but by the end of 1966, they formed but 13 percent.[16] The following data indicate the scope and rate of the movement of Africans into higher-level jobs. Between May and October 1967, the number of Europeans in supervisory grades decreased in sixteen out of the twenty-six departments; in only four departments did the number remain constant; and in only five did it increase. Conversely, the number of Africans in these same grades increased in sixteen departments, remained unchanged in five, and decreased in only four. Where increases in the number of African supervisors have taken place, the rate of increase has ranged from 33 percent to 333 percent. In the underground departments, the government and the companies have agreed on a program which will Zambianize over two-thirds of the posts at the mine captain level by the end of 1972. Even more dramatic changes have been introduced in the personnel departments, where all personnel managers were Zambians by the end of 1969. These figures, combined with the mines' expansion of training facilities, indicate the strong current of upward mobility which has been introduced within the pattern of racial stratification in the mining industry.

Ironically, upward mobility appears to have produced an increased sensitivity to racial discrimination among the upper stratum of African workers. I frequently encountered evidence of this. Again and again, it was the better-off workers and staff employees who asserted the grievances over the racial structure of the mines. The intervening variable between mobility and sensitivity appeared to be a sense of relative deprivation.

The introduction of increased numbers of African employees into higher jobs has increased the opportunity for these Africans to evaluate their own position against that of the European employees. Increased mobility has produced an increase in the incidence of Africans and Europeans holding similar jobs; and as table 28 reveals, the African promotee is confronted with a white counterpart who earns from 165 percent to 264 percent more than himself, not including differences in quasi-monetary benefits.

Moreover, many Africans achieving supervisory grades are convinced that the companies extend less authority to them than to their European counterparts and predecessors. Thus, during my stay, there were at least two protests by newly appointed African shift bosses. They struck in protest against a mine captain who would not allow them to penalize workers directly, although European shift bosses could do so; they had first to clear the penalties with their superiors.[17]

Such negative reactions are not confined to the union member-

TABLE 28

The Dual-Wage Structure: Wage Differences in Localized Jobs

Job designation	Expatriate salary as percentage of local	Expatriate earnings as percentage of local[a]
Shift boss	165	183
Training officer, Grade II	179	199
Senior mine layout d. man	185	206
U/G foreman	192	214
Rockbreaker boss-craftsman	250	279
Mining sup. I-sen. operator I	256	286
Crane driver	264	294

Source: Robert F. Halvorsen, "Wages Policy in the Zambian Copper Mining Industry" (Paper submitted to the Department of Economics, Harvard University, 27 May, 1968, typescript), exhibit 2. The data were collected while the dual-wage structure was in force. While a single basic wage has been implemented, the expatriate bonus will perpetuate a disparity in actual earnings.

[a] Includes allowances, bonuses, etc.

ship alone. The leadership of the union branch is itself composed disproportionately of employees from the upper levels of the African labor force. One-third of the branch executives occupied training posts for supervisory positions, even though supervisors constituted less than one-tenth of the total labor force. The case of the former Rhokana branch vice-chairman, Maxwell Kapengwe, reveals how the branch executive experiences relative deprivation in common with other advanced employees. A form II graduate, Kapengwe was a highly educated employee by prevailing standards and therefore received rapid promotion. Within eighteen months he became a pump attendant underground, a job of immense responsibility because of the danger of underground flooding. The job was formerly held by a European. When he was promoted, Kapengwe regarded the difference between his own salary and that of his European predecessor as an insult to himself and as proof of the disadvantages which Africans encountered on the mines. Moreover, he condemned the continued presence of the European employee in the same work area as an expression of the company's distrust of his ability to fulfill his responsibilities. Although benefiting from the mobility within the racially stratified structure of the company, Kapengwe became deeply sensitive to the racial structure of the mines. He experienced his newly won status as painful instead of rewarding, and used his position as branch vice-chairman to broadcast his discomfort.[18]

Mobility thus leads to an increased sensitivity to the racial structure of the mines among those who hold jobs in the upper categories. Moreover, since education, literacy, income and length of service correlate with occupancy of advanced positions (table 29) it is only to be expected that this group would be the opinion

TABLE 29

Comparison, African Supervisors with Other Local Employees, Rhokana

	Supervisors	Other employees
Education		
None	7%	55%
Primary or higher	75%	37%
No information	18%	8%
Average length of service (months)	98	94
Average income (kwacha per month)	121.05	66.34

Source: From a 20 percent systematic random sample of the African labor force.
Note: All those with staff jobs are counted as supervisors. There are more staff than supervisors, however, as clerical and technical workers are designated staff as well.

leaders influencing the attitudes of the mass of the workers toward the industrial structure.

STATUS INCONSISTENCY AND LABOR MILITANCY. The increased unwillingness of the mass of the workers to accept racially based patterns of stratification is not to be explained solely in terms of the views of their superiors, however. There are other factors increasing the rebelliousness of the lower strata. One of the most important is the contradiction they perceive between their subordinate industrial status to European miners and their political preeminence in independent Zambia. To most mineworkers, political independence meant triumph over foreign, European rule. The victory over the European is a great source of pride and satisfaction. Tales of how Europeans were first confused, then bewildered, and in the end, terrified and cowed by the daring and self-assertion of the Africans during "the struggle" are still told and retold with relish. For many African employees, the dominance they possess over the Europeans in the political realm is difficult to reconcile with their subordination to the white man in the industrial sphere. As stated by the labor department, "the ordinary Zambian does not only cherish political freedom for its own sake but looks beyond politics to the field of economics where he feels he must have the same amount of freedom as in politics." [19]

Added to the problem is the increased hostility of the expatriates themselves. There is evidence that the greater the advancment of the African workers, the greater the resistance of the European miners. Thus, when in the late 1950s Roan and Mufulira mines increased the access of Africans to higher-level jobs, a survey of European miners found the white employees of these two mines to be more opposed to African advancement than the European workers at other mines on the copperbelt.[20] There is also evidence that the discrepancy between their economic and political authority in independent Zambia has rendered the Europeans more assertive and arbitrary in their exercise of managerial authority; thus the memorandum written by the parliamentary secretary to the minister of labor in which he contends that "European mineworkers [have] since 20th October, 1962, become increasingly contemptuous of the Africans and provocative." [21] The popular slogan, "Politics is theirs; the economy is ours," expressed the Europeans' determination to reassert their dominance in independent Zambia and to do so in the economic sector. Status inconsistencies produced by self-government are thus experienced by both blacks and whites. The result is a pattern of challenge and provocation between the races in their day-to-day relationships on the mines.

The branch executive members also are aware of the contrast between political authority and economic subordination. The branch chairman at Rhokana frequently expressed his disgust at the company's reluctance to discipline supervisors who had uttered racial insults or provocative criticisms of independent Zambia.[22] At one time he obtained a strike vote from workers in the refinery after a European foreman called an African worker a "Kaffir."[23] In two other cases, he encouraged work stoppages over racial insults. As he explained his actions: "We Africans are very poor. We are not well educated. But we Africans are *abene ba Zambia.* [Freely translated, the rightful inhabitants of Zambia.] It is our government now. The Europeans must learn to behave here, because they do not rule us any longer."[24]

Racial inequality thus promotes the types of demands which the government seeks to curtail. Increased mobility generates the conditions under which Africans increase their demands for greater pay; for the more advanced the African workers, the more apparent the disparity between African and European conditions of service. The inconsistency between their newly won political supremacy and their all too familiar experience of subordination to the white man provokes many African employees to resist the authority of their foremen and bosses. The supervisors' commands to work hard fall victim to the attempts by the Africans to establish consistency between their racial and economic statuses. These patterns also impinge on the last tenet of government policy: the curtailment of strikes. The social structure of the mines often lends racial overtones to the workers' demands, and when a demand acquires a racial dimension, the probability of strike action nearly doubles (table 30). And the local branch leaders, themselves employees in the mining com-

TABLE 30
Racial Incidents and Strikes, Copperbelt, 1950–68

Racial involvement	Percentage strikes	Percentage not strikes	Total number of incidents
Present	44	56	62
Absent	26	74	514

munity, directly experience the tensions of this community and share the militant attitudes of the rank and file.

Patterns of Leadership Mobility

There is a last factor which helps to explain the difference in the responsiveness of national and local officials to the government's labor policy: the factor of upward mobility. In a sense, union office holding is a temporary thing. The rate of turnover among Head Office officials has indeed been impressive. Since 1960 there have been five union presidents, five general secretaries, six vice-presidents, and four deputy general secretaries (table 31). Moreover, it is not simply a matter of offices changing

TABLE 31
The Head Office since 1960

Office	Number of different incumbents
President	5
Vice-President	6
General Secretary	5
Vice General Secretary	4
Treasurer	2
Vice-Treasurer	3

hands; the body of officeholders has altered as well. Thus, of the 1960 officeholders, only two remained in office in 1968.

It is difficult to account for the departure of Head Office unionists. Some were voted out of office for misfeasance; others took jobs with prominent corporations. But what is of significance here is the degree to which union officials utilized their prominence in the Mineworkers' Union to achieve positions in government.

One example is John Chisata. Chisata became union president following the removal of Lawrence Katilungu in late 1960. He then stood as a UNIP candidate in the key district of Mufulira—the one copperbelt town in which UNIP's chief rival, the ANC, continued to draw significant support. Following his victory and UNIP's later formation of a government, Chisata won promotion to the rank of parliamentary secretary. In 1964 Chisata retired from his union post to devote full time to his governmental career. Another example is Matthew Deluxe Nkoloma. Nkoloma had been one of the most illustrious early leaders of the union; in 1963 he had returned to union work after the colonial government lifted its ban on his union activities. Nkoloma soon left the union a second time, however. A Kitwe city councillor and chairman of Kitwe's largest UNIP branch, Nkoloma, in 1960, was promoted to the position of assistant to the minister of state in the Western Province. Other Head Office officials have assumed governmental duties on a part-time basis. Edward Mubanga, the former general treasurer of the union, and John Sichone, its current deputy general secretary, received government appointments to posts in the ZCTU. Cosmos Mweene, a former general secretary, served as the president's representative to North Korea. Matthew Mwendapole, another early luminary in the union, twice stood as a UNIP candidate for the National Assembly. Thus, prominence at the national level of the union translates into the possibility of a career in government (tables 32 and 33).

TABLE 32
Government Experience by Head Office
Officeholders in the 1960s

Number currently employed by the government	4
Number who have done work in government service	4
Number with no government experience at all	10
Total number Head Office leaders since 1960	18

TABLE 33
Current Status of All Head Office
Officeholders in the 1960s

Still in office	6
Staff job in union	2
Officeholders at branch level	2
Government service	4
Company employment in job outside the union's jurisdiction	1
Fired by company	1
Deceased	2
Total Head Office since 1960	18

Mobility at the Local Level

Insofar as union officials at the branch level perceive the possibility of advancement, however, they look not to the government but to the mining companies. To the best of my knowledge, only one branch official has achieved prominence in governmental affairs; branch officials must first achieve Head Office posts before they can bring themselves to the attention of the political elite.[25] However, union branch leaders do possess prospects of higher jobs in the mining industry, provided they possess the requisite education. As one senior company official stated:

> Let's face it. If a chap can control his fellows in the union, he'll be able to control them for us. He's a valuable man and we'll have our eyes on him. We're not out to break the union this way. We want the best employees we can get, and if we find them in the union, we're not going to refuse to offer the chap a job, just because he's a union official.[26]

The companies therefore look to the pool of active trade unionists as potential high-level employees. Advanced jobs, however, tend to be incompatible with continued office holding in the union. Personnel officers cannot hold office in the union and in many cases are not even allowed to hold union membership; until 1967 no employees holding staff jobs could be represented by the union. To accept the job offer of the companies is therefore to have to surrender one's union position.

Both Head Office and branch officials thus stand at the boundaries of the union. The Head Office officials can move up to governmental roles, and the branch officials can undertake advanced jobs with the mining companies. In both cases, therefore, union officeholders possess possibilities for advancement. But the effects of these possibilities on the union officeholders appear to differ between the two levels.

At the Head Office level, the prospect of promotion to a government job appears to produce a willingness to conform to the norms and standards of the government itself. While this is terribly difficult to document, there is some evidence for the assertion. John Chisata, as president of the union, strove to quell strikes by his members; so national-minded did Chisata become that he once cancelled a union strike so as not to threaten the electoral prospects of UNIP, the dominant party.[27] Edward Mubanga also utilized his influence within the union to bring it into a closer relationship with the governing party. In 1966, John Sichone allowed UNIP to endorse him in a trade union election and stood on a "platform" of union responsibility for national development (see chapter 7). To a certain degree, the conforming behavior of the Head Office officials appears to result from anticipatory socialization. For insofar as the union leaders seek government positions, they must signify their incorporation of the government's viewpoint to qualify for these positions. The minister of home affairs made this clear to a group of trade unionists.

> It would be wise for Union leaders to know that there are many vacancies in the Government services which have not yet been filled. . . . But jobs will not be given to people who are the cause of trouble and friction. The Government does not want Union leaders, M.P.'s or Parliamentary Secretaries who cause trouble. . . . The Government also needs Ambassadors . . . but here again, it will be difficult for the Government to choose the right people, because there are a number of trouble makers amongst the Unions, and these persons are not, therefore, to be trusted.[28]

If the prospect of advancement open to the Head Office leaders leads to conformity with the government's conception of the role of labor, the prospect of advancement available to branch officials appears to lead to a different kind of reaction. Evidence suggests that branch leaders who have been offered high company posts tend either to lose interest in union activities or to engage in militant and disruptive union activities before eventually succumbing to the company's offer. The second kind of reaction is of interest at this point in the analysis.

One example is Augustino Nkole, leader of the Roan branch of the Union in the late 1950s and early 1960s. As part of their advancement plan, the mining companies had opened a limited number of formerly European jobs to African workers at ex-patriate terms of service. Nkole was among the African employees nominated for training for one of these positions. Had he accepted, he would have qualified for a European miner's salary, as well as for a house in the European township; he would also have had to surrender his post as branch chairman. During Nkole's leadership, Roan branch became one of the most disruptive branches on the mines: the number of strikes increased, the number of racial incidents rose, and disputes were forced to a higher level (table 34). The rate of increase in all these matters

TABLE 34
Nkole Era at Roan

	Roan		Other mines	
Percentage of disputes that were:	1950-56	1957-63	1950-56	1957-63
Racial	3	27	8	11
Non-racial	97	73	92	89
Strikes	12	45	20	46
Not strikes	88	55	80	54
Conciliated	12	14	16	4
Arbitrated	0	2	0	0

was far in excess of the rate of increase elsewhere on the copper-belt. Under Nkole, Roan formed the "ginger group" on the mines. Finally, however, Nkole succumbed to the company's offer; in 1963, he accepted his advanced job and took up residence in the European township.[29]

A second example is Elijah Kabungo, the branch organizing secretary at Broken Hill Mine in the early 1960s. Soon after assuming his union post at Broken Hill, Kabungo was offered a job in the company's community services department. During his tenure in office, Kabungo organized a series of strikes in protest over bonus payments, discriminatory conduct by supervisors, and job-grading practices by management. However, in a bewildering switch over, Kabungo, at the climax of his efforts, changed sides and accepted the company's offer.[30]

While the mobility prospects of the Head Office officials promote behavior in conformity with government policy, the mobility prospects of local branch officials thus appear to produce the
opposite. Local officials, confronted with the possibility of crossing
over from union office to an advanced company position, tend to
amplify rather than dampen conflict in industrial relations. One
reason for the discrepant response of branch and Head Office
officials would appear to be the conflict they experience as a result
of the opportunities open to them. The Head Office and the
government and the local branch and the companies are all to a
degree in conflict relations; but overlaying the conflict between
the companies and the local branch is the dimension of race. For
a branch official to surrender his union post for a company
appointment is not only to cross from the workers' to the em-
ployer's side, but also to cross over from the side of the African
to the white man. To reduce the conflict experienced in the offer
of an advanced job, the branch official may passionately champion the most extreme demands of the African labor force against
the companies, and thereby reestablish consonance in the relationship between himself as union leader, the African work
force, and the "enemy"—the European-dominated mining companies. Branch leaders may thereby become most militant just
when they are most tempted to become company men.

Perhaps the most appropriate way of representing the different
psychological pressures upon the two leadership levels is in the
notation of balance theory. Thus, both sets of leaders are in conflict situations (chart 6). However, overlaying the psychological

Chart 6. Similarity of Conflict Positions, Branch and Head Office.

conflict of the local branch leaders is the added element of race; while this racial dimension operates for the local leaders, it does not for the Head Office (chart 7). As the diagram suggests, for the local leaders, the racial dimension reinforces the conflict engendered by the prospects of a company job offer, while, for the Head Office leaders, there is no such reinforcement of the conflict created by the prospects of a government position. The local branch leaders are therefore placed in a stronger conflict situation, and are motivated to more militant action to reduce the strains which they experience.[31]

Chart 7. Contrasting Conflict Positions, Branch and Head Office.

6 The Transmission of Government Policy

We now turn to an examination of the relationships between the Head Office and the branch leaders of the union. Given the conflict between government policy and the interests of labor, it must be assumed that in the absence of incentives to induce cooperation, only the direct and forceful exertion of power will enable government policy to prevail. It is precisely the lack of such power at the Head Office level that explains the persistent advocacy of the workers' interests by the local branch officers of the union.

Power Relations within the Union

One index of the distribution of power within the union is the relative access of Head Office and branch officials to the bodies which govern significant union activities. Basically, the union's activities can be divided into two spheres: goal attainment and organizational maintenance. In both areas, the bodies determining the performance of these functions are composed overwhelmingly of branch level officials.

The primary goal of the union is the attainment of concessions from management. Grievances must be brought forward, assigned to the negotiation agenda, and bargained for. I have already noted that the vast majority of such grievances are handled by the branch structures of the union. But even at the national level, branch officials dominate the bodies which control goal attainment procedures. Agenda items emanate from local branch committees, composed solely of branch officials.[1] The selection of items for the negotiating agenda takes place at the union's Annual Conference; of the fifty-five members of the Conference in 1967, forty-eight came from the union branches. And the Negotiating Committee of the union, which bargains with the Copper Industry Service Bureau, recruits seven of its eleven members from the branches, and only four from the Head Office of the union.[2]

The bodies that superintend the maintenance of the union's structure follow a similar pattern. Recruitment of leadership, for example, is controlled by the Annual Conference and the Supreme Council. The Head Office leaders depend for their posts on the votes of delegates to the Annual Conference; and as noted above, over 80 percent of these delegates come from the local branches. Recruitment to nonelected positions is controlled by the Supreme Council. Appointments to staff positions, promotions, and the determination of rates of pay—all these decisions are reviewed and ratified by the Supreme Council of the union. Of the thirty-one Supreme Council members in 1967, twenty-four come from the branch level of the union. The suspension, dismissal, or penalization of union officers are also activities performed by the Council, and thus also fall under the control of a branch-dominated structure.

The Performance and Conduct of Union Structures

To infer the distribution of power in an organization from the composition of its formal structures is not an entirely satisfactory procedure. It must be determined if the bodies formally vested with control actually exercise that control and if the branch officials in these bodies do in fact dominate their proceedings. Only then can we be relatively certain of inferences about the allocation of power.

I was able to piece together a complete sequence of goal attainment activities, following workers' grievances from the branch level to the negotiating committee, and thence to actual negotiations at the Chamber of Mines. This was not an easy task and a perfect sequence of data could be obtained only for 1963 (table 35). The data validate the importance of the branches. Of the sixty-seven grievances proposed for national-level negotiations at the Annual Conference, fifty-seven, a full 85 percent, originated among the branches. Of the seventeen items selected for the final negotiating agenda, fourteen—or 82 percent—were branch resolutions. And of the seven items in which the union

TABLE 35
Negotiation Items, by Origin

	Total number	Number from branches	Number from Head Office
Items submitted for industry-wide negotiations	67	57	10
Items selected for negotiating agenda by the Annual Conference	17	14	3
Items won or compromised in negotiations at the industrial level	7	5	2

Source: Report on Annual Delegates Conference, May 1963, Ja/9, Vol. 8. Agenda, Supreme Council Meeting, 30–31 August 1963, Ja/9, Vol. 8.

attained victories or compromises in the negotiations, five or 71 percent came from the branch level of the union. It must be remembered that national-level negotiations in 1963, as in any year, represent but a part of goal attainment activities by the Union; 96 percent of the grievances were handled by the branches alone.

There is a similar pattern in the area of institutional maintenance. The data suggest that the bodies formally assigned power over this process do, in fact, exercise their power, and that the preponderance of local branch leaders in these bodies therefore accurately reflects the distribution of power in the union. In 1966 the Supreme Council fined and suspended the general secretary when he arbitrarily transferred a staff member from the Head Office to a branch of the union. That same year the Supreme Council also stripped the general treasurer of every office he held in the union; he had been a national-level leader of the union for nearly a decade. In 1967 the Supreme Council fined the branch officers at Rhokana £15 each for their failure to file an annual report and their misuse of union transport.

The process of leadership recruitment most dramatically reveals the power of the local branches. Perhaps the most striking example was the 1961 overthrow of Lawrence Katilungu as president of the union. In the 1950s, Katilungu was among the most illustrious leaders in Central Africa. It was he who organized the first branch of the Mineworkers' Union at Rhokana Mine; it was also Katilungu who federated local branches into a national-level union with the power to negotiate industry-wide agreements. In 1952, he startled the colonial government and the industry by presiding over a successful three-week strike which resulted in substantial concessions to the mineworkers' demands. Because of his absence from Northern Rhodesia in 1956, Katilungu escaped the government's wholesale arrest of union and nationalist party leaders; starting with few experienced leaders, he rebuilt the union into a powerful representative of the mineworkers' interests. Despite his immense prestige and proven effectiveness as a leader, and despite his incumbency of the union presidency since its inception, Katilungu, in 1960, was voted out of office by the Supreme Council of the union. A principal reason for his fall was his inability to control a key local in the union—Roan Antelope, under the chairmanship of Augustino Nkole.

Disagreements between Katilungu and Nkole began in 1958, when Katilungu attempted to transfer from Roan a branch clerk whom Nkole liked and depended upon. Nkole refused to allow Katilungu to remove the clerk. In 1959 Nkole and Katilungu again clashed. Nkole's branch secretary, one Chisunka, was both a popular and belligerent union official and was in constant trouble with the mining companies. Katilungu found Chisunka an embarrassment, and upon his dismissal by the company in 1959, refused to appeal Chisunka's case on behalf of the Roan local. Nkole was reportedly outraged, and compelled the Head Office to reverse the decision. When Chisunka was again dismissed in 1960, however, Katilungu stood by his refusal not to defend the branch secretary. Katilungu's decision in part accounts for the efforts by the leadership at Roan to supplant him as president. In the 1960 Head Office elections, Roan nominated Sylvester Nkoma—a prominent early unionist who had just returned from detention—to stand against Katilungu in the elections for the presidency of the union. When Nkoma's candidacy failed, Roan began agitation for Katilungu's removal. Katilungu's long absences from the country, and his assumption of a seat on the Monckton Commission—a commission boycotted by both

nationalist parties in Northern Rhodesia—increased his vulner-
ability to Roan's attacks,* as did the relative failure of the 1960
wage demands. But it was Katilungu's alienation of a second
local which appeared to give Roan a decisive advantage.

In early 1960, Katilungu led an effort to suspend the Chibuluma branch of the union. Chibuluma had long been involved
in a dispute over the company's decision to close down its hospital facilities; repeated protests by the branch leaders, combined
with unconstitutional local branch action, finally provoked Katilungu to suspend the local, thus alienating the entire branch
leadership. Roan, in sympathy with Chibuluma, passed a unanimous vote of no-confidence in Katilungu; and the two branches
allied to sponsor a similar motion at the next Supreme Council
meeting. At the behest of Roan and Chibuluma, the Supreme
Council formed a committee in November 1960 to determine
branch-level opinion on whether or not Katilungu should be
removed. All the branches but one voted overwhelmingly against
him, and on 1 January 1961, Katilungu was dismissed from the
presidency of the Mineworkers' Union.[3]

Katilungu's fall is but the most dramatic example of local
branch power over the process of leadership maintenance and
recruitment at the national level. In the main, local branch leaders
exert this power less dramatically, exacting adjustments from the
Head Office on a day-to-day basis. Thus, when I asked the general secretary of the union about campaign techniques in Head
Office elections, he denied the existence of campaigns as such;
rather, he indicated that Head Office leaders win votes by performing their everyday duties in a way that wins the support of
the local leaders. As he stated:

The Head Office . . . people rely on the branch leaders for

---

* The Monckton Commission was appointed to investigate the operations of the federal system and to recommend ways of improving it.
Because the terms of the Commission did not include making recommendations on the possibility of secession from the Federation, the nationalist parties decided to boycott the Commission. See discussion in
chap. 7.

their reputations and popularity. . . . the best way to stay popular is by giving good advice on their branch matters, such as during negotiations. If your advice on three or four things leads to achievement for the branch level, then you are all right.[4]

Not only do the Head Office leaders make sure they assist the branch leadership; they also scrupulously avoid alienating them. The best example of this is their constant referral back to the Supreme Council of almost all important decisions. During negotiations, for example, the Head Office constantly convenes and reconvenes the Supreme Council to consider new company offers and to establish new bargaining positions. An awareness of the necessity of preserving popularity among the local branch leaders thus breeds in the Head Office a desire to perform their duties in a way that will increase their support among the branches and a desire to refrain from activities that will compromise their standing with the local leadership.

The Powerlessness of the Head Office

If the Head Office of the union fails to commit the union to a regulative role and to enforce the government's development labor policy, it is thus in large part because the distribution of power in the union places the Head Office at a great disadvantage. The crippling effects of local preeminence are perhaps best illustrated in the following notes from a Supreme Council meeting in January 1963. President Chisata had called the meeting in an attempt to curb the rising levels of strikes and thereby help "our new African Government."

The meeting was opened by the President, Chisata, who said that the reason it was called was on account of the strikes at present taking place on the Copperbelt, and that ways and means must be found to end these continual stoppages. . . .

The Chibuluma Branch Secretary reported that his branch would go on strike at 2 a.m. on Saturday 5/1/63, the reason for the strike being that a member of the Union was beaten up by a foreman and a policeman. . . . The Head Office officials pointed out that if the Branch . . . had notified the Head Office of their intention to call a strike, Head Office officials could have intervened and the strike could have been avoided.

A member of the Roan delegation . . . reported that the Roan Antelope would go on strike again.[5]

The Head Office was thus completely countered by the locals, and was apparently unwilling even to try to reverse the decisions they had taken.

An equally telling illustration of the powerlessness of the Head Office is given in table 36. For every dispute, I attempted to

TABLE 36
Role of Head Office
(N = 576)

Percentage of cases in which Head Office:	1950–63	1964–68
Dampened local	4	2
Was passive	5	9
Took over dispute	21	11
Exacerbated dispute	6	0
Was not involved	64	78

determine the role played by the Head Office. Most often, the Head Office did not enter the dispute. Other times it took a passive role (e.g., collected information about the dispute), took over the dispute, dampened the activities of the local, or exacerbated the dispute. It might be expected that given the Head Office's responsiveness to government's labor policies after self-government in Zambia, it would less frequently exacerbate disputes and much more frequently dampen them in comparison with the colonial era. As shown in table 36, this expectation is ill-founded. The Head Office reduced the frequency with which it exacerbated disputes; but it also dampened them less often. In short, since self-government, the Head Office more often took no action at all.[6]

The Union as a Structure of Communications

There is another reason for the union's failure to serve as an agency of government policy: the structural resources at the command of the local leaders limit their ability to reach and influence their members.

THE NETWORK OF OFFICEHOLDERS. Union leaders can easily receive communications from their members, but they experience great difficulties in disseminating communications downward. The union maintains a network of officials throughout the plant area, and it takes considerable pains to insure that the workers know the identity of their shop stewards. Each shop steward must prove his popularity among the workers by collecting twenty-five names on a nomination paper before he receives confirmation by the union. Moreover, the branch executive repeatedly lectures the shop stewards on the necessity of being constantly prepared to accept their members' grievances. To guarantee that shop stewards transmit the grievances through to the branch executive, union leaders require them to report into the union offices on the way home from work. The union maintains its office between the plant area and the township, so that the stewards and aggrieved workers as well can easily stop by at the end of their shifts.[7] The union leaders thus maintain themselves as a "captive audience," open to the receipt of messages from their members.

Unfortunately, while suited to receiving messages from the membership, the union is ill-suited for the transmission of messages to the rank and file. For whereas the leaders are a captive audience for their members, the membership is not captive from the point of view of the leaders themselves. Indeed, the whole notion that the membership and union come into contact when the membership has grievances institutionalizes the selective exposure of the membership to the union officials. Structured as it is to respond to its members when they are aggrieved, the union is not structured so as to maintain constant contact with its members, and thereby expose them on a continuing basis to the viewpoints the union may wish to communicate.

Contributing to this deficiency of the union is the small number of channels it maintains between the leaders and their followers. All told, at Rhokana branch, the union maintains fifty-two shop stewards and fifteen branch officers.[8] There is no evidence that the number of officers is too few for detecting the grievances of the members; when the members feel the union fails to give them satisfaction, it is not for want of being able to find a union official to speak with. But there can be no question that in the face of a membership of over 10,000 the union possesses an insufficient number of officials to transmit messages to the bulk of the employees. The union simply cannot reach its membership on a continuous, face-to-face basis, given the number of officials at its command. Union leaders recognize this fact, and express considerable frustration at their inability to get their point of view across to the members.

UNION MEETINGS. Recognizing this deficiency, the union leaders employ an alternate form of communication: the public meeting. At Rhokana, as at the other copper mines, the union acquired a large meeting ground in the midst of the mine townships. On the top of an anthill—the podium characteristic of most copperbelt organizations—the union constructed a large, covered platform in which it installed a microphone and loudspeakers. When the branch leaders schedule a meeting, they lease a soundtruck from the Head Office and circulate throughout the townships "shouting the meeting." At the scheduled hour, or more characteristically an hour after the scheduled hour, they commence their addresses to the members.

The public meeting represents an improvement over the network of union officials, for it increases the ability of the union leaders to reach the mass of their followers. However, there is evidence that the improvement is only a slight one. In comparison with other institutions on the copperbelt, the union holds infrequent public meetings. From June to November 1962, for example, UNIP held forty-one public meetings and the union only sixteen (table 37). Granted, the level of party activity was at a height over this period; it was preparing for the October election

TABLE 37
Meetings, June–November 1962

	Mineworkers' Union			UNIP		
	Number of meetings	Average attendance	Number of towns on the copperbelt at which meetings were held	Number of meetings	Average attendance	Number of towns on the copperbelt at which meetings were held
June	9	964	7	7	1,446	1
July	0	0	0	7	3,650	4
August	2	425	2	8	1,829	5
September	2	45	2	6	4,967	4
October	2	290	2	9	1,930	3
November	1	24	1	4	1,300	3

Source: Reports, June–November 1962, File 100.20.7D. No information for 15–30 November 1962.

which was to lead to the formation of the first African government in Zambia. But the union too was at a peak of activity: it was at the climax of its dispute over the advancement issue. It not only conducted an industry-wide strike in this period, but also participated in a major commission of inquiry, the Morison Commission. The assertion that the union holds relatively few public meetings receives further verification from the fact that during my fourteen months of research in Kitwe, the union held only two public meetings, whereas the party held eight.

Not only are meetings relatively infrequent, they also are poorly attended. I was able to collect attendance figures for all four mines over a one-year period. Only at one mine did the average attendance exceed 10 percent of the members; and in the case of two of the mines, the figure was 5 percent or less (see table 38). These data too receive confirmation from my own observations. The two meetings at Rhokana mine were attended by no more than 150 persons each, or about 2 percent of the

TABLE 38

Acts of Participation

Proportion of employees who:	Mufulira	Roan	Nchanga	Rhokana
Attend meetings	16%	4%	10%	5%
Vote in union elections	24	26	24	17
Vote in strike ballots	59	96	88	66
Strike	71	73	62	68

Source: Meetings data: Reports, 1 November 1961, to 15 November 1962, File 100.20.7H. Election data: Report on 1967 election, from the office of the Assistant Labour Commissioner. Strike ballot: Report, November 1954, Department of Labour, Ha/43, Vol. 1. Strike: Reports, January–March 1954, Ha/43, Vol. 1.

Note: For participation in the strike, I picked the least favorable day, i.e., the one with the lowest participation in the strike. Note that the figure is further depressed by the compulsory attendance at work of essential service workers.

membership; the size of the crowds at party meetings averaged in the thousands.

Union officials not only solicit the views of their members at these public meetings; they cannot avoid expressions of members' opinions. Before attending Annual Conferences and Supreme Council meetings, branch officials often call public meetings and gather items to place on the negotiating agenda. For example, at a meeting in Chibuluma branch, members of the audience came forth with the following complaints:

Why is the number of overtime hours not marked on the new pay sheet? We do not know whether our overtime pay is correct. . . .

Can the Union not press for better uniforms for messengers? They should be as good as the police.

The foreman at the machine shop just whistles when he wants to call an African—as if he was calling a dog. . . .

Group 1 labourers are forced to work in stopes when they are unskilled for such work.

The [company] promised that the groups of machine and spanner boys would be raised, but they are still the same.[9]

But even if the Union officials do not solicit members' viewpoints, the mass of the mineworkers freely offer them from the floor of the meeting. Thus, during a meeting at Rhokana, branch officials were subject to abuse from underground lashers who demanded to be transferred from lashing duties; smelter workers shouted that their jobs should be regraded and that the companies had promised to do this two years previously; and other underground workers protested bitterly about the conduct of a European mine captain.[10] Union officials regard such meetings as the primary means by which they can learn of their members' demands, and are philosophic about the pressures exerted by members in the course of these public sessions.

The efficiency with which meetings transmit members' demands to the union officials is not, however, matched by the efficiency with which meetings enable union officials to transmit to the members messages of moderation and restraint. The presence of members at meetings does not insure their acceptance of the union's viewpoint; when union officials seek to preach restraint at public meetings, their message is often rejected out of hand. For example, at Rhokana in 1965, "The branch Chairman reminded the audience that the President [Dr. Kaunda] . . . was against unconstitutional or wild-cat strikes" and was shouted down.[11] And in 1967, the chairman was nearly assaulted when he urged a meeting of strikers to return to work so that he could take their case to the companies.[12] Moreover, the presence of members at union meetings does not even ensure their exposure to the union's point of view; when union speakers express opinions at variance with those of the miners, the audience frequently disbands. Thus, for example, after the union signed the unpopular agreement of 1964 in which they accepted the dual-wage structure, the Rhokana branch commenced a series of meetings to win back members who had begun to resign from the union; several of these meetings disintegrated when the leadership tried to defend the agreement and to criticize workers who had commenced strikes in opposition.[13]

I failed to record the frequency with which meetings did break up in this manner; despite this oversight, my impression was that the failure of union meetings was a surprisingly frequent phenomenon, suggesting the union leaders' inability to communicate views which differ from those held by the mineworkers themselves. Indirect evidence for this interpretation exists in the variations of attendance figures at meetings. The data for the Chibuluma branch indicate that the greatest attendance at union meetings takes place just prior to strike action. Over 1961 and 1962, attendance at meetings rarely exceeded 350 persons. But in the period from April to June 1962, when the union was preparing strike action, the average attendance climbed to over 800 persons. This fluctuation suggests that union leaders can get the members to expose themselves to their views only when the members can be fairly certain that the views of the leaders will be in support of their own desire for militant action.[14]

Additional evidence for this assertion is the data presented in table 38, displaying the relative frequency of four acts of membership participation. All four represent occasions on which the branch leadership brings the membership into contact with the union. They differ, however, in that participating in or voting for a strike represents an act in which the leadership encourages the members to express their demands, whereas attending a meeting represents an act in which the leadership gains the opportunity for communicating its opinions to the members. Voting in a union election represents a relatively neutral act along this dimension. The relative frequency of the four acts therefore suggests that the union leaders can easily reach their members when the contact enables the workers to express or to act for their demands; but not when such contact affords the chance of disseminating the leaders' point of view.

The union leaders themselves recognize the deficiencies of their communication resources. As the president of the union stated:

We have a new government, and it is our government. We are a new country and we have to do things differently now —take up a new way of doing things to work hard in development. The main difficulty with all this is to tell all this to the man in the shop. . . . We can not reach him, and it is very difficult to express this to them.[15]

At the time I was in Zambia, the Head Office had become alarmed at this inadequacy of the union and was planning to supplement its face-to-face structure with mass media of communication. It was planning to introduce a newspaper and a series of radio programs. Its efforts received a severe blow, however, with the death in 1968 of the union's publicity officer. Until a replacement could be found, the Head Office bought space in an inside page of the house tabloid of the Anglo-American Corporation, *The Miner*. As 51 percent of the miners at Rhokana are illiterate in English, and as vernacular languages abound, this medium was relatively ineffective. The Head Office also planned large-scale worker education programs under the auspices of the ZCTU; it hoped that the creation of such programs will afford it additional means of instilling "responsibility" into the labor force. Very little had been done in this direction by the time I completed my research. Meanwhile, the Head Office had to utilize the union's communication structure, with all the weaknesses that we have just described.

The Attitudes of the Mineworkers

The ineffectiveness of the union stems not only from the poverty of the structural resources available to its local leaders, but also from the way in which the characteristics of the local mining community strengthen and reinforce the militant labor attitudes toward industrial relations.

SOCIAL HOMOGENEITY. A primary cause of the reinforcement of the mineworkers' attitudes is the near total occupational homogeneity of the mineworking community. Only employees of the mine companies are allowed to reside in the mine townships. Moreover, the companies attempt to house all their employees, so that few mineworkers reside outside of the company towns.[16] The most dramatic result is the creation on the copperbelt of two relatively distinct communities: those governed by the municipalities, which contain persons from a wide variety of occupations, and those run by the mining companies, in which mineworkers alone reside. Table 39 illustrates the degree to which the mine-

TABLE 39
Township Composition, Employed
Northern Rhodesian Citizens

	Nkana Township	Kitwe Township
Mineworkers	11,180	36
As percentage of total	99	2
Other workers	118	2,545
As percentage of total	1	98
Total	11,298	2,581

Source: Compiled from District Summary, Kitwe, 1946 Census of African Employees, F4/A/709.
Note: Assumes domestic workers in Nkana are employees of European miners. If this assumption is dropped, the proportion of Nkana residents who are miners reduces to 81 percent.

workers were segregated from the nonmining communities in 1946. Figures submitted to the Brown Commission of Inquiry indicate that the trend persists: in 1966, all but 5 percent of the home dwellers in the Nkana township were mine employees; and if the domestic servants of European employees are counted as mine employees, the figure drops to 2 percent.[17]

The mineworkers are naturally differentiated by status. We have two indicators of status: pay group and education. Tables 40 and 41 indicate the distribution of the African mineworkers by these criteria.

Despite the social variation introduced by these status criteria, two significant phenomena must be noted. The first is the degree of homogeneity within the distributions. Well over half of the mineworkers concentrate in the three bottom pay groups at Rhokana, and a full two-thirds have received less than a primary education. The second phenomenon is the structure of the mine townships.

TABLE 40
Pay Groups of African Mineworkers, Rhokana

	Number	Percentage	Cumulative percentage
Local staff	1,322	12.5	100.0
Senior operator I	33	0.3	87.5
Senior operator II	42	0.4	87.2
Leading operator I	197	1.9	86.8
Leading operator II	240	2.3	84.9
Operator I	216	2.1	82.6
Operator II	775	7.4	80.5
Operator III	972	9.2	73.1
Operator IV	594	5.6	63.9
Helper II	1,064	10.0	58.3
Helper III	2,734	26.0	48.3
Workmen	2,346	22.3	22.3
Total	10,535	100.0	

Source: Compiled from Rhokana Corporation, Manpower Services Department, Monthly Report, 24 January 1968, Files, Manpower Services Department.

Within the mine townships there is little correlation between occupation and residence. The companies maintain a gradation of houses, running from relatively abysmal two-room dwellings,

TABLE 41
Educational Attainment of African Mineworkers, Rhokana

Educational attainment	Number	Percentage
Uneducated	1,114	51
Infant schooling	332	15
Lower primary	336	15
Upper primary	113	5
Secondary	66	3
No information	222	10
Total	2,183	99

Source: From a 20 percent systematic random sample of the labor force.

located in high-density areas, to relatively luxurious six-room homes, sited in low-density townships. While a miner must be well paid to live in the better housing, most well-to-do miners dwell among their less-prosperous fellows. There are several reasons for this. Expatriates are guaranteed low-density housing, so few vacancies exist for advanced Africans. Many local employees prefer to pay lower rents so as to meet school fees or to purchase capital goods, such as vans, with which to supplement their incomes. Moreover, houses are allocated on a point system; less well paid employees with large families and greater seniority may gain prior access to the better housing.[18] Despite the companies' efforts to persuade higher-level workers to move to better areas in the townships, miners of a wide variety of income levels thus dwell in each housing area.[19]

The result of these housing patterns is to frustrate the emergence of divergent viewpoints among the mine employees— variant viewpoints based on different occupational levels. It can be hypothesized that when discussions of labor matters take place in the mine townships, they cut across status groupings. People of similar income are not isolated and cannot communicate solely among themselves. Spatial patterns thus reduce the potential for the emergence of sectional viewpoints within the labor force. While the structure of the township cannot explain the origins of the mineworkers' militant attitudes, it thus does help to explain their persistence and intensity.

OVERCOMING SOCIAL HETEROGENEITY. It is easy to oversimplify in emphasizing the high degree of social homogeneity in the mine community. African supervisors and laborers inevitably come into conflict and disagree. Moreover, such factors as tribal background and provincial origin introduce major sources of social variation in the work force of the mines. I recorded over one hundred different tribes among the workers at Rhokana. As noted in table 42, even when grouping the tribes into major ethnic clusters, the variety and diversity of tribal backgrounds remain. And table 43 indicates that residents of every province in Zambia are represented in the mine's labor force. However in the context

TABLE 42
Ethnic Background, Rhokana

Tribal group	Number	Percentage
Luapula group	310	14
Bemba, Mambwe	597	27
Lamba	172	8
Tonga, Ila, Lenje	165	8
Ndembu, Lovale	133	6
Lozi	41	2
Chewa, Ngoni	158	7
Others, Alien	607	28
Total	2,183	100

Source: From a 20 percent systematic random sample of the labor force.

Note: The groupings are based upon ethnographic similarity, and are made in partial conformity with the categories employed by J. Clyde Mitchell in his demographic surveys of the copperbelt. See, for example, J. Clyde Mitchell, "A Note on the Urbanisation of Africans on the Copperbelt," *The Rhodes-Livingstone Journal* 12 (1951): 20–27.

of the mine community, such status or tribal variations are frequently overridden by a single shared characteristic: the attribute of race.

The racial attribute is able to reduce the effects of other characteristics because, in the context of the mine community, race is seen by most mineworkers as the most salient social background factor; in the mine community, wealth, authority, and the perquisites which establish major differences in life styles distribute on racial lines. The attribute of race thus organizes and explains so many variations on the mines that it becomes one of the most powerful single predictors of the social and economic differences which are salient to the members of the mining community. And when it is realized that conflicts between labor and management take place across this racial dimension, it can be seen why so much of the African workers' thinking on labor issues becomes organized about racial categories. Management does something

TABLE 43

Province of Origin, Rhokana

Province	Number	Percentage
Barotse	61	3
Central	173	8
Eastern	109	5
Northern	615	28
Luapula	112	5
Southern	14	1
Northwestern	121	6
Western	25	1
Alien	401	18
Don't know	552	25
Total	2,183	100

Source: From a 20 percent systematic random sample of the labor force.

Note: Disparities between this and the preceding table largely result from the mine's failure to discriminate in its records between Tonga in Zambia and Malawi, Mambwe in Zambia and Tanzania, Lamba in Zambia and the Congo, and so forth.

"because they are Europeans"; a laborer is fired "because he was an African"; African workers are more frequently injured and killed "because the whitemen want to prove that we cannot run our own mines safely"; and production falls "because the European miners want to injure the country and show that we Africans cannot rule ourselves." [20]

These patterns of thought generate tremendous social pressures to prevent people from taking a position on labor matters which diverges from that of the majority of the black community. For example, when the African workers in the upper occupational categories established an independent organization for the conduct of labor relations in the early 1950s, the majority of the members of the Mineworkers' Union branded the members of the new association "sell-outs," betrayers of the Africans, and black Europeans. So great was the opposition to the new association that even when it was recognized by the mining companies, hundreds of eligible workers refused to join (table 44). The pressures were so intense that many high-level workers accepted demotions instead.

Not only are pressures exerted to override occupational variations in opinion; mineworkers strive to reduce variations based on tribal difference as well. The best study of this phenomenon is the work of A. L. Epstein. In his study of the Roan branch of the Mineworkers' Union in the early 1950s, Epstein notes the mineworkers' conviction that the skills relevant to leadership in tribal affairs are not relevant to the defense of the Africans' interests as industrial workers. He recounts how the mineworkers voted overwhelmingly to abolish the institution of tribal elders as a mediator between the companies and the labor force; and how the tribal elders, when they encroached into the field of labor relations, were subject to abuse and even assault by the mineworkers. While Epstein interprets his observations primarily as evidence of the operation of class instead of tribal social relationships in the urban social setting, he also notes that the perception of racial differences in the mining community promotes the rejection of tribal divisions and the endorsement of racial unity. When interacting among each other, Epstein concludes, African mineworkers still note tribal variations and adjust their relationships accordingly; but when interacting across racial boundaries, such variations become irrelevant. In his own words, "The evi-

TABLE 44
Refusal to be Represented by Staff Association

Number of workers	Rhokana	Nchanga	Mufulira
Falling under Staff Association when recognized, December 1955	803	528	574
Refusing to go into staff positions as of August 1956	311	75	151
Accepting cut in pay rather than becoming staff	228	...	85

Source: Verbatim Testimony, Branigan Commission, 24–25 October 1956, and 1 November 1956.

Note: Roan figures not available.

dence of the present study shows that in situations involving the total field of Black-White relations the tribal factor tends to be overborne." [21]

I saw nothing to contradict Epstein's findings, and much to support them. Tribal variations still functioned in social relations. Bemba teased Ngoni; informal visiting tended to take place within and not across tribal groupings; and marriage partners were selected from within tribal clusters. Indeed, in some respects, the potential for tribal divisions had increased since Epstein's time. In August 1967, Zambia experienced a severe political crisis. During elections to UNIP's Central Committee, Lozi candidates lost out to candidates from other tribes. In response, and in protest over the supposed lack of governmental expenditures in Barotse Province, there arose a new party, termed the United Party (UP), which drew the support of large numbers of Lozi tribesmen. These events led to severe political tensions in the Rhokana townships—tensions which resulted in minor, if bloody, clashes between UNIP youths and UP supporters.[22] Nevertheless, when it came to relations between the mineworkers and the companies, tribal background was still regarded as totally irrelevant. None of the strains which arose in the field of interparty and interethnic competition engendered rivalries or dissention within the sphere of labor relations. And had attempts been made to introduce discrepant outlooks on labor relations among the various tribes, they would certainly have been resisted with pressures approaching coercion, just as they were in Epstein's time.

Adding to the power of the racial factor to override divergent points of view is the increased potential for the emergence of industrial consciousness among the mineworkers. The days of "target," short-term employment are over at Rhokana. The labor force has stabilized: in 1968 the employees of Rhokana Corporation had worked for the company for an average of nearly eight years. This degree of stability suggests a strong commitment to industrial employment and a heightened potential on the part of African employees to perceive and defend their interests as working men.[23]

Thus, while the potential for discrepant viewpoints on labor relations exists, given the social variety of the mine labor force, the potential is simply not realized. The isolation of the mining communities, the spatial structure of the mine townships, and the pervasive pattern of racial stratification, all contribute to the stabilization and reinforcement of uniform attitudes on labor matters. Social variations within the labor force fail to translate into divergent opinion, and the radical attitudes of the workers fail to encounter opposition or dissent. The union leaders, enjoined to implement government labor policy, thus confront a difficult task.

Attitudes toward the Union

The attitudes of the workers toward the union leaders themselves present a further difficulty. In the workers' eyes, the leaders lack legitimacy.* They are unable to convince the mineworkers that they are sensitive to their demands and determined to advance their interests.

THE CONSEQUENCES OF THE LEADERS' CONCEPTION OF THEIR ROLE. In a lecture to a group of shop stewards, the general secretary outlined the union's conception of the role of its leaders. He defined the role of the shop stewards as "defending members and winning cases." He went on to explain, however, that the shop steward must act only on "good cases"; these, he stated, are ones in which the members had not in fact violated a plant rule. The rationale offered by the general secretary was trenchant and informative. On the one hand, if shop stewards seek to achieve popularity for the union by appealing all cases, they will in fact lose the support of the members in the long run, for the union's record of winning cases will be compromised by the losses it will suffer in fighting for members who were clearly in the wrong.

---

* Legitimacy we define as a relationship between leaders and followers in which the followers accord their leaders the right to adhere to and to propound policies, irrespective of their agreement with the content of these policies.

On the other hand, the shop stewards must remember that the union, if it is to win cases, has first to win the respect of management. By screening the cases in advance, it can win the reputation of advancing only genuine grievances, and thereby win serious consideration in its dealings with the company.[24]

The general secretary's point was clear. Union leaders must invest an acceptance of company rules in exchange for respect from the company. Leaders' acceptance of management's rules takes various forms. In its quest for respect, the Head Office enjoins the shop stewards "to be an example. Work hard. Don't come to work late, and don't leave [unfinished] work behind when you leave; then you will have management's respect and be in a good position to advance your cases." [25] More dramatically, the leaders go beyond a mere acceptance of the management's rules to an active communication of them. Thus, shop stewards are asked to "explain all the rules of the plant; make sure you have your members know them, so that when you take up their cases they won't be wrong and you will win them." [26] And in extreme, but not infrequent cases, the union's acceptance of management's rules takes the form of enforcement of these rules. Thus, at the time of strikes, the union leaders actively exhort their members back to work; only by so doing can they get management to negotiate with them the members' grievances.[27]

The union leaders thus seek to invest cooperation with management in exchange for respect and cooperation. The result is costly, however, in that the leaders thereby lose the regard of many of the members. They are accused of being "collaborationist"; they receive the epithet of "sell-outs"; and they are viewed as persons accepting and working in terms of the illegitimate authority of the European management. Their apparent insensitivity to the subordinate position of their members in the industrial structure costs them the respect of their fellow employees.

EFFECTIVENESS AND PERCEPTIONS OF POWER. The general secretary asserted in his lecture to the shop stewards that his strategy of collaboration *could* win legitimacy for the leaders of the Mineworkers' Union. Collaboration would increase effectiveness, and from the effectiveness of the union could stem its legitimacy. It is impossible to test the general secretary's assertion as the data for a direct test do not exist. What evidence does exist, however, suggests that while he is correct in stating that the union's approach renders it effective, he is wrong in assuming that the union's improved performance results in increased legitimacy.

Evidence for the effectiveness of the union is the proportion of cases in which the union gains victories or compromises and the proportion of cases in which it suffers defeats. Over its history, the union has gained as great a proportion of favorable outcomes (36 percent) as it has suffered setbacks (38 percent).[28] Since self-government, the union's effectiveness has increased (table 45).

TABLE 45

Effectiveness by Year

Outcomes	1950–63	1964–68
Victories	15%	18%
Compromises	19%	25%
Losses	43%	27%
Don't know	23%	31%
Total	382	194

While the union gained victories or compromises in 34 percent of its cases before self-government, since self-government the proportion has increased to 43 percent. Conversely, while the union lost 43 percent of its cases before self-government, it has lost only 27 percent of its cases since 1963.

Further evidence of the union's effectiveness is its apparent ability to win those kinds of cases which the mineworkers care most deeply about. Taking the propensity to strike for a given issue as an indicator of the intensity of feeling about the matter, we can determine the union's performance on issues of critical importance to the membership. As shown in table 46, there is a slight positive coefficient of rank order correlation between intensity and the union's ability to gain wins or compromises; in other words, the union tends to be most effective on the matters which are of the greatest concern to the rank and file.

TABLE 46
Effectiveness and Intensity

Issue	Rank of frequency of strikes	Rank of frequency of wins or compromises
Bonus	1	1
Task	2	6
Labor flow	3	8
Supervisor	4	2
Hours	5	9
Jurisdiction	6	11
Wages	7	3
Clothing	8	10
Union rights	9	7
Township	10	5
Dismissal	11	4

$r_s = +.16$

Lastly, the data suggest that the branch level of the union—which makes the most immediate impact on the workers—is fully as effective as the Head Office. Thus, table 47 reveals a positive

TABLE 47
Effectiveness at Branch Level

Issue	Rank of frequency at branch	Rank of frequency of wins or compromises
Hours	1	9
Bonus	2	1
Supervisor	3	2
Dismissal	4	4
Task	5	6
Clothing	6	10
Labor flow	7	8
Township	8	5
Union rights	9	7
Wages	10	3
Jurisdiction	11	11

$r_s = +.34$

coefficient of rank correlation between the tendency for cases to arise at the branch level and the ability of the union to gain wins or compromises in these matters. Breaking down the kinds of outcomes of union action directly by union level reveals little difference between the branches and the Head Office (table 48).

TABLE 48
Effectiveness and Union Level

	Victories	Compromises	Losses	Don't know	Total
Branch	17%	20%	36%	27%	427
Head Office	26%	23%	39%	12%	70
Both	6%	24%	53%	17%	79

They suffer the same proportion of losses and they gain the same proportion of compromises; the Head Office does possess a superior record in obtaining "wins" from the management, however.

The image of the union gleaned from the data is that of a fairly effective organization. It is able to obtain favorable outcomes as frequently as not, and in more recent times, in the majority of the cases it undertakes. Its record is best in the kinds of cases its members appear to care the most about. And the units to which its members are most directly exposed are in no way weaker than the other units of the organization. Despite its record of effectiveness, however, the legitimacy of the union remains highly in doubt. At Rhokana branch, the union's effectiveness was not recognized as such. The primary reason for this appeared to be that many of the mineworkers interpret the branch leaders' cooperation with the mining companies as prima facie evidence of their weakness. "*Intungulushi shama Union, tee sana* [Union leaders, they're hopeless]." "They don't know how to fight." "They're cowards in front of Europeans." "When there is trouble they hide in their houses." I encountered these comments frequently. They strongly suggest that while the union leaders may be able to trade cooperation with management for increased success in handling grievances, they fail to achieve a reputation as strong and effective champions of the interests of African labor. For the very tactic employed creates an impression of their weakness and ineffectuality.

SOCIAL RANK AND UNION LEGITIMACY. The performance of the union leaders undermines their legitimacy in yet another way. For not only do they appear to work closely with management; they appear to profit unduly from this relationship. It was widely felt at Rhokana branch that union leaders receive disproportionate benefits from the company. The workers believed that union leaders received higher incomes, had better jobs, and lived in better areas of the mine townships than did other workers on the mines. For whatever reason, many of these beliefs were true. Union leaders do earn better incomes; while the mean wage at Rhokana was K75.40 per month, shop stewards earned on the average K82.68, and branch executives and committee members earned K93.26. Because of their higher salaries, branch officials do tend to live in the more prosperous section of the mine townships. And in any given department there is a high probability that the union officials will possess a better job than that held by the average employee. Thus, using an index of income to rank jobs, we find that in four of the five departments which employ the vast majority of the work force at Rhokana mine (over 80 percent), the union representatives tended to possess better jobs than the average worker.[29]

The greater advantages of the union officials are not unexpected and, in themselves, might not be damaging. But when they are viewed in conjunction with the tactic employed by the union, these advantages are very damaging indeed. It is not difficult for union members to believe that their leaders, in cooperating with management, seek to obtain advantages for themselves. Rather than obtaining respect as the champions of the workers' demands, the leaders instead appear to function as a privileged group, attempting to evoke cooperation from the workers in exchange for personal benefits.

The very factors which undermine the legitimacy of the union's leaders operate with particular force to weaken their ability to restrain and control workers' demands in conformity with government policy. Should the leaders enjoin their members to contain wage demands, respect supervisors, work hard, or refrain from striking, their statements would be interpreted as reflecting the leaders' identity of interests with the management, their weakness in the face of the white men, or their desire to further ingratiate themselves with the company. This became evident when the leaders sought to get their members to return to work after wildcat strikes. Speeches to the workers were greeted with cries of "sellout," "coward," "*tamukwete amaka* [you have no strength]." Even if the branch leaders were strongly motivated to render the union an output structure, they would therefore most likely fail; for their messages of restraint would be discounted by the members, given their attitudes toward the leaders themselves. The failure of the union leaders to convince their followers of the effectiveness of the union as an input structure thus undermines the union's ability to function as an effective output agency for the greater political system.

7 The Union and the Party

The political leaders of Zambia possess a variety of reasons for wanting the party to control the Mineworkers' Union. While an economic motive prevails at the present time and was explicit in the most recent attempt to assert party authority—which we describe below—their desire to place UNIP in control of the union predates their dedication to a development labor policy. Their political motives for party domination derive from their experiences with the Mineworkers' Union in the preindependence period.

Relationships at the National Level

The party and union were formed at virtually the same period. With the prospect of federation in the early 1950s, the leaders of the two organizations determined on closer cooperation, and for a time, it appeared that the union would indeed play an important role in the nationalist movement. In 1952, the African National Congress formed a Supreme Action Council to plan and, if necessary, to order a total withdrawal of labor so as to cripple the colonial government. The president and secretary of the Mineworkers' Union held seats on this council (table 49).

TABLE 49
Supreme Action Council, African National Congress

L. C. Katilungu	Mineworkers' Union
Simon Kaluwa	Mineworkers' Union
Dixon Konkola	African Railway Workers' Trade Union
Simon Zukas	Anti-Federation Action Committee
Kenneth Kaunda	Chinsali Branch, ANC
E. Chisenga	Kitwe African Society
S. Mununga	Representing Chief Mununga

Source: *Freedom Newsletter*, 4 March 1952.

The link between the union and the nationalist movement was further strengthened through the Trade Union Congress. The congress' executive was dominated by unionists who were committed to a politically activist role for the trade union movement; moreover, the congress maintained a political subcommittee which formulated plans for politically supportive action by labor. In both these bodies, leaders of the Mineworkers' Union occupied prominent positions (tables 50 and 51).

TABLE 50
Executive Officers, Trade Union Congress, August 1952

Office	Name	Union
President	Dixon Konkola	Railway Workers
Vice-President	Robinson Puta	Mineworkers' Union
General Secretary	Matthew Nkoloma	Mineworkers' Union
Executive Member	Jameson Chapoloko	Mineworkers' Union
Executive Member	Justin Chimba	Unknown

Many of the early leaders of the Mineworkers' Union endorsed a conception of trade unionism which affirmed the nationalist cause. The most influential spokesman for this viewpoint was Simon ber Zukas, an expatriate with close personal ties to the leaders of both the African National Congress and the Mineworkers' Union. In two early pamphlets he wrote:

TABLE 51
Political Action Subcommittee, 1952

Office	Name	Union
Chairman	Dixon Konkola	Railway Workers
Secretary	Matthew Nkoloma	Mineworkers' Union
Member	Paul Kalichini	Industrial Workers
Member	Jonathan Mubanga	Municipal Workers
Member	Chanda	Railway Workers
Member	Matthew Mwendapole	Mineworkers' Union
Member	Jameson Namitengo	Mineworkers' Union
Member	Jameson Chapoloko	Mineworkers' Union
Member	Gordon Chindele	Mineworkers' Union

The trade union movement must take part in the political struggle of the country. For trade unions to divorce themselves would mean that they acquiesce in the oppression of the people as a whole.[1]

Now is the time to awaken the mineworkers and educate them in trade unionism. The leaders must not lose sight of the fact that a trade union must act politically in defense of its members. It must act and take an interest . . . in the Government of the country. When the struggle against Federation begins, the Mineworkers' Trade Union must be ready to take strike action because this is the only real weapon available to the African workers as they have no vote.[2]

Several key officials of the Mineworkers' Union—Puta, Chapoloko, Nkoloma, Chindele, Mwendapole, and others—strongly endorsed Zukas' interpretation of the role of the union.[3] Their responsiveness reflected the consonance of their economic objectives with the nationalist goals of ANC. That African advancement formed a major objective of the newly formed union;[4] that the color bar was a major grievance shared by all Africans; and that the whole political issue of federation revolved around the relative position of Africans and white men—these principles underlay the belief that the cause of the Mineworkers' Union and the nationalist movement were one.

THE USE OF STRIKES. The early structural and ideological affinities between the union and the African National Congress failed to last, however. One of the principal issues that divided the two organizations was their differing attitudes toward the use of strikes for political purposes.

The first break came in 1952 when the government deported Zukas for conduct "dangerous to peace and good order." Zukas' allies in the union sought to strike in protest over this action. However, the president of the union, Lawrence Katilungu, frustrated their plans.

On 8th April, when it became known in Kitwe that the High Court had found against Mr. Zukas . . . certain Africans set themselves up as an "action committee" to foment an immediate widespread stoppage of work . . . as a means of showing active sympathy with him.

Meetings of Africans were addressed by various speakers and by the early evening of the 9th April, it seemed certain that most African workers either through conviction or fear would not turn out the following morning. Late the same evening, however, Katilungu decided that he would take a hand and use his influence to prevent any stoppage. He toured the various Mine African Townships as well as holding meetings at several places in Kitwe, telling his African audiences to work as usual on the following day. Most of them did.[5]

It was Katilungu's conviction that the union should not become embroiled in political controversy; that its job was to fight for a better economic position for the African employees; that the union could do more for the economic position of the Africans than the politicians would ever accomplish; and that the union should refrain from annoying the companies and government any more than was absolutely necessary to achieve its objectives. As a result, Katilungu strongly opposed any use of the union's strike weapon for political reasons.[6]

Katilungu's position brought the union into direct conflict with the congress in 1953. In June 1952, the British government published a White Paper announcing its intention to implement the Federation of Rhodesia and Nyasaland; the congress determined to protest the policy in every way possible. The congress campaign was consummated in March 1953, when Nkumbula, the president of the congress, publicly burned a copy of the White Paper and announced a two-day general strike, termed a Two-Day National Prayer. In his speech, he stated:

> Both the Delegate Conference and the Supreme Action Council . . . have decided that should Federation be imposed against the opposition of the Africans, measures would be taken to paralyse the industries of this country. Among the industries that would be hard hit are farming, the railways,

mining, and the general workers' industries. The Union leaders have at these meetings put in express terms that their unions are behind the African National Congress.[7]

However, while the strike commenced in other industries, it did not materialize in the mines, and lacking this support, it failed. As Epstein states: "On the Copperbelt the African miners completely ignored the 'strike.' Nkumbula bitterly denounced Katilungu." [8] "Thereafter, although there were still strong Congress supporters within the Union leadership, there was open hostility between the two organizations." [9]

The union leaders' resistance to political strikes persisted throughout the nationalist period. In 1954 the Mineworkers' Union again frustrated a general strike. The General Workers' Union had struck over a wage demand, and following a prolonged work stoppage, the employers, with government support, served notice to over one thousand striking employees. The Trade Union Congress, with the backing of nationalist leaders, called for sympathetic strikes to protest the action. While radical elements in the Mineworkers' Union determined to cooperate with the congress, the president again overrode them. Robinson Puta, chairman at Nchanga, succeeded in getting his branch out on strike, but no other branch followed. This strike also failed.[10]

Similarly, eight years later, UNIP formulated a highly secret "master plan." The plan reputedly specified a series of levels of protest against the colonial regime; it was reported that stage three called for large-scale, sympathetic strikes in support of the party's objectives. While this stage was never reached in the nationalist struggle, it would have in any case failed. For the Mineworkers' Union resolved not to support it.

A meeting of the [Supreme] Council was held on the 11th of January to discuss the action to be taken should U.N.I.P. call for a strike. . . .

It was agreed that the Union could not as a Union take part in a political strike, but that Union members as individuals should be at liberty to do so; the Union would not make representations to the Companies on behalf of the strikers who were discharged.[11]

THE ESTABLISHMENT OF A UNITED LABOR FRONT. Equally as disturbing as the union's refusal to strike was its reluctance to participate in a united labor front.[12] The union's reluctance was made manifest in its failure to maintain membership in the Trade Union Congress (TUC).

From the early days of its formation, the congress functioned as the political wing of the labor movement and represented an organized form of expression for labor's political positions. Issuing draft proposals for constitutional reform in Northern Rhodesia, providing employment for labor leaders who had lost their jobs for engaging in political activities, and formulating official worker opinion on the political controversies of the day, the TUC represented the semiofficial political voice of labor in the nationalist period.[13] For the party leaders, it was extremely important that all unions be brought within, and kept within, the field of the TUC; only in this way could the nationalist movement achieve the advantage of unified support. It was therefore galling when the Mineworkers' Union in 1960 withdrew from the Trade Union Congress and stood aloof from its efforts to organize united labor support for self-government and independence. From the point of view of the nationalist leaders, the union's action represented an assertion of the paramountcy of its own interests above those of the national cause.

There were a number of reasons for the union's withdrawals from the TUC. Occasionally, the splits resulted from natural differences in interests between the federated unions. Being the biggest and wealthiest union in Northern Rhodesia, the Mineworkers' Union frequently felt that it was making a disproportionate contribution to the coffers of the TUC. One of the reasons for its 1960 breakaway was Katilungu's disgust with the refusal of several other unions to help meet the TUC's expenses.[14] A second reason was the influence of international labor organizations. The Mineworkers' Union received financial support, scholarships, and travel funds from affiliates of the International Confederation of

Free Trade Unions (ICFTU), while other unions in Northern Rhodesia maintained ties with the World Federation of Trade Unions (WFTU). Attempts by the foreign organizations to gain preeminence for their local backers in the TUC led to increased conflict between the Mineworkers' Union and other member unions. Moreover, the very availability of external resources amplified the scope of the conflict, for it enabled the groups to organize and support competing unions in their rival's fields of jurisdiction. The 1960 breakaway of the leaders of the Mineworkers' Union in part resulted from their anger at the WFTU backing of rival unions in the congress. And their breakaway again in 1963 was in part to protest the formation of the United Mineworkers' Union, a union supported by their WFTU-backed opponents.[15]

While these factors go far to explain the reluctance of the Mineworkers' Union to adhere to the TUC, there remains a more important reason: its distinct reluctance to subject itself to political influence. A principal reason behind the initial break between the Mineworkers' Union and the TUC in 1960 was the politically motivated opposition of other unionists to Katilungu, the president of the Mineworkers' Union. Katilungu had chosen to participate in an official government commission which was boycotted by both UNIP and the ANC. Moreover, he had initiated political contacts with European and other African leaders to form a party in opposition to the two dominant nationalist parties. Other leaders in the TUC opposed this attempt to further fragment the nationalist movement and Katilungu resented their attempts to impose political pressures upon him.

Following Katilungu's removal from the presidency of the Mineworkers' Union in 1960, the union refederated with the Trade Union Congress, now named the United Trade Union Congress (UTUC). The UTUC served as the labor wing of the United National Independence Party. Its president, Chivunga, was a former UNIP official; Wilson Chakulya, the general secretary, had earlier been detained for making a seditious speech at a UNIP meeting; and the treasurer, Albert Kalyati, was an active UNIP supporter.[16] Furthermore, the UTUC supported UNIP's commitment to industrial action in support of political objectives.

Chivunga, for example, at one point telegraphed Kaunda that the congress "unanimously supported UNIP demands on N. R. Constitution. Workers will take positive action [against] any imposition of constitution not assuring African majority." [17]

It was precisely on the issue of the congress' power to control industrial action for political purposes that the Mineworkers' Union again split from the united labor movement. Ironically, however, this time it was not in response to a UTUC call for a political strike; rather it was in opposition to the congress' attempts to prevent a strike that would have had adverse political consequences. Throughout 1961, the Mineworkers' Union had engaged in difficult and protracted wage negotiations. Failing to gain its objectives in negotiations, the union subjected the issue to conciliation; and when conciliation also failed, the union, in April 1962, went on strike. Three weeks into the strike, the government appointed the Morison Commission to investigate the dispute. Out of respect for the commission, the union adjourned the strike; but following the dissolution of the commission in July, the union resolved to renew strike action.

UNIP, along with the UTUC, opposed this decision. UNIP feared the disruption of the October general elections—elections which would lead to the formation of the first African government in Northern Rhodesia. As indicated in a circular issued by the Ndola Regional Office, UNIP viewed the union's action as an assertion of its interests without regard for the national cause.

> The United National Independence Party . . . unequivocally persuades all workers on the mines . . . to go to work. . . . The proposed strike is misguided, treacherous, and suicidal. . . . The strike will serve the interests of our enemy who will be happy to see the coming October election disrupted. We appeal to everybody to go to work for your own interest and that of your country. . . . [The actions] of the present leadership of the trade union of the mines . . . are misguided by reactionary forces inimical [sic] to African interests.[18]

Another regional secretary wrote:

Dear Comrades,

Tell all our people that anyone true sons and daughters of the soil that United National Independence Party does not agree to strike . . . because . . . the strike will spoil our forthcoming elections. . . . [Do not be] an enemy of the African Cause.[19]

Through these letters and the local UNIP branches, the UNIP leaders applied pressure on union members to cancel the strike. It was through the UTUC, however, that the party applied pressure on the union leaders.

In a meeting with the president and secretary of the union, Chivunga, the president of the UTUC, argued intensely that the strike could cause a postponement or cancellation of the elections, and all UNIP's efforts would come to naught. Moreover, it would demonstrate the irresponsibility of the Africans and discredit their leaders; European voters would be alienated, and the new African government would lack the confidence of the outside world. He urged that the union apply for arbitration "as a temporary measure." Failing to persuade the union leaders to reverse their decision, the UTUC arranged a series of meetings between the UNIP leaders and the union officials. It was at these meetings that the union was persuaded to cancel its proposed resumption of the strike.[20]

While they cooperated with the UTUC and UNIP, the leaders of the union were deeply angered at the exertion of political pressure in what they regarded as an industrial matter. They demanded a public apology from the regional secretaries, and the national party leaders extracted one. In addition, the union again withdrew from the congress, refusing to participate in what they regarded as a politically motivated labor movement. Despite repeated attempts to rejoin the Mineworkers' Union with the UTUC, UNIP failed to reestablish unity in the labor movement until the month before independence.[21]

ELITE PERCEPTIONS OF THE UNION. The union's refusal to strike for political purposes or to participate in the UTUC created intensely negative attitudes toward the union on the part of the political leaders. These attitudes were expressed in varying contexts and in different ways. The central themes, however, were that the leaders of the Mineworkers' Union were selfish, politically unreliable, and insensitive to appeals for national consciousness.

In reference to the union's withdrawal from the congress, one politician wrote:

> Without identifying myself with any particular group, I think (and this view is shared by many) the split is detrimental. . . . The bid for power, selfishness, and lust for prestige have made certain leaders fall easy victims to the Imperialist tactics and machinations to split the united front in the Labour Movement—[the importance of] Unity cannot be overestimated at this crucial time of transition.[22]

The mineworkers' determination to "go it alone" was wrong, because:

> The Trade Union Movement . . . should indissolubly be linked up with the struggle for freedom, Independence, and . . . unity. . . . A trade union movement . . . cannot divorce itself from the national struggle for political Independence. . . . [Therefore] the first duty of all organizations existing in a colonial territory is for these forces in that country to unite in the fight for the nation's liberation.[23]

As the struggle for independence drew to a close, the political leadership perceived a new implication to the political unreliability of the Mineworker's Union: the prospect that the union would fail to contribute to the development of the new nation. This lent a new sense of urgency to their conviction that the union must be controlled. As one commentator analysed the efforts of the political leaders to rejoin the Mineworkers' Union with the Congress of Trade Unions: "Kaunda must gain a hold on N[orthern] R[hodesia's] labour force. He needs a united and controllable labour movement which will be prepared to submerge its own interests in a formidable post-independence national effort." [24] And one regional party official stated, with notable vitriol:

Many of the leaders [of the Mineworkers' Union] are opportunists with no national interests at heart. They are a committed bunch who, if left alone, would cripple the economy of the country to nothingness.

With an exception of a few of them, these people did not feel the slightest bitterness of the struggle to liberate the country from foreign rule. In the election [of 1962] they even made it difficult for us to reach our goals. [25]

These attitudes gave rise to the conviction that party officials should control the union. In the preindependence period, the primary purpose of exerting such control was to purge the union of political enemies and bring it into the center of the nationalist struggle. In the postindependence era, the motive was to supplant the trade union leaders with party loyalists who would bolster the nation's economy and the government's ability to implement its development program.

Relationships at the Local Level

At the local level also, the party leaders vigorously seek to supplant union leaders with party personnel. The motivations of these local leaders are more parochial, however, deriving from the structure of the local mining community and the relationships between the union and party leaders within it.

THE TOWNSHIP COUNCIL. The chief instrument of the party in the mining community is the Mine Township Council. The council is an advisory body to management, and expresses the viewpoints of the miners on township matters: the conditions of roads, sanitation facilities, public markets, clinics, health facilities, taverns, and so forth. Until 1962 the local leaders of the Mineworkers' Union held seats on the council; at Rhokana mine in 1962, of the twelve council posts, six were held by the Mineworkers' Union and one each by the Staff and Mines' Police Associations. All the members of the local branch executive of the union sat on the Township Council.[26]

The union, however, was highly critical of the councils. Union leaders felt that whenever they demanded changes in the townships through the council, the management insisted that the issue was a matter for collective bargaining and not a matter for discussion in an advisory body.[27] Because they could not obtain concrete concessions through the councils, the union leaders, in 1962, boycotted their proceedings. As the general secretary of the union wrote the Chamber of Mines: "The . . . Councils are not serving any useful purpose. In the circumstances, all our representatives at the various Branches will not cooperate in the continuation of these councils, i.e., their membership is withdrawn as with effect from 24th September 1962." [28] In the election following the union's action, UNIP candidates took over the vacant council positions. The councils have remained under the party's control ever since.[29]

While we will analyze the operations of the councils in greater detail in the following chapter, it is sufficient here to note that the council and the union branch represent the two arenas for indigenous leaders in the local mining community. Almost inevitably, these two centers of power have come into conflict. The conflicts arise from three major phenomena: overlapping jurisdictions, overlapping constituencies, and what we will term "symmetric clientage."

SOURCES OF LOCAL HOSTILITY. UNIP, through the council, is preoccupied with township affairs, while the union concentrates on matters arising in the plant area. Despite the separate focus of the two organizations, many issues cut across their spheres of concern. For example, because the mining company owns the houses which its employees live in, the level of the rents is a matter for union negotiations. The party, as the spokesman for the township residents, champions the cause of reduced rentals, and places enormous pressure on the union to achieve lower rental charges. The union, however, has been unable to achieve substantial reductions. The natural result is that the party and union spokesmen come into conflict, and the party leaders view the union's failure as evidence of its incompetence. Another such issue is the status of employees working in the community services department of the mines. The functions of the department fall under the surveillance of the council, and the status of its employees is thus of direct concern to the council; but the employees fall under the jurisdiction of the union. The efforts of the council to penalize or assist these employees thus brings it into conflict with the union. For example, when a housing officer at Rhokana was found to be corrupt, the Rhokana council protested to management and the officer was punished; the union's efforts to protect the employee gave rise to hostile reactions from the council. In addition, when the council sought better conditions of service for tavern workers, the union protested its interference in a matter which the union regarded as its own concern.[30] As a result of these encounters, the UNIP leaders at Rhokana became convinced that the union was seeking to frustrate and to undermine the council.

Not only do the union and council often deal with common issues; they also possess identical constituencies, and their overlapping constituencies are a second source of conflict. The mine employees belong to both the union and party and they generate competition between the two in order to advance their interests. I witnessed numerous instances of this phenomenon at Rhokana mine. One worker had injured an eye while working in the tank house; unable to obtain rapid compensation from the union, he took the case to the party so it could arrange for assistance from the labor officer.[31] The union had been unable to obtain permanent contracts for tavern waitresses; the waitresses therefore turned to the party for assistance.[32] In several instances, local employees found their promotion blocked by workers who were not Zambian citizens; being impatient, they bypassed the union and attempted to get the party to petition the Ministry of Home Affairs to expel the alien workers.[33]

Thus the party serves as an agency for appeals and as a refuge for those who are dissatisfied with the union. While the constituencies of the party and union are identical, many of the most vocal members of the party's constituency are those who have failed to find satisfaction from the union and turned to the party instead. The nature of this constituency naturally creates a belief on the part of UNIP officials that the union leaders are incompetent and that they could do a better job were they to hold positions of power in the union. Equally as important, the fact that the party leaders are approached by persons who are disillusioned with the union encourages a belief that the union has little support and could easily be taken over.

The third major source of conflict between the party and the union is what we term "symmetric clientage." For some purposes, the union leaders rely on the party; and for many purposes, the party leaders must rely on the union. To understand the hostility of the local UNIP officials toward the union, it is more valuable to explore the second of these relations.

For a variety of reasons, the local party officials are in frequent difficulties with the company. A significant proportion of the councillors are recent promotees to low-level supervisory posts.[34] Because the management is determined that Zambianization will not lower productivity on the mines, the new supervisors are under close scrutiny and receive frequent reprimands and warnings from company officials.[35] In addition, European supervisors, when they detect a political official in their crews, reportedly single out the official for frequent disciplinary action.[36] For whatever reason, a large number of the party officials have had to rely on the union to defend them against company action; and many have not been satisfied with the union's performance. Thus, for example, the chairman of the UNIP branch I studied had been frozen in his rank and denied training for twelve months after an altercation with his supervisor; he was convinced that had the union leaders "not been so lazy," he would have received a lighter penalty.[37] A similar case arose with a councillor from Mindolo township at Rhokana. He was returned to the ranks after failing to perform satisfactorily as a shift boss, and he too was convinced that the union leaders could have prevented his demotion.[38]

What particularly incites the hostility of the UNIP officials, however, is not the belief that the union leaders are lazy; it is their conviction that the union uses its power with the companies to coerce them. Instead of protecting party officials and UNIP supporters, the union is believed to employ its power to victimize those officials who are placing inordinate pressure on the union.

The best illustration of this pattern, and the one most frequently cited by the local party leaders at Rhokana, was the case of the former vice-chairman of the union branch. The vice-chairman was an active UNIP supporter; and while holding union office, he worked vigorously to attack racist supervisors. During his tenure, he defended men who had struck over racial insults and repeatedly threatened to precipitate strikes over racial issues. The local party officials, themselves deeply preoccupied with abolishing racial discrimination, enthusiastically supported his actions. By contrast, the union leaders found the vice-chairman's conduct embarrassing, for the company's attitude toward the union perceptibly hardened in the face of his provocative conduct. The vice-chairman possessed a poor work record, and soon faced dismissal for sleeping on the job. The union branch executive refused to defend him and was evidently glad to get rid of the "trouble maker." The local UNIP officials, however, were irate, for they felt that the union had deprived them of one of their most powerful supporters.[39]

In a similar case, the local party leaders vigorously urged the union to insist that the company dismiss a racist foreman. The union pressed the case for over two months, but made little progress. The party leaders followed the union's performance in the case through a UNIP official in the personnel department. In meetings with the union, the party leaders used their confederate's reports to make detailed criticisms of the union's tactics. The union soon discovered the source of the party's intelligence and threatened "to get him in trouble with the companies." The party leaders were furious with the union. It was not merely the threat that incited the UNIP officials; but also the idea that any African miner could use the power of the European management to victimize a fellow black worker.[40]

Because of overlapping jurisdiction and constituencies, and because of symmetrical clientage, the local party and union officials are in a perpetual state of conflict. The local party officials express intense hostility toward their union counterparts and regard them as rivals. They are convinced that the trade unionists intend them harm. They feel the union leaders are incompetent and that they can easily displace them. Nationally inspired UNIP attacks on the union activate and reinforce these preexisting attitudes at the local level and receive the enthusiastic support of the local party.

UNIP Efforts to Control the Mineworkers' Union: Three Cases

The Fall of Katilungu

The first case concerns Lawrence Katilungu's removal from the presidency of the Mineworkers' Union in December 1960 and the part UNIP played in his removal. As noted by the colonial government, "the breaking of Katilungu's power in the [Mineworkers' Union] and in the [Trades Union Congress] and his replacement by a UNIP nominee was an important aim of the party." [41] The party had good reason to seek Katilungu's removal. He operated actively in opposition to UNIP; and the colonial government, in conformity with its own interests, actively, if gingerly, supported Katilungu as an alternative to the nationalist party.

Katilungu long sought to avoid intermingling politics and trade unionism. But when the nationalist movement split he found it necessary to choose between ZANC and ANC; he chose the latter. As noted by a local reporter, Katilungu "called upon the union . . . to support Mr. Nkumbula and his African Congress and not to follow the 'new thing called Zambia which is trying to divide our people in their ceaseless struggle for freedom and independence.' " [42] Later, after ZANC had reformed as UNIP, Katilungu reiterated his support of ANC and his opposition to UNIP. As UNIP was banned on the copperbelt at the time, his endorsement of ANC represented a tremendous blow to the party.[43] Katilungu did not stop at merely weighing the balance between competing nationalist groups, however; he set out as well to form a "responsible" nationalist party, based on the most "respectable" elements of the African population as defined by the colonial value system. Thus, in October 1960, he announced his intention to form a party based on his union, the African members of the federal parliament, the chiefs, and members of the European clergy. As he stated:

> We shall be traditionalists. We shall not allow talk of democracy to destroy or undermine the powers and respect of the Chiefs. . . . The Chiefs are more responsible than any politician living in the country at the moment. There is not a single politician who has ever signed a treaty with the British Empire.[44]

To increase his power within this conservative coalition, Katilungu developed his relationship with Chitimukulu, paramount chief of the Bemba; he exchanged frequent visits with Chitimukulu and organized elaborately deferential receptions for him on the copperbelt.[45]

While countering UNIP, Katilungu sought official support for his position. Pointing out that UNIP's backers in the labor movement received funds from the WFTU, he attempted to convince the colonial government that his opposition to UNIP represented opposition to communism. As he noted: "Already Communism is entering this country through irresponsible political and trade union organizations. Communist ideologies could be very dangerous in the near future, especially to our well organized trade unions." [46] In this manner, he built a reputation as the preferred spokesman for African interests in the eyes of the colonial government. In response, the government refrained from harassing Katilungu, despite his violation of numerous laws regulating trade union officials. Personal use of union funds was officially illegal and the government, through the registrar of trade unions, utilized this law to harass "undesirable" leaders in the union movement. In the case of Katilungu, however, the registrar contended: "It would have been the easiest thing in the world over the last four years to have harried him, . . . initiated legal action, and generally antagonized him. We have got much further in the long run by accepting his weaknesses." [47] The governor endorsed the registrar's tactic as "both wise and politic." [48] The government went beyond a tacit support of Katilungu, however. For example, Katilungu was in Lagos at the time dissident elements were organizing his dismissal from the Mineworkers' Union. Learning of this, the government contacted Katilungu, urged his return, and sought to postpone the meeting at which his leadership was to be challenged.[49] That government efforts were to no avail is less significant than the fact that they were made at all.

UNIP's CAMPAIGN. UNIP therefore viewed Katilungu as an opponent, and rightfully so. It mounted a two-pronged attack, applying pressure through its branches on the local union leaders while backing UNIP supporters in the Congress of Trade Unions. On both fronts, UNIP sought to convince the leadership of the Mineworkers' Union that political premises should govern their evaluation of Katilungu's conduct as a union leader.

Local UNIP branches mounted an increasingly vituperative campaign, criticizing and abusing Katilungu at party meetings in the mine townships. The criticism carried over to union meetings, where shouts against the union president began to rise from the audience.[50] Unfortunately for Katilungu, he provided UNIP with abundant material for censure. For one, he agreed to serve on the Monckton Commission—the commission whose job it was to review the Federation of Rhodesia and Nyasaland and to make recommendations for alterations in its structure and operations. In so doing, he appeared to betray the nationalist parties and to sell out to the federal government. UNIP made these allegations one basis for its campaign. Secondly, in remarks widely quoted in the Federation's press, Katilungu made a damaging critique of the value of self-government; returning from Nigeria, he announced at a meeting of the union:

> I have heard people say that, as soon as they get self-government, they will be able to sit down without working and money will come rolling up to their doors. But you can take it from me . . . that there are more economic difficulties in the countries with self-government than in this country at the moment.[51]

On the one hand, the government and European politicians cited Katilungu's remarks as reasonable observations by a responsible African spokesman; on the other, UNIP branches broadcast them as a clear sign of Katilungu's opposition to the nationalist aspirations of the African population.

During 1959–60, UNIP mounted a parallel attack through the Congress of Trade Unions. The congress had always played an intermediary role between the labor movement and the nationalist parties. While unions would not take political stands—i.e., provide transport or endorsements for political parties, propose amendments to the country's voting laws, etc.—the TUC frequently did so.[52] When Katilungu joined the Monckton Commission, his opponents sought a vote of political censure in the TUC; in retaliation, Katilungu, who was the president of TUC, expelled from the meeting all unions in arrears with the congress, thus effectively excluding all but the mineworkers' unions.[53] The expelled unions formed a Reformed Trade Union Congress (RTUC), and within a year identified their body with UNIP. To undermine Katilungu's position, the RTUC sponsored a dissident mineworkers' union, led by a former lieutenant of Katilungu, Gordon Chindele.[54] Meeting with local UNIP representatives and union leaders, they urged Katilungu's overthrow. And they held public rallies in the mine townships, often sharing the platform with UNIP speakers, to marshal support for their opposition to Katilungu.[55]

ASSESSMENT OF UNIP's EFFORTS. To a certain degree, UNIP's campaign succeeded. Certainly, Katilungu was removed from office at the end of 1960.* What is striking, however, is the degree to which the union leaders who deposed Katilungu based their actions on nonpolitical standards. The very actions which provoked censure based on political norms were evaluated by the

---

* Katilungu went on to become the acting president of ANC. His political career was cut short by his death in November 1961 in an automobile accident. At the time of the accident, Katilungu was on his way to the Luapula and Northern Provinces to organize support for ANC.

union leaders in terms of their standards of conduct for trade unionists. They criticized Katilungu's work on the Monckton Commission not solely as evidence of his political unreliability, but also because of his inability to fulfill his union duties while serving on the commission. That Katilungu continued to draw full salary while absenting himself added import to this critique.[56] Katilungu's favorable comparison of economic conditions in Northern Rhodesia with those in the independent states of Africa was given a political interpretation by some; but the trade union leaders were more upset by the harmful impact of the statements on the union's bargaining position.[57] Moreover, their criticisms of Katilungu's active opposition to UNIP were not based solely on his betrayal of the nationalist movement. They also stemmed from the premise that union leaders should not involve the union in any form of politics, for this would both divide the union and violate the union's agreement with the companies. As stated by a reporter who interviewed Katilungu's opponents in the Head Office: " 'Either Katilungu remains a trade unionist, or he becomes a politician. He can't be both.' was [the] general reply in interviews." [58] And as stated by the union investigatory commission, which was asked to advise on the problem of Katilungu:

> We advise all Officials and members of the Union, during all sorts of political upheavals in our country, not to let opportunists disrupt the Organisation that you have built. . . . Do not allow politicians to ply their political trade at your expenses [sic]. Know the difference that Politicians have their place . . . trade unions fight for the betterment of the workers.[59]

In the view of the trade union leaders, Katilungu was weakening the union, by using it for his political advantage and by exposing it to attack by other politicians.

The case of Katilungu documents the first major conclusion in this portion of my study: UNIP is able to remove political opponents from positions of leadership in the Mineworkers' Union. Supporting evidence is the series of purges at the branch level which followed Katilungu's removal. At Nchanga, for example:

On the 1st of October [1962] the Vice Chairman of the
Branch . . . contacted the Labour Officer and stated that the
members of the Executive who did not support the United
National Independence Party were in fear of their lives. . . .
They stated that on or about the 30th September a note
appeared in the form of a petition stating their names, saying
that they were bad leaders and should be dismissed from
office.[60]

In October, they surrendered their positions in the union.[61]
Similar purges of ANC supporters took place at Bancroft and
Ndola Copper Refineries.[62]

Our second conclusion is that while the party can succeed in
inserting political considerations in decisions of union leaders, it
can do so only marginally. For despite the party's success in removing Katilungu, the union leaders apparently based their decisions largely on non-political norms; they utilized the conven-
tional standards for evaluating the behavior of trade unionists.

The United Mineworkers' Union

The formation of the United Mineworkers' Union (UMU) in
1963 represents the second major attempt by the party to gain
control of the union. UNIP had several reasons for backing a
rival union in the mining industry. First, UNIP and ANC were
wed in an unstable governing coalition at the national level, and
UNIP was determined to consolidate the support of all African
organizations to win sole control of the government in the 1964
elections. Secondly, the Mineworkers' Union had withdrawn from
the UTUC in 1962 and thereby disrupted the UNIP-dominated
labor movement. In retaliation, the UTUC helped to form the
United Mineworkers' Union, and sought to use it to regroup the
mineworkers into the labor wing of the party. UNIP supported
the UTUC's action.

In September 1963, at the urging of Wilson Chakulya and
Jonathan Mubanga, the general and deputy general secretary of
the UTUC, the Central Council of the Mines African Staff Association resolved to affiliate with the UTUC, to alter its name

to the United Mineworkers' Union, and to seek to organize and represent all African mineworkers.[63] In so doing, the UTUC and the Association committed themselves to a jurisdictional conflict with the Mineworkers' Union.

The UTUC disseminated propaganda in support of UMU, provided funds, and placed staff, offices, office equipment, and transport at its disposal. At public meetings in the mine townships, the UTUC condemned the Mineworkers' Union and advocated merger. Slogans such as "Unity Now," "Solidarity Forever," "AMU is dead," and "Better agreements through UMU" became catchwords at UTUC meetings.[64] By the first week in October, the general secretary of the Staff Association was able to write the UTUC acknowledging "receipt of ten thousand membership cards, twelve receipt books, and one thousand letter heads" as UTUC support for the establishment of the United Mineworkers' Union. He added, "We also appreciate your suggestion that you should negotiate on our behalf with the motor company to enable us to get a car through the UTUC on . . . hire purchase agreements." [65] In addition, the UTUC seconded (assigned) its own paid organizers to UMU. In Roan, for example, the UTUC maintained a local labor council to advise and assist local unions; with the formation of UMU, the chairman of the local labor council moved into its offices and commenced recruiting members for the United Mineworkers' Union.[66]

As in the campaign against Katilungu, the party used its own apparatus to supplement the efforts of the UTUC. To a high degree, local UNIP officials occupied positions of influence within the Staff Association; they employed their joint offices to realize the objectives of one union in one industry. At Rhokana, for example, the chairman of the Staff Association held party office as a councillor in the Mine Township Council; and of the six UMU organizers, four held branch or section offices in UNIP. These officials vigorously campaigned to dislodge members from the Mineworkers' Union.[67] Even more dramatic was the case of Broken Hill, where five of the seven UMU local executive officers were UNIP officials and UNIP's section and Youth League officials served as UMU organizers. In Broken Hill, the party's constituency chairman was the chairman of UMU as well.[68] Although no concrete data are available to support the contention, the impression is strongly conveyed that such patterns also existed at the other mines.

Besides working from within the Staff Association, UNIP also lent support from without. The regional party press endorsed UMU while deriding the Mineworkers' Union. Thus, in an article entitled "African Miners Must Unite," the Kitwe party paper declared:

> A close examination of the two African Unions on the mines reveals one unfortunate fact that African miners lack an effective organisation to represent them, fight for their better conditions—better pay, better homes and social facilities and to redress their grievances.
>
> UMU has a Seasoned leadership which could be very effective. . . . It embraces energetic and brilliant young men who could tackle the mining companies. . . .
>
> AMU [the Mineworkers' Union] has the masses alright and what is more they can go on strike and force the mines to crawl on their knees, but AMU is crippled by lack of leadership. Besides the well furnished offices and the few shillings they wring out of the Chamber of Mines after every 18 months, nothing seems to be cooking at London House [the location of the Head Office].[69]

The UNIP Youth League sold membership cards for UMU and distributed forms to be used to cancel subscriptions to the Mineworkers' Union. Moreover, despite opposition on the part of senior UNIP officials, the youths intimidated union leaders, going so far as to invade the Head Office in Kitwe and to assault the local branch chairman at Mufulira.[70] At public meetings, local UNIP officials advocated support for the UMU campaign. Thus, for example, the Kitwe regional secretary strongly endorsed UMU in public speeches in May and October 1964.[71]

UNIP also utilized its access to governmental power to assist UMU's efforts to supplant the Mineworkers' Union. Two weeks after the Staff Association resolved to become the United Mine-

workers' Union, an "UMU delegation visited Lusaka where . . .
they met [the minister of labor]. . . . After describing the current position, [he] assured them of support." [72] At the minister's
urging, the leaders of the Mineworkers' Union met with the
UMU leaders to discuss amalgamation; but the two delegations
failed to reach accord.[73] In April 1964, the Ministry of Labour
registered UMU, thus granting it legal recognition. This act
provoked the acting president of the Mineworkers' Union to
declare: "I am now satisfied that the Minister [of Labor] is
somehow behind the present situation in the mining industry.
. . . I am more convinced than ever before that there are people
within the Government circles who wish . . . to see [the Mineworkers' Union] collapse and the UMU wear our boots." [74]

When the mining companies sought clarification of the government's position on UMU, the minister of labor advised them
that UMU "was a properly constituted and registered trade
union" and that the companies should "negotiate with . . . UMU
on the question of demarcation of interests as between UMU and
[the Mineworkers' Union]." [75] And when the leaders of the
Mineworkers' Union sought an interview with the minister of
labor, they were firmly instructed that they must form a joint
delegation with the UMU leaders.[76]

Government spokesmen utilized their public positions to attack the Mineworkers' Union, urge amalgamation with the UMU,
and advocate the overthrow of the current union leadership. For
example, after a bitter attack on Musonda, Chima, and Namitengo, three Head Office leaders, "The Minister [of Labor and
Mines] ended his speech by saying that UNIP only wanted one
union in one industry, and the people should choose their own
leaders, but not men like Musonda, Chima, and Namitengo." [77]

The response of the leaders of the Mineworkers' Union to the
UMU campaign was at first surprisingly moderate. In December 1963, the Head Office of the union agreed in principle to a
merger with UMU, but only of the membership of the two organizations; the leaders of UMU would not be given top posts
in the amalgamated union. As the general secretary of the Mineworkers' Union wrote:

The Supreme Council of my union expressed wholeheartedly its willingness to receive members of the Mines African Staff Association back into the fold of the . . . African Mineworkers' Trade Union [sic]. Furthermore it has strongly endorsed in clear terms No merger could be intertained [sic] but members of the Mines African Staff Association were at liberty at any time to join this Union.[78]

Later, the leaders of the Mineworkers' Union resisted more strongly. When in the early months of 1964 Rhokana Corporation informally met a delegation of the UMU, the leaders of the Mineworkers' Union denounced the company for "violating its recognition agreement," going "behind our backs," and seeking to "split and divide" the established union in the industry. The union leaders hardened their position by announcing that under no conditions would they accept UMU into the union.[79]

When UNIP openly entered the fray, the union leaders became deeply concerned about the role of the government in the UMU affair. As one observer noted:

Head Office officials were extremely annoyed at a report [that] a UNIP official attacked the leaders of the M[ineworkers'] U[nion] and supported UMU. As a result of this statement the Union officials have said that the UNIP officials must have had the backing of [the minister of labor] or even been instructed by [him] to make that statement.[80]

For most union leaders, the specter of UNIP backing for UMU presaged the assertion of government control. Following the emergence of overt UNIP support for UMU, one observer wrote: there is "a genuine apprehension on the part of the . . . Union to avoid becoming involved in . . . Government control . . . which they fear will take place if U.M.U. . . . gain[s] control."[81] The direct entrance of the minister of labor into the UMU campaign strengthened the union's fear, and nearly precipitated an open breach between the union and the government. Following the minister's recognition of UMU, and his speeches on behalf of the association, the acting president of the Mineworkers' Union declared, "The Mineworkers' Union no longer has confidence in the [minister of labor] and are not prepared to meet him." [82] His colleagues in the Head Office offered profuse apologies for his statement and publicly withdrew it. [83] Thus, the deputy general secretary wrote the minister of labor: "As decided by our Supreme Council . . . it is as it has always been, the policy of this Union to cooperate and maintain confidence in the Government and the party in power as well as all the Ministers." [84] The Supreme Council dispatched the acting president for a study tour outside of the country, and made clear that it was determined not to break openly with the government. Although unprepared to openly oppose the government, neither was it prepared to give in to what many leaders regarded as a government-inspired attempt to control the union. The union leaders therefore continued their public campaign in opposition to UMU and its efforts to undermine the Mineworkers' Union.

THE FAILURE OF UMU. Despite the backing of the Trade Union Congress and UNIP, UMU failed in its attempt to displace the Mineworkers' Union. Measured in terms of the number of members it "captured," UMU, even at its peak, failed to make significant inroads into the union's membership (table 52). At

TABLE 52
Penetration of United Mineworkers' Union

	Mufulira	Nchanga	Rhokana	Roan
a. Mineworkers' Union potential membership	7,758	5,361	7,910	6,342
b. Mineworkers' Union actual membership	6,226	4,405	6,132	5,446
c. Percentage potential members in Mineworkers' Union (b/a)	80	82	78	86
d. UMU membership	94	176	1,922	389
e. Percentage Mineworkers' Union members "captured" by UMU (d/b)	2	4	31	7

Source: File 100.47, vol. 15.
Note: The figures for UMU membership represent for each mine the maximum number of members ever obtained by UMU. The figures represent the number of union subscriptions cancelled in favor of UMU.

Rhokana, UMU gained a full 30 percent of the union's membership but the figures from the other mines suggest that Rhokana represented the height of UMU's penetration. Insofar as UMU received UNIP support, therefore, the failure of UMU clearly represented a defeat for UNIP's attempts to displace the leadership of the Mineworkers' Union with leaders of its own preference and choosing.

Perhaps the principal reason for UMU's failure was the manner in which it was perceived and evaluated by the mineworkers themselves. For one, UMU originated from the Staff Association and both the association and its leaders were peculiarly suspect. The association was founded as a breakaway from the Mineworkers' Union in 1952, and received recognition from the mining companies in 1955. As noted earlier, the mineworkers strongly resisted the formation of the association, feeling that it was company-inspired (see chap. 6). By recognizing the association, they believed, the companies sought both to remove the more able workers from the Mineworkers' Union and to divide and thus weaken their employees. Credence was lent the workers' suspicions by the no-strike clause in the association's constitution; for not only did the clause make the association appear weak, but it also cast it in the form of a strikebreaker.[85] Adding to the unpopularity of the association was the political role played by some of its most prominent leaders. Just as the association appeared to serve as an agency of the Europeans in the sphere of industrial relations, its leaders appeared to have served as the "front-men" for the Europeans in the sphere of politics. Thus, for example, Godwin Mbikusita Lewanika, the founder of the association, had held a post in the federal parliament.[86] Peter Chibuye, a leader at the time the association became UMU had run as a candidate for the United Federal Party (UFP), the party which united the European settler population in Northern and Southern Rhodesia. Other officers were known to be former members of the UFP.[87] The past role of the association in the history of the labor movement and the role of its leaders in the political history of the nation therefore rendered it suspect in the mining community.

The mineworkers also appear to have perceived that UMU was politically inspired and to have distrusted it as a result. For example, at one meeting, UMU and UTUC leaders commenced a biting denunciation of the Mineworkers' Union and cited the consistency between the goals of UMU and those of the party. An observer of the meeting noted, "Many in the audience began drifting away saying that they had not come to listen to politics, but had been [promised] trade union matters." [88] Similarly, when asked what they had felt about UMU, many miners stated that politically, UMU was "quite good," but that in trade union matters, "politicians, what can they know about it?" [89] The miners appear to regard industrial and political activities as distinct spheres of behavior, and because of this, UMU could not automatically claim their allegiance as a representative of their industrial interests.

Lastly, there is the factor of effectiveness. A large part of UMU's success can be accounted for in terms of the inefficacy of the Mineworkers' Union, for UMU's membership increased following the union's acceptance of the 1964 dual-wage settlement. The miners regarded this settlement as a poor one. UMU made the agreement a focus of its attacks on the union, and gained support as a result.[90]

However, UMU itself foundered on its own ineffectiveness. The mining companies consistently refused to recognize UMU. They opposed any effort to include all workers under one union; supervisors, they felt, would be open to victimization without a union of their own.[91] Because UMU was refused recognition by the companies, it was unable to negotiate on behalf of its members. Penalties were inflicted on staff members without recourse to union representation; dismissals could not be challenged; and when the staff's agreement lapsed, the companies implemented new rates of pay for staff categories without having to consult representatives on their behalf. New job gradings and promotional routes were also imposed on the staff without formal negotiations.[92] Because UMU could not gain company recognition, it could not effectively defend the interests of its members in these and other matters. And as a result, it lost support among the mineworkers.[93]

The 1966 Elections

The last major attempt by UNIP to influence the selection of union leaders came in the postindependence era. Following the embarrassing settlement of January 1964, the Mineworkers' Union had reopened wage negotiations with the companies. After months of fruitless negotiations, the union scheduled strike action. The registrar of trade unions ruled, however, that before a strike ballot could be taken, the union leaders had first to submit themselves to elections; under the letter of the law, he contended, it was doubtful that the current leadership legally held office. The subsequent unilateral declaration of independence by Rhodesia caused the union leaders to cancel their strike. The elections, however, were held as scheduled, and UNIP determined to contest them.

UNIP had several reasons for entering the elections, but the primary one was its fear that the union would disrupt the government's economic program. In 1965 the government was formulating its first national development plan and this lent a new sense of urgency to its development efforts. Moreover, the Rhodesian rebellion gave rise to a sense of grave economic crisis. While union leaders had cancelled a strike and moderated their wage demands in response to the Rhodesian situation, the government nonetheless felt it imperative to strengthen its ability to cope with the economic disruption which the crisis entailed. Largely in response to these pressures, in December 1965, the UNIP National Council appointed a committee to draft a new party constitution; the purpose was to integrate the trade union and cooperative movements more closely with the governing party. In reference to the proposal, President Kaunda was quoted as saying, "We want loyal party leaders also to control the cooperative and labor movements. . . . We cannot afford the luxury of calling this undemocratic." [94] Apparently in accordance with this policy, UNIP sought to incorporate the Mineworkers' Union into the party, and therefore entered the union elections.

The elections fell into two stages. The union first conducted branch elections, and then election to the Head Office. During the second stage, which took place at the Annual Conference, local officials acted as electors for the national leadership. UNIP intervened at both stages.

At the local level, UNIP regional secretaries attempted to pack and control the meetings at which nominations were made for union office. Thus, in Rhokana, Nchanga, Chibuluma, Roan, and Mufulira, the party transported people from the municipal locations to the meetings in the mine townships at which the nominations were made. At Nchanga, when shop stewards and officials attempted to make nominations, the party supporters shouted them down. In addition, when a government labor officer checked UNIP nominations against a list of mine employees, members of the crowd invaded the speakers' platform and attempted to destroy the list.[95]

The party also nominated candidates for the election. At several mines, UNIP endorsed some of the union's candidates and challenged others;[96] at most mines, however, UNIP filed a complete slate of candidates in opposition to those of the union. Evidence from Rhokana indicates that when UNIP did nominate candidates for office, it nominated its own local officials: of the six UNIP candidates, one was a constituency official and three were local branch officials. In addition, three held office on the Township Council.[97]

UNIP also sought to insure that the union officials withdrew from the elections. Thus, in Chibuluma, the UNIP regional secretary sent copies of the following notice to local union officials:

LAST WARNING

It has come to our knowledge that you all intend to contest today's nomination at the Public meeting.

Realising that you are all members of UNIP we have decided to sound a very big warning to you all. Yesterday you all were informed in writing of the Party's decision, and it seems some elements amongst you have decided to defy the party. If you are a true member, don't accept any nomination today because acceptance of such nomination will be regarded as direct political war against UNIP and we shall not hesitate to challenge the enemy with all the ruthless powers at our disposal.

The party will therefore expel any member for life who wants to fight these elections and confiscate all party cards that such a member may hold. Today we are ready for big political showdown. . . . We still humbly ask you to stand down beloved brother.

UNIP says "hands off from today's nomination. He that has ears to hear, let him hear."

Regional Secretary[98]

There is no indication that the threats contained in this letter received the support of national party leaders.

The trade union leaders were curiously silent throughout UNIP's campaign. Besides their professions at public meetings that "we are all UNIP," [99] the leaders had nothing more to say. In private, however, they expressed strong indignation. In the words of one observer, "the Union leaders took the UNIP letters as an insolent insult. They made the Union people very angry. 'We are as good UNIP members as anybody else,' they said." [100] They also expressed their conviction that the party's intervention in the elections represented the government's attempt to gain control of the union. As the president of the union stated at a meeting with officials of the Congress of Trade Unions:

> The cause of the trouble was because the Government wished to take over the Union and also intended to take over the Railway Workers' Union and wanted U.N.I.P. supporters to become the leaders of the [Mineworkers' Union]. He further stated that in the end, the Government would take over all the small unions in the country and he reminded those present that the present leaders of the [Mineworkers' Union] were all U.N.I.P. supporters and he could not therefore understand why the Government wanted other U.N.I.P. members to be leaders of the [Union].[101]

THE FAILURE OF UNIP's CAMPAIGN. UNIP largely failed in its attempt to capture branch offices, and thereby control the election of national officers, as well. Of the fifty-three branch delegates elected to the Annual Conference of the Mineworkers' Union, only twelve were UNIP candidates.[102] UNIP's failure is even greater than these figures suggest, however; for the party was able to secure the selection of twelve candidates only by winning the support of leading elements in the union's own hierarchy. Thus, it was the general treasurer of the union who secured a compromise between union and party officials at Mindolo and Chibuluma. The compromise allowed a joint slate of candidates to pass through uncontested. The twelve UNIP candidates who succeeded in reaching the Annual Conference were those who benefited from the initiative of the general treasurer.[103] As an independent force in the local union elections, therefore, UNIP appears to have failed to control the selection of union leaders.

Failing at the local level, UNIP sought to control the selection of leaders at the union's Annual Conference. There, the party abjured frontal attacks of the kind that had failed at the branch level and instead let it be known whom they would like to have as president and general secretary of the union. It is reported that the party's director of elections selected the approved UNIP candidates and advertised the selections.[104] The motivations of the party were clearly understood by everyone concerned. As one of the party's candidates explained it, "The party had confidence in us to run the union in conformity with what was required by economics—less strikes, more responsible demands, and so forth." [105]

The party was no more successful at the Annual Conference than it had been at the branch level: both candidates failed to gain posts in the Head Office. One candidate explained his failure in this manner: "The leaders had confidence in me to run the Union, but they couldn't vote for me as a Union man; they took me to be party." [106] As one of the Head Office leaders explained his opposition to the party's choices: "These people were good Union members but they were talked to by the [UNIP] people. This is difficult to explain, Mr. Bates; it didn't mean that they were bad unionists—they were already leaders. But the position was this: we vote for *Union* leaders." [107]

The impression of union autonomy is further strengthened by

events subsequent to the elections. At a meeting of the Supreme Council, the general treasurer was penalized for his role in the elections by being stripped of office. As a letter to the personnel manager of Rhokana Corporation makes clear, the treasurer was subject to complete expulsion from the union hierarchy.

> You have no doubt received letter T5/A/Vol V/65 from the General Secretary of this Union in regard to the expulsion of [the General Treasurer] from Union leadership.
> We wish to lay emphasis on this point, by registering the same feeling in the strongest terms in order that he must not be allowed to take part in representing our members at the plants and elsewhere as a shop steward.[108]

The party's candidate for general secretary suffered a similar fate. Hitherto deputy general secretary of the union and a full-time official at the Head Office of the union, he was demoted to the lowly post of branch clerk and posted to Broken Hill, the relatively isolated branch at which he had begun his union career nearly a decade before.[109] Through these actions, the union penalized those who had attempted to introduce political standards into the selection of union leaders, and removed from positions of power those who had proved sensitive to external sources of influence.

These case studies reveal an intriguing pattern. The contrast between the fate of UNIP's efforts to unseat Katilungu and its two later campaigns suggests that the party can effectively influence the union up to the point of securing unanimous UNIP membership among union officials; beyond that point, the party appears unable to control the selection of union leaders. This pattern is crucially important; for it delineates precisely the boundaries of the influence of the dominant party over peri-political organizations in this and perhaps other political systems. And it suggests as well the limits upon UNIP's ability to penetrate and control the sphere of industrial relations in the copper industry.

Reasons for UNIP's Success

We need not look far for an explanation of the party's ability to purge union offices of nonparty members. As we have noted, the union exists in a nearly totally UNIP environment (see chap. 2). UNIP candidates have won all the lower-roll parliamentary elections on the copperbelt, UNIP controls every urban and township council, and all the copperbelt mayors are UNIP. Not to belong to UNIP is to deviate in a major way; for many, not to belong to the party is both to render oneself politically unacceptable and to flaunt one's political disloyalty. To occupy a major position on the copperbelt while resisting membership in the party is therefore to violate a basic social and political pattern; the pressures generated against such deviance are incredibly strong and sometimes violent. It is therefore not surprising that the party successfully imposes membership as a requirement for public office in the union. What needs to be explained is its inability to influence selection among trade union leaders who are all UNIP members.

Reasons for UNIP's Failure

Such an explanation can be based largely on the properties of the union itself. The union's leadership is largely differentiated from that of the party. The leaders place high value on the organization and its traditions. And they possess norms for evaluating and selecting among fellow leaders that are both separate from and inconsistent with the criteria employed by the party. These characteristics help to render the union an autonomous organization.

There is a low incidence of joint office holding between the union and party: only one officer in the 1969 Head Office held a party position; none of the branch executive at Rhokana held a party post; and but three of the fifty-two shop stewards at Rhokana held offices in the party. Moreover, those who hold office in the union persist in their union posts for a very long time; there is no evidence of a circulation among the union and party structures. The 1969 Head Office leaders had held office for an average of 11.3 years and the local executive officials at Rhokana had worked as union leaders for an average of 9.9 years. Moreover, as shown in the cohort pyramids (tables 53 and 54), the Head Office of the union is traditionally composed of a core of officials who have held office for a long period of time.[110]

Given these attributes of the union leaders, we can begin to understand why the party is unable to influence the selection of union personnel. The union leaders are separate from the party; from their point of view, the party leaders are outsiders and they naturally resent their intrusion. Thus, the statement of the union committee investigating Katilungu's behavior: "Know the difference that politicians have their place in the legislative council and other councils in the land," with the clear implication that they

TABLE 53

Head Office: Date First Elected

Head Office by year	Number initially elected to Head Office, by year																	
	'49	'50	'51	'52	'53	'54	'55	'56	'57	'58	'59	'60	'61	'62	'63	'64	'65	'66–67
1949	6																	
1950	6	0																
1951	6	0	0															
1952	5	0	0	1														
1953	5	0	0	1	0													
1954	5	0	0	1	0	0												
1955	3	0	0	1	0	0	2											
1956	3	0	0	1	0	0	2	0										
1957	1	0	0	0	0	0	0	0	3									
1958	1	0	0	0	0	0	0	0	2	3								
1959	2	0	0	0	0	0	0	0	2	1	1							
1960	2	0	0	0	0	0	0	0	2	0	0	2						
1961	1	0	0	0	0	0	0	0	2	0	0	2	1					
1962	2	0	0	0	0	0	0	0	1	0	0	2	1	0				
1963	1	0	0	0	0	0	0	0	1	1	0	2	1	0	1			
1964	1	0	0	0	0	0	0	0	1	0	1	0	0	0	1	3		
1965	1	0	0	0	0	0	0	0	1	0	1	0	0	0	0	2	1	
1966–67	0	0	0	0	0	0	0	0	1	0	1	0	0	0	0	2	0	3

Note: In 1957 there are several cases of double officeholding. For any given year (row), the table shows the year in which the occupants of that year's Head Office were first elected to a Head Office position.

TABLE 54

Head Office: Date Elected to First Union Office

Head Office by year	Number of Head Office officials elected to first union office, by year																	
	'49	'50	'51	'52	'53	'54	'55	'56	'57	'58	'59	'60	'61	'62	'63	'64	'65	'66–67
1949	6																	
1950	6	0																
1951	6	0	0															
1952	6	0	0	0														
1953	6	0	0	0	0													
1954	6	0	0	0	0	0												
1955	6	0	0	0	0	0	0											
1956	5	0	0	0	0	0	0	0										
1957	3	0	0	0	0	0	0	1	0									
1958	3	0	0	1	0	1	0	1	0	0								
1959	3	0	0	1	0	1	1	0	0	0	0							
1960	3	0	0	1	1	0	0	0	0	0	0	1	0					
1961	3	0	0	1	1	0	0	0	0	0	0	1	0	0				
1962	3	0	0	1	1	0	0	0	0	0	0	1	0	0	0			
1963	2	0	0	1	1	1	0	0	0	0	0	1	0	0	0	0		
1964	1	1	0	1	1	2	1	0	0	0	0	0	0	0	0	0	0	
1965	1	1	0	1	0	1	1	1	0	0	0	0	0	0	0	0	0	0
1966–67	0	1	0	1	1	1	0	1	0	0	0	0	0	1	0	0	0	0

Note: For 1956 one case is unknown. In 1957 there are cases of double office-holding. For any given year (row), the table shows the year in which the occupants of that year's Head Office were first elected to a post in the union.

do not have a place in the trade union movement.[111] Thus, too, the statement of the general treasurer: "Please do not get mixed up. We are all members of U.N.I.P., but don't bring politics into Union matters." [112]

Not only does the union possess a leadership that is highly differentiated from that of the party; it also possesses a highly valued, and distinctive, set of traditions. When I observed the opening of a meeting of the union's Supreme Council, the chairman commenced the meeting by reviewing the union history, its many struggles for better wages, and how, despite the colonial government's detention of its leaders, the union rose again to defend the interests of its members.[113] The leaders take great pride in the union's tradition. And, as the Committee of Four shows in its condemnation of Katilungu's political activities, this pride translated directly into a censure of those who would disrupt the Union for political purposes.

> We advise all Officials and members of the Union, during all sorts of political upheavals in our country, not to let opportunists disrupt the Organization that you have built which has won a prominent place in the economy of this country. . . . If you now allow other persons to come in and break up this organization that you have worked so hard for, then you are not fit to live.[114]

Also significant are the norms and standards by which union leaders evaluate fellow officials and choose amongst them as candidates for high office. The primary criterion is the number and magnitude of the steps which an official has taken to assist in winning concessions from the companies and to help other officials in gaining favorable settlements from management. Thus, as we have noted, the general secretary emphasises the need to campaign for union office by providing advice in negotiations to local branch leaders (see chap. 6); and Katilungu's threat to the union's bargaining position contributed to his loss of support in the Supreme Council. Given these norms for evaluating candidates for high union office, party personnel are placed at a severe disadvantage. Because they operate outside and independently of the union's hierarchy, they are not in a position to make immediate and visible contributions to the union. Nor are they in a position to build up the record of contributions to union officers which is necessary to qualify for high positions. Moreover, lower union leaders resist attempts at lateral entry. Not only do they feel that lateral entry will block their own promotions; but also, they feel that the transfer into high office of inexperienced persons cheapens the contributions which they have made to the union.[115] According to the norms of their organization, they feel that they have every right to expect gratitude and promotions for the work they, and not the party leaders, have done.

There remains another reason for UNIP's inability to influence the selection of union officials. As an institution, the union strives for concessions from the mining companies, and, as we have noted, the leadership adapts its behavior to the rules of the companies in order to increase their capacity to gain such concessions. We would hypothesize that the union leaders adapt to company standards in their selection of union leaders as well; and that as a result, in their electoral choices, they penalize persons whose qualifications lie in the sphere of party politics.

The companies have long sought to prevent the incursion of party activists into trade union affairs. When the union commenced a series of jurisdictional strikes against the Staff Association in 1956, the companies perceived a political element in the strikes and persuaded the colonial government to detain almost the entire leadership cadre of the union.[116] After Katilungu formed a putative "detente" with the nationalist leaders in 1957, the companies, in exchange for the renewal of a checkoff agreement, compelled the union to forbid the use of union funds or facilities by political parties.[117] These and other actions demonstrate the companies' resistance to the encroachment of politics into trade union activities. The companies' efforts appear to have created in the Mineworkers' Union a pronounced and persistent suspicion of overtly political activities. Indeed, it would almost appear that built into their conception of a trade unionist is the attribute of being uninvolved in party affairs. To further the goals of their organization, the leaders of the union therefore appear to have accommodated the management's standards in their notions of the qualifications for union office.[118]

Everything we have discussed so far explains the resistance of the union's leaders to the party's attempts to control the union. But what about the mineworkers themselves? UNIP, like the union, organizes the African mineworkers; but in the elections we have discussed, the workers too resisted the incursions of the party into the union. How can this be explained? We would hypothesize that the workers' continued electoral support of the officials of the Mineworkers' Union simply represents their assessment that their interests are best served by the union leaders.

Although the union and party organize the same population, the scope of their concerns bear upon different aspects of the people they organize. The manner in which the two organizations address themselves to the workers structures the way in which the workers orient themselves to the two organizations. The workers look to the party for assistance in some matters and to the union for assistance in others.

The union addresses itself to the mineworkers as working men and organizes on the basis of mine departments. The party, however, addresses itself to the workers as township residents and organizes on the basis of neighborhoods. Thus, it is the party which contests positions on the Township Council. In its activities on the council and in the townships, the party concerns itself with roads, housing conditions, law and order, market prices, and other affairs that affect the mineworkers as township residents. As a result, the mineworkers conceive the party leaders as possessing expertise in these matters and grant their requests for votes in the council elections. They feel, however, that it is presumptuous for the party leaders to claim expertise in industrial relations. For it is the union which deals with wages and conditions of service; and it is the union leaders who possess the necessary expertise in these matters: knowledge of the union's agreement with the companies, the disciplinary code, appeal procedures, and national legislation governing pension rights, health insurance, and so forth. The mineworkers freely accord the party the right to comment on the union's performance in industrial matters, especially when the union's conduct bears on national policy. But they do not feel that the party leaders possess the expertise to defend their interests as industrial employees. For this reason, they withhold their votes from party officials in union elections. As we quoted one comment about UMU: "Politically, UMU was quite good," but on trade union matters, "politicians, what can they know about it?"

We cannot say that the workers resist the party's campaigns for fear of the government's takeover. Despite the union leaders fear, they did not, as we have seen, use this theme in their campaigns against the party. Moreover, the party leaders, as we have seen in the UMU campaign, did not chastise the union leaders for failing to carry out the government's labor policy; instead, they emphasized the union's inability to get higher wages and better conditions of service. In their campaigns against the union, the party leaders emphasized their dedication to the fulfillment, not the curtailment, of the workers' demands. On the part of the workers, the rejection of UNIP's campaign was therefore not an act of resistance to the government or its policies. Rather, it was a selection among competing claimants to expertise as representatives of their interests as mine employees. So long as the union leaders were UNIP, the workers were satisfied as to their political loyalty. And once satisfied that all claimants were loyal, they selected those who they felt were most knowledgeable in industrial matters.

8 UNIP and Government Labor Policy

In failing to gain control over the union, UNIP has failed to obtain control over the industrial power and incentives with which to implement government policy. Nonetheless, there exists a domain in which the party can function. Through public speeches, agitation, the exertion of pressure on union leaders, and the proffering of assistance to them, the party can attempt to implement the government's program. I contend that within its limited domain, the party functions to a much greater extent than the union as an output structure.*

The Party and Labor Policy

Local UNIP leaders are militants. They repeatedly and strongly protest the patterns of racial discrimination on the mines; and they vigorously strive to implement the government's policies of social justice. Because the party organizes the Township Council, it is in a position to attempt to abolish inequitable practices in public facilities. For example, during my stay at Rhokana, UNIP councillors mounted a campaign against the matron at the non-fee-paying hospital.† The company had appointed a new matron and instructed her to increase the efficiency and economy of the hospital administration. The councillors regarded her innovations as discriminatory, however, and as attempts by the company to lower the standards of the hospital used by the majority of the Africans. Through the Township Council, they demanded satisfaction in the matter, and the companies partially granted it. The councillors mounted similar campaigns against discrimina-

---

* The material on the party is drawn from the Kitwe region and the local UNIP branches in the Rhokana mine townships.

† The matron is the head administrator in the hospital. She reports to the chief medical officer of the company.

tory practices at the mine mess, the mine club, and the recreational center.[1]

With regard to racial discrimination in the plant areas, the party urges the union to punish racist behavior. Local branch leaders mounted prolonged and dogged campaigns against supervisors whom they regarded as racists. When a supervisor at the tank house reportedly insulted a senior African employee, telling him that he smelled and calling him a "Kaffir," the local party officials determined to rid themselves of the man. Placing enormous pressure on the union to get him suspended, they also sought to generate resistance by his subordinates, thereby rendering his removal or transfer the only alternative open to management. During my research, similar campaigns were mounted against one "nine-by-nine," an obese and unpopular mine captain, and another management official at Mindolo Shaft.[2]

Local officials also seek to advance the rate of Zambianization. For example, they collected reports of promotions or training of non-Zambians and transmitted these to the union;[3] they achieved the breakup of one work gang that was composed of aliens and the promotion of Zambian employees into that gang;[4] and local officials conducted continuous campaigns of harassment of Rhodesian and Malawian officials in the personnel department whose posts they felt should belong to Zambian employees.[5] Moreover, branch officials won the right to review applications for Zambian citizenship that were filed by mine employees, and used that right to prevent aliens from winning access to training and promotional opportunities.[6] In their efforts to abolish racial discrimination and accelerate Zambianization, the local party leaders thus reveal their strong identification with the racial and economic interests of the miners.

While local UNIP leaders militantly champion the interests of the mineworkers, they also reveal a capacity to identify with the government's formulation of the public interest and to work for its development labor policy.

The branch officials exhort their people to work hard. At many of the meetings, they called for *"buyantanshi n'incito,"* faithfully portraying the relationship between hard work and national development. Moreover, they poured scorn on those who went absent from work or arrived too drunk or sleepy to perform their jobs. Such offenses, it was argued, demonstrated a lack of respect for the nation. In addition to making speeches, party officials also upbraid individual offenders. When one official discovered that his neighbor was in peril of losing his job for frequent absenteeism and drunkenness, he strongly abused him, pointing out his responsibilities to his wife and children and his failure to heed "the words of our President and party leaders." [7]

The party leaders take a more active role against strikes. When they occur, the party places itself at the disposal of the union for the purpose of achieving a rapid return to work. For example, when underground workers struck at Rhokana mine, the general secretary of the union kept the assistant minister of state informed of the situation, noting that his support and the support of the local party could prove useful. While in this particular case UNIP backing was not necessary, in other cases the support of UNIP officials was used to secure the return to work of mine laborers.[8] During a similar strike at Bancroft, for example: "U.N.I.P. . . . officials . . . stated that they would go into the townships . . . to persuade the strikers to return to work." The next morning, officials addressed the strikers; and a company spokesman reported:

> that he was most impressed by the strong line taken . . . in condemning strike action. [The UNIP officials] informed the lashers that the Government had no sympathy for employees who went on strike before the machinery for settling disputes had been exhausted even if the grievances were genuine.[9]

The strikers returned to work. Particularly impressive is the party's ability to keep its own local officials from striking and to discipline those who violate its policies. During an industry-wide strike in 1966:

> Party officials were at first scared to go back to work due to the fear of intimidation to themselves or their wives. After the President's broadcast [calling for a return to work], they

met in their branches and the branches met together with the Regional Secretary, and they went back to work. They also sent observers to the mine gates to observe intimidation and picketing, and reported their names. When they found [three junior officials] were picketing . . . they suspended them and informed the secretaries of the Region and Constituencies. The Regional Secretary . . . got all the mine branches together. He took the names of those officials who stayed at work and sent these to the companies for consideration due to their service to the companies and to the Government.[10]

The party's discipline in this regard contrasts sharply with that in the union, where local branch leaders often precipitate strike action in the face of opposition from the Head Office officials.

With regard to the government's injunction that workers are not to challenge the power of supervisors, the party, unlike the union, reveals an ability to make its local officials conform to the government edicts. Thus, for example, a supervisor in the power plant found an employee showering early and compelled him to return to work until the shift was over; the employee became abusive, whereupon the supervisor suspended him. The local party officials, noting that the supervisor was an alien, organized an informal court and demanded that the supervisor attend. The supervisor contacted the regional secretary, who advised him to attend and to report afterwards on the activities of his subordinate party officials. The regional secretary collected the supervisor's reports and obtained from the personnel department further evidence on the victimization of supervisors; he used this information to rebuke the lower party officials for undermining the authority of supervisors and thereby disrupting copper production.[11] This case took place shortly after my arrival at Rhokana, and no other one arose thereafter. Similarly, when the Mineworkers' Union won the right to represent supervisors as well as common employees, the local party officials met with the union's branch officials and demanded assurances that the union leaders would not use the union to victimize staff employees. They did so at the behest of the regional secretary and, I believe, out of a genuine regard for the wishes of the government.[12]

Despite their loathing of racial inequities, the party leaders also support the government's wages policy. Thus, while the regional secretary felt that it was wrong for Europeans to earn more than Africans doing similar work, he shared the government's view that mine wages were high in relation to those of the rest of the nation, and that if they were to increase further, Zambia's development would be endangered. He was puzzled and angered at the mineworkers' desire for even further increases.[13] The local branch officials agreed that wage increases should not take place now, although they felt that they were justified. As a local branch secretary stated, because the government opposes increases, "they would not be good now"; but "Mr. Bates, as you can see, we are very poor. We cannot buy fine furniture, good food, automobiles, radios, or television sets. The companies are oppressing us. We live in poverty. We need better wages." Like the other mineworkers, this official did not view himself as wealthy compared with the rest of the nation; he viewed himself as poverty-stricken, and strongly wished that his wages were higher. He and other branch officials, however, refused to demand union action for higher wages or to use the party to agitate for wage increases: "we cannot do that unless we are told by the Regional Secretary that it is all right."[14] While the local party officials did not preach the virtues of wage restraint, they did allow senior officials to do so at their public meetings. In addition, they actively defended the government's position when dissenters queried them at local party sessions.[15] At one party meeting, members protested that the Mineworkers' Union should "get us pay like the Europeans"; in rebuttal, the branch secretary stated, "That is a good demand, but it is too early. The Union promised our Government that it would hold the line for four years."[16] In this manner, the local party officials attempted to dampen, or at least postpone, the workers' demands.

UNIP thus tries to implement both streams of government labor policy at the local level. In one crucial respect, therefore, the party reveals its superiority to the union: its local officials reveal a willingness not merely to defend the workers' interests, but also to moderate and contain their behavior in conformity with government policy. In this respect, the ruling party is a superior output structure.

Campaigns and Local Party Officials

One of the reasons for the opposition of local union figures to government labor policy was the failure of the government to campaign effectively for the union's support. The government did not create a sense of national status and importance among the local branch officials, or expose them intensively to the content of government policies. These two factors help to explain the contrasting ability of UNIP to gain adherence to government policy at the local level.

I have already noted the frequency with which members of the Central Committee, in their capacity as ministers, visit the Kitwe Region on the copperbelt. These tours of the national dignitaries are organized and conducted by UNIP; the party's central role in the Kitwe area and its direct link with the national center are thereby repeatedly demonstrated. Morever, not only the assistant minister and regional secretary perform prominent roles in these receptions; great care is taken to involve the branch people as well.

When a minister arrives at the airport, the regional secretary and assistant minister stand prominently to the fore; they are the first to greet the minister as he steps off the plane. They do not monopolize his time or attention, however; rather, they promptly channel him to the local officials and publicly introduce each of them to the visiting dignitary. From discussions with local branch leaders, I gained the distinct impression that this was one of the most important rewards of holding office. To be made to feel near to the holders of national power, and to know that others have witnessed your proximity to them, is one of the most gratifying benefits of being a local party leader. This involvement in the national level of power, however superficial it may appear to an outside observer, nonetheless appears to serve as a strong in-

ducement to local party officials to conceive of their role in national terms and to feel a responsibility to acquire and defend
national points of view on matters of public policy.

UNIP frequently establishes links between branch officials and
the national center. One index of the frequency of this phenom-
enom is the high rate of ministerial touring. Another index is the
frequency of national campaigns to rally public support for public
policies. These campaigns are almost always channeled through
UNIP. For example, when Zambia decimalized her currency, the
party made the teaching of the new denominations into a major
campaign. Senior officials spent long hours explaining the conversion rates to local branch officials, who in turn passed the explanation on; the names of the new currency—*kwacha* and
ngwee—were integrated into party slogans.[17] In another campaign, local officials were called upon to explain the reasons behind reductions in petrol supplies and school places, both of which
had caused widespread criticism. The branch leaders were made
to feel that it was their responsibility to defend the national government and to maintain public confidence in its ability to overcome these problems.[18]

There is a similar approach to the government's labor policy.
Thus, when President Kaunda initiated a drive for increased
productivity on the mines, he did so by calling a series of seminars on the copperbelt. Party officials down to the branch level
were transported to the convocations; they were forcefully reminded of their roles as "the backbone of the nation" and
exhorted by government ministers to impress upon their members
the necessity for hard work, respect for supervisors, increased
productivity, etc. Interviewing a local branch official after the
meeting, I was impressed by the tremendous gratification and
excitement he had derived from the long meetings with the
president and ministers, and by the strength of his conviction
that it was his national duty to insure that his branch members
understood what he himself had seen and heard.[19] Government
labor policy received further impetus from the campaigns in support of national development. The campaigns centered about a
series of conventions and seminars. It was the duty of local party

officials to attend these seminars; on the copperbelt, they focused on the government's views of the role of labor in national development.

Labor policy is further disseminated in the context of the government's campaign to develop and transmit Humanism, the official ideology of Zambia. President Kaunda conceives Humanism as a doctrinal alternative to communism and capitalism. Communism, he asserts, places ideas above men, while capitalism subjugates men to material things. Humanism, by contrast, places man at the center of society's concerns.[20] Promulgating his philosophy and his plans for its implementation at the UNIP Annual Conference of 1967, the president initiated a campaign for its dissemination. The campaign took the form of UNIP-sponsored seminars. At the meetings, the president himself, his ministers, or the minister of state expatiated on the doctrine to local party officials. They took the opportunity to stress the role of labor in the development of a prosperous economy able to bring benefits to the "common man" in Zambia.[21]

Mobility in UNIP

An examination of the pattern of mobility within UNIP also helps to explain UNIP's superior ability to evoke adherence to the government's program from its local officials. It suggests that the opportunities for advancement open to the local branch leaders strongly motivate them to accept the viewpoints articulated by their political superiors.

Many of the lower level officials of UNIP are intensely ambitious and fervently desire to better their positions in the party. Some believe that they are fully as qualified for top positions as those that now hold them, and therefore strive to attain equivalent posts. For example, lower-level officials knew that the registrar of trade unions, a former local UNIP official, held less than a standard VI education; his arrival in a chauffeur-driven car and receipt of a superscale salary caused intense jealousy on the part of these officials and expressions of intent to move up where "I can go around like that." More realistic aspirations focus at the regional level. Many officials seek no more than to attain regional posts and to become known, respected, and prestigious persons in the Kitwe area. Although the level of the positions to which most aspire is therefore low, the intensity of their ambitions is still high.

The intensity of these aspirations is revealed in the tensions of the election periods. Candidates become extremely nervous; through friends and intermediaries, they monitor closely the conduct of their opponents, the sentiment of lower-level officials with strong followings, the turnout at the polls, and the conduct of the polling officials. Officials lose their composure. Before and after elections, they are liable to argue and fight. And those who were friends and had worked closely together become distant during the elections, either because they have friends who have become rivals or because they themselves are contesting a single party position. Measured in terms of the tensions of the election period, the ambitions for office are thus very strong.[22]

In seeking to better their position in UNIP, party officials are confronted with closely refined ranks within the party structure. There are four local levels of officeholding: the section, branch, constituency, and region. An official at one level can improve his standing in the party by contesting offices at the next. Moreover, within a given level, not all offices are equally attractive. An official holding a junior office, such as publicity chief or vice-treasurer, can enhance his position by seeking a higher post within the cabinet, such as deputy chairman or even branch secretary. Given the aspirations for higher office, the increments of rank in the party therefore serve to keep these aspirations alive; for the party structure presents a continuous series of realistic targets to which those with ambitions can aspire.

An analysis of one constituency election and three branch elections provides evidence for this argument. Each level had eight posts: the chairman, secretary, treasurer, publicity chief and their lieutenants. By our coding scheme, the single constituency election therefore involved eight vacancies and the three branch elections involved twenty-four. For each of the elections, I recorded two kinds of information: the party level from which the person came who filled a given vacancy and, if the person did not cross levels in the election, the post he held previous to the election.

The information suggests that, despite the frequency of elections, there was a good deal of continuity in the pattern of office
holding. Of the twenty-four branch vacancies, sixteen were filled
by branch-level people; and of the six constituency vacancies for
which information could be obtained, half were filled by former
constituency officers (table 55). The information on branch elec-

TABLE 55
Mobility in UNIP by Level

Vacancies at:

Filled from:	Constituency	Branch
Constituency	3	0
Branch	3	16
Section	0	5
Other/Don't know	2	3

tions suggests that a high degree of continuity of officeholding
exists within given party levels (table 56): of the twenty-four

TABLE 56
Mobility in UNIP by Post

Branch vacancies in:

Vacancies filled by:	C	V-C	S	V-S	T	V-T	PC	VPC
Branch officer								
Chairman	2							
Vice-Chairman	1							
Secretary			2					
Vice-Secretary				3				
Treasurer		1	1					
Vice-Treasurer						2		
Publicity Chief							2	
Vice Publicity Chief								2
Sections		1			2	1	1	
No office		1		1				
Youth								1

Note: The abbreviations in the column headings correspond to the office titles
in the stub column.

vacancies in the branch, thirteen were filled by persons who had held the same office before the election.

The data also confirm the existence of gradations within the party. The party levels appear to be ranked. The branch receives officers from the branch and the sections, but not from the constituency; and the constituency receives officers from the constituency and the branch, but not from the region or the section. Thus, there appears to be a hierarchy between the levels: people move up from the section to the branch and thence to the constituency, and no one moves down from the region to the constituency, from the constituency to the branch, or from the branch down to the section. This last bit of information is contained in table 57, where it is shown that no branch official moved into section office.

TABLE 57
Mobility in UNIP

	Movement to branch office[a]								Constitu-ency	Section	No office	Youth
	C	V-C	S	V-S	T	V-T	PC	VPC				
Branch officer												
Chairman	2								1			
Vice-Chairman	1											2
Secretary			1						2			
Vice-Secretary				3								
Treasurer	1	1									1	
Vice-Treasurer					2						1	
Publicity Chief						2					1	
Vice Publicity Chief					1	2						

[a] Abbreviations as in table 56.

Tables 56 and 57 confirm the gradation of posts within a given party level. The grouping of the entries within a sector defined by a diagonal across the matrix shows that in no case was an office filled by a person who formerly held an office of higher title. Thus, the vice-chairmanship was never filled by a chairman; the post of secretary was never filled by a former chairman or his deputy; and so on. Rather, all movements were directed upward: treasurers became deputy chairmen or secretaries, a vice-chairman became chairman, and a deputy publicity secretary moved up to treasurer. To a great degree, control over the selection of personnel in the party is hierarchically distributed. The branch reconstructs section cabinets, the regional secretary empowers the branch to reshuffle its officers, and in December 1967, the regional secretary created and filled a whole new set of offices at the constituency level.* Documentation of the importance of such administrative action in filling party positions is to be found in table 58. Counting the purge

TABLE 58
Reasons for Leaving Office

Number of times a person left branch office:

For constituency office	3
For higher branch post	4
Because asked to resign by the party	5
Total	12

of two officers that took place at the time of our departure, twelve offices were vacated at the branch level during our research; almost one-half of these were forcefully rendered vacant by the party administration.

Given the control by the party hierarchy over the selection of personnel, lower party officials seek to impress upon their superiors their fitness for promotion. As part of this process, they acquire many of the attitudes and viewpoints of their superior officers. This was made clear by the behavior of the secretary of the branch we studied. One of his great ambitions was to become secretary or chairman of the constituency. When it became known that the

* Up to that time, there had been one constituency party in Kitwe. In December, the regional secretary subdivided Kitwe into two constituencies; the division largely paralleled the boundary between municipal and mine townships in the area. He did so because, as he put it, there tended to be more "troubles" on the mines and he needed to stay in closer touch. He himself nominated the first set of officers to fill the constituency posts.

regional secretary intended to create a new constituency, the branch secretary became intensely aware of the regional secretary. He felt that the regional secretary was watching him and evaluating his abilities. He formulated ideas as to what the regional secretary regarded as desirable qualities among his party officials, and strove to exhibit these qualities in his party work. Conscientiously performing his duties, he rendered himself conspicuous among other branch officials and won the regional secretary's nomination to a constituency post.[23]

Thus, the party confronts its officers with a series of ranks, both within and between the party levels. The frequent party elections and the intense ambitions of the officers encourage the party personnel to enhance their standing in the party. While their attempts produce conflict, they also encourage conformity with the dictates of party superiors. For to a high degree, the successful passage of a junior official from one level to the next is mediated by the actions of his superiors. The pattern of mobility in the party thus helps to explain the acceptance of government policies by the lower ranks of UNIP officialdom.

The Distribution of Power in UNIP

In our description of UNIP's support for the government's program, we noted a second source of UNIP's superiority over the union. When conflicts between public policy and the interests of the miners did penetrate into the party structure, the regional secretary was able to compel adherence to the public interest. The data thus suggest that in addition to possessing the necessary incentives and sanctions to motivate party officers to adhere to government policy, UNIP possessess a structure of power which enables its superior officials to impose public policy upon dissident local leaders.

Power over Goal Attainment

UNIP is functionally diffuse, even when only its manifest functions are considered. The party performs a wide range of activities for the national political system, in part because the national political elite assigns a large variety of tasks to it. Among other things, UNIP has been required to: gather intelligence, teach the electorate how to vote, eradicate the social barriers of class and tribe, organize patriotic rallies and celebrations, teach Humanism, and so forth. The abundance of party goals makes it impossible to analyze the distribution of power by examining the performance of a single set of tasks, as could be done with the union. Nonetheless, we can approximate a similar approach to the problem. For the goals of the party, multiple though they be, are reduced to weekly party agendas. An analysis of the control over the agenda of local party units would therefore suggest the distribution of control over the goal attainment function.

UNIP's local branches draw up weekly agendas. In the branch we studied, the branch chairman and secretary write the agenda and present it for approval to other members of the branch cabinet. The agenda is usually impressive and contains a large variety of tasks and assignments for the party activists to perform. Typically, it would include at least one meeting of the Mine Township Council, a meeting with the Womens' Brigade or Youth League, a meeting with a management body (either a member of the personnel department or a ward committee of the community development program), at least one branch cabinet meeting, a meeting with the regional secretary or constituency officials, possibly the organization of a demonstration or rally, and a public meeting of some sort—either under the auspices of the branch or sections or the Township Council. Not included in the agenda are activities which the party must perform but cannot anticipate, such as the adjudication of family disputes or the apprehension of offenders in the township who are in some way disturbing the peace. The party activists must undertake all these activities on "free time," that is, after their return from work on the mines.

The regional secretary maintains a similar weekly agenda. He circulates it to the branch officers so as to inform them of his intentions. His typical weekly program would include: a reception for officials at the airport; a speech before one or two community groups, such as mission societies; a meeting with the party branches; a meeting with the Regional Development Committee; another with the minister of state and his assistants; a caucus with party municipal councillors; a discussion with some union group; a report to the minister of state on political cases; the organization of elections to lower party posts; and so forth. As with the branch agenda, the program of the regional secretary does not include obligatory tasks whose timing cannot be foreseen, such as intervening in wildcat strikes and investigating incidents of political violence.

While these agendas give a flavor of the activities of UNIP, that is not their importance for the analysis. It is apparent that each level in the party constructs and pursues its own, relatively autonomous weekly program. But what is of greatest importance is that the regional office can at any time totally supersede the agenda of the local branches. The local branch can posit and pursue its own goals, and is encouraged to do so; but it is also conditioned to regard regional instructions as possessing preferred status and instructed to incorporate regional items into its program when the regional secretary so desires.

The regional secretary was observed inserting items into the branch agenda on numerous occasions. Sometimes he would insert only one or two items; for example, when the regional agenda indicated a Saturday afternoon meeting on the mine townships to discuss the president's new program for cooperatives, that afternoon was reserved for the region on the branch's agenda. Sometimes the regional secretary would appropriate dates already reserved by the branches for their own activities. Thus, the branch had at one time reserved a Thursday afternoon for a meeting of the Township Council. The regional secretary notified the branch secretary that he would arrive in the township with the assistant minister that afternoon, and the branch officials withdrew from the council meeting, giving preference to their meeting with the regional secretary. On other occasions, the regional secretary would take over the branch's entire schedule. This often happened, for the Kitwe Region had frequently to host foreign visitors, international delegations, and presidential parties from Lusaka. The preparation of these functions would involve at least a week's time. The Women's Brigade would practice songs and brew beer; the party branches would receive briefings on the schedule of speeches, receptions, and local inspections; and the local officials would inform the people of the name and status of the visitor, his schedule, when they must greet him, and why it was important to make a favorable impression upon the dignitary. Throughout this period, the agenda of the local branches would be totally at the command of the regional secretary and for a relatively long period of time.

Thus, while the local units usually decide upon and perform their own activities in relative isolation from the regional office, the regional secretary can supersede the local agenda when he wishes to do so. This strongly suggests that the distribution of power is hierarchical in UNIP, with power concentrating in the regional office.

Power over Internal Maintenance

An analysis of the performance of organizational maintenance functions corroborates this inference. UNIP's primary maintenance activities are the collection of finances and the selection of leadership personnel. UNIP obtains a large part of its revenues from the sale of party cards. Party cards are crucial documents on the copperbelt. Whenever a person seeks assistance from UNIP, he must produce the most recent party card to receive consideration; failing that, he must purchase a new one before his case will be handled. In extreme cases, only the possession of the most recent card will insure personal safety; for in times of political tension, the party youths use possession of a UNIP card to distinguish friends and enemies.

The regional secretary is in charge of the distribution of cards and the collection of remittances. He receives a new shipment of cards early each year, and registers the serial numbers of his allotment. He then apportions a series of serial numbers to each branch, and transmits the appropriate cards to the branch secretary. Only given numbers are legitimate in a region, and enemy parties issuing counterfeit UNIP cards can therefore be detected, as can criminals who sell false cards and pocket the proceeds.

The branch treasurer is in charge of the marketing of party

cards. He too divides the cards by the serial numbers and issues one series to each section. The section treasurer makes the actual sales and remits the proceeds to the branch which in turn returns the funds to the region. By party "law," following the regional secretary's transmission to a branch of a series of cards, the equivalent funds must be returned to the regional office in one month's time.[24]

The regional secretary strives to insure that all the funds do in fact revert to his office. For example, the branch we studied had difficulty recovering funds from one of its sections; the branch officers notified the regional secretary who empowered them to threaten the section with police action. Another time, the branch treasurer spent the proceeds from the sale of UNIP cards on clothing for his children; in this case too the regional secretary empowered the branch officers to threaten prosecution at law. In both cases, the regional secretary recovered his funds.

The regional secretary is thus armed with auditing controls over the issuance of cards and with coercive powers over the collection of money from their sale. Party funds flow to this office and cannot remain at the lower levels of the party. In financial matters, therefore, power would appear to lie with the regional secretary.

Control over the recruitment and selection of party officials also appears to be hierarchically distributed. As noted in the discussion of mobility in UNIP, a given level of the party can control the selection of officers at the next lower level. The best illustration of this took place at the time the regional secretary created a new constituency in Kitwe. Not only did the regional secretary thereby create new posts in the party hierarchy, but he also filled them with officers of his own choosing. The process did not stop there; the new constituency cabinet nominated the successors to the positions at the branch level which they had just vacated. The new branch officers were promoted from the ranks of the section officials; and it was the branch cabinet which nominated persons to fill the vacated section posts.

Another illustration is the ability of the branch cabinet to purge dissident section officers. For several weeks in the Kalela branch, the officers in Kamanga section conducted a running feud with their branch cabinet. Two of the section officials had attempted to gain charters for an ex-servicemen's club by directly approaching the mine's community development officers, thus sidestepping the branch cabinet and offending the party officials. The cabinet officers, utilizing their power as township councillors, persuaded the Community Development Ward Committee to deny a charter to the club, and thus earned the enmity of the section leaders. The Kamanga section officers then began to spread rumors about the branch cabinet, and to boycott branch meetings; when they did attend meetings, it was only to harass the branch officers. The branch cabinet retaliated by calling for new elections in Kamanga section; at the election meeting, they proposed an approved slate of officials, and spoke eloquently on their behalf. By forewarning these officials of their intentions, the branch leaders were able to insure a large turnout of sympathetic voters and insure the selection of their choices.[25] Kalela branch similarly reconstituted Milner section, whose officials had proven to be apathetic and ineffectual.[26]

In both the selection of party officials and the collection of finances, therefore, higher party units control the performance of internal maintenance activities. In conjunction with the analysis of goal attainment activities, this finding supports the inference that power in UNIP is distributed hierarchically. The acceptance of government labor policy by the lower ranks of the party can therefore, in part, be explained in terms of the distribution of power in the party.

UNIP and the Mineworkers

In this portion of our study, we move from an analysis of the relationships within the party structure to an analysis of the relationships between the party and the mineworkers themselves. I contend that in comparison with the branch leaders of the union, local party leaders possess a much greater ability to propound and propagate public policies which are at variance with the interests of the mineworking community.

UNIP as a Structure of Communications

Like the union, the party officials are well equipped to detect and transmit the grievances of their members. UNIP officials are expected to be available to their members and responsive to them. They are instructed to insure that their identity and location are well known to all township residents; some officials even maintain signs on their houses, thereby marking the location of UNIP leaders. The officials maintain an open house for their members, and encourage people to bring their cases to them freely. For example, a whole series of cases was brought to the home of the Kalela branch chairman: a woman brought her marital problems to him; he was asked to intervene in a dispute between the brother and lover of a young woman; and he was called out on several occasions to investigate instances of overcharging at the market. Senior branch officials instruct their juniors always to be available for such cases; to determine quickly and accurately the facts of the case; to settle the matter if it is in their power; and if not, to take it to those with the power to do so. In this manner, the party maintains itself as a captive audience to the mineworkers.

The party officials go a step further to insure their captive status. They do not merely await the arrival of cases; they also tour the township so that people can bring matters to their attention. Branch officials circulate through the entire area in their domain, and section officials perambulate through their areas as well. The regular schedule of such touring enables members to find their party officials and to communicate their grievances.

UNIP, therefore, like the union, is sensitive to the upward communication of views and grievances. Peculiar to the party, however, is the practice of turning occasions for upward communications into occasions for the downward transmittal of political information and points of view. When a person comes to the party, he is interrogated. He is asked for his party card. He is asked the name of his section officials. If his complaint has a "political element," as in the case of market prices, he is queried about government policy toward the matter. Should the plaintiff not possess a party card, he is instructed to purchase one before his case can be considered; the opportunity is taken to teach him the name and residence of his section treasurer, as well as the meaning and significance of the document. Should the plaintiff not know the names of his section officials, he is told to learn them; only when he acquires this information is his case considered. Government policies are also explained and elaborated during the course of these proceedings. In this manner, the occasion for upward communications becomes an occasion for impressing knowledge of the party's structure and viewpoints upon the township residents.

THE NETWORK OF PARTY OFFICIALS. The party goes beyond case work in its attempt at downward communications. For UNIP seeks to render its membership a captive audience to the party's point of view. One method is to utilize its network of party officials to maintain close and intensive contact with the membership. By dividing and subdividing the party structure, the UNIP leaders both increase the number of active officials in the township and achieve total and relatively uniform coverage of the residential areas. As noted earlier, the party maintains a set of constituency officials for the mine townships; including the Youth League and Women's Brigade, they number 24. UNIP then divides the Rhokana mine townships into four party branch areas: Kalela, Chamboli, Wusikili, and Mindolo. All told, these branches engage the services of 96 officials. The branches subdivide into sections. There are thirty-four sections in the mine townships; with 24 officials for each section, the total number of UNIP officials in the Rhokana townships rises to 936.

The system of dividing party officials into branches and sections distributes political sources over the entire township; by preventing the clustering of UNIP officials, it insures that party officials will be present in all residential areas. In addition, it portions the population itself into sufficiently small units that the officials can maintain continuing face-to-face contact with their members. For example, in the branch we studied, there were 168 officials and 2,177 houses, or one UNIP official for every thirteen households (table 59). Thus, party officials are able to maintain near-total coverage of the mineworkers; each official need visit but

TABLE 59
Network of Party Officials: Kalela Branch

Section	Section officials	Houses	Ratio
Milner	24	317	1:13
Kamanga	24	444	1:19
Kapwepwe	24	480	1:20
Sikota Wina	24	349	1:15
Kaunda	24	480	1:20
Kalulu	24	107	1:4
Total	144	2,177	1:15
Branch officials	24		
Grand total	168	2,177	1:13

thirteen or so houses, and this can be achieved simply by walking the length of the street he lives on.

The efficiency of the system was demonstrated repeatedly during my research. For example, the branch secretary would receive notice of a meeting in the morning. Recruiting youths, he would write notices to every section publicity secretary; the publicity secretary organized youths to write notices to the houses in his area and delivered the announcements that evening. Within seven hours, every household in the branch was informed.[27] The mineworkers could not avoid messages the party wished them to receive, so widely and densely distributed is the network of party officials.

PUBLIC MEETINGS. Like the union, UNIP has won the right to use a large meeting ground on the mine townships. It too has constructed a platform on an anthill at one end of the grounds, and installed a public address system with speaker equipment loaned by the Government Information Department. Before public meetings, sound trucks circulate about the mine townships blaring political slogans and the time and date of the meeting. They make the rounds of the townships for a full day before the meeting and again the next morning. Following up on the second tour come droves of UNIP youths. Herded by section officials, they enter every yard and house, checking that everyone has left for the meeting or is making preparations to attend. Where obvious reluctance is shown, the youths sometimes use force; despite the disapproval of Main Body leaders, the pots of women who are cooking are sometimes toppled into the fire, or sometimes broken, and the reluctant members severely abused. Through the youths, each section recruits its members into the greater audience, and the party reduces selective attendance at its meetings.

In comparison with the union, the party holds frequent meetings and gains high attendance. Thus, table 37 in chapter 6 indicates that at times of peak effort for both the union and party, the party was much more active in organizing public meetings. In every month but one, it held more meetings than the union; and in every month without exception, it achieved a greater average attendance. During my stay in Zambia, public party meetings were still periodic and important features of life in the mine townships. As seen in table 60, UNIP held five meetings in the mine

TABLE 60
Party Meetings

Date	Site	Speaker
July 1967	Chamboli	Vice-President Kapwepwe
July 1967	Trade Fair	President Kaunda
July 1967	Chamboli	Minister of Local Government and Housing, Sikota Wina
Sept. 1967	Mindolo	Minister of State and assistant
Oct. 1967	Chamboli	Local officials
Dec. 1967	Wusikili	Minister of State and assistant
Jan. 1968	Airport	President Kaunda
Mar. 1968	Airport	President Kaunda

townships themselves and conducted three meetings at the airport and fairgrounds, both immediately adjacent the mine townships. By comparison, the union held but two meetings over the same period. While I did not attempt precise counts of attendance at these meetings, it was obvious that the union achieved audiences of one to two hundred people, while the party's audiences numbered in the thousands.

UNIP meetings are not occasions for upward communications. The speakers do not solicit comments from the audience, for this is not the purpose for which the meetings are held. Moreover, it is considered disrespectful to shout anything but comments of agreement from the meeting floor. Rather, the whole intent is to capture and hold the public's attention and focus it on information concerning the party's structure, activities, policies, and programs. Speakers "warm up" the crowd with attention-gaining exhortations and involve the audience by gaining its participation in a mutual exchange of political slogans. The national anthem is then sung, and great care is taken that due respect is shown during the singing of the anthem. When someone has his hands in his pockets or moves from his place during the anthem, the "master of ceremonies" is liable to stop the anthem, have the offender apprehended, and exhibit him before the audience for public shaming. People are thus put in a dutiful and respectful frame of mind. During the speeches, party officials distribute youths about the perimeter of the meeting grounds to prevent any exodus. Youths are also used to break up inattentive congeries in the crowd. When the load of one-way communications has been too heavy, attention is won back by the singing of political songs or the performances of talented and comical entertainers. Three to four hours of intensive downward communications are thereby achieved.

During the proceedings, speakers present party officials and announce their names and offices; where there have been promotions or transfers, the change of offices is carefully detailed. Speakers devote additional time to describing party activities: events in the local council, campaigns against mini-skirts and traffic violators, card sales, price control measures, and so on. But the bulk of their efforts is devoted to explaining and elaborating national policies, such as on drunkenness, productivity, poor work habits, strikes, tribalism, and so forth. The whole performance thus centers on the transmittal of information and viewpoints from the officials on the platform to the mineworkers on the meeting grounds.

REINFORCEMENT. UNIP follows up large public meetings with smaller, more intimate, face-to-face sessions. In the weeks that follow important pronouncements at the large sessions, the branch officials convene smaller public meetings and introduce the principal themes of the rally into their speeches before these smaller sessions. In these meetings, the audience will be several hundred persons. In turn, the section officials pick up the themes and emphasize them before groups of thirty or forty persons.

Selective attendance is not allowed to play a part in these smaller sessions. While youths were used to gain full attendance at the larger meetings, social pressures are applied to gain attendance at the smaller sessions. A section official knows many of the families in his area; through his knowledge and the reports of his fellow officers, he knows who attends or fails to attend his section meetings. The local officials organize and sustain intense social pressures on habitual nonparticipants. The wives of the faithful cajole the wives of those who are reluctant. UNIP officials pay them visits to persuade them to attend. Should these efforts fail, the people are increasingly isolated. Social contacts are withdrawn and visiting becomes infrequent. Women no longer loan cooking equipment or firewood; the children of the offenders are not fed when they come to play, and the children of the faithful are discouraged from playing in the yards of the unwelcome. Gossip mounts about the nonparticipant, focusing on his wealth, pride, selfishness, or lack of social involvement. Should he deviate too far, when he is away at work, UNIP youths will abuse his wife and children; at night, they will throw stones on his tin roof or pound loudly on his door. Gradually, he will be compelled either to withdraw entirely from the township or to reenter the fold of the UNIP faithful.[28]

At the smaller meetings, the principal tenets of UNIP policy are reiterated once more. The smaller sessions enable the party officials to tailor their presentations much more carefully to the audience and to evoke a collective understanding of the content of the policy. For example, when Zambia introduced its new currency, the proclamation was made at large public rallies. The names of the new units—*kwacha* and *ngwee*—became political slogans. But the task of explicating the system in detail was largely performed in the smaller sessions. Armed with charts and posters, the branch and section officials indicated how two *kwacha* were the equivalent of a pound and one *kwacha* the same as ten shillings. And they took particular care to indicate the relationship between *ngwee* and pence. This last was most important, because so many purchases would be made in these smaller denominations; it was also the most difficult, because ten *ngwee* did not convert exactly into twelve pence. Using familiar examples— the cost of fish, of rolls and buns, and of joints of sugar cane— they illustrated the proper conversions. The officials then solicited questions and invited people forward to attempt the conversions themselves.

This process of communications is similarly employed to introduce relatively unpopular messages and with apparently telling effect. When there were strikes underground in the mines, the party activated its machinery to present the government's viewpoint on the matter. No large rally was held, as officials felt that a large meeting would provide the workers with an opportunity for shouting their complaints to the podium, rather than providing UNIP officials with the chance to explain the necessity for restraint to the workers. Instead, the party activated its network of section leaders and organized a series of small face-to-face sessions with the underground employees. Youths circulated to the houses of the underground workers and brought them to meetings. At the meetings, the party officials collected the grievances of the workers and expressed great sympathy with them. They then went on to point out the effect of strikes on the mines and the country; to show how much the government was doing for the workers and how much it had accomplished since independence; and to encourage the workers to return to their jobs so as "not to spoil our independence and help our enemies."[29] There is no way of telling how much of an impact this had, but there can be no doubt that the party's efforts assisted in securing a return to work; the miners reported to their jobs the next day.

Attitudes toward UNIP

I have argued that even had the union branch leaders advocated government labor policy at the local level, they would have been unable to motivate the workers to accept it, because the union leaders lacked legitimacy. The factor of legitimacy also helps to explain the superior capabilities of UNIP.

THE POLITICS OF CONFRONTATION. UNIP's main instrument in its relationship with the companies is the Township Council. While it conducts its affairs with the company through the council, UNIP's position is in no way analogous to that of the union. The union is able to make, negotiate and win substantive claims from the mining companies; and the mining companies formally acknowledge its right to do so. The Mine Township Council, however, is only advisory. It is called upon to review and comment upon the company's regulation and conduct of the markets, the clinics and hospitals, and the sanitary facilities of the townships. The companies regard the council solely as consultative, and they grant it no right to propose or negotiate for substantive concessions.[30]

UNIP councillors recognize and resent their position. They know that the companies extend them no right to make claims upon management, and thus no purchase for a collaborative relationship. They freely compare their position with that of the union and express strong resentment at what they regard as the union's more favorable position. They feel slighted; and given UNIP's paramountcy in the nation, their resentments are intensified.

Receiving no recognition and few concessions from management, UNIP councillors feel no obligation to exchange concessions in return. They feel no necessity for evoking support from their followers for the company's regulations or respect for the company's point of view. They need not serve as company spokesmen, for they have received nothing from the companies that

would engender so high a level of regard for the companies' interests. As a result, instead of operating in a collaborative relationship with company spokesmen, they develop a relationship of
sustained confrontation.

This pattern manifests itself in the meetings and deliberations
of the township councillors. The powerlessness of the councillors
again and again transforms into hostile and provocative statements. When issues come forward that the councillors feel
strongly about, they voice their resentment at their inability to
force the companies to comply with their wishes. For example,
the councillors sought to evict from a tearoom a man they felt
had obtained the premises under false pretenses. They dispatched
a letter to the personnel manager; the reply was long delayed,
and this gave rise to hostile comments. Even after they had gained
a favorable decision, there was little satisfaction, for it was many
weeks before the man was evicted. Again and again, speakers
reverted to the point as proof of how little respect the council
received from management.[31] That UNIP ruled outside the mine
townships only made matters worse. The first time I sat in on a
council meeting, I was asked why "our brothers in the municipal
areas have a real council and we do not?" And again and again,
at moments of frustration, the councillors made themselves even
more unhappy by noting that in Zambia as a whole, UNIP governed.

The realization that UNIP had no purchase on the companies
frequently translated into vitriol. Occasionally the councillors
asked company spokesmen to appear before the council to clarify
company policy in a given area. The results often approached
chaos. Refusing to confine their comments to subjects falling
within the official's sphere of competence, the councillors confronted him with the full range of their grievances. Issues where
the company had shown bad faith and matters where the company had made evident the low regard in which it held the Township Council were revived and dwelt upon. The councillors
derived much satisfaction from these confrontations, and after the
meetings, freely broadcast the blows they had rained on the com-

pany official and the discomfort he had evidenced during these sessions.

That the councillors thus abuse the company accounts for much of their popularity. The officials are seen as strong and brave. It is widely known that they do not quail before the company officials. Instead, they are known to champion the feelings of the miners. Unlike the union officials, the councillors are not seen as disseminating company regulations and cooperating with management; instead, they are seen as protesting company policies and confronting management personnel. As a result, the authority of the UNIP councillors is not corrupted by any involvement or cooperation with the European authorities; instead, their legitimacy is augmented by their posture of confrontation against this deeply resented element of the mine community.

PERCEPTIONS OF UNIP POWER. Ironically, despite its inability to achieve significant concessions from the mining companies, UNIP is regarded as an immensely powerful advocate of the interests of its members. The reason for this is clear. While having no claim upon the companies, the party does possess the backing of the government. Moreover, the local party officials have proven their ability to utilize this backing effectively.

A convincing illustration of the benefits of access to government power arose during my stay at Rhokana. As noted, the council advises the company on the regulation of the township markets. One of the principal items marketed is fish, which forms an important element of the local diet. For the miners, *"munani ukwabula isabi, tefyakulya* [relish without fish is not fit to eat]." The price of fish is regulated by the government; but the fish vendors, pleading rising transport costs, raised their prices above the legal minimum. This constituted a direct threat to the party's position, for the council had to reverse the unpopular price rise in order to stave off damaging criticism from its price-conscious members. The vendors did not stop there, however. At the instigation of their union president, they also sought direct control over the market itself. They sought the power to allocate stalls, to regulate the quality of goods, to examine and calibrate the scales, and to make improvements. These demands represented further challenges to the party, for the overseeing of such tasks fell to the council; moreover, the allocation of market stalls represented a crucial element of party patronage. The conflict came to a head, however, when the marketeers' union began to collect rent for the stalls; the income of the council was immediately threatened, and the council had either to sustain this loss of income or reverse the union's actions.

The council's first reaction was to demand that the companies act to enforce its position. Only the companies could reverse the price rise, for the markets were on company property. Moreover, the union's collection of rents amounted to defrauding the company and not the council, for the council itself had no rights in law. Only the company could prosecute the offending union. The councillors lobbied vigorously to press the company into action. They formed a special council committee, wrote letters to the personnel manager, sent delegations to the personnel department, and filled pages of the council minutes with speeches in support of rapid action. During all this activity, their sense of inefficacy and frustration mounted; for the situation compelled them to realize that it was their lack of power over the companies that made them unable to take action on the matter.

So irate did they become that the councillors finally invoked the government's backing. They sent a delegation to Lusaka to meet with the minister of local government and housing. The minister handled the situation with alacrity and skill. On the one hand, he dispatched his parliamentary secretary to rebuke and to activate the management. On the other, he himself accelerated the work of a commission on fish prices. In addition, he received the local UNIP councillors with dignity and charm. Stating his intention to reduce fish prices, he consented to announce the reduction at a public meeting in the mine townships. The phrase he used that was most quoted afterwards was: "From this moment, you are real councillors." Despite their demeaning position with respect to the companies, in the eyes of the government, it was the councillors who had power.

The councillors won a famous victory in their conflict with the marketeers. The minister announced the price reduction before a vast audience; and while he spoke, they shared the platform. His announcement that "the price of fish is now two shillings sixpence a pound" was greeted with cheers and the shouted exchange of political slogans. The local UNIP branches were indeed powerful, for they had gained the backing of a minister from Lusaka to defend the interests of their followers.[32]

The marketeers incident was but the most dramatic illustration of the party's power. On a day-to-day basis, the party repeatedly illustrates its capacity to utilize government power for the benefit of its members. Thus, when people need the police, they turn to the branch officials; it is they who can get the police to listen and respond. Thus, too, when Europeans make subversive comments, the people report them to the party; for it is the party which can get the special branch to investigate. The local UNIP leaders thereby achieve reputations as strong and powerful advocates of the interests of their followers.

SOCIAL RANK AND PARTY LEGITIMACY. There is yet another reason for UNIP's legitimacy. For unlike the union, UNIP officials do not appear to prosper from their relations with the companies; rather, they appear to suffer. At first glance, this popular belief would not appear justified. An examination of the social background of the township councillors reveals that in comparison with the union, they occupy positions of advantage. There is a greater proportion of staff employees in the council than there is in the union's local executive; while 7 percent of the union officials hold staff positions, a full 43 percent of the councillors do so. Moreover, the average councillor earns a greater income; thus the local union officials earned roughly K80 a month while the local party officials earned over K100 per month. These realities stand in contradiction to the popular belief concerning UNIP and its position in the mining community. The contradiction is resolved, however, by ignoring the attributes of the UNIP officials and noting their actual behavior.

In part, UNIP's image of "suffering" has already been explained. The party leaders' denunciation of the mining companies and their portrayals of the company's insensitivity to their position create the notion that they are victimized. Moreover, as we have argued previously, the very fact that many UNIP officials occupy top positions in the mines renders them the most expert witnesses of the racial structure of the industry. Their verbal portrayals of their plight create the conviction of suffering and oppression.

There is an additional reason for UNIP's ability to overcome the "objective reality" of its position and to transform it into an image of suffering. The officials consciously work at doing precisely that. They realize the dangers of appearing prosperous, for they know that those who do too well in their jobs at the mine become unpopular among the mass of the workers. They therefore redouble their efforts to identify with the position of the vast majority of the mineworkers concentrated at the lower pay levels. They publicly champion their demands for nicer houses, cleaner townships, better clinics, better communal toilets and wash stands, and cleaner roads and passageways. And by providing firewood for funerals, sitting at wakes, defraying the expenses of those who are injured, and visiting and socializing throughout the township, they seek to communicate that they have not become "too proud."

There are other indications of the determination of party officials to bridge the gap between their position and that of their followers. Some have forsaken the opportunity of moving to the bigger houses to which their jobs entitle them; pointing out the saving in lower rents, they also note their fears for their popularity and following.[33] In one case, a councillor actually decided not to seek a further promotion to which he was entitled. Knowing that he would receive a big house and an increment in pay, he knew too that his political standing would be threatened: "People would say I had 'sold out.' They would think I am proud and begin shouting at me. I couldn't do it, Mr. Bates. Politically, I would be finished."[34] In their actual conduct and behavior, therefore, the officials seek to overcome the impression of benefiting from the companies and to transmit an image of being one with those who fall victim to the oppressive aspects of the corporate structure.

By contrast with the local union leaders, the party leaders have won the right in the eyes of their members to express viewpoints that may be at variance with the interests of the members. When party leaders demand that their members contain their demands for better wages and conditions, followers do not suspect that they are afraid of management, sold out to the Europeans, or without the power to stand up to the company. Instead, they pay attention and listen with respect, for the UNIP officials are believed to be strong, sensitive and vigorous spokesmen of their interests. Functioning effectively in an input capacity, they have legitimated their output roles as well. Yet we are left with the undeniable fact that the government's policy of restraint has failed. If all I have said suggests the strength of UNIP as an output structure, why then is UNIP ineffective in gaining support for this policy?

UNIP's Restricted Role

In part, of course, I have already explained the failure of UNIP. Despite its dedication to regulating the mineworkers in conformity with government policy, there is very little the party can actually do. Were UNIP to intervene directly in the process of industrial relations, then, of course, the case would be different. The party, functioning as a union, could concur with management's sanctions on strikes, negotiate wage scales and bonus schemes tied to productivity, establish incentive schemes to reward those who work hard, and fail to extend union protection to those who contested the authority of supervisors. Other parties, elsewhere, have done as much.[35] But UNIP cannot utilize such rewards and such sanctions, for, as we have seen, it has failed to gain control of the union. Instead of actually taking a direct role, the party is left with a peripheral one. It can intervene at moments of severe deviation from the government's policies, as it does in the case of strikes. It can exhort the workers to harder work, obedience, and greater discipline. And it does defend the policy of wage restraint, even if it dare not propound it. In all of these things, the party leaders appear to gain greater respect for their viewpoints than the leaders of the union could ever receive. But these activities are only marginal to the sphere of industrial relations.

There is another way of phrasing UNIP's problem. Because the party lacks direct access to the conduct of industrial relations, it is left with an almost purely communications role in the mine townships. The party fulfills this role with dedication and skill. But it lacks the rewards and sanctions to gain actual cooperation with the program; it lacks access to the inducements necessary to transform the workers' respectful attention into cooperative behavior.[36]

UNIP's Search for Legitimacy and the Failure of Government Strategy

There is another set of reasons for UNIP's failure, and these stem from the party's search for legitimacy, which centers on the abolition of the inferior status of African miners in the copper industry. The party champions Zambianization, fights to abolish discriminatory practices in mine facilities, and seeks to purge racist supervisors from the ranks of management. In its quest for legitimacy, UNIP strives to be seen in combat with the European management and renews and sustains the theme of racial oppression. And UNIP, like the government, seeks to exchange its championship of the mineworkers' demands as Africans for their cooperation as industrial workers.

It is my belief that this advocacy of racial justice in fact produces greater, not less, militancy on the part of the workers. The cause of this is not to be found in UNIP or in the nature of its campaigns. Rather, it is in the structure of the mining community. Given the racially stratified mining community, it is almost impossible to differentiate the interests of the mines' employees as workers from their interests as Africans.

On the mines, to be a worker is to be an African, and to be an African is almost certainly to be a worker. To demand that the basic wages of Africans be equal to those of Europeans is thus to set the stage for a large wage claim by the workers. To protest the racist conduct of European supervisors is to protest against the use—or misuse—of managerial authority. To coerce Europeans who insult Africans is to establish a situation in which supervisors fear to exercise their authority and in which management fears to enforce the government's injunction to work hard. It is almost impossible, therefore, to trade off contributions to the workers in the sphere of racial justice for concessions to the government in industrial relations.

Furthermore, UNIP, in the cause of racial justice, insistently presses for African advancement in the mining industry. But, as we have noted, there is a strong tendency for African advancement to heighten, not dampen, the militancy of industrial relations. Insofar as the party does improve the racial status of mine employees, it therefore sets in motion forces which tend to perpetuate and perhaps strengthen the radical character of industrial relations.

There is a final reason for the failure of the party and government to consummate an exchange between the interests of the employees as workers and as Africans: despite the vigorous efforts of UNIP and the government, racial inequity still prevails in the mining industry. We have seen that African personnel are advancing into the supervisory ranks on the mines and that one full department—the personnel department—is totally Africanized. Party and governmental pressure have rendered management sensitive to the necessity of penalizing racist conduct by company supervisors and the companies have agreed to allocate all facilities by status and rank, rather than by race. The 22 percent wage increase of 1966 significantly reduced the disparity in African and European wage levels. And the negotiation of a single basic wage scale has at last closed the gap between the basic wages of local and expatriate workers.

Despite these impressive steps toward social justice, racial stratification still permeates the social and economic structure of the industry. Allocating facilities by rank rather than by race nonetheless means that the best facilities remain largely for Europeans. Basic wages may be equal, but Europeans will still hold the best-paying jobs and receive an expatriate bonus. Authority remains largely concentrated in the hands of expatriate officials.[37] UNIP and the government may have made great progress in enhancing the economic position of the Africans. But for the mass of the mineworkers, the pattern of racial inequity remains highly visible and their sense of racial deprivation remains powerful and profound. Given the intensity of their demands for racial equality, many miners do not feel that the progress which has been made warrants major concessions to UNIP and the government. In its attempts to persuade the miners to reciprocate with concessions to government policy for the progress which has been made, the party and the government face strikingly unfavorable terms for the trade.

9   Zambian Mineworkers and the Study of Development

Students of labor and development contend that the labor policies of developing nations are largely dictated by the commitment of their elites to the goal of rapid development. I find this to be true for Zambia. What makes the thesis so convincing is Zambia's near-total reliance on copper. The government's policy toward mine labor is but one of many policies designed to protect and utilize mining revenues for the attainment of rapid development. Given its dependence on the taxable earnings of the copper industry and its commitment to rapid economic development, it is easy to account for the government's exhortations to work hard, obey supervisors, restrain wage demands, and abstain from strike action.

My analysis corroborates a second principal hypothesis in the field: that the role assigned to trade unions in developing societies is productionist in nature. The Zambian government repeatedly proclaims that the proper role of labor is to contribute to production, and thereby to enhance the taxable earnings of industry. And it repeatedly outlines to trade union leaders the necessity of structuring the conduct of the workers so as to conform with this productionist role.

Insofar as this study thus corroborates relatively established propositions in the field, it contributes new data for old concerns. I have attempted to go beyond the preoccupations of previous analysts, however, by asking: Given a development labor policy, what determines the degree to which it succeeds or fails? And given the new role for trade unions in developing nations, what determines their ability to fulfill that role?

One of my principal contentions is that the answers to these two questions partially coincide; the development labor policy of the government fails in part because the union is unable to fulfill the productionist role assigned it by the government.

The failure of the union, derives largely from the lack of agreement within the union as to whose interests are paramount—those
of the workers or the government. While government succeeds to
a surprising degree in making the Head Office leaders conceive of
their interests as being the public interest, the interests of the local
branch officials remain those of the workers. This disagreement
results in the inability of the union to perform as a coherent and
cohesive organization in support of the government's program.
Equally as important as the fact of disagreement is the pattern of
disagreement within the union. The policy is denied union support where it is needed most: at the branch level, where closest
contact is maintained with the workers. And because the pattern
of disagreement parallels the distribution of power in the union,
the ability of the union to give organized support to the government's policy is further diminished.

Also significant is the nature of the relationship between the
local branch leaders and the mineworkers themselves. The local
leaders simply do not possess the resources necessary to induce the
members of the mining community to act contrary to their conception of their interests. The union's structure is ill-suited for
downward communications, especially when the viewpoints they
wish to transmit are at variance with the interests of the workers.
Moreover, the local branch leaders lack the legitimacy required to
obtain the workers' support for the government's program.

The union is thus an unreliable instrument for government
policy. And from the government's point of view, its reliability is
further diminished by its persisting autonomy from the governing party. In seeking to explain the failure of the government's
policy, however, we are compelled to acknowledge that the union's
failure also results from the very militancy of the attitudes it is
called upon to alter. The demands of the workers for equality and
the racially stratified structure of the mining community make it
extremely difficult for the union or the government to reduce and
contain the militant nature of labor relations in the copper industry.

There remains the problem of determining the general relevance of this analysis. Several considerations lead me to believe that what was found to be true in Zambia may well be true elsewhere. The most important is that the factors cited are highly general in nature. One factor is the existence of radical leaders at the local level. This is an unspectacularly common phenomenon, but while commonplace, it gains great importance when applied to the study of development labor policies. It should be of general value in explaining the failure of other unions to implement development programs.[1] Another is the union's decentralized power structure. In keeping with their role of detecting and advancing membership interests, many trade unions possess decentralized structures of power. Insofar as this frustrates the ability of national leaders to impose collective policies on the union, this attribute should also help explain the inability of unions elsewhere to implement development policies.[2] A third factor is the structure of communication. It can be assumed that most unions make contact with their members on a case basis, that is, when grievances arise; and it is generally found that union meetings are poorly attended, the finding being phrased in terms of membership apathy.[3] In this study, I found these two phenomena to be extremely valuable in explaining the inability of the union to disseminate government programs. Also important is the failure of the government's campaign for union support to penetrate to the local branch level. The confinement of political communications to the level of national elites and the failure of government programs to penetrate to the lower social strata are general characteristics of developing systems.[4] This factor too should therefore be relevant to explanations for the failure of unions elsewhere to fulfill development roles.

A last set of factors was of great importance: the attributes of the social structure of the mining industry. These too should be of relevance elsewhere. Foreign, racially alien managers dominate other economies in Africa, although this is rapidly changing. One need only think of the Levantines, the Asians, the British, and the French, all of whom have occupied commanding positions in the economies of many African nations. As to the occupational homogeneity of the mine townships, this also has been related to the militancy of the labor force of mines and other industries in other countries; thus, it too should help to explain the failure of productionist labor policies in other settings.[5]

The factors which we employed to explain the failure of the Mineworkers' Union to assist in the implementation of the government's development labor policy operate in other unions and in other nations. Insofar as this work has charted now ground in the study of labor and development, it has done so, therefore, with concepts that are more than parochial in nature. Other analysts should find them useful and other studies should bear out their explanatory power.

The Case of Zambia and Development Theory

In this study of the implementation of a development labor policy in Zambia, I have addressed myself to processes which range beyond the confines of the field of labor and development and impinge upon the more general concerns of development theory.

In seeking to regulate the behavior of the mineworkers, the government of Zambia, in the terms of development theory, is attempting to intervene in its economic environment. The government attempts to implement its policies through the union and party. In the terms of development theory, this represents an attempt to use structures which specialize in the articulation of demands for the purpose of regulation and control. To increase its capacity, the government of Zambia, like the governments of many other African nations, attempts to employ input structures to perform output functions.

In the body of this study, comparative data was presented on the response of the union and party to the government's labor policy. While the two organizations operate in separate domains, and while neither succeeds in implementing the government's program, it is nonetheless apparent that the party more readily served as an output structure than did the union. The contrasting responses of the union and party therefore offer an opportunity for formulating hypotheses about the ability of organizations to undertake output functions in developing political systems.

For convenience, in the following paragraphs, I use a common term—intermediate organizations—to refer to the union and party. The term highlights their common characteristic of spanning the gap between the national government and major groups in its environment. It is this characteristic, after all, which renders these organizations attractive means for reaching and influencing key groups in the political system.

The Determinants of Output Capabilities

In my analysis of the union and party, I focused on three sets of relationships: those between the organization and the government, those between the superior and local officials within the organization, and those between the local officials and the members. In the last resort, the ability of an intermediate organization to regulate its members determines its effectiveness as an agency of government policy. I therefore label our propositions concerning the last set of relationships as propositions about the *effectiveness* of the organization. Propositions concerning relations between local officials and their superiors, we label transmission propositions. We measure *transmission* in terms of the ability of the organization to gain cooperation with government policy from its local officials. And those propositions that characterize the relationships between the government and the officials of an organization we label responsiveness propositions. *Responsiveness* we measure in terms of the willingness of the leaders of an organization to utilize their organization as an agency of government policy.

The scheme is appropriate to the analysis of output functions, for it is sensitive to the flow of policy from the governmental center, through the hierarchy of the intermediate organization, and down to the rank and file. Moreover, it is appropriate to the data, and captures the essential differences between the union and the party. Neither the party nor the union was effective in implementing the government's policy. But in terms of its responsiveness to the government's program, and its ability to transmit policy to the local level, UNIP was a superior output agency. In capturing these distinctions, the scheme takes on an additional virtue: it highlights the several elements that go into the formation of an overall output capability. Our threefold breakdown enables us to make comparisons along the variety of dimensions inherent in the notion.

RESPONSIVENESS. Our study suggests that the ability of intermediate organizations to implement government policies depends upon the willingness of their leaders to do so. In turn, the responsiveness of the leaders of intermediate organizations depends upon the ability of government to expose them to the content of its policies while furnishing inducements for their support. Inducements include the attribution of national status, the conferment of prestige, and the prospects of mobility into the political sector. These factors account for variations in the response of the national and local leaders of the union. Moreover, the contrasting response of union and party leaders relates to their different levels of exposure to government policies and to the contrasting material and psychic benefits that accrue to them as a result of their cooperation.

TRANSMISSION. The ability of an organization to serve as an output structure depends upon its capacity to evoke cooperation with government policy from its local leaders. When the organization lacks the ability to transmit policies to the local level, then it is unable to implement these policies among its members. The union's failure to serve as an output structure stems in large part from its inability to gain adherence to the government's policies among its local leaders. By contrast, the party does gain such cooperation. In this respect, the party is a superior output structure.

The ability of an intermediate organization to serve as an output structure depends upon its distribution of power. Organizations in which power distributes hierarchically are better able to implement policies than those with a decentralized distribution. A hierarchical distribution facilitates the imposition of policy upon lower-level leaders, the penalizing of deviance from the viewpoints of the center, and the provision of rewards to subordinates who are loyal to the central point of view. Thus, the party secures the fidelity of the local branch leaders to government policy, while the union does not, in part because the distribution of power in the party favors the regional secretary to a greater degree than the power distribution of the union favors the Head Office. The ability of an intermediate organization to evoke coopera- tion at the local level depends upon the mobility pattern within that organization. Where local leaders utilize the organization as a means of advancement, and where their access to higher posi- tions is mediated by those advocating conformity with govern- ment policy, then leaders of the organization have the power to reward and punish subordinate officials and to evoke cooperation with the government's viewpoint. Thus, differences between the responses of local union and party leaders correspond to differences in the degree to which government spokesmen mediate their pros- pects for advancement. However, where promotion entails too great a shift in values and norms of conduct, a "boomerang" effect may result. The mobile official may resolve the conflict engendered by his aspirations through the adoption of radical, "counterelite" behavior: thus the radical behavior of union branch officials which we discussed in chapter 5.

EFFECTIVENESS. The capacity of an organization to serve as an output structure depends upon its ability to communicate down- ward to its members. The most important determinant of this ability is the organization's capacity to render its members a cap- tive audience. The number of officials; the ratio of officials to mem- bers; the frequency with which officials initiate contacts with their members; and the frequency, size, and demeanor of meetings ap- pear to be the most significant determinants of the organization's ability to capture its members for purposes of communication. Also important is the presence or absence of cell units in which leaders can present and defend government policies before small audi- ences, achieve a high degree of participation and involvement on the part of the members, and utilize social pressures to achieve an acceptance of the leaders' point of view. Differences in the effec- tiveness of the union and party as channels for downward com- munications stem from differences in these properties.

The ability of intermediate organizations to assist in the imple- mentation of government policies is a function of the legitimacy of their leaders in the eyes of the members. A leader is legitimate when his followers concede him the right to formulate and propound policies despite their disagreement with the content of these policies. In intermediate organizations, legitimacy is gained when the leaders convince their followers that they are sensitive to and willing to defend their interests. The greater usefulness of the party as an output structure derives in large part from the greater legitimacy of its leaders.

While an intermediate organization may possess an adequate structure of downward communications and sufficient legitimacy to disseminate government policy, it will not be an effective output structure unless it possesses resources for rewarding or punishing the behavior of its members. While UNIP possesses many of the elements necessary to serve as an effective output structure, it lacks this ability to reward and punish the mineworkers; as a result, the party fails to motivate them actually to cooperate with the policies it so vigorously broadcasts at the local level.

Lastly, the ability of an organization to serve as an effective output structure is a function of the intensity of the attitudes of its members which the organization is asked to modify. The basic attitudes which government strives to alter are in fact deeply held, and the militant attitudes of labor are deeply anchored in the social organization of the mining community. The overall failure of the union and party in implementing government labor policy is thus a function of the intensity of the attitudes which the two organizations had been asked to counter.

The Relationship between Input and Output Capabilities

There remains a last basic question: Is there a necessary contradiction between an intermediate organization's ability to perform input and output functions in a political system? The data strongly suggest there is not.

Rather than being incompatible with the performance of an output function, the performance of an input function would appear to be a prerequisite of an organization's ability to regulate and control the behavior of its members. The two are not contradictory. Rather the two must go together; for the intermediate organization to succeed as an output structure, it has also to succeed as an input structure. The intervening factor is legitimacy. Leaders of intermediate organizations legitimize their position by performing input roles; and their legitimacy enables them to propound and seek to enforce unpopular policies. Thus, the party is a superior output agency because its leaders acquire a reputation as fearless and powerful spokesmen for the interests of the members. By contrast, the union leaders appear unwilling to champion the interests of their members against the European management; failing to convince their members of their ability to perform input functions, they lack the legitimacy required to perform an output function.

While the performance of output and input functions must go together, in our study they did not do so. There seem to be special conditions under which input capabilities translate into output capabilities, and one of these is the presence of social differentiation.[6] The importance of differentiation is underscored by the dilemma which so painfully confronts the leaders of the Mineworkers' Union. They are dedicated to the advancement of the demands of the mine employees as working men; but it is precisely these demands which they are asked by government to moderate and contain. And unless they can sponsor the demands of the workers, they lose the ability to restrain them. Were the union to serve other interests of its members besides their interests as industrial laborers, it could then exchange services to its members in the nonindustrial sphere for concessions in labor relations.[7]

The assertion that UNIP fails to become an effective output structure, despite its vigorous championship of the interests of its members, further illustrates the role of social differentiation in the transformation of input into output capabilities. UNIP leaders dedicate themselves to the betterment of their members as Africans, while striving to regulate their behavior as industrial workers. But it is precisely the lack of differentiation between the interests of its members as workers and Africans that makes it impossible for the party to transform its input capabilities into output performance. Were the interests separate, indulgences in the one field could be exchanged for concessions in the other. But lacking the differentiation of interests, the tactic is confounded.

The data suggest other factors which limit the capacity of input organizations to perform output functions. These constraints are structural in nature.

While an organization may be equipped to perform input functions, it may lack the properties necessary for the performance of output functions. Thus, the union possesses a structure well suited to the performance of input functions; it can detect and transmit upward the demands of the members. However, the union structure is inadequate for the performance of output functions. In contrast to the party, the union does not furnish its leaders with means of rendering their followers a captive audience, and therefore cannot insure the transmission of their viewpoints to the rank and file. A comparison of the union and party structures suggests the additional properties which an intermediary organization must possess to function as an output structure: a large and pervasive network of officials and a cellular structure, with inclusive, lower-level membership units through which officials can agitate in support of their points of view.

The data also suggest that an organization should possess a hierarchical distribution of power in order to perform output functions. A decentralized power structure suffices for the performance of input functions. Lower-level leaders are in a better position to detect the grievances of the members than are leaders at the center; and where the organization is designed to fulfill the demands of its members, it is appropriate that the lower-level leaders have the power to act in response to these demands. However, when the organization is designed for the implementation of policy from the leaders at its center, then a hierarchical power structure is more appropriate. Thus, the decentralized power structure of the union is perfectly in keeping with its role as an input structure, but frustrates the ability of the Head Office to commit the union to the enforcement of a development labor policy. UNIP, however, is able to secure adherence to central policies by its lower-level units. In comparison with the union, therefore, UNIP is better able to disseminate and strive to implement government policy at the local level.

A last structural requisite for the performance of output functions is access to inducements and sanctions. If the organization is to gain adherence to policies from its members, it must be able to reward those who cooperate and penalize those who do not. Thus the lack of access to such resources frustrates UNIP's ability to perform effectively as an output structure.

The answer to the initial question, therefore, is that an intermediate organization *must* perform input functions in order to serve as an output structure. However, as we consider the data, this initial proposition acquires a series of limiting conditions. The input capabilities of an organization translate into output capabilities only when the interests of its members are differentiated and when additional structural features are acquired. That the racial structure of the mines reduces the differentiation of the interests of the miners, and that both UNIP and the union lack the necessary structural properties, means that in the end neither the party nor the union can serve as an effective output structure. And it is in part because the intermediate organizations lack these properties and operate under these social conditions that the government of Zambia fails in its attempts to implement its development labor program.

10 Postscript

This study has dealt with the immediate pre- and postindependence period in Zambia. At the time I left the field—May 1968—the government had been in power for but three and one-half years. In this postscript, my analysis is carried briefly into the later years of the postindependence era.

Since the research was completed, the government has vastly increased its efforts to harness the copper revenues for development purposes, by nationalizing the mines and by attempting vast increases in mineral production. In August 1969, President Kaunda announced the government's intention to purchase a controlling share of the assets of Roan Selection Trust and Anglo-American Corporation. In November of that year, the government and companies announced the mechanics of the takeover. The government purchased 51 percent of the book values of the companies, as assessed on 30 December 1969, making the purchase in government bonds. The payments are to be made in installments over the next several years, and are to be accelerated should the industry prove exceptionally profitable.[1] RST and AAC have reincorporated as Roan Consolidated Mines and Nchanga Consolidated Copper Mines. They will operate under management and sales contracts, and will thus continue to produce and sell copper, but as contractors rather than proprietors of the mines. The government now appoints six of the eleven directors of each company, including the chairmen of the boards.[2]

The government vested control of the copper industry in the newly formed Zambia Industrial and Mining Corporation. The Corporation has two major subgroups: the Mining and Industrial Development Corporation (MINDECO), which controls the mining companies, and the Industrial Development Corporation (INDECO), which promotes the development of new industries in Zambia. President Kaunda is chairman of the parent corporation. Andrew Sardanis, the president's chief economic advisor, is managing director of the parent body and chairman of both subsidiaries.[3] (See Appendix 2.)

The government is thus the primary, direct recipient of the revenues of the copper industry. And the mining industry has been incorporated into the bureaucratic-cum-managerial structure whose principal function is to sponsor industrial development in Zambia. The nationalization of the mines thus represents an institutionalization of the relationships between the government, the copper industry, and the developing sectors in Zambia, as they were conceived of at the time of our study. There are indications that the expected correlative in labor policy is also coming to pass: a more direct appreciation by government of the consequences of labor militancy for its development objectives. Thus, following the nationalization of the mines, President Kaunda stated:

> The revolutionary measures we have taken of controlling a number of major industries in the country means one very important thing and this is that if the workers decisively put their shoulders to the wheel and greater profits accrue, . . . the Government and therefore the people would benefit from these profits through our share of fifty-one percent.[4]

More dramatically, he "reminded Zambian workers that the nation's share of the profits of the mining industry is K 87 for every K 100 profit and appealed to them to work hard and increase production in the interests of the nation."[5] Referring to a strike in another government-owned industry, President Kaunda equated the strike with a strike against the people of Zambia and a blow to their economic well-being.[6] It is therefore apparent that nationalization has clarified the link between the conduct of labor and the success of development efforts, and strengthened the government's resolve to curtail the militancy of labor.

The government has also promoted the rapid expansion of the mining industry. At the urging of government, the companies have reopened Bwana Mkubwa and Kansanshi mines; developed means for recovering and processing low grade and oxidized ores; and opened two new mines—Baluba and Kalengwa. Moreover, in a national referendum, the government acquired the power to alter fundamental rights in property through parliamentary enactment. It used this power to assume title to all mineral deposits in the country. Having acquired these properties, the government encouraged foreign companies to enter into joint mining ventures; so far, it has registered six such companies.[7]

Within the mining industry, the patterns of tension and conflict in labor relations have persisted since my field work was completed. The roots of these tensions are familiar: the determination by Africans to receive the same wages as expatriates working on similar jobs. The union and companies agreed to negotiate a single basic wage scale for the mining industry which would cover expatriate and local workers alike. Following a massive, industry-wide job evaluation, they negotiated the new wage structure. The result was an increase in basic wages of 10 percent, one-half being retroactive to 1 November 1969, the date of the termination of the last contract.[8] During the course of these negotiations, Rhokana Corporation, the mine I had studied, experienced several strikes, the origins of which should be familiar to the readers of this book.

The instigators of one strike were African winding engine drivers—workers who occupy one of the elite jobs in the mines.* A driver who had participated in the strike was quoted as saying: "Since we took the job from expatriates we have carried it on in a responsible manner. . . . There have been no reports of accidents or damage to engines. But . . . we have not received equal shares with the expatriates."[9] There have also been strikes in Nchanga, and these were also precipitated by high grade employees: section bosses, who protested the racist conduct of an expatriate superior.[10] The contemporary tensions in labor re-

---

* Winding engine drivers operate the hoists which lower the cages down the mine shafts. They are responsible for the lives of the one hundred or so men in the cage and for the smooth flow of labor, ore, and equipment between the surface and underground departments.

lations in the mines thus remain similar to those which I observed during the study.

In the face of the failure of its labor policy, as documented in this study, the government has made a new departure in its labor program: a trend away from voluntarism and toward more direct public intervention in labor relations. In August 1969, President Kaunda announced a wage freeze. It is to last until the government institutes a Wages, Prices, and Productivity Council, which will be empowered to investigate all proposed wage increases and to make recommendations concerning their acceptability. As an incentive to labor productivity, the council will "give virtually automatic approval to increases where effective payment-by-results (piece-rate) schemes had been introduced." [11] The council is to file its recommendations with another new body, the Industrial Court. The court is to be empowered to make binding judgments on all proposed wage increases and trade disputes referred to it by the Ministry of Labour. There are no provisions for appeal. The court will award wage increases only when it finds indisputable evidence of concomitant increases in labor productivity.[12] In conformity with this policy, the Mineworkers' Union and the mining companies have agreed that under the terms of the new wage agreement, the union will cooperate in implementing measures for achieving greater efficiency and reducing production costs.[13] The government has thus heightened its efforts to implement the wage tenet of its labor policy and to stem the postindependence flow of inflated wage demands.

These efforts have been accompanied by fiscal and monetary measures, designed to curtail the rapid inflation of the late 1960s. The government has increased income and excise taxes, the discount rate, and charges for bank loans. Paralleling its freeze on wages, the government has frozen prices. Even more dramatically, it has used its power over the major retail stores, which it nationalized in 1968, to reduce prices on basic consumer goods. The inflation of the 1960s has thus precipitated a vastly increased level of government intervention in the economy, and, by recent reports, these efforts are meeting with some success.[14]

The last major change has been in the sphere of union-government relations. Immediately following the nationalization of the mines, the government consummated its policy of cooptation by appointing the president of the Mineworkers' Union to the board of directors of the Zambia Industrial and Mining Corporation and the general secretary to the board of INDECO. This measure was paralleled by similar appointments in other industries. Cooptation has intensified a second trend which we noted in our study: the growth of the cleavages between the national and local levels of the union. Almost immediately after the government announced its appointments, local branch leaders at Roan demanded the resignation of the union's president. Accusing him of "selling out," they challenged his ability to negotiate effectively against a company which he now helped to manage.[15] However, there was an intriguing denouement to this incident: the Head Office successfully insisted on the dismissal of the dissident local leaders and a senior Head Office official who had apparently supported them. This suggests that the Head Office has enhanced its power position since the time of my field work. If this is true, it bespeaks an increased capability on the part of the union to implement government policy.[16]

There was a generational element to this split. Several of the protesting local leaders were prominent preindependence leaders in the union. The purged Head Office official had secured national office before independence and had become union president in 1965; however, in 1968, he was displaced to the honorary post of chairman. The reason given was that he was illiterate in English and thus an embarrassment to the other union leaders; with him as president, the other officials felt unable to convince the government that the union possessed a dynamic and effective leadership, able to cope with the industrial problems of a developing nation. The Head Office's purge of this official and the Roan branch officers therefore represents a successful attempt to consolidate its power position and to enforce upon the "old unionists" its conception of the responsible role of the union in a postindependence society.

In the union elections of November 1970, the generational split again opened when a former president of the union challenged the incumbent president, David Mwila. At the height of the struggle between UNIP and the union, it had been this former president who had issued the statement of no confidence in the minister of labor (see chap. 7). In the 1970 elections, he successfully sought the chairmanship of the dissident local at Roan; he was soundly defeated, however, in his quest of the presidency at the Head Office level. Following his defeat, the government appointed him to a public office which required that he surrender his position in the union. The current Head Office thus once again survived a resurgence from the branch level of the old generation of trade unionists.[17]

The government is sensitive to the growing disparity between the viewpoints of the national and local officials, and has moved to counter the trend. It has insisted on the formation of works councils at the local plant level. In these councils, the management will consult with local union officials in making industrial decisions. Management, it is hoped, will thereby come to appreciate labor's point of view; equally important, labor will also learn to appreciate the perspective and problems of management. In addition, the Congress of Trade Unions has increasingly focused its training programs on local branch officials. Branch leaders are now being schooled in the government's labor policy and in the implications of labor militancy for the economy of the nation. Soon they will attend the government's Mulungushi Citizenship Training College, where they will be instructed in the essential techniques of labor organization and collective bargaining, in government economic policy, and in the philosophy of Humanism.[18] In these ways, the government has attempted to involve the local branch leaders in programs which expose them to public officials and public policies and to instill in them a broader perspective on the role of labor in their industries and their nation.

A last event which must be mentioned is the Turner report. Alarmed at the failure of its labor program, the government requested the United Nations Development Programme (UNDP) to conduct a study of wages, productivity, and economic development in postindependence Zambia. The UNDP dispatched H. A. Turner, professor of industrial relations at Cambridge Uni-

versity, and he filed a report which was truly distressing.[19] According to Turner, less than one-quarter of the increase in the
gross domestic product which had taken place since independence
in Zambia was due to increase in output; more than half was
the result of the increased price of copper. Average productivity
had decreased 12 percent since independence, despite vast increases in capital investment. On top of the decline in productivity, industrial discipline had broken down and wages had risen.
The overall import of the report was clear: the workers had failed
to contribute their share to Zambia's development effort. Zambia's
economic growth had resulted not from its own efforts, but from
the price of copper—a factor largely outside of Zambia's control.

The report occasioned heated controversy in Zambia. The basis
of the criticism was simply that the report was too antilabor. Thus,
as his critics point out, Turner failed to acknowledge the debilitating effects of UDI on productivity, the supply of fuels and raw
materials, and the rising cost structure of Zambia's economy. He
ignored the adverse consequences for labor productivity of the
state of race relations in postindependence Zambia, and the flight
of experienced managers and skilled manpower. Just as Turner
argued that Zambia's economic growth was caused by factors
beyond its control, Turner's critics stress that the poor performance
of Zambia's workers resulted from factors largely beyond the control of the workers themselves.[20]

On two things Turner and his critics agree: after independence
in Zambia, productivity declined and wages rose. They disagree
on the reasons for the decline, with Turner placing the onus on
labor and his critics emphasizing the impact of a host of other
factors, and particularly Rhodesia's UDI. Turner and his critics
also disagree on the impact of wage increases on inflation in
Zambia. In this debate, I clearly side with Turner's critics. The
emphasis should be placed on the complex of factors which influence the conduct of the mineworkers—for example, the effects
of racial structure of the mining community, the impact of independence on stratification patterns in the mines, and the properties of the organizations which influence the mineworkers' be-

havior. While I side with Turner's critics, however, I am too aware of the limitation of this study to believe that it will extinguish the controversy. Nor would I aspire to do so. For only such debates can generate new ideas, new hypotheses, and new alternatives for decision makers in Zambia.

Appendix 1   Evaluation of Quantitative Data

The single largest body of quantitative data employed in this study is composed of information on labor disputes at Rhokana, Nchanga, Mufulira, and Roan for the years 1950 to 1968 (the life of the Mineworkers' Union). Largely on the basis of this information, I drew inferences concerning the state of pre- and post-independence labor relations; the contrasting responses of the Head Office and local branches of the union to government labor policy; and the causes of local branch radicalism.

To collect the data, I culled the monthly reports filed by the labor officers stationed in Kitwe, Chingola, Luanshya, and Mufulira. These reports covered the activities of the labor officer and recorded his observations on subjects of concern to the labor department: housing, sanitation, labor migration, township conditions, and so forth. Concentrating on the sections on labor relations, the occurrence of labor disputes in the mines were noted. For each dispute, the following information* was collected:

A. Who initiated the dispute?
   1. The workers
      a) Their department   c) Their grades
      b) Their job   d) Their shift
   2. The union alone

B. What was the issue of the dispute?
   1. Wages   7. Labor flow
   2. Task   8. Supervision
   3. Bonuses   9. Union rights
   4. Hours   10. Jurisdiction
   5. Township conditions 11. Other
   6. Clothing

* A copy of the code book, which is more detailed, is available on request.

C. What was the method of settlement?
1. Who were the parties to the dispute?
   a) The local branch
   b) The Head Office
   c) The labor officer
   d) The level of management
2. What was the role of the Head Office?
3. To what level did the dispute escalate?
   a) Negotiations
   b) Conciliation
   c) Arbitration

D. What was the course of the dispute?
1. Was there a strike?
   a) If so, how long?
   b) If so, how many workers were involved?
   c) If so, was it official or unofficial?
2. How long did the dispute go on?
3. What was the outcome? Was it a union
   a) Victory?   c) Loss?
   b) Compromise?   d) Don't know?

While the data are intriguing, there are major gaps; and these restricted their use in the study. There is almost no information on the number of workers involved in each dispute; as a result, I could not determine the causes of different magnitudes of disputes. Secondly, the information on who initiated the dispute is very spotty. As a result, it was impossible to determine what kinds of workers were more militant than others, and thus specify more precisely the causes of worker radicalism. Nonetheless, the data did support extensive sections of the analysis; and they must therefore be scrutinized critically.

In evaluating the data, I tried to answer three questions. How well did I cover the data? How well do the results correspond with records kept by independent sources? And how much were the data affected by the predispositions of those that filed the reports in the first place? That is, how much selective reporting was there by the labor officers who wrote the reports from which the data were gathered?

Reliability

I assessed my own performance by comparing the counts extracted from the monthly reports of the labor officers with the counts made from the same reports by the labor department itself. The obvious comparison would have been between my data and the data published in the annual reports of the labor department. However, an examination of the annual reports revealed that the department included varying proportions of the incidents reported by its field officers. Some years, the department appears to have included only those incidents which met the legal requirements for a labor dispute, while in other years, it did not apply this stricture. This variation in the rules for including or excluding information from monthly reports nullified the value of the annual reports as a standard for evaluating my coverage of this material. Moreover, the annual reports aggregated the information in all the copper mines while my data covered only Rhokana, Nchanga, Roan, and Mufulira. As a result it would have been difficult to interpret differences that appeared; and this would have been particularly difficult for those periods during which new mines came into production.

There was another standard available, however: the data submitted by the labor department to the Branigan Commission of 1956. Because the labor department was trying to prove the irresponsibility of the Mineworkers' Union in its submissions to the Branigan Commission, the department reported every incident in the mines that came to its attention over the period 1951-55. As the department did not filter information coming from its officers in the field in compiling these counts, its submission could form a standard for evaluating my own coding. Moreover, the data were gathered at a time in which the only mines in production were the four for which I too had gathered data. Differences between my counts and those of the labor department therefore could not be attributed to differences in the number of mines or miners.

A comparison of my data with the tables in the Branigan testimony reveals that in any given year, the two counts did indeed differ. Over a five-year period, however, my counts almost precisely correspond to the department's records (table 61). This

TABLE 61
Incidents with No Loss of Work

Year	My count	Count of Labour Department	Difference
1951	5	3	+2
1952	2	4	−2
1953	6	5	+1
1954	5	7	−2
1955	14	13	+1
Total	32	32	—

result suggests that the data are presented in the monthly reports in a manner which makes it difficult to decide what is and what is not an incident, and therefore what should or should not be counted; but that this difficulty is not so great as to produce significantly different counts by different analysts over a large number of cases. In other words, I was able to code the reports well enough to consider my data reliable over a large number of cases, but not well enough to consider them reliable when the number of cases is small.

Criterion Validity

To evaluate the data through a comparison with an independent source, I looked for compilations kept by the mining industry. The Copper Industry Service Bureau (CISB) compiled quantitative data on labor relations only intermittently. However, for a little over a year it kept fairly precise counts of the frequency of work stoppages.

I compared my counts with the CISB records for the period September 1963 to December 1964 (table 62). The result is a small difference between my counts and those of CISB. It is evi-

TABLE 62
Number of Work Stoppages

Period	My count	CISB count	Difference
Last quarter 1963	17	18	−1
1964	24	30	−6
Total	41	48	−7

dent that the labor department recorded fewer work stoppages than the mines themselves experienced, however.

To test the data further, I broke down work stoppages into constitutional and unconstitutional strikes. Further sorting the data by mines, I compared the four-fold breakdowns with CISB's records (table 63). The results were heartening. While the tend-

TABLE 63
Constitutionality of Stoppages
(By mine)

Constitutionality of work stoppages	Rhokana		Nchanga		Roan		Mufulira	
	My data	CISB data	My data	CISB data	My data	CISB data	My data	CISB data
Unconstitutional	1	1	18	22	3	3	2	4
Constitutional	0	0	0	0	0	0	0	0

ency toward undercounting persisted, no tendency toward misclassification appeared. The mines and the labor department both agreed that none of the strikes were constitutional, and they portrayed similar distributions of strikes among the four mines.

Selective Reporting

The last test I applied was to assess the degree to which the content of the reports was influenced by their authorship, and thus failed to reflect what "really" took place on the mines. One way of assessing the effect of the reporters themselves was to determine whether or not different labor officers tended to file different accounts of labor relations at the same mine. To determine the degree to which such selective reporting took place, I located cases in which a labor officer for a given mine was displaced by a successor and then compared the reports of the two officers. The number of cases for which it was possible to make such comparisons was small, as it was necessary to have two years of reports for each labor officer in order for the number of incidents to be large enough to make meaningful comparisons. However, I was able to ferret out one suitable comparison for each mine. I then compared the relative frequency with which different agencies—union branch, Head Office, and the labor officer himself—were reported as participating in disputes, and the relative frequency of peaceful as opposed to lost-work incidents.

The results of the comparison suggest that the contents of the reports were not influenced by the interests or reporting habits of the officers themselves (table 64). For a given mine, succeeding

TABLE 64
Selective Reporting

	Union agency involved							Severity			
	Branch		Head Office		Labour officer		No strike		Strike		
Mine/Year	N	%	N	%	N	%	N	%	N	%	N
Mufulira											
1949–50	15	100	0	0	0	0	12	80	3	20	15
1953–54	20	91	1	4.5	1	4.5	17	85	3	15	20
Roan											
1950–51	11	85	2	15	0	0	11	100	0	0	11
1952–53	18	66	6	23	3	11	16	89	2	11	18
Rhokana											
1957–58	7	58	1	8	4	33	7	100	0	0	7
1959–60	1	50	0	0	1	50	1	100	0	0	1
Nchanga											
1957–58	21	88	2	8	1	4	21	100	0	0	21
1960–61	6	86	1	14	0	0	5	84	1	16	6

Note: The N's for the "union agency involved" are greater than for "severity of disputes," since for any given dispute, more than one agency may be involved. Percentages refer to the proportion of agency actions taken by a given agency, rather than the proportion of labor disputes that the agency was involved in.

labor officers tend to report similar relative frequencies of peaceful and lost-work disputes. So too in their portrayals of the relative frequency with which different agencies become involved in mine. The last agreement is made more striking by the case of Rhokana Corporation. While labor officers are portrayed as less likely to be involved in disputes than either the Head Office or branch at Roan, Nchanga, and Mufulira mines, labor officers are reported to be more likely than the Head Office to be involved in disputes at Rhokana. Were this distinctive pattern an artifact of the man who wrote the reports for Rhokana, then it would be doubtful that the pattern would persist through a succession of labor officers.

In conclusion, therefore, the data do not appear to have been affected by the authorship of the records from which they were gleaned, for different labor officers file similar reports for a given mine. Nor do the results appear to have been biased by performance in coding; my counts agree fairly closely with those made from the same data by the labor department, when the number of cases is large. Lastly, my records accord with those kept by an independent source, CISB, save insofar as my data slightly underrepresent the number of incidents that take place on the mines. So long as the data are not employed to make precise statements, they should therefore tend to be reliable and valid. And so long as they are not used to make statements about absolute values, they should support generalizations about labor relations in the mines. In this study, I have attempted to respect these limitations while making inferences from this data.

Appendix 2   Structure of Ownership of the Mines

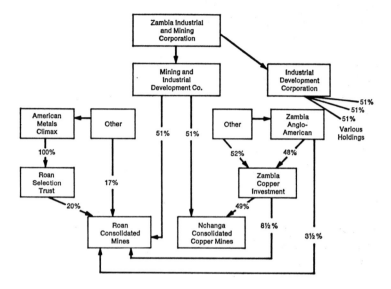

Adapted, with permission, from *Zambia Business Mail,* 15 April 1970.

Notes

The following conventions have been adopted in citing archival materials:

Where the note reads "File" followed by a number (generally 100 or above), the materials are from the collection of the Copper Industry Service Bureau, Kitwe.

Where the note reads "File" and then a letter (e.g. File A19) the materials are from the files of Rhokana Corporation, Nkana. The sole exception is in the case of files numbered S; these are CISB files, save where specifically noted otherwise.

Where the note cites file numbers reading "Sec/ . . .", the file is from the Secretariat of the colonial government, and is located in the National Archives of the Republic of Zambia.

Where the note begins with any other combination (e.g. Ja/ . . . or Hl/ . . .), the file is a labor department file and is also in the National Archives, Lusaka.

Chapter 1

1 Clark Kerr et al., *Industrialism and Industrial Man*. The appendix to that book lists the other studies published by the participants in the "Inter-University Study of Labor Problems in Economic Development." Most relevant to this study have been John T. Dunlop, *Industrial Relations Systems*; Charles A. Myers, *Labor Problems in the Industrialization of India*; Reinhard Bendix, *Work and Authority in Industry*; Frederick Harbison and Ibrahim Abdelkader Ibrahim, *Human Resources for Egyptian Enterprise;* Val R. Lorwin, *The French Labor Movement*; and Daniel L. Horowitz, *The Italian Labor Movement*.

2 Kerr et al., *Industrialism*, p. 32.

3 Ibid., pp. 60–61, 110–11, and 204–07.

4 Accounting for the variety of labor policies in the industrializing nations is the predominant but not exclusive concern of the authors. A second major concern is with the creation and stabilization of the labor force. A third is with the properties of trade unions in developing areas, a subject of preoccupation in this book also.

5 See, for example, Bruce H. Millen, *The Political Role of Labor in Developing Countries*; Sidney C. Sufrin, *Unions in Emerging Societies*; Walter Galenson, "Introduction," in *Labor and Economic Development*, ed. Walter Galenson; Elliot J. Berg and Jeffrey Butler, "Trade Unions," in *Political Parties and National Integration in Tropical Africa*, ed. James S. Coleman and Carl G. Rosberg, Jr.

6 William H. Friedland, "Basic Social Trends," in *African Socialism*, ed. William H. Friedland and Carl G. Rosberg, Jr., p. 19.

7 Galenson, "Introduction." The following studies point out that most often, the conversion to a productionist role is involuntary; Berg and Butler, "Trade Unions"; G. E. Lynd, *The Politics of African Trade Unionism;* and Jean Meynaud and Anisse Salah-Bey, *Trade Unionism in Africa.*

8 One of the few attempts to answer these questions is made by William H. Friedland in his article, "Labor's Role in Emerging African Socialist States," in *The Role of Labor in African Nation-Building*, ed. Willard A. Beling, pp. 20–38.

9 Martin L. Kilson, "Authoritarianism and Single-Party Tendencies in African Politics," *World Politics* 15 (1963): 262–94; Immanuel Wallerstein, *Africa: The Politics of Independence*; Coleman and Rosberg, *Political Parties.*

The major studies of the postindependence position of trade unions as interest groups are by Berg and Butler, "Trade Unions"; and Michael F. Lofchie and Carl G. Rosberg, Jr., "The Political Status of African Trade Unions," in *The Role of Labor in African Nation-Building*, ed. Willard A. Beling.

10 James S. Coleman and Carl G. Rosberg, Jr., "Introduction," in Coleman and Rosberg, *Political Parties*, p. 7.

11 For a discussion of these notions in development theory, see Gabriel A. Almond and G. Bingham Powell, Jr., *Comparative Politics*, pp. 25–30; Gabriel A. Almond, "Introduction," in *The Politics of the Developing Areas*, ed. Gabriel A. Almond and James S. Coleman; David Easton, "An Approach to the Analysis of Political Systems," *World Politics* 9 (1957): 383–400, later expanded in book form in David Easton, *A Systems Analysis of Political Life.*

12 For an admirable statement of both sides of the issue, see the discussion in Ioan Davies, *African Trade Unions.* In his concluding chapter Davies indicates the international implications of the superimposition of the cold war struggle upon this already heated issue. One of the most thoughtful and balanced statements of the second

position is to be found in the concluding paragraphs of Meynaud and Salah-Bey, *Trade Unionism*.

Chapter 2

1   L[ewis] H. Gann, *A History of Northern Rhodesia*, pp. 181–82.
2   J. W. Davidson, *The Northern Rhodesian Legislative Council*, p. 69.
3   Robert I. Rotberg, *The Rise of Nationalism in Central Africa*, p. 108.
4   Davidson, *Legislative Council*, p. 103.
5   Rotberg, *Nationalism*, p. 202.
6   Ibid., p. 203.
7   Richard C. Hall, *Zambia*, p. 124.
8   Rotberg, *Nationalism*, p. 212.
9   A. L. Epstein, *Politics in an Urban African Community*, pp. 160–61.
10   The best treatments of this period are David C. Mulford, *The Northern Rhodesia General Election* and *Zambia: The Politics of Independence, 1957–1964;* Rotberg, *Nationalism;* and Margaret Rouse Bates, "UNIP in Postindependence Zambia: The Development of an Organizational Role" (Ph.D. diss., Department of Government, Harvard University, 1971).
11   See Ian Scott and Robert Molteno, "The Zambian General Elections," *Africa Report* 14 (1969): 42–46.
12   See William J. Barber, "Federation and the Distribution of Economic Benefits, "in *A New Deal in Central Africa, ed.* Colin Leys and Cranford Pratt, pp. 81–97; and the discussion in Richard L. Sklar, "Zambia's Response to U.D.I.," *Mawazo* 1 (1968): 11–32.
13   For a discussion of these reforms, see Dennis L. Dresang, "The Civil Service in Zambia," draft version of a chapter to be published in *Government and Politics in Zambia,* ed. William Tordoff (forthcoming). Of the fifty-three district governors appointed after the reforms, only seven were civil servants; the remainder were UNIP personnel. Ibid., p. 41. Also, *Times of Zambia*, 26–28 August 1969; *Zambia Mail*, 8–10 October 1970, and 9–10 November 1970.
14   Edward Clegg, *Race and Politics,* p. 37.
15   Gann, *A History*, p. 119.
16   Clegg, *Race,* p. 37.
17   Gann, *A History*, pp. 254–56.
18   Ibid. See also, Robert E. Baldwin, *Economic Development and Export Growth.*
19   For materials on these events, see the secretariat file entitled Labour

Disturbances on the Copperbelt, May 1935, Sec/Lab/67, vols. 1 and 2. See also, Epstein, *Politics,* pp. 28–31, 64–65.

20 Secretariat, Strike by Africans on the Copperbelt, 1940, Sec/Lab/78, vol. 4.

21 Epstein, *Politics.* This is the major hypothesis of the historical portions of his study. For another excellent study of this period, see Elena L. Berger, "Labour Policies on the Northern Rhodesian Copperbelt, 1924–1964" (Ph.D. diss., Nuffield College, Oxford University, 1969).

22 Ibid., p. 31.

23 Ibid., p. 65.

24 Report on The Strike of African Employees of Rhokana Corporation 28 March to 5 April 1940, by the District Commissioner, Sec/Lab/78, vol. 4, pp. 26–27, 46–47.

25 For materials on these intermediate stages, see files J2/52/17–19. Also, The Development of Machinery of Negotiations for African Workers in the Copper Mines, 13 May 1946, J2/52/17.

26 Notes on the Events Leading to the Formation of the African Mineworkers Union (no date), Ue/3, vol. 1.

27 Materials on the planning of Comrie's appointment are contained in J4/(52/20). Materials on the positions of the main power groups, including the European Union, are contained in Sec/Lab/125. See also Notes on a Meeting Held in the Government Offices Kitwe on Monday the 28th October 1946, J2/52/18, pp. 1–7.

28 The work of this commission is covered in file J4 (52/20).

29 Monthly Reports of the Trade Union Labour Officer, November 1947–July 1948, Sec/Lab/126. See also J. R. Hooker, "The Role of the Labour Department in the Birth of African Trade Unionism in Northern Rhodesia," *International Review of Social History* 10 (1965): 1–22.

30 Epstein, *Politics,* p. 100.

31 P. K. Lomas, "African Trade Unionism on the Copperbelt of Northern Rhodesia," *South African Journal of Economics* 26 (1958): 110–22.

32 This entails largely excluding Chibuluma and Bancroft Mines, as well as Chambishi. Figures are from the Ministry of Labour, *Annual Report of the Department of Labour 1965.*

Chapter 3

1 President Kaunda, "Speech to the Governing Council of the Zambia Congress of Trade Unions," Press Release, Zambia Information Serv-

ices, 29 November 1965, p. 15 (hereafter cited as "Governing Council").

2 Republic of Zambia, Office of National Development Planning, *First National Development Plan, 1966–1970* (Lusaka: Office of National Development and Planning, July 1966), pp. 5–6 (hereafter cited as ONDP, *First National Development Plan*).

3 Ibid., pp. 40–41.

4 Ibid., pp. 56–60.

5 President Kaunda, "Governing Council," p. 15.

6 There is evidence that the interindustry differentials in wages do not merely reflect differences in the skill of the labor forces. Using education as an index of skill, note the comparisons in table 65.

TABLE 65
Average Annual Cash Earnings
of African Males, 1965
(£ per year)

Education	*Mining*	*Secondary, Nonmining*
Secondary	769	572–622
Upper Primary	562	359–392
Other	409	197

Source: Figures on mining are calculated from a 20 percent systematic random sample of the personnel records of Rhokana Corporation. Figures on nonmining are calculated from table 2 of John B. Knight, "Wages and Zambia's Economic Development" (Paper prepared for the Institute of Economics and Statistics, Oxford University, 1968, mimeographed). To appear in Charles Elliot, ed., *Constraints on the Economic Development of Zambia* (Nairobi: Oxford University Press, forthcoming).

7 ONDP, *First National Development Plan*, p. 31.

8 Ibid., p. 11.

9 Department of Economics, University of Zambia, "Taxation in the Mining Industry" (Paper submitted to the Ministry of Finance, Republic of Zambia, 1968. Typescript).

10 The best single discussion of the government's reaction to Rhodesia's declaration of independence is contained in Richard L. Sklar, "Zambia's Response to U.D.I.," *Mawazo* 1 (1968): 11–32.

11 Ministry of Labour, "Background Paper on Discipline at Work for the Ndola Labour Conference of Trade Unions" (Photocopy, Author's Collection, 29 July 1967), p. 6.

12 Ministry of Labour, "Livingstone Labour Conference 7th and 8th April 1967," Press Release, Zambia Information Services, 9 April 1967, p. 2 (hereafter cited as "Labour Conference").

13 Ibid., p. 3.

14 President Kaunda, "Speech to Luanshya-Ndola Productivity Seminar" (Photocopy, Author's Collection, 6 January 1968), p. 5.

15 Minister of Labour, "Speech to Labour Relations Course, Kitwe," Press Release, Zambia Information Services, 25 February 1967, p. 10 (hereafter cited as "Labour Relations Course").

16 Ibid., p. 5.

17 Minister of Labour, "Comments at Luanshya-Ndola Productivity Seminar" (Photocopy, Author's Collection, 6 January 1968), p. 6.

18 Ministry of Labour, "Labour Conference," p. 2.

19 Minister of Labour, "Speech to Conference of Trade Unionists," Press Release, Zambia Information Services, 29 July 1968, p. 4 (hereafter cited as "Conference of Trade Unionists").

20 Minister of Labour, "Labour Relations Course," p. 10.

21 Ibid.

22 *Zambia Pilot,* April 1965, p. 17.

23 Minister of Labour, "Conference of Trade Unionists," p. 5.

24 Ministry of Labour, "Labour Conference," p. 1.

25 Ibid., p. 4.

26 Copper Industry Service Bureau, Memorandum to General Managers on the Trade Union and Trade Disputes (Amendment) Bill, 20 November 1964, File 100–20, vol. 22.

27 Minister of Labour, "Conference of Trade Unionists," p. 8.

28 Verbatim Testimony, Brown Commission of Inquiry, 21 June 1966, pp. 74–75. Also, see Robert E. Baldwin, "Wage Policy in a Dual Economy—the Case of Northern Rhodesia," *Race* 4 (1962): 73–87. This single article appears to have greatly influenced government policy.

29 Assistant Labour Commissioner, "Speech to the Congress of Trade Unions," Press Release, Zambia Information Services, 9 December 1967, p. 5 (hereafter cited as "Speech to Trade Unions").

30 Minister of Labour, "Labour Relations Course," p. 5.

31 Minister of Labour, "Speech to the First Annual Conference of the

Z. C. T. U.," Press Release, Zambia Information Services, 16 July 1967, p. 3 (hereafter cited as "First Annual Conference").

32 Republic of Zambia, Ministry of Labour, *Hard Work and Happiness,* p. 1.

33 Ibid.

34 The University of Zambia, "Some Key Statistics of the National Development Plan" (Paper submitted to a Faculty Seminar on National Development, 14 June 1967, Lusaka. Mimeographed), p. 1.

35 Ministry of Labour, *Hard Work and Happiness,* p. 1.

36 President Kaunda, "Speech to the National Council of the United National Independence Party at Mulungushi," Press Release, Zambia Information Services, 19 April 1968, p. 1 (hereafter cited as "Mulungushi Speech").

37 Republic of Zambia, *Government Paper on the Report of the Commission of Inquiry into the Mining Industry (Brown Report, 1966),* p. 3 (hereafter cited as *Government Paper*).

38 Ibid.

39 President Kaunda, "Speech to Chingola Rally," Press Release, Zambia Information Services, 12 January 1966, p. 6 (hereafter cited as "Chingola Rally").

40 President Kaunda, "Mulungushi Speech," p. 6.

41 President Kaunda, "Governing Council," p. 23.

42 President Kaunda, "Mulungushi Speech," p. 5.

43 Ministry of Labour, "Labour Conference," p. 4.

44 Minister of Labour, "Labour Relations Course," p. 6.

45 *Zambia Pilot,* June 1964, p. 7.

46 *Zambia Pilot,* March 1964, p. 5.

47 Verbatim Testimony, Brown Commission of Inquiry, scattered throughout.

48 Republic of Zambia, *Government Paper,* pp. 3–4.

49 Republic of Zambia, *Government Paper,* p. 1.

50 Ibid., p. 3.

51 Ibid., p. 4.

52 President Kaunda, "Chingola Rally," p. 4.

53 Assistant Labour Commissioner, "Speech to Trade Unions," p. 6.

54 President Kaunda, "Governing Council," p. 23.

55 Interview, Assistant Labour Commissioner, Kitwe, 7 July 1967.

56 Minister of Labour, "Conference of Trade Unionists," p. 7.

57 President Kaunda, "Chingola Rally," p. 6.

58   President Kaunda, "Governing Council," p. 25.
59   Assistant Labour Commissioner, "Speech to Trade Unions," p. 4.
60   Republic of Zambia, *Government Paper,* p. 3.
61   Ibid., p. 4.
62   President Kaunda, "Chingola Rally," p. 4.
63   Minister of Labour, "Labour Relations Course," p. 10.
64   Minister of Labour, "Conference of Trade Unionists," p. 6.
65   Assistant Labour Commissioner, "Speech to Trade Unions," p. 6.
66   Minister of Labour, "First Annual Conference," p. 5.
67   Minister of Labour, "Conference of Trade Unionsts," pp. 4, 3.
68   Assistant Labour Commissioner, "Speech to Trade Unions," p. 3.
69   Minister of Labour, "Conference of Trade Unionists," p. 6.
70   President Kaunda, "Governing Council," p. 18.
71   Assistant Labour Commissioner, "Speech to Trade Unions," p. 4.
72   Minister of Labour, "First Annual Conference," p. 4.
73   President Kaunda, "Governing Council," p. 7.
74   In the elections of 1962, 1964, and 1968, UNIP swept all of the
     lower-roll seats on the copperbelt. In 1964, ANC contested nine of
     eleven seats in the Western Province and got 8 percent of the vote. In
     1968, it contested fifteen out of eighteen seats, and received 18 percent
     of the vote. See David C. Mulford, *The Northern Rhodesia General
     Election;* Elections Office, "Analysis of Polling: Northern Rhodesian
     General Election 1964" (Lusaka, 28 January 1964. Mimeographed);
     Parliamentary Elections Office, "Analysis of Polling: Zambia General
     Election 1968" (Lusaka, n. d. Mimeographed).
         Within two years after independence, UNIP controlled all but one
     of the municipal and township councils on the copperbelt. The sole
     "laggard" was Mufulira; and by the end of 1966 UNIP controlled
     this council as well. All the mayors on the copperbelt belong to UNIP.
         In Nkana, the mine township of Rhokana Corporation and the
     township from which most of the case materials in this book are
     drawn, no ANC candidate has entered an election for the council
     since 1962—the first year in which political parties put up candidates
     for council posts. Of the thirty-two township councillors holding
     office in 1968, only six faced opponents in the elections and none of
     their opponents were members of ANC.
         Political opposition in Zambia has centered in the Southern Prov-
     ince and in some areas of the Central Province; these retain their
     loyalty to ANC. In the 1968 elections, the Lozi areas of Barotse Prov-

ince switched their support from UNIP to ANC; this followed the growth and eventual banning of the United Party (UP), led by a former cabinet minister, Mundia. The UP rose in response to Lozi outrage over the defeat of Lozi candidates in the 1967 elections to the UNIP Central Committee and their growing feeling of neglect in the allocation of development funds. Following riots and the assassination of a UNIP official on the copperbelt, UP was banned and Lozi disaffection was expressed through votes for ANC. For a good introduction to the Barotse situation, see chapter 6 of David C. Mulford, *Zambia: The Politics of Independence, 1957–1964,* pp. 211–28. See also Robert I. Rotberg, "Tribalism and Politics in Zambia," *Africa Report* 12 (1967): 29–35; and Ian Scott and Robert Molteno, "The Zambian General Election," *Africa Report* 14 (1969): 42–46.

While the potential for political opposition prevents direct government intervention in labor relations, evidence also exists that were this potential to be realized, the level of intervention would increase dramatically. Thus, during the 1966 strikes, six trade unionists were detained. Of these, five were persons who the government believed supported the opposition party in Mufulira, and one was a person whose criticism of local UNIP officials had been widely quoted in the press. Despite the wide-scale strikes, no other union officials were arrested. The presence of a *threat to* support the opposition party thus appears to be the controlling factor in reducing coercion. (*Times of Zambia,* 7 April 1966; 30 April 1966; 17 September 1966.)

It is useful to refer to other cases in evaluating the amount of coercion used in Zambia. Certainly, compared with Tanzania, there is indeed little coercion in the field of labor policy. See the accounts of G. E. Lynd, *The Politics of African Trade Unions,* and William Tordoff, "Trade Unionism in Tanzania," *The Journal of Development Studies* 2 (1966): 408–30.

75 President Kaunda, in criticism of the railway workers and workers in other state-controlled industries, *Zambia Mail,* 3 April 1970. In chap. 10, we discuss the government's recent innovations in labor policy.

Chapter 4

1 Interview, 27 May 1967.
2 Interview, 1 June 1967. Note also the following interchange between the general secretary of the Union and Father Quinn, a University

of Zambia economist who was a member of the board of inquiry: *Quinn:* Would you feel that more should be done to train not only trade union organizers but to have the rank and file to see their importance in the economy of Zambia today?

[*General Secretary*]: I am sure that this is very important, sir, that is very important indeed, but, as I said earlier, most of our members do not understand the economic implications at all, but at least it is our duty to see that we explain this to them.

Verbatim Testimony, Brown Commission of Inquiry, 13 June 1966, pp. E1–2.

3 Talk delivered to Ministry of Labour, Labour Relations Course, 14 June 1967.

4 Interviews at the Copper Industry Service Bureau, 3–8 May 1967. Notes on meeting of MUZ local branch officers with the Mines Police, 28 May 1967. Inserted into the agreement between the companies and the union was a new clause, paragraph 1.1.3(b) which states, "The Union agrees that it will not take disciplinary action against any employee . . . on account of the performance of his duties, and in particular of any supervisory duties, as an employee of the Company" (Copper Industry Service Bureau, *Local Conditions of Employment and Service* [Kitwe: Copper Industry Service Bureau, 1968]).

5 Talk delivered to Ministry of Labour, Labour Relations Course, 14 June 1967.

6 Interview, 27 May 1967.

7 Report on Supreme Council Meeting, 8 January 1963, File 100.20.71. The Head Office expanded to seven members in 1967.

8 See the discussion of the wages tenet of the government's development labor policy in chap. 3.

9 See the discussion of the wages tenet of the government's social justice policy in chap. 3.

10 See Republic of Zambia, *Report of the Commission of Inquiry into the Mining Industry,* 1966, pp. 28–29. With regard to the Head Office's efforts to terminate strikes of 1966, note the following: "The impression was left with officials of the Ministry of Labour and Social Development that because of UDI in Rhodesia, the Union leaders felt that they should try and finalise a long outstanding matter which might embarrass the Government directly or indirectly" (Interview, Permanent Secretary, Ministry of Labour, November 1967). Tyson Simposha, in his testimony before the Brown Commission, corroborates this position: "Then UDI came and they (the Head Office)

held another meeting and explained about UDI and that we should not strike, so we agreed" (Verbatim Testimony, Brown Commission of Inquiry, 13 June 1966, p. F3). There is also evidence that the union's Head Office accepted the 1964 agreement, which included the dual-wage structure, out of regard for the national welfare. Thus, in the Brown Commission of Inquiry, the president of the union testified: "These were the first days of a new African Government . . . and the Union, or the people negotiating, did not want to embarrass the Government with possible industrial unrest and strikes and [we] knew the importance of this big copper industry to the country" (ibid., 3 June 1966, p. E10); however in 1964 the Head Office may have wanted any form of agreement, so as to counter the attacks of the United Mineworkers' Union. See chap. 7.

11 Minutes of Zambianization Committee, 20 September 1967 and 16 October 1967, File 100.65, vol. 6.

12 Minister of Labour, "Do Not Employ Aliens," Press Release, Zambia Information Services, 25 August 1967, p. 1.

13 "Zambianization of All Mine Personnel Managers," Press Release, Zambia Information Services, 21 September 1967, p. 1; "Mining Companies Agree to Major Zambianization Programme," Press Release, Zambia Information Services, 21 June 1967.

14 Data for Roan Antelope Mine indicate a decrease of 22 percent in absenteeism over the same period. However, the number of lateness-at-work, leaving-work-early, and negligent-performance-of-duty offenses increased 534 percent, 305 percent, and 68 percent respectively. Ministry of Labour, "Comments at Luanshya-Ndola Productivity Seminar" (Photocopy, Author's Collection, 6 January 1968), p. 9.

15 Two other factors could explain these increases, and must be ruled out before the increases can be accepted as established rather than apparent. One is the Zambianization of the supervisory grades of the mines, and the other is an alteration in the severity of penalties for the reported offenses. The two could possibly go together: African supervisors might be less willing to punish their compatriots, and so their compatriots may have become increasingly unruly.

We can rule out Zambianization as a direct source of increased indiscipline. The Zambianization Committee was established in 1966, and the Zambianization program began in earnest only in 1967. However, an examination of the penalty records presented in the text reveals that substantial increases in the number of offenses predated the Zambianization program. The sole exception to this is in insubordination; but here our data for the four largest mines on the copperbelt reveal that protests against supervisors increased well before the supervisors were drawn from the ranks of the local workers (table 66)

TABLE 66

Protests against Supervisors by Year

	1950s to 1960	1961	1962	1963	1964	1965	1966	1967	1968
Number of protests	33	1	5	10	5	3	4	17	5
Protests as percentage of all demands	9	9	24	22	19	43	67	22	38
Total no. of demands	364	11	21	45	27	7	6	79	13

A second possible cause for the increase in offenses could be greater leniency in penalization. Data for May and June 1967 at Rhokana mine allow us to rule out this factor as well (table 67). There are seven degrees of severity in the mines' penalty code. Interpreting each level as a position on a continuum, we can compare the average severity of penalties meted out for each offense over the two-month period.

The tabulation reveals that there has not been a uniform increase in the leniency of penalization. As a result, we cannot conclude that the increase in the frequency of offenses reported in the text is attributable to a decrease in the severity of penalization. Moreover, were increased leniency the cause of increased indiscipline, then decreases in the average severity of offenses should associate with increases in the totals figure in our tabulation. In three cases out of four, however, increased leniency associates with a *decrease* in the frequency of offenses over the two-month period.

A third possible hypothesis is that changes in the composition of the labor force increased the rate of indiscipline. The only major change in this period was an increase in the average length of employment. This change cannot explain the rise in indiscipline, however, for decreases, rather than increases, in the average length of

TABLE 67
Offense by Penalty, May–June 1967

	Absenteeism		Sleeping on duty		Failure to obey		Refusal to obey	
Penalty	May	June	May	June	May	June	May	June
1. Warnings	172	214	1	4	109	116	1	0
2. Severe warnings	76	84	0	2	59	38	5	2
3. Final warnings	27	27	14	7	8	10	7	9
4. Comprehensive final warnings	9	12	2	5	2	3	3	6
5. Suspension	3	6	13	8	17	16	6	9
6. Demotion	0	0	1	0	1	1	0	0
7. Discharge	14	8	2	2	2	0	3	0
Total	301	351	33	28	198	184	25	26
Average severity[a]	1.84	1.70	4.12	3.68	1.84	1.74	3.80	3.85

Source: Personnel Department, Disciplinary Analysis, General File on the MUZ, Chief Industrial Relations Officer, Rhokana Corporation.

[a] The formula for determining average severity is: $\dfrac{\text{Number of Penalties} \times \text{Offense Level}}{\text{Total}}$.

service should correlate with indiscipline. See Clark Kerr et al., *Industrialism and Industrial Man,* chap. 5.

16 This is not true at Mufulira, where large-scale mechanization has been introduced into aspects of underground operations. These figures do not include Mufulira.

17 There are several other points to be made about our measures. The average grade of oxide ores extracted at Rhokana fell from 2.2 to 2.01 percent in copper content over this period. However, as none of our productivity measures are based upon the volume of the output of copper, the decline in the grade of the ore does not affect our conclusions. The extraction of ore becomes more difficult with time; but this four-year period with which we are concerned is not sufficiently long to make a significant difference in our measures, and certainly not long enough to account for the magnitude of the decreases.

It is instructive to observe the movement of alternative measures of productivity. When we use the average number of short tons of copper

TABLE 68
Average Number of Short Tons of Copper per Man Year

Year	Output (thousand tons)	Local employees	Tons per man year	Change per year
1963	635.0	35,568	169	+4.1%
1964	707.9	39,203	181	+6.6
1965	754.8	40,391	187	+3.2
1966	645.9	42,475	152	−18.7
1967	679.3	42,936	158	+3.9
1968	733.0	42,989	170	+7.6

Source: Computed from figures contained in Copper Industry Service Bureau, *Copperbelt of Zambia Mining Industry Year Book* [*various years*] (Kitwe: CISB, various years).

produced per man year, we obtained the pattern depicted in table 68. The clear implication is that while the productivity of the workers consistently improved over the period of independence, it was severely harmed by the disruptions resulting from the Rhodesian rebellion in 1965. While this is a crucially significant observation, our objective is to measure worker effort. The above index is influenced by such factors as the introduction of new technologies, the bringing into production of newer mines with richer ores at shallower levels, the availability of fuel supplies, and so forth. Thus, while the measure is valuable for many purposes, it is less sensitive than our measure to the factor with which we are concerned.

Despite the pattern of increasing productivity, however, the overall level in 1968 remained below that of the first full year of independence, 1965, and the net increase fails to warrant the more than 30 percent increase in average mine wages.

18 Some may argue that productivity declined because of the promotion of "less skilled" African labor. However, since the Zambianization program began several years after productivity began to decline, we can rule out this hypothesis. There is evidence of a recent upward shift in these measures. Thus, in 1968, record figures were being recorded by several crews in Mindolo shaft at Rhokana; their efforts were publicized in *The Miner*—the household journal of Anglo-American Corporation (Zambia).

19 This information was collected from government and company reports on labor disputes on the four principal mines on the copperbelt;

Chingola, Luanshya, Kitwe, and Mufulira. Among the items noted for each dispute were: who made the demand, the issue, the agencies handling the dispute, the level reached by the dispute, and the outcome. The data cover the period from the formation of the union to 1968. Please refer to Appendix 1.

20 *Business and Economy of Central and East Africa,* September 1967, p. 8.

21 For a discussion of recent trends and future prospects in the price of copper, see "Dark Cloud with a Copper Lining," *Forbes,* 1 March 1970, pp. 26–40.

22 John B. Knight, "Wages and Zambia's Economic Development" (Paper prepared for the Institute of Economics and Statistics, Oxford University, 1968), p. 10. The paper is to appear in Charles Elliot, ed., *Constraints on the Economic Development of Zambia.* The estimate is for 1964. The Rhokana figures are drawn from Rhokana Corporation, Cost Report for June 1967, Files, Manpower Services Department. The Rhokana estimate does not include the cost of capital depreciation in the estimate of total costs of production.

23 See William J. Barber, "Federation and the Distribution of Economic Benefits," in *A New Deal in Central Africa,* ed. Colin Leys and Cranford Pratt, pp. 81–97.

24 Ministry of Labour, "Wages Settlement(s)," Press Releases, Zambia Information Services, November 1966 to October 1967.

25 Verbatim Testimony, Brown Commission of Inquiry, 12 June 1966, pp. A10–11.

26 Knight, "Wages," p. 11. Our discussion throughout this section draws heavily on Knight's research. We are grateful for his permission to use these materials and he is not responsible for our interpretations.

Applying a least squares regression to changes in earnings in mining and nonmining sectors over the period of 1955 to 1964, Knight finds that the best fitting equations are:

$$N_t = 2.844 + 0.289 \, M_t; \ r^2 = .631; \text{ significance level} = 1\%$$

$$N_t = 2.023 + 0.329 \, M_{t-1}; \ r^2 = .601; \text{ significance level} = 1\%$$

N is the annual absolute change in average earnings in the nonmining sectors; M is the annual absolute change in average earnings in mining. As Knight states: "the second equation implies that an annual increase in mining earnings produced, on average, an annual increase in nonmining earnings about one third as large, with a time lag of three months. The mining sector acted as a 'wage leader' for the rest of the wage-employment economy."

27 Richard L. Sklar, "Zambia's Response to U.D.I.," *Mawazo* 1 (1968): 16 and 22.

28 Knight, "Wages," p. 27.

29 Ibid., p. 16.

30 Republic of Zambia, *Monthly Digest of Statistics* 5, no. 6 (June 1969): 49. The index is for the whole country, all items, lower incomes.

31 For 1969 recurrent expenditures will remain the same as in 1968 at $280 million. Capital expenditures will decline from their 1968 level of $236 million to $189 million. *Times of Zambia*, 30 January 1969.

32 Reported in Knight, "Wages," p. 27.

33 There are, of course, strategies for coping with the dilemmas which face Zambia. Inflation represents an opportunity, as well as a disadvantage, for rising prices can call forth investments in increased production. And decreasing trade balances can be offset by import substitutions. As a result of these considerations, the government has promoted investments in the production of goods currently being imported. By manipulating tariffs and terms of credit, it has facilitated the construction of local bottling plants and assembly works; above all, it is emphasizing the expansion of the agricultural industry so as to curtail rising food imports. Zambia is a high-cost producer, however, and by protecting Zambia's market so as to facilitate import substitution, the government is imperiling another of its economic objectives—entry into the East African Common Market. This result has been noted in President Kaunda, "Address at the Opening of the Second National Convention, Kitwe," Press Release, Zambia Information Services, 22 December 1969, p. 10; see also Knight, "Wages," pp. 18–19.

34 The statistics and the warning are both drawn from President Kaunda. Ibid., p. 9. See also Charles Elliot, "Humanism and the Agricultural Revolution," in *After Mulungushi: The Economics of Zambian Humanism*, ed. Bastiaan de Gaay Fortman.

35 President Kaunda, ibid., p. 8. See also Kevin P. Quinn, "Labour and Zambian Humanism," p. iv; *After Mulungushi*, pp. 152–53.

Chapter 5

1 Interview with Jameson R. Namitengo, 27 May 1967.

2 Copper Industry Service Bureau, Memorandum to General Managers

on the Trade Union and Trade Disputes (Amendment) Act, 1964, 11 December 1964, File 100.60.

3 Interview, Jonas Ponde, 23 May 1967. Interview with Ron Taylor, 15 November 1967.

4 John Sichone, deputy general secretary of the Mineworkers' Union, held the post of deputy general secretary of ZCTU from 1965 to 1967. The former deputy general treasurer of the union was a committee member of the ZCTU over the same period. The former acting president of the Mineworkers' Union currently holds an executive office in the ZCTU.

5 Notes taken at Supreme Council meeting, 22 January 1967.

6 Anglo-American Corporation, "Zambia First National Convention, Achievement in Our Developing Land in Kitwe—January 11th to the 15th" (Paper prepared February 1967, following the First National Convention, January 1967, Kitwe. Typescript); Republic of Zambia, *National Convention on the Four Year Development Plan, Kitwe;* Ministry of Labour, *Livingstone Labour Conference.* The information on the seminars was collected personally by the author. The government had begun to involve the lower ranks of the union in similar functions at the time our research was drawing to a close.

7 Computed as a simple product of the number of incidents times the days spent resolving each incident for those cases where the second datum is known. Rounded off to the nearest 500.

8 Since these data were collected, the companies and the union have negotiated a single basic wage for the industry, and Europeans and Africans who hold the same job now receive the same basic pay. Nonetheless, the Europeans also receive an "expatriate bonus" designed to recruit them to Zambia, and they continue to cluster in the better-paying jobs. While the highly visible pattern of the dual-wage structure will no longer prevail, the racially skewed distribution of income will nonetheless persist in the mining industry. The settlement is reported in the Copper Industry Service Bureau, "Memorandum of Agreement" (Photocopy, Author's Collection, 15 May 1969), and the *Zambia Mail,* 8 September 1970.

9 Industry-wide figures for the section bosses, shift bosses, and foremen underground indicate that on 5 May 1967 there were 616 expatriates and 95 locals serving in these categories. This figure of 15 percent localization is, of course, much lower than that for Mindolo Shaft a year later. Copper Industry Service Bureau, "Progress of Zambianization," 5 May 1967, File 90.14.91B.

10 A chart at Rhokana mine projects the future manning structure of
    the concentrator. A line drawn between the section bosses and shift
    foremen demarcates the extent of localization "for the foreseeable
    future," in the words of the training officer for the department. Inter-
    view, 7 July 1967.

11 Memorandum, CISB to Group Headquarters, 23 June 1967, File 100.9,
    vol. 10. This policy is based on the stated belief that all the African
    workers would demand appliances once it is known that some ob-
    tain them.

12 Report by Special Subcommittee on House Rental Policies, 13
    September 1965, File 100.9, vol. 8. Republic of Zambia, *Report of the
    Commission of Inquiry into the Mining Industry*, 1966, p. 62. Rent
    was consolidated into the basic pay of local employees in 1964.

13 Rhokana Corporation, "Response to Inquiries by the Commission"
    Submission to the Brown Commission of Inquiry, 1966), Appendix II.

14 Republic of Zambia, *Report of the Commission of Inquiry*, p. 65. In
    May 1969, the union and companies agreed to a minimum leave
    of twenty-one days for *all* employees in the industry (Copper Industry
    Service Bureau, "Memorandum of Agreement").

15 For a report on the activities and achievements of the Zambianization
    Committee, see the Republic of Zambia, Ministry of Labour, *The
    Progress of Zambianization in the Mining Industry*.

16 Central Statistical Office, *Monthly Digest of Statistics* 4, no. 5 (July
    1968):2.

17 To insure that Zambianization does not produce greater inefficiency,
    the companies submit new African supervisors to close scrutiny and
    supervision. Naturally, the Zambian promotees regard this as under-
    mining their position of authority. See Verbatim Testimony, Brown
    Commission of Inquiry, 27 May 1967, p. B 8.

18 Verbatim Testimony, Brown Commission of Inquiry, 16 June 1966,
    pp. G8–J6. Appeal of Maxwell Kapengwe, 27 October 1967, Dis-
    ciplinary Files of the Chief Industrial Relations Officer, Rhokana
    Corporation. Interviews with the Personnel Manager and Kapengwe's
    colleagues at Rhokana.

19 Ministry of Labour, "Background Paper on Discipline at Work for
    Ndola Labour Conference of Trade Unions" (Photocopy, Author's
    Collection, 29 July 1967), p. 1.

20 National Institute for Personnel Research, in association with The
    Institute for Social Research, University of Natal, "The Attitudes of
    White Mining Employees Towards Life and Work on the Copper-
    belt," vol. 2, p. 110.

21 Parliamentary Secretary to Minister of Labour, 22 December 1962, Ja/9, vol. 8. The October date refers to the pre-self-government elections.

22 *Zambia Mail,* 8 March 1968.

23 *Times of Zambia,* 25 November 1967. Also General Manager, Rhokana Corporation to Senior Labour Officer, 25 November 1967, File M.13(i). See also the letter entitled "Watchdog Bosses" by M. Ngenda, Lusaka, *Zambia Mail,* 3 November 1967.

24 Interview, 19 May 1967.

25 Hankey Blackskin Kalanga, recently deceased. He was fired from the mines for holding an illegal union meeting while he was branch chairman at Rhokana.

26 Interview, Eric Bromwich, Industrial Relations Advisor, Roan Selection Trust, 8 April 1967.

27 This took place in July 1962, when the Mineworkers' Union was about to resume a strike on a wages dispute; the strike had been suspended out of regard for the Morison Commission. UNIP feared that the strike would disrupt the general elections scheduled for October of that year. For details, see chap. 7. For an analysis of the correlates of "national-mindedness" see Lars Clausen, "On Attitudes Towards Industrial Conflict in Zambian Industry," *African Social Research* 2 (1966): 117–38. We are indebted to this article for suggesting the term.

28 Report, 4 June 1964, File 100.60.

29 Monthly Reports, African Mineworkers' Union, July 1961 to July 1963, Ja/9, vol. 8. Also, General Secretary to all Branch Secretaries, 15 July 1963, Ja/9, vol. 8.

30 Reports, Incidents at Broken Hill, Ha/43, vols. 4 and 5. Telex, CISB to Group Headquarters, Salisbury, 28 February 1964, File S.6. Telex, CISB to Group Headquarters, Salisbury, 28 March 1964, File S.7, vol. 2. Bruce Kapferer, Untitled papers presented to departmental seminars of the Department of Sociology and Social Anthropology, Manchester University, 1966. Typescript.

31 See Roger Brown, "Models of Attitude Change," in R[oger] Brown et al., *New Directions in Social Psychology* (New York: Holt Rinehart, and Winston, 1962). This analysis, even more than other parts of the study, is highly tentative. It is no more than a series of hypotheses drawn from the qualitative data available. Still required is a comparative analysis of the behavior of branch officials with and without prospects for high-level jobs in the companies, and systemat-

ically collected data that the Head Office leaders look to the government as a source of future employment more frequently than to the mining companies.

Chapter 6

1 See, for example, Proceedings of Branch Committee Meeting, 13 March 1963, File 100.20.7A.

2 Note on Composition of ZMU Negotiating Committee, 4 December 1967, File 100.65, vol. 1.

3 *Northern News,* January 1960, 31 May 1960. Extensive materials contained in Ja/9, vol. 7, National Archives, Lusaka and File 100.20.7D, Copper Industry Service Bureau, Kitwe.

4 Interview, Edwin Thawe, 14 May 1967.

5 Report on the Supreme Council Meeting, 8 January 1963, File 100.20.71.

6 Further evidence for the divergence between the Head Office and local branch leaders is contained in the following: "The President and the Secretary [of the Mineworkers' Union] admitted that there was a tendency on the part of Branch officials of the Mineworkers' Union to precipitate a crisis, in the event of disagreements with employers, before consulting them because top leaders might suggest constitutional methods of settling differences" (Minutes of the Parliamentary Secretary of the Ministry of Labour and Mines, 22 December 1963, Ja/9, vol. 8). The pattern obtained at an earlier date as well. Thus the comment of the Kitwe labor officer: "The Union Head Office policy is acceptable and realistic. In Rhokana and Chibuluma branches it would be unwise to accept that this change of attitudes has permeated to branch level. Lack of militant action is invariably interpreted at branch level as lack of activity" (Monthly Report, Kitwe, April 1957, File 100.47). See also Report on Conciliation Procedures, Broken Hill, 31 January 1951, H/1.

7 Field observations in union branch offices, May through June 1967.

8 The fifteen branch officers included nine committee members and six members of the branch executive.

9 Report, 27 April 1960, File 100.20.7F.

10 Interviews, 22 June 1967.

11 Report by Personnel Manager, Rhokana Corporation, 21 November 1965, File A 25.

12 The company's policy is not to negotiate an issue until the workers return to work.

13 Reports, January–July 1964, File 100.47, vol. 8. Also note the follow-
    ing account of the union's efforts to get workers to return to their
    jobs at Nchanga in March of 1966: "The General President, Milambo,
    outlined the complaints of the ZMU members at Nchanga and gave
    a comprehensive background to these complaints. . . . In strongest
    terms, he appealed for a return to work. . . . There was an im-
    mediate adverse reaction, and the crowd shouted that they would
    not under any circumstances return to work before their demands
    were achieved. It was stated that the return to work would be taken
    as weakness by the companies as had happened in the old Federal
    and colonialist days. Milambo came in for severe criticism, with it
    said he was dull and useless and should never have signed the agree-
    ment" (Report, 16 March 1966, File 100.22, vol. 34).

14 Attendance figures from Reports, January 1961 through December
    1962, File 100.20.7F.

15 Interview with David Mwila, President of the Mineworkers' Union,
    5 June 1967.

16 The sole exceptions, to the best of our knowledge, are at Nchanga
    and the Ndola Copper Refineries, where some of the workers live
    in the municipal townships. This section extensively draws upon
    and reinterprets the analysis contained in A. L. Epstein, *Politics in
    an Urban African Community.*

17 Rhokana Corporation, "Housing and Social Services" (Submission
    to the Brown Commission of Inquiry, 1966), p. A10.

18 See the statement of the Community Services Manager to the Town-
    ship Council in Rhokana Corporation, Minutes of the Mine Township
    Council, 27 February 1967, Files, Chief Community Services Officer.
    Also, CISB, Memo to Group Headquarters, 23 June 1967, File 100.9,
    vol. 10; Note for Group Industrial Relation Managers, February
    1967, File 100.9, vol. 9; and Rhokana Corporation, "Housing and
    Social Services."

19 It is the companies' belief that by establishing a spatial separation
    between the supervisors and the workers they can create the social
    distance necessary to the authority of the supervisor and thereby im-
    prove labor discipline.

20 Comments frequently heard in the field.

21 Epstein, *Politics,* p. 240. See also the discussion of J. Clyde Mitchell,
    The Kalela Dance.

22 In the August 1967 elections to the Central Committee of UNIP,
    electoral alliances were formed between the leaders of the Bemba and

Tonga on the one hand and the leaders of the Lozi and the Nyanja-speaking tribes of the Eastern Province on the other. See account of Robert I. Rotberg, "Tribalism and Politics in Zambia," *Africa Report* 12 (1967): 29–35. For a discussion of interparty competition and ethnicity, see Ian Scott and Robert Molteno, "The Zambian General Elections," *Africa Report* 14 (1969): 42–46.

23 Note the changing rate of turnover among local laborers recorded in table 69.

TABLE 69
Turnover of Local Labor,
Copper Industry

Year	Annual African percentage turnover
1952	60.1
1953	52.0
1954	47.6
1955	125.8
1956	27.6
1957	33.4
1958	42.7
1959	27.9
1960	30.2
1961	22.8
1962	17.7
1963	9.3
1964	8.3
1965	8.4

Source: Copper Industry Service Bureau, "Company Submission" (Submission to the Brown Commission of Inquiry, 1966), Appendix 7.

24 Edwin Thawe, General Secretary of the Mineworkers' Union, Speech to Labour Relations Course, 14 June 1967, notes taken by the author.
25 Ibid.
26 Ibid. Also emphasized by the union's organizing secretary in Rhokana in his talk to local shop stewards, 7 May 1967, notes taken by the author.

27 During our research in Rhokana, the union leaders suffered tremendous abuse from striking members but nonetheless were unstinting in their efforts to get their members back to work.

28 In 25 percent of the cases, we were unable to ascertain or to judge the outcome of the union's action.

29 Indicative of the consequences of this is the following passage from our field notes: "At Muhongo's workpoint, a shop steward announced the union's coming meeting. His announcement was greeted with cries of 'To Hell with the union. We give you five shillings a month and you haven't even promised us what you are going to do. . . .' Part of the antagonism derived from the fact that it was known that the shop steward had just purchased a new van and that he had just received a new hat, i.e., he had just received a promotion. He had been a leading operator, but he is now a section boss."

Chapter 7

1 Rhodesia Study Club, *Newsletter* 1, no. 2 (November 1948): 4.

2 Rhodesia Study Club, *Newsletter* 1, no. 13 (October 1949): 4.

3 Personal communication, Dr. David C. Mulford, 17 June 1968.

4 The implementation of the recommendations of the 1948 Dalgleish Commission was an early demand of the union. The commission had advocated African advancement.

5 Monthly Report, April 1952, Ha/43, vol. 1.

6 For example: "Katilungu, in addressing a general meeting of the Broken Hill branch of the Union took the opportunity of rebuking the branch for its preoccupation with political matters. He made it clear that membership in the Congress and the Trade Union were not at all incompatible but that the Trade Unionist must hold his first loyalty to the Union. His opinion was that the African people had most to gain from economic advancement and the Trade Union was the body which could best achieve this" (Monthly Report, July 1953, Ha/43, vol. 4).

7 A. L. Epstein, *Politics in an Urban African Community*, p. 161.

8 Ibid.

9 Ibid., p. 162.

10 Monthly Report, October 1954, C/1814/14.

11 Digest no. 1 of 1962, 14 January 1962, File 100.20.7H.

12 In 1956 the government detained over forty leaders of the Mineworkers' Union for allegedly striking for political purposes. Included among the detainees were Nkoloma, Puta, Chapoloko, Nkoma,

Chindele, Mwendapole, and others who had adhered to a "Zukasite" interpretation of the role of the union. Katilungu remained untouched, officially because he was out of the country at the time of the strikes. In the contemporary mythology of the union, as well as in the eyes of the colonial government at the time, the series of rolling strikes (three days at one mine, followed by three days at another) represented nationalist acts of political protest. The evidence for this assertion is unimpressive, however.

The immediate "cause" of the strikes was a jurisdictional dispute. Following the Staff Association's refusal to cooperate with the union's strike of 1955, the mines had recognized the association. The union had concurred at the time; but when in 1956, the companies placed the bulk of a newly localized group of jobs in the association's jurisdiction, the Mineworkers' Union began its strikes. The union did receive verbal encouragement from the African National Congress; and as table 70 shows, a small proportion of the detained unionists

TABLE 70
Union-Party Overlap, 1956

		Of those detained	
Branch	*Total from Mineworkers' Union detained*	*Number who were party officials*	*Number who were members, TUC Political Action Subcommittee*
Mufulira	10	0	0
Rhokana	14	3	4
Nchanga	5	1	1
Roan	11	1	1
Total	40	5	6

Source: Evidence Volumes, Branigan Commission of Inquiry.

Note: Not recorded in the table are the smaller union branches; the exclusion does not affect the pattern.

were active in the congress and in the Political Subcommittee of the Trade Union Congress. However, the actions of the union were neither instigated nor organized by or in conjunction with the congress. The origins and form of the strikes conform to the pattern of one of the typically most strenuous forms of industrial conflict:

a jurisdictional dispute. (See Evidence Volumes of the Branigan Commission of Inquiry. *Central African Post,* 11 June 1956. Materials in the collection of the Afrika Studiecentrum, Leiden, Holland. Interviews with Matthew Mwendapole, 10 and 14 April 1967.) Also note that during the strike, the supposedly militant nationalist Nkoloma, was quoted as "expressing concern about A.N.C. [support], for this was entirely a Union dispute" (Assistant Labour Commissioner to Deputy Labour Commissioner, 27 June 1956, C/1828). See also Elena L. Berger, "Labour Policies on the Northern Rhodesian Copperbelt, 1924–1964" (Ph.D. diss., Nuffield College, Oxford University, 1969).

13 See the numerous reports contained in File 100.20.7H.

14 *Northern News,* 2 May 1960.

15 For a discussion of the ICFTU and WFTU rivalry, see Report, 19 November 1961, File 100.20.7H. Also, Area Secretary to General Secretary, UTUC, n.d., Ja/128, vol. 2. For materials on the formation of rival unions, see File 100.60, vol. 2, and Ja/128, vol. 2.

16 Personal communication, Dr. David C. Mulford, 17 June 1968.

17 Ibid.

18 Circular, Regional Secretary, Ndola, 7 July 1962, File 100.25, vol. 4.

19 Circular, Regional Secretary, Kitwe, Kalulushi, Mufulira, 7 July 1962, File 100.25, vol. 4.

20 General Circular, President of the UTUC to Affiliated Unions, July 1962, Ja/128. See also, N.R. Chamber of Mines to Group Headquarters, Salisbury, 13 July 1962, File 100.20.5, vol. 4.

21 In April 1963, Mr. Simon Kapwepwe, the treasurer of the United National Independence Party and now vice-president of UNIP and Zambia, chaired a "unity election" between the warring factions. As the UTUC stacked the election meeting, the Mineworkers' Union refused to accept the new slate of officers and withdrew once again. In May 1964, elections were held once again. By this time, a falling out between Chakulya and Chivunga had split the UTUC itself and the Mineworkers' Union allied with the Chakulya faction. In July 1964, Kapwepwe again chaired a unity meeting and persuaded the principal protagonists—Chisata, Chakulya, Chambeshi, Mwiinga, Kalyati, Chivunga, Mubanga, and others—to leave the labor movement for government positions. Forming a new UTUC, he brought a united, if depleted, labor movement to independent Zambia. Subsequent government legislation created a new Congress of Trade Unions after independence. Elections to the congress were not held until May 1967.

The Mineworkers' Union participates in the new congress. For reports on these events, see the numerous reports in File 100.60, vol. 2 and File 100.20.7H. *Financial Mail,* October 1963, June 1964, July 1964, November 1964, and May 1965. *Africa 1963,* August 1963. *Africa 1964,* August 1964. See also the material in File Ja/128, vol. 2.

22   *Zambia Pilot,* June 1963, p. 9.

23   *Zambia Pilot,* October 1963, p. 10.

24   *Africa 1963,* August 1963.

25   *Zambia Pilot,* April 1965, p. 15.

26   Minutes, African Township Advisory Committee, 29 March 1956, File 100.54.J.

27   Interview, secretary of the Rhokana branch of the Mineworkers' Union, 6 May 1967.

28   Letter from the General Secretary of the Mineworkers' Union to the Secretary of the Chamber of Mines, 3 October 1962, Ja/9, vol. 8.

29   Interview, Chief Community Services Officer, 7 July 1967.

30   Minutes, Meeting with Branch Executive, MUZ, 10 January 1968, General File on the Mineworkers' Union of the Chief Community Industrial Relations Officer, Rhokana Corporation. Also, interview, UNIP Branch Secretary, 6 October 1967.

31   Interview, Branch Chairman of UNIP, 13 December 1967.

32   Interview, Branch Secretary of UNIP, 6 and 30 October 1967.

33   Field notes, 25 September 1967, and 8 March 1968.

34   Forty-three percent of the councillors are staff-grade employees. Also indicative of their high position in the mines is table 71. All the

TABLE 71
Union and Party Officeholders, by Income

	Quartiles				
	1st	*2nd*	*3rd*	*4th*	N
All workers	25%	25%	25%	25%	2,098
Councillors	8	42	28	23	26
Trade unionists	39	27	19	16	64

workers are ranked by income and the ranks divided by quartiles; the union leaders are included for purposes of comparison.

35   Interview, Personnel Manager, Rhokana Corporation, 23 March 1968.

36 This was asserted by the party leaders on frequent occasions.
37 Interview, Rhokana Branch Chairman, 13 December 1967.
38 Interview, 5 July 1967.
39 Interviews, 7 and 12 January 1968.
40 Interview, 5 January 1968.
41 Personal communication, Dr. David C. Mulford, 17 June 1968.
42 *Northern News,* 11 December 1958. For Katilungu's earlier flirtation with politics, and the union's adverse reaction to it, see *Northern News,* 11 November 1957; 27 November 1957; 3 December 1957.
43 *Northern News,* 28 October 1960.
44 *Northern News,* 10 September 1960.
45 *Northern News,* 12 May 1959, and 9 July 1959.
46 *Luntandanya,* 24 September 1960.
47 Letter from the Registrar of Trade Unions to the Ministry of Labour, 3 November 1959, File Ja/9, vol. 6.
48 Ibid., minutes on the letter.
49 Record Note, 18 November 1960, Ja/128, vol. 1.
50 Memorandum on the Position of Lawrence Chola Katilungu, 12 December 1960, Ja/9, vol. 7. Note also the assessment of the assistant executive officer: "This determination of the members [to abuse Katilungu] cannot be doubted as having been derived from shouts of encouragement at U.N.I.P. public meetings" (ibid.).
51 *Northern News,* 19 May 1960.
52 Over the period 1959–60, the Congress organized a boycott of South African goods (which failed), formed a political committee to prepare a submission to the 1960 Constitutional Conference and to work for closer links with nationalist political parties (from material contained in Ja/128, vol. 2). Also, the Congress channeled funds to UNIP, bought Land Rovers for the party and spoke for UNIP on behalf of the African labor force (Personal communication, Dr. David C. Mulford, 17 June 1968).
53 Registrar of Trade Unions to Assistant Labour Commissioner, 25 February 1960, Ja/128, vol. 1. See also *Northern News,* 2 May 1960.
54 Report, 28 May 1963, File 100.60, vol. 2. Also, Record Note, 19 November 1962, Ja/128, vol. 2.
55 See the numerous reports contained in Ja/128, vol. 2.
56 *Northern News,* 22 November 1960. Assistant Executive Officer to Labour Commissioner, 17 December 1960, Ja/9, vol. 7. Report on Supreme Council Meeting, 4–6 November 1960, Ja/9, vol. 7.
57 *Northern News,* 31 May 1960 and 3 January 1961. *African Mail,* 9 September 1960.

58 *African Mail,* 27 December 1960. See also the reports on the attitudes of Katilungu's colleagues in the Head Office contained in Record Notes, 16 July 1960 and 4 November 1960, Ja/9, vol. 7.

59 Report of the 4 Man Committee to Ascertain Support for L. C. Katilungu, 9 December 1960, Ja/9, vol. 7.

60 Monthly Report, October 1962, Ha/43, vol. 5.

61 Ibid.

62 As a labor officer reports the incidents in Bancroft: "There has been strong action at Union meetings during the month against Congress Officials holding office in the trade union. Not long ago a list of names was handed the African Personnel Manager by the Union with a request that they be moved from their jobs" (Monthly Report, December 1962, Ja/9, vol. 8).

63 Report on the Meeting of the Central Council, MASA, 21-22 September 1963, File 100.47, vol. 8.

64 Notes on a Gathering of African Employees, 22 July 1964, File A.20. Telexes, CISB to Group Headquarters, Lusaka, 15-22 May 1964, File S.7, vol. 2.

65 General Secretary, UMU to UTUC, 10 October 1963, File 100.47, vol. 8. See also Report on MASA, 24 November 1963, File 100.47, vol. 8.

66 Monthly Report, Luanshya, October 1963, Ja/9, vol. 4.

67 Office Holders, Staff Association, 30 March 1964, File A.20.

68 Bruce Kapferer, Untitled papers presented to departmental seminars of the Department of Sociology and Social Anthropology, Manchester University, 1966. Typescript. Also, Telexes, ZINCOROUS Broken Hill to Chamber of Mines, 31 October, 25 November, 27 November, 1963, File 100.20, vol. 25.

69 *Zambia Pilot,* March 1964, p. 3.

70 Report, 10 June 1964, File 100.20 7D.

71 UMU Public Meeting, 7 May 1964 and UNIP Public Meeting, 11 October 1964, File S.6.

72 Personal communication, Dr. David C. Mulford, 17 June 1968.

73 General Secretary, UMU, to Minister of Home Affairs, 14 January 1969, File 100.47, vol. 8.

74 *Northern News,* 23 April 1964.

75 Record of a meeting between the Minister of Labour and the two Groups of Mining Companies, 1 July 1964, Ja/9, vol. 8. CISB Memorandum on United Mineworkers' Union to General Managers, 1 June 1964, File 100.47, vol. 12.

76 *Northern News,* 22 May 1964.

77 Report, Public Meeting, Chamboli, 6 June 1964, File S.6.
78 Letter, General Secretary, NRAMTU, to Secretary General, MASA, 30 December 1963, File 100.20. 7.
79 Report, 25 May 1964, File A.19.
80 Report on Annual General Congress, 26–28 September 1964, File 100.47, vol. 15.
81 Report, 4 June 1964, File 100.60. See also Annual General Congress, 26–28 September 1964, File 100.47, vol. 15.
82 *Northern News,* 22 May 1964.
83 Press Release by Mineworkers' Union, 26 June 1964, Ja/9, vol. 8. Report on the Supreme Council Meeting, 22 June 1964, File 100.20, vol. 26.
84 Letter, Deputy General Secretary to Minister of Labour and Mines, 27 June 1964, Ja/9, vol. 8.
85 See the testimony of Matthew Nkoloma in Verbatim Testimony, Branigan Commission of Inquiry, 26 and 31 October 1956, pp. H5–13.
86 *Northern News,* 5 November 1957.
87 Report on Administration and Current Affairs in MASA, July 1963, File 100.47, vol. 8. Also, Meeting at Chamboli, 11 November 1963, File 100.47, vol. 8.
88 Monthly Report, October 1963, Ja/9, vol. 4.
89 Field notes. Also to be noted is the statement of the general president of the Mines African Police Association, in which he "stressed that . . . the UTUC acts as [a] political organization . . . and as a result [is] not interested in Union matters" (Notes on MASA Supreme Council Meeting, 30 October 1963, File 100.47, vol. 8).
90 Verbatim Testimony, Brown Commission of Inquiry, 26 May 1966, p. A1. Telex, Chamber of Mines to ANMERCOSA Salisbury, 29 June 1964, File 100.47, vol. 8. Minutes, Meeting of Branch Executive and Personnel Manager, 3 March 1964, File 100.47, vol. 8.
91 CISB Memorandum on United Mineworkers' Union to General Managers, 1 June 1964, File 100.47, vol. 12. Personnel Manager, Rhokana Corporation, to Branch Secretary, UMU, 29 April 1964, File A.20. See also the contents of File 100.47, vol. 14.
92 Republic of Zambia, *Report of the Commission of Inquiry into the Mining Industry,* 1966, p. 27.
93 Toward the end of UMU's existence, the Council sent out the following letter: "Dear Comrade: I thank you for the support you gave both to MASA and UMU in the past. You couldn't have done better

then. But by today you, and other men of your class in the Mining Industry, have lost plenty in hard cash and other benefits due to lack of representation" (Circular No. SA/32/173/64, 17 December 1964, File 100.47, vol. 14).

94 *Zambia News,* 12 December 1965.

95 The purpose of the list is to insure that all nominees for union posts are employees of the mines. Monthly Report, December 1965, File 100.20, vol. 32. See also *Times of Zambia,* 23 December 1965 and 5 February 1966.

96 An example of the party's endorsement of a union nominee is UNIP's support of David Mwila for branch chairman in Mufulira. Interview, 12 May 1967. See also *Times of Zambia,* 8 February 1966.

97 Personnel Manager to Acting General Manager, 23 December 1965, File A.25. Report to General Manager, Rhokana Corporation, 11 June 1965, File S.6.

98 Regional Secretary, Kalulushi, to All Office Bearers, Zambia Mineworkers' Union, Chibuluma, n.d., File 100.20, vol. 32.

99 Cosmos Mwene, General Secretary, in the *Times of Zambia,* 23 December 1965.

100 Interview, 28 March 1968.

101 Report, 27 January 1966, File 100.60, vol. 3.

102 Verbatim Testimony, Brown Commission of Inquiry, 8 June 1966, p. B8. There are no figures available for the election returns. However, we do have returns for a union election in which a local UNIP branch intervened. At Rhokana in May 1967, the branch backed Kapengwe for secretary and Chitente for financial secretary, while strongly opposing Machuta for chairman. The branch's failure to influence the outcome of the election is revealed in table 72.

TABLE 72

Votes for Officers, Union Branch Elections, 1967

Chairman		*Secretary*		*Financial Secretary*	
Kabuswe	124	Kaoma	578	Chitente	611
Machuta	557	Sinwawa	104	Yumbe	307
Mbewe	283	Kapengwe	294		
		Supaile	114		

Source: Returns are from the office of the Assistant Labour Commissioner, Kitwe. Information on party activities from interviews on 11 June 1967.

103 Interviews, 28 April 1967; 12 June 1967; and 28 March 1968.
104 Ibid.
105 Interview, 30 May 1967.
106 Ibid.
107 Interview, 12 June 1967.
108 Nkana Branch Secretary to Personnel Manager, Rhokana Corporation, 10 January 1966, File A.19.
109 Interviews, 30 May 1967, and 12 June 1967. Later the Supreme Council reinstated Sichone and penalized the general secretary for demoting him.
110 Further, there is no evidence that union officials are influenced by a desire to cross over to the party hierarchy; were this desire present then the party could influence the union while not being structurally linked to it. While union officials may become party officers after having lost union jobs, I do not know of a single case where a leader quit a union post in preference for a position in UNIP. And while many union officials have taken positions in the government, I know of but three instances where they have undertaken government posts which involved party duties as well. The cases in point are Messrs Chapoloko and Nkoloma and the late Mr. Kalanga.
111 Report of the 4 Man Committee, Ja/9, vol. 7.
112 *Times of Zambia,* 8 February 1968.
113 Strike Diary Report on a Public Meeting, Chamboli, 1 May 1962, File S.9.
114 Report of the 4 Man Committee, Ja/9, vol. 7. See also, Meeting at Chamboli, 11 November 1963, File 100.47, vol. 8.
115 See, for example, the speeches reported in Meeting at Chamboli, 11 November 1963, File 100.47, vol. 8.
116 See note 12 and the account of David C. Mulford, *Zambia,* pp. 44–46.
117 Record of Decisions Reached at the 2nd Meeting of the Executive Committee, 14 January 1958, File 100.20.22, vol. 2. Memo, Secretary of Chamber of Mines, 8 June 1959, File 100.20.22, vol. 2. Record of Decisions, Executive Committee, 24 August 1959, File 100.20.22, vol. 6. Also note the following speech by the African personnel manager for Rhokana mine in 1957: "Mr. P. G. Lendrum . . . speaking as someone to whom many Africans have taken their troubles over the past years, has warned African employees of Rhokana Corporation to be careful of the things political agitators are saying on mine property. . . . 'I want you to sit back and listen carefully

and ask yourselves the question: how much are you going to allow people who do not work on this mine, who do not live here, people who know nothing of the struggles and difficulties we have gone through together—how much are you going to allow these people to influence your lives? You can be proud of the many things which you and your representatives have won. You are the highest paid African miners in Southern Africa. . . . This has been achieved without the "politicians" . . . ' He said he was speaking strongly because he did not want to see all that the African employees and their organisation and the management had struggled to get being destroyed by the big talkers" (*Luntandanya, 28* September 1957). See also speeches in *Luntandanya,* 11 March 1961.

118 Interviews, Head Office, 1967–68. Also see Report on Politics and the Mineworkers' Union, 29 March 1960, File 100.20.7D. Report, 28 November 1962, File 100.20.7A.

Chapter 8

1 Interviews with the Personnel Manager, Rhokana Corporation, 22–23 March 1968. See also UNIP's efforts to abolish racial segregation in change houses. Telex, Rhokana to ANMERCOSA, 29 October 1966, File A. 19.

2 See also Telex, CISB to Group Headquarters, 14 June 1966, File 100.20.YC. Occasionally, UNIP officials directly reprimanded expatriate personnel for their racist conduct; see Telex, CISB to Group Headquarters, 17 December 1964, File 100.41. For a discussion of racial cases, see Chief Industrial Relations Secretary to Resident Secretary, Ndola, 27 October 1964, File 100.65, vol. 5.

3 Interview, 17 November 1967.

4 Interview, 30 October 1967.

5 For particular instances, consult materials in File 100.56.B.

6 Interviews, 8 March 1968, and 25 September 1967. The protests were made directly to the Ministry of Home Affairs. See, Letter from Permanent Secretary, Ministry of Home Affairs, to Permanent Secretary, Ministry of Labour, 15 June 1967, File 100.65, vol. 3.

7 Interview, 8 January 1968.

8 Interview, General Secretary, Mineworkers' Union of Zambia, 23 June 1967.

9 Telex, CISB to Group Headquarters, 23 September 1967, File 100.65.

10 Interview, 8 April 1968. In 1966, the UNIP National Council urged

the government to take "stern measures" against strikers (*Times of Zambia,* 2 November 1966). In 1965 the UNIP Provincial Council for the copperbelt did likewise (*Times of Zambia,* 5 November 1965). In late April 1966, the party committed its local machinery to getting the mineworkers back to work as a prelude to the convocation of the Brown Commission (*Times of Zambia,* 11 April 1966).

11 Interview, with Personnel Manager, Rhokana Corporation, 4 May 1968.

12 Interviews, 31 May 1967 and 9 June 1967.

13 Interviews, 6 October 1967 and 7 July 1967.

14 Interviews, 6 October 1967 and 3 February 1968.

15 Ministers and other high party and government officials who spoke at meetings sponsored by UNIP in the mine townships often harped on the development tenets of government policy, including the necessity for wage restraint. We witnessed several spirited defenses by local party officials of the government's desire not to have rapid wage increases.

16 Interview, 31 October 1967.

17 Interviews, 6 October 1967 and 12 December 1967. These terms had been slogans during the independence struggle, but they had fallen out of usage. One *kwacha* equals ten shillings, and an *ngwee* is one one-hundredth of a *kwacha.*

18 Notes by the author on the meeting of the Regional Party, 28 January 1968.

19 This took place at the series of Productivity Seminars at Luanshya, Kitwe, and Mufulira in January 1968; also at a meeting with President Kaunda on 9 March 1968.

20 See His Excellency, Dr. K. D. Kaunda, *Humanism in Zambia and a Guide to Its Implementation* (Lusaka: Government Printer, 1967). Also, Republic of Zambia, *Address by His Excellency Dr. Kenneth D. Kaunda, President of the Republic of Zambia, to the Mulungushi Conference and a Guide to the Implementation of Humanism in Zambia* (Lusaka: Government Printer, 1967).

21 The Humanism campaign began in Kitwe in December 1968, with the regional secretary and assistant minister giving speeches to local party units who in turn "passed on the word." The regional secretary for Kitwe also spoke on Humanism before civic and religious groups, and got Rhokana Corporation, the mining company in his town, to agree to stress the relevance of Humanism in its training courses. Interviews, 11 December 1967 and 22 March 1968.

22 Observations over the period of constituency elections, 28 January
     1968, and branch elections, mid-February 1968.
23 Interviews, 17 November and 12 December 1967.
24 Stressed by the branch chairman, himself a former treasurer, in his
     instructions to the new treasurer and vice-treasurer, 5 May 1968. Also,
     discussions 15 December 1967, and 24 March 1968.
25 Minutes, 28 September 1967, 21 October 1967, 27 November 1967,
     7 December 1967, 15 January 1968, and 24 January 1968, File on
     the Kalela Planning Committee, kept by the Community Development
     Officer, Rhokana Corporation. Also, field notes, 19 February 1967,
     and 2 March 1968.
26 Interviews, 13 April 1968 and 15 April 1968.
27 This was done on repeated occasions during our stay. For an im-
     portant discussion of section organizations in Luanshya, see P[eter]
     Harries-Jones, " 'Home-boy' Ties and Political Organization in a Cop-
     perbelt Township," in *Social Networks in Urban Situations,* ed. J.
     Clyde Mitchell, pp. 297–349.
28 Field notes, 23 February 1968; 8 April 1968; 10 May 1968; and 19
     May 1968. In the cases we witnessed, the Main Body officials were
     simply informed that the Youth League intended to resort to coercive
     tactics. They dared not block the efforts of the youths. They feared
     being called cowardly for opposing militant action, and they especially
     feared such accusations by the women. At no time, however, did the
     Main Body leaders initiate such actions, or give public support for
     them. They did not like these tactics, but they could not act against
     them. Nonparticipants fell into three major cotegories: foreigners—
     Rhodesians and Malawians; members of the Watchtower sect; and
     well-to-do mine employees. The sensitive position of these deviants
     made it impossible for us to study them. Active opponents to UNIP—
     members of ANC and UP—were rare among the members of the
     mining community; it was believed that the few who did exist were
     drawn from the Lozi and Tonga tribesmen, and especially from the
     well-to-do members of these tribes.
29 Field notes, 8 July 1967; 12 December 1967; and 19 May 1968.
30 "Constitution of the Rhokana Mine Townships Council" (Photocopy,
     1967, Author's Collection); Notes for Discussion with United Nations
     Advisors on the Incorporation of Mine Townships, 6 March 1968, File
     100.5.
31 Minutes, Rhokana Mine Townships Council, May through August

1967, Files of the Chief Community Services Officer, Rhokana Corporation.

32 Field notes from June through July 1967. Minutes, Rhokana Mine Townships Council, Markets and Trading Committee, April–July 1967, Files of the Chief Community Services Officer, Rhokana Corporation. Special File on Fish Traders, Chief Community Services Officer, Rhokana Corporation. Also, materials contained in File D.4, vol. 3.

33 Thus, the branch chairman and secretary both delayed for months moving from their low-grade houses to better houses to which they were entitled; the houses they remained in were deemed substandard by the companies and slated for demolition and renewal.

34 Interview, 23 February 1968.

35 Isaac Deutscher discusses the role of the Soviet Communist Party in his chapter, "Russia" in *Comparative Labor Movements,* ed. Walter Galenson. See also Emily Clark Brown, "The Local Union in Soviet Industry," *Industrial and Labor Relations Review* 13 (1960): 192–215, and the discussion of the industrial role of the East German Communist Party in Reinhard Bendix, *Work and Authority in Industry.*

36 The sole source of party patronage is the Mine Township Council. And aside from the free beer it distributes on Independence Day, it has no favors to disburse. It does allocate market stalls, but these are few in number. Moreover, they can be given only to retiring miners of long service who want a source of income so as to remain in town. Their allocation is therefore of little use in influencing those who are still working in industrial jobs. As to roads, health services, and houses—the council can only advise on these. Responsibility for their maintenance is exercised by the community services officers, who are responsible to the Personnel Manager.

37 For a review of the progress of integration of mine facilities, see Telex, CISB to all General Managers, 8 August 1967, File 100.65, vol. 4 and the series of replies to this telex contained in that file.

Chapter 9

1 For descriptions of this phenomenon in England and France, respectively, see B[enjamin] C[harles] Roberts, *Trade Unions in a Free Society,* and Val. R. Lorwin, *The French Labor Movement.*

2 An interesting deviant case is Norway, where unions have assisted in implementing policies of wage control and restraint. One of the

reasons offered to explain this phenomenon is the centralized structure of power in Norwegian trade unions. See Walter Galenson, "Scandinavia," in *Comparative Labor Movements*, ed. Walter Galenson. For a discussion of the structure of power in United States trade unions, see Phillip M. Marcus, "Organizational Change: The Case of American Trade Unions," in *Explorations in Social Change*, ed. George K. Zollschan and Walter Hirsch (Boston: Houghton Mifflin Company 1964).

3   For an intriguing deviant case, see Seymour Martin Lipset, Martin Trow, and James Coleman in their analysis of the International Typographical Union in *Union Democracy*. For a discussion of this subject in an African union, see David R. Smock, *Conflict and Control in an African Union*.

4   See Lucian W. Pye, "Introduction" and "Models of Communications Systems," in *Communications and Political Development*, ed. Lucian W. Pye (Princeton: Princeton University Press, 1963).

5   Note Lipset's analysis of worker radicalism in terms of the isolation of industrial communities in *Political Man* (Garden City: Doubleday and Company, 1960). For a discussion of the effects of residential isolation on radicalism among miners, see Clark Kerr and Abraham Siegel, "The Inter-industry Propensity to Strike, An International Comparison," in *Industrial Conflict*, ed. Arthur W. Kornhauser, Robert Dubin, and Arthur M. Ross (New York: McGraw-Hill Book Co., 1954), pp. 189–212.

6   This supports Almond's contention that there is a direct relationship between increased differentiation and increased output capabilities. See Gabriel A. Almond and G. Bingham Powell, *Comparative Politics*, especially pp. 208–12.

7   An interesting illustration of this solution is the case of Soviet unions in the 1920s. As in Zambia, a large proportion of the Soviet labor force was composed of recent immigrants into the urban areas. Soviet unions in part gained the ability to restrain the demands of their members as industrial employees by serving their interests as urban immigrants. See Isaac Deutscher, "Russia," in *Comparative Labor Movements*, ed. Walter Galenson, pp. 480–574.

Chapter 10

1   The government will accelerate the payments to the companies when two-thirds of the dividends earned by the government from the mining industry exceeds the planned installments.

2 Anglo-American Corporation, "Announcement to Shareholders," 17 November 1969. Roan Selection Trust, "Announcement to Shareholders," 17 November 1969.

3 *Zambia Mail,* 30 January 1969.

4 President Kaunda, "Address at the Opening of the Second National Convention, Kitwe," Press Release, Zambia Information Services, 12 December 1969, p. 17.

5 Personal communication, 7 January 1970.

6 *Zambia Mail,* 3 April 1970.

7 Formerly the government did possess "mineral rights," but these amounted solely to the right to collect royalties for the use of mineralized lands; the actual property rights to these mineral deposits had devolved from the British South Africa Company to RST and AAC. See: "Zambia," *African Diary* 9 (30 April to 6 May 1969): 4427, and 9 (28 May to 3 June 1969): 4465; "Zambia," *Keesings Contemporary Archives* (30 August to 2 September 1969): 23534–23536. Under these arrangements, the government has granted licenses to firms from Yugoslavia, Japan, Rumania, Italy, Canada, and Switzerland. *Zambia Mail,* 4 April 1970.

8 *Zambia Mail,* 26 May 1970 and 8 September 1970.

9 *Zambia Mail,* 31 March 1970. As happened frequently in the immediate post-independence period, the local branch secretary of the union attacked the management for provoking the strike, while the general secretary of the union attacked the workers for an illegal work stoppage (*Zambia Mail,* 21 and 22 January 1970).

10 *Zambia Mail,* 27 February 1970.

11 President Kaunda, "Address," p. 13.

12 Ibid., p. 16.

13 Mineworkers' Union of Zambia and Copper Industry Service Bureau, "Memorandum of Agreement" (Photocopy, Author's Collection, 15 May 1969); *Zambia Mail,* 8 September 1970.

14 The combined consumer price index for higher and lower incomes for all itemes rose only 2.6 percent between November 1968 and February 1970 (*Zambia Business Mail,* 27 May 1970). While these measures have slowed the rate of inflation, they also have adversely affected employment. Thus, the government reports that in 1968 employment actually fell by 0.3 percent; the locus of decline was principally in the contruction industry, and among non-Africans. Republic of Zambia, Ministry of Development and Finance, *Economic Report, 1969* (Lusaka: Government Printer, 1970), p. 19.

15   *Zambia Mail,* 24 February 1970, p. 1.

16   We must be cautious in this assessment, however. Following these dismissals, President Kaunda found it necessary to speak out against dangerous rumors which were being spread at Roan. The rumors contended that the government planned to fire all the mineworkers and rehire them as civil service employees. The Head Office's power to dismiss the local Roan officials may not, therefore, validly indicate its degree of effective control over the local. *Zambia Mail,* 25 May 1970.

17   *Zambia Mail,* 19 October 1970; 14, 17, 21 November 1970.

18   *Zambia Mail,* 9 January 1970; 23 March 1970; 31 March 1970.

19   United Nations Development Programme, Technical Assistance Sector/International Labour Office, *Report to the Government of Zambia on Incomes, Wages, and Prices in Zambia.*

20   The critics of Turner base their attacks on the analysis of wages, prices, income and productivity contained in the Republic of Zambia, Office of the Vice-President, Development Division, *Zambian Manpower.* For debates on the Turner report by government and university economists, see *Zambia Mail,* 12 February 1970, p. 2; and *Zambia Business Mail,* 4 March 1970, p. 7; *Times of Zambia,* 1 May 1970 and 8 May 1970.

Selected Bibliography

Bibliographies

Friedland, William H. *Unions, Labor and Industrial Relations in Africa: An Annotated Bibliography.* Cornell Research Papers in International Studies, 4. Ithaca: Center for International Studies, Cornell University, 1965. (For studies of labor in Africa.)

Gifford, Prosser. "An Initial Survey of the Local Archival and Published Materials for Zambian History (1895–Independence 1964)," *African Social Research,* no. 1 (1966), pp. 59–84. (For materials in the archives of the government of the Republic of Zambia.)

University of Zambia, Institute for Social Research. *A Complete List of the Publications of the Former Rhodes-Livingstone Institute.* Lusaka: Institute for Social Research, 1966. (For works on Zambian sociology, history, and ethnography.)

Books and Articles on Labor and Development
and on Development Theory

Almond, Gabriel A. "Introduction." In *The Politics of the Developing Areas,* edited by Gabriel A. Almond and James S. Coleman. Princeton: Princeton University Press, 1960.

Almond, Gabriel A., and G. Bingham Powell, Jr. *Comparative Politics: A Developmental Approach.* Boston: Little, Brown and Company, 1966.

Bendix, Reinhard. *Work and Authority in Industry.* New York: John Wiley and Sons, 1956.

Berg, Elliot. "French West Africa." In *Labor and Economic Development,* edited by Walter Galenson. New York: John Wiley and Sons, 1959.

Berg, Elliot. "The Development of a Labor Force in Sub-Saharan Africa." *Economic Development and Cultural Change* 13 (1965): 394–412.

Berg, Elliot, and Jeffrey Butler. "Trade Unions." In *Political Parties and National Integration in Tropical Africa,* edited by James S. Coleman and Carl G. Rosberg, Jr. Berkeley and Los Angeles: University of California Press, 1964.

Brown, Emily Clark. "The Local Union in Soviet Industry: Its Relations with Members, Party, and Management." *Industrial and Labor Relations Review* 13 (1960): 192–215.

Coleman, James S., and Carl G. Rosberg, Jr. "Introduction" and "Conclusion." In *Political Parties and National Integration in Tropical Africa,* edited by James S. Coleman and Carl G. Rosberg, Jr. Berkeley and Los Angeles: University of California Press, 1964.

Davies, Ioan. *African Trade Unions.* Harmondsworth, Middlesex: Penguin Books, 1966.

Deutscher, Isaac. "Russia." In *Comparative Labor Movements,* edited by Walter Galenson. New York: Russell and Russell, 1968.

Dunlop, John T. *Industrial Relations Systems.* New York: Henry Holt and Company, 1958.

Easton, David. "An Approach to the Analysis of Political Systems." *World Politics* 9 (1957): 383–400.

Easton, David. *A Systems Analysis of Political Life.* New York: John Wiley and Sons, 1965.

Friedland, William H. "Basic Social Trends." In *African Socialism,* edited by William H. Friedland and Carl G. Rosberg, Jr. Stanford: Stanford University Press for the Hoover Institution on War, Revolution, and Peace, 1964.

Friedland, William H. "Labor's Role in Emerging African Socialist States." In *The Role of Labor in African Nation-Building,* edited by Willard A. Beling. New York: Praeger, 1968.

Friedland, William H. *Vuta Kamba: The Development of Trade Unions in Tanganyika.* Stanford: Hoover Institution Press, 1969.

Friedland, William H., and Dorothy Nelkin. "Labor in the Post-Independence Period." Paper delivered at the Annual Meeting of the African Studies Association, November 1967, in New York. Mimeographed.

Friedland, William H., and Carl G. Rosberg, Jr. "The Anatomy of African Socialism." In *African Socialism,* edited by William H. Friedland and Carl G. Rosberg, Jr. Stanford: Stanford University Press for the Hoover Institution on War, Revolution, and Peace, 1964.

Galenson, Walter. "Introduction." In *Labor and Economic Development,* edited by Walter Galenson. New York: John Wiley and Sons, 1959.

Galenson, Walter. "Scandinavia." In *Comparative Labor Movements,* edited by Walter Galenson. New York: Russell and Russell, 1968.

Georgulus, Nikos. "Post-1964 Trends in the Tanzania Unions: A Commentary." Paper delivered at the Annual Meeting of the African Studies Association, November 1967, in New York. Mimeographed.

Harbison, Frederick H. "Egypt." In *Labor and Economic Development,* edited by Walter Galenson. New York: John Wiley and Sons, 1959.

Harbison, Frederick H., and Ibrahim Abdelkader Ibrahim. *Human Resources for Egyptian Enterprise.* New York: McGraw-Hill Book Company, 1958.

Hirschman, Albert O. *Journeys Toward Progress: Studies of Economic Policy-Making in Latin America.* New York: The Twentieth Century Fund, 1963.

Holt, Robert T., and John E. Turner. *The Political Basis of Economic Development: An Exploration in Comparative Political Analysis.* New York: D. Van Nostrand Company, 1966.

Horowitz, Daniel L. *The Italian Labor Movement.* Cambridge: Harvard University Press, 1963.

Kannappan, Subbiah. "The Tata Steel Strike: Some Dilemmas of Industrial Relations in a Developing Economy." *The Journal of Political Economy* 67 (1959): 489–507.

Kerr, Clark; John T. Dunlop; Frederick Harbison; and Charles A. Myers. *Industrialism and Industrial Man.* New York: Oxford University Press, 1964.

Kilson, Martin L. "Authoritarian and Single-Party Tendencies in African Politics." *World Politics* 15 (1963): 262–94.

Kilson, Martin L. "Tensions and Dynamics of Single-Party Systems: Case of the Erst-While Convention Peoples' Party." Prepared for delivery at the Annual Meeting of the American Political Science Association, September 1968, in Washington, D.C. Mimeographed.

Lofchie, Michael F., and Carl G. Rosberg, Jr. "The Political Status of African Trade Unions." In *The Role of Labor in African Nation-Building,* edited by Willard A. Beling. New York: Praeger, 1968.

Lorwin, Val R. *The French Labor Movement.* Cambridge: Harvard University Press, 1954.

Lynd, G. E. *The Politics of African Trade Unionism.* New York: Praeger, 1968.

Mathur, A. S. "Statutory Dispute Settlement in India." In *The Challenge of Industrial Relations in the Pacific-Asian Countries,* edited by Harold S. Roberts and Paul F. Brissenden. Honolulu: East-West Center Press, 1965.

Mehta, Asoka. "The Non-Statutory Approach to the Settlement of Industrial Disputes in India." In *The Challenge of Industrial Relations in the Pacific-Asian Countries,* edited by Harold S. Roberts and Paul F. Brissenden. Honolulu: East-West Center Press, 1965.

Meynaud, Jean, and Anisse Salah-Bey. *Trade Unionism in Africa: A Study of Its Growth and Orientation.* London: Methuen and Co., 1967.

Millen, Bruce H. *The Political Role of Labor in Developing Countries.*
Washington, D.C.: The Brookings Institution, 1963.
Morris, Morris David. "Trade Unions and the State." In *Leadership and
Political Institutions in India,* edited by Richard L. Park and Irene
Tinker. Princeton: Princeton University Press, 1959.
Myers, Charles A. *Labor Problems in the Industrialization of India.*
Cambridge: Harvard University Press, 1958.
Norman, John. *Labor and Politics in Libya and Arab Africa.* New York:
Bookman Associates, 1965.
Parsons, Talcott, and Neil J. Smelser. *Economy and Society.* New York:
The Free Press, 1965.
Pye, Lucian W. *Aspects of Political Development.* Boston: Little, Brown
and Company, 1966.
Roberts, B[enjamin] C[harles]. *Trade Unions in a Free Society.* London:
Hutchinson of London for the Institute of Economic Affairs, 1959.
Roberts, B[enjamin] C[harles]. *Labour in the Tropical Territories of the
Commonwealth.* London: G. Bell and Sons, 1964.
Roberts, B[enjamin] C[harles], and L. Greyfie de Bellecombe. *Collective
Bargaining in African Countries.* London: Macmillan with the Interna-
tional Institute for Labour Studies, 1967.
Scott, Roger D. "The Determination of Statutory Minimum Wages in
East Africa." *The Canadian Journal of African Studies* 1 (1967): 143–
53.
Scott, Roger. *The Development of Trade Unions in Uganda.* Nairobi:
East African Publishing House. 1966.
Seidman, Joel; Jack London; and Bernard Karsh. "Political Consciousness
in a Local Union." *Public Opinion Quarterly* 15 (1951): 692–702.
Smock, David R. *Conflict and Control in an African Union.* Stanford:
Hoover Institution Press, 1969.
Sufrin, Sidney C. *Unions in Emerging Societies: Frustration and Politics.*
Syracuse: Syracuse University Press, 1964.
Taborsky, Edward. "The Class Struggle, the Proletariat, and the Develop-
ing Nations." *Review of Politics* 29 (1967): 370–86.
Tordoff, William. "Trade Unionism in Tanzania." *The Journal of
Development Studies* 2 (1966): 408–30.
Wallerstein, Immanuel. *Africa: The Politics of Independence.* New York:
Vintage Books, 1961.
Warren, W. M. "Urban Real Wages and the Nigerian Trade Union
Movement." *Economic Development and Cultural Change* 15 (1966):
21–36.

Case Study Materials

BOOKS

Baldwin, Robert E. *Economic Development and Export Growth: A Study of Northern Rhodesia, 1920–1960.* Berkeley and Los Angeles: University of California Press, 1966.

Bancroft, J[oseph] Austen. *Mining in Northern Rhodesia.* London: The British South Africa Company, 1961.

Barber, William J. *The Economy of British Central Africa: A Case Study of Economic Development in a Dualistic Society.* Stanford: Stanford University Press, 1961.

Breese, Gerald. *Urbanization in Newly Developing Countries.* Englewood Cliffs, New Jersey: Prentice-Hall, 1966.

Brelsford, W. V. *The Tribes of Northern Rhodesia.* Lusaka: Government Printer, 1957.

Clausen, Lars. *Industrialisierung in Schwarzafrika: Eine Soziologische Lotstudie zueier Grossbetriebe in Sambia.* Bielefeld: Bertelsmann Universitätsverlag, 1968.

Clegg, Edward. *Race and Politics: Partnership in the Federation of Rhodesia and Nyasaland.* London: Oxford University Press, 1960.

Commission for Technical Cooperation in Africa South of the Sahara. *Absenteeism and Labour Turnover: Proceedings under Item 1 of the Sixth Inter-African Labour Conference.* Abidjan: CCTA, 1961.

Copper Industry Service Bureau. *Copperbelt of Zambia Mining Industry Year Book for* [*various dates*]. Kitwe: Copper Industry Service Bureau, various dates.

Davidson, J. W. *The Northern Rhodesian Legislative Council.* London: Faber and Faber for Nuffield College, 1948.

Elliot, Charles, ed. *Constraints on the Economic Development of Zambia.* Nairobi: Oxford University Press, forthcoming.

Epstein, A. L. *Politics in an Urban African Community.* Manchester: Manchester University Press on behalf of The Rhodes-Livingstone Institute, Northern Rhodesia, 1958.

Fortman, Bastiaan de Gaay, ed. *After Mulungushi: The Economics of Zambian Humanism.* Nairobi: East African Publishing House, 1969.

Franck, Thomas M. *Race and Nationalism: The Struggle for Power in Rhodesia-Nyasaland.* London: Allen and Unwin, 1960.

Franklin, Harry. *Unholy Wedlock.* London: Allen and Unwin, 1963.

Gann, L[ewis] H. *A History of Northern Rhodesia: Early Days to 1953.* London: Chatto and Windus, 1964.

Gouldner, Alvin W. *Patterns of Industrial Bureaucracy*. Glencoe: The Free Press, 1954.

Gouldner, Alvin W. *Wildcat Strike*. Yellow Springs, Ohio: The Antioch Press, 1954.

Gray, Richard. *The Two Nations: Aspects of the Development of Race Relations in the Rhodesias and Nyasaland*. London: Oxford University Press, 1960.

Hall, Richard. *Zambia*. New York: Praeger, 1965.

Hall, Richard. *The High Price Principles: Kaunda & the White South*. New York: Africana Publishing Corporation, 1970.

Kaunda, Kenneth. *Zambia Shall Be Free*. London: Heinemann, 1962.

Legum, Colin, ed. *Zambia, Independence and Beyond: The Speeches of Kenneth Kaunda*. London: Thomas Nelson and Sons, 1966.

Leys, Colin, and Cranford Pratt. *A New Deal in Central Africa*. New York: Praeger, 1960.

Lipset, Seymour Martin; Martin A. Trow; and James S. Coleman. *Union Democracy: The Internal Politics of the International Typographical Union*. Garden City: Anchor Books, 1962.

Little, Kenneth. *West African Urbanization: A Study of Voluntary Associations in Social Change*. Cambridge: Cambridge University Press, 1965.

McCulloch, Merran. *A Social Survey of the African Population of Livingstone*. The Rhodes-Livingstone Papers, no. 26. Lusaka: The Rhodes-Livingstone Institute, Northern Rhodesia, 1956.

Mason, Philip. *Year of Decision*. London: Oxford University Press, 1960.

Mayer, Philip. *Townsmen or Tribesmen*. Cape Town: Oxford University Press, 1961.

Mitchell, J. Clyde. *African Urbanization in Ndola and Luanshya*. Rhodes-Livingstone Communication, no. 6. Lusaka: The Rhodes-Livingstone Institute, Northern Rhodesia, 1954.

Mitchell, J. Clyde. *The Kalela Dance: Aspects of Social Relationships among Urban Africans in Northern Rhodesia*. The Rhodes-Livingstone Papers, no. 27. Lusaka: The Rhodes-Livingstone Institute, Northern Rhodesia, 1956.

Mitchell, J. Clyde. *An Outline of the Sociological Background to African Labour*. Salisbury: Ensign Publishers, 1961.

Mitchell, J. Clyde, ed. *Social Networks in Urban Situations*. Manchester: Published for The Institute for Social Research, University of Zambia, by Manchester University Press, 1969.

Mulford, David C. *The Northern Rhodesia General Election*. Nairobi: Oxford University Press, 1964.

Mulford, David C. *Zambia: The Politics of Independence, 1957–1964*. London: Oxford University Press, 1967.

Mwewa, Parkinson B. *The African Railway Workers' Union, Ndola, Northern Rhodesia*. Rhodes-Livingstone Communication, no. 10. Lusaka: The Rhodes-Livingstone Institute, Northern Rhodesia, 1958.

National Institute for Personnel Research in association with The Institute for Social Research, University of Natal. "The Attitudes of White Mining Employees Towards Life and Work on the Copperbelt." 2 vols. Mimeographed. Kitwe: Copper Industry Service Bureau, 1960.

Northern Rhodesia Chamber of Mines. *Northern Rhodesia Chamber of Mines Year Book [various dates]*. Kitwe: Northern Rhodesia Chamber of Mines, various dates.

Pauw, B[erthold] A[dolf]. *The Second Generation: A Study of the Family among Urbanized Bantu in East London*. Cape Town: Oxford University Press, 1963.

Powdermaker, Hortense. *Copper Town: Changing Africa*. New York: Harper and Row, 1962.

Rotberg, Robert I. *The Rise of Nationalism in Central Africa: The Making of Malawi and Zambia, 1873–1964*. Cambridge: Harvard University Press, 1965.

Sanger, Clyde. *Central African Emergency*. London: Heinemann, 1960.

Simms, Ruth P. *Urbanization in West Africa: A Review of Current Literature*. Evanston: Northwestern University Press, 1965.

Southall, Aidan, ed. *Social Change in Modern Africa*. London: Oxford University Press for the International African Institute, 1961.

Southall, Aidan W., and Peter C. W. Gutkind. *Townsmen in the Making: Kampala and Its Suburbs*. Kampala: East African Institute of Social Research, 1957.

Stokes, Eric, and Richard Brown, eds. *The Zambesian Past: Studies in Central African History*. Manchester: Manchester University Press for The Institute for Social Research, University of Zambia, 1966.

Thompson, C. H., and H. W. Woodruff. *Economic Development in Rhodesia and Nyasaland*. London: Dennis Dobson Limited, 1954.

United Nations Educational, Scientific, and Cultural Organization (UNESCO)/International African Institute. *Social Implications of Industrialization and Urbanization in Africa South of the Sahara*. Paris: UNESCO, 1956.

Warmington, W. A. *A West African Trade Union*. London: Oxford University Press for the Nigerian Institute of Social and Economic Research, 1960.

ARTICLES

"Mining Labour in Northern Rhodesia." *International Labour Review* 33 (1936): 721–26.

"Native Labour in Northern Rhodesia." *International Labour Review* 39 (1939): 75–85.

Baldwin, Robert E. "Wage Policy in a Dual Economy—The Case of Northern Rhodesia." *Race* 4 (1962): 73–87.

Bettison, David G. "Factors in the Determination of Wage Rates in Central Africa." *The Rhodes-Livingstone Journal* 28 (1961): 22–46.

Clausen, Lars. "On Attitudes towards Industrial Conflict in Zambian Industry." *African Social Research* 2 (1966); 117–38.

Epstein, A. L. "Linguistic Innovation and Culture on the Copperbelt, Northern Rhodesia." *Southwestern Journal of Anthropology* 15 (1959): 235–53.

Epstein, A. L. "The Network and Urban Social Organization." *The Rhodes-Livingstone Journal* 29 (1961): 29–62.

Gann, L[ewis] H. "The Northern Rhodesian Copper Industry and the World of Copper, 1923–52." *The Rhodes-Livingstone Journal* 18 (1955): 1–18.

Gluckman, Max. "Tribalism in Modern British Central Africa." *Cahiers d'études africaines* 1 (1960): 55–70.

Gulliver, P. H. "Incentives in Labour Migration." *Human Organization* 19 (1960): 159–63.

Hooker, J. R. "The Role of the Labour Department in the Birth of African Trade Unionism in Northern Rhodesia." *International Review of Social History* 10 (1965): 1–22.

Lomas, P. K. "African Trade Unionism on the Copperbelt of Northern Rhodesia." *South African Journal of Economics* 26 (1958): 110–22.

Mitchell, J. Clyde. "A Note on the Urbanisation of Africans on the Copperbelt." *The Rhodes-Livingstone Journal* 12 (1951): 20–27.

Mitchell, J. Clyde. "Africans in Industrial Towns in Northern Rhodesia." In *His Royal Highness the Duke of Edinburgh's Study Conference on the Human Problem of Industrial Communities within the Commonwealth and Empire*. Vol. 2. London: Oxford University Press, 1957.

Mitchell, J. Clyde. "Aspects of Occupational Prestige in a Plural Society."

In *The New Elites of Tropical Africa,* edited by P. C. Lloyd. London: Oxford University Press for the International African Institute, 1966.

Mitchell, J. Clyde, and A. L. Epstein. "Occupational Prestige and Social Status among Urban Africans in Northern Rhodesia." *Africa* 29 (1959): 22–40.

Moore, R. I. B. "Native Wages and Standard of Living in Northern Rhodesia." *African Studies* 1 (1942): 142–48.

Phillips, E. A. B. "General Trends in Training for Management with Special Reference to Rhokana Corporation Limited." Paper submitted to the Seventh Commonwealth Mining and Metallurgical Congress, May 1961, no place. Mimeographed.

Prain, R[onald] I. "The Problem of African Advancement on the Copperbelt of Northern Rhodesia." *African Affairs* 53 (1954): 91–103.

Prain R[onald] I. "The Stabilization of Labour in the Rhodesian Copperbelt." *African Affairs* 55 (1956): 305–12.

Prain, R[onald] I. "The Stabilization of Labour in the Rhodesian Copperbelt." In *His Royal Highness the Duke of Edinburgh's Study Conference on the Human Problem of Industrial Communities within the Commonwealth and Empire.* Vol. 2. London: Oxford University Press, 1957.

Rheinallt, Jones J. D. "The Effects of Urbanization in South and Central Africa." *African Affairs* 52 (1953): 37–44.

Rotberg, Robert I. "Tribalism and Politics in Zambia." *Africa Report* 12 (1967): 29–35.

Scott, Ian and Robert Molteno. "The Zambian General Elections." *Africa Report* 14 (1969): 42–46.

Sklar, Richard L. "Zambia's Response to U.D.I." *Mawazo* 1 (1968): 11–32.

Vilakazi, Absolom L. "Non-Governmental Agencies and their Role in Development in Africa: A Case Study," *African Studies Review* 13 (1970): 169–202.

Waldstein, Nan S. "The Struggle for African Advancement within the Copper Industry of Northern Rhodesia." Mimeographed. Cambridge: Center for Internationl Studies of the Massachusetts Institute of Technology, 1957.

Waldstein, Nan S. "The Indigenous African Trade Union Movements of Nigeria, the Federation of Rhodesia and Nyasaland, French West Africa, and the Belgian Congo." Mimeographed. Cambridge: Center for International Studies of the Massachusetts Institute of Technology, 1960.

Wallerstein, Immanuel. "Ethnicity and National Integration in West Africa." *Cahiers d'études africaines* 3 (1960): 129–39.
Wallerstein, Immanuel. "The Political Role of Voluntary Associations in Middle Africa." In *Urbanization in African Social Change: Proceedings of the Inaugural Seminar Held in the Centre of African Studies, University of Edinburgh,* edited by Kenneth Little. Edinburgh: Centre of African Studies, 1963.
Wallerstein, Immanuel. "Voluntary Associations." In *Political Parties and National Integration in Tropical Africa,* edited by James S. Coleman and Carl G. Rosberg, Jr. Berkeley and Los Angeles: University of California Press, 1964.
Welensky, Roy. "Africans and Trade Unions in Northern Rhodesia." *African Affairs* 45 (1946): 185–91.
Williams, R. W. "Trade Unions in Africa." *African Affairs* 54 (1955): 267–79.

Official Publications

FEDERATION OF RHODESIA AND NYASALAND

Central Statistical Office. *Census of Production, 1962, 1963, and 1964.* Salisbury: Central Statistical Office, 1962, 1963, 1964.
National Accounts of the Federation of Rhodesia and Nyasaland, 1954–62. Salisbury: Central Statistical Office, 1963.
Report of the Commissioner of Taxes for the Year[s] Ending 30 June 1955–30 June 1963. Salisbury: Government Printer, 1956–64.

GREAT BRITAIN, COLONIAL OFFICE

Report of the Nyasaland Commission of Inquiry. Cmnd. 814. London: HMSO, July 1959.
Northern Rhodesia: Proposals for Constitutional Change. Cmnd. 1295. London: HMSO, 1961.
Northern Rhodesia: Proposals for Constitutional Change. Cmnd. 1423. London: HMSO, June 1961.
Report of the Advisory Commission on the Review of the Constitution of Rhodesia and Nyasaland. Cmnd. 1148. London: HMSO, October 1960.

NORTHERN RHODESIA

"Report and Award of the Arbitrator C. W. Guillebaud, Esq., CBE." Lusaka, January 1953. Mimeographed.

Report of the Commission of Inquiry into Unrest on the Copperbelt July–August 1963. Lusaka: Government Printer, 1963.

Department of Labour. *Trade Unions and How They Work.* Lusaka: Government Printer, 1964.

Department of Labour. *Annual Report of the Department of Labor for* [*various years*]. Lusaka: Government Printer, various years.

Ministry of Finance. *Estimates of Revenue and Expenditures for the* [*various years*]. Lusaka: Government Printer, various years.

Ministry of Finance, Income Tax Department. *Annual Report for the Year* [*s*] *1948–1954.* Lusaka: Government Printer, 1948–55.

REPUBLIC OF ZAMBIA

An Outline of the Transitional Development Plan. Lusaka: Government Printer, 1965.

National Accounts 1964–1965 and Input-Output Table 1965. Lusaka: Central Statistical Office, November 1966.

National Convention on the Four Year Development Plan: Kitwe, 11th–15th January 1967. Lusaka: Government Printer, 1967.

First National Development Plan, 1966–1970. Lusaka: Office of National Development and Planning, July 1966.

Report of the Commission of Inquiry into the Mining Industry, 1966. Lusaka: Government Printer, 1966.

Government Paper on the Report of the Commission of Inquiry into the Mining Industry (*Brown Report, 1966*). Lusaka: Government Printer, 1966.

Official Verbatim Report of the Debates of the National Assembly. Lusaka: Government Printer, various years.

Monthly Digest of Statistics. Lusaka: Central Statistical Office, various years.

Ministry of Finance. *Estimates of Revenue and Expenditure* (*Including Capital Expenditure*) *for the* [*various years*]. Lusaka: Government Printer, various years.

Ministry of Finance, Department of Taxes. *Annual Report for the Period 1st June 1964 to the 30th June 1965.* Lusaka: Government Printer, 1966.

Ministry of Labour. *Hard Work and Happiness: Towards Labour Stability, Social Justice, and Equitable Welfare.* Lusaka: Ministry of Labour and Social Development, 1966.

Ministry of Labour. *Livingstone Labour Conference.* Lusaka: Government Printer, 1967.

Ministry of Labour. *Annual Report of the Department of Labour: 1964–1966.* Lusaka: Government Printer, 1965–68.

Ministry of Labour. *The Progress of Zambianization in the Mining Industry.* Lusaka: Government Printer, 1968.

Office of the Vice-President, Development Division. *Zambian Manpower.* Lusaka: Government Printer, 1969.

UNITED NATIONS

Economic Commission for Africa, Food and Agricultural Organization. *Economic Survey Mission on the Economic Development of Zambia.* Ndola: Falcon Press, 1964.

United Nations Development Programme, Technical Assistance Sector / International Labour Office. *Report to the Government of Zambia on Incomes, Wages and Prices in Zambia: Policy and Machinery.* Lusaka: Government Printer, 1969.

Files of the Copper Industry Service Bureau, Kitwe

Many of these files run several volumes; for example, File 100.20 on the Mineworkers' Union of Zambia runs over thirty volumes.

File 30.8.8	Zambia National Provident Fund
File 80.1.2	Change Over from Ticket to Daily Paid
File 100.3	African Labour Classification, Rates of Pay
File 100.3.2	Classification
File 100.3.3	Wages
File 100.5	Cost of Living
File 100.5.3	Budget Survey
File 100.20	General, Zambia Mineworkers' Union
File 100.20.1	Meetings with Executive Council, ZMU
File 100.20C	Rhokana, ZMU Meetings
File 100.20.4.C	Local Disputes, Rhokana
File 100.20.7.C	Reports, Rhokana
File 100.20.7.I	Mineworkers' Union Youth Movement
File 100.20.22	Subscriptions
File 100.20.24	Shop Stewards
File 100.20.31.A	Minutes of the MJIC, ZMU
File 100.41	African Labour
File 100.41.1	1963 Copperbelt Unrest
File 100.42	Tribal Representatives
File 100.46.11	African Advancement into Staff

File 100.47   Mines Local Staff Association
File 100.47.1   Meetings with MLSA
File 100.47.2   Meeting with Local Branches, MLSA
File 100.47.3   Salary Claims, MLSA
File 100.47.4   MJIC, MLSA
File 100.50   Labour Rationalization
File 100.52   *Mwabombeni*
File 100.60   Trades Union Congress
File 100.61   National Union of Mineworkers
File 100.65   Mineworkers' Union of Zambia
Verbatim Testimony, Branigan Commission of Inquiry, 1956.
Verbatim Testimony, Brown Commission of Inquiry, 1966.
Verbatim Testimony, Commission of Inquiry into Copperbelt Unrest, 1963.

Files of Rhokana Corporation Limited, Nkana

Personnel Manager Files, M.13 (MUZ.CISB)
Personnel Manager Files, S.6 (CISB)
Personnel Manager Files, A.25 (African Mineworkers' Union)
Personnel Manager Files, A.40 (MASA)
Personnel Manager Files, General File
Files, Chief Community Services Officer
Files, Chief Industrial Relations Officer
Files, Manpower Services Department

Files of the National Archives, Lusaka

SECRETARIAT FILES

African Labour Corps, Monthly Reports. Sec/Lab/65.
Africans and the Mineworkers' Union, Progress of African Trade Unions. 52/20, 21.
Arbitration, Compulsory and African Representation. Sec/Lab/106, 107.
Arbitration, Voluntary. Sec/Lab/116.
Boss Boys Associations and Tribal Representatives. Secretariat 10/14/1D; J/1, 2; 52/17–19.
Circulars, Ministry of Labour and Mines. Sec/Lab/233.
Copperbelt African Mineworkers Dispute. Sec/Lab/150.
Departmental Histories. Secretariat E/2709/4; 93/417.
Department of Labour and Mines, Organisation and Staff. Sec/Lab/100.
Industrial Advisor: Functions. Sec/Lab/115.
Industrial Conciliation and Arbitration. Sec/Lab/123, 124.

Industrial Councils, Policy. Sec/Lab/112.
Mineworkers' Union N.R. Sec/Lab/84; 94–96.
Mineworkers' Union of N.R. and Mining Companies. Sec/Lab/108, 109.
Nchanga Mines Dispute. Sec/Lab/130, 132.
Salaried Staff Association. Sec/Lab/160.
Strike by Africans on the Copperbelt. Sec/Lab/78, 79; 104; 136–139.
Trade Unions, African. Sec/Lab/125–128.

DEPARTMENT OF LABOUR FILES

African Advancement. Ue/3, volumes 1–3.
African Mineworkers' Union. Ja/9, volumes 7 and 8.
African Trade Unions. C/1821.
African Trade Unions, Monthly Reports. C/1831/1.
African Trade Union Congress. C/1821/4.
Arbitration, General Policy. C/1937.
Confederation, Trade Union Formation, C/1822/u.
Federal Trades Union Congress. C/1822/3.
Industrial Relations, Policy. C/1815/m.
Labour Reports. C/1828.
Northern Rhodesia African Mine Workers' Trade Union. C/1821/2.
Reports of Labour Officers. C/1814/14.
Stoppages in Mining Industry, Commission 1957. Z.P.26.
Trade Disputes. H/1; Ha/44; Ha/58–65; Ha/67, 68; Hb/1a; Hc/1a;
    Hd/1a; Hg/1a; Hh/1a; Hb/142, vol. 3–Hb/163; Hc/97–Hc/106;
    Hd/95–Hd/106; He/62n; He/67; He/77–81; Hf/68; Hf/74, 75;
    Hf/77–83 Hf/85–91; Hg/60; Hg/81; Hh/134–155; Hi/41–48; Ha/34,
    vols. 1–4; Ha/43, vols. 1–5 Ja/9, vols. 1–6; C/1819/LC.
Trade Unions. C/2101/1, vols. 1, 2; C/2101/1/LC, vols. 1, 2.
Trade Unions, Formation and Origins. C/1820/5.
Trade Union Government. Ja/73, vols. 1 and 2.
Trade Union Registrar, Ja/30, vols. 1 and 2.
Trade Union Registration. C/2101/2.
Trade Union Rules. C/2101/3.
Training, Trade Unions. C/1822/1.
United Trade Union Congress. Ja/128, vols. 1 and 2.

Newspapers and Dates Consulted

The African Mineworker (Kitwe) 1953–55.
Business and Economy of Central and East Africa (Ndola) 1967–68.
The Central African Examiner (Salisbury) 1957–63.

The Central African Mail (Lusaka) 1962–65.
The Central African Post (Lusaka) 1950–57.
The Financial Mail of Zambia (Ndola) 1966–67.
The Miner (Kitwe) 1962–63.
M.O.S.S.A. (Kitwe) 1953.
Mwabombeni (Kitwe) 1962–63.
The Northern News (Ndola) 1958–64.
The Times of Zambia (Ndola) 1964–68.
The Union News (Kitwe) 1963.
The Voice of U.N.I.P. (Lusaka) 1963–65.
The Zambia Business Mail (Lusaka) 1969–70.
The Zambia Mail (Lusaka) 1964–70.
The Zambia Pilot (Kitwe) 1963–65.
Zambia Workers (Lusaka) 1965–66.

Unpublished Materials

Bates, Margaret Rouse. "UNIP in Postindependence Zambia: The Development of an Organizational Role." Ph.D. dissertation, Department of Government, Harvard University, 1971.

Berger, Elena L. "Labour Policies on the Northern Rhodesian Copperbelt, 1924–1964." Ph.D. dissertation, Nuffield College, Oxford University, 1969.

Halvorsen, Robert F. "Wages Policy in the Zambian Copper Industry." Paper submitted to the Department of Economics, Harvard University, 27 May 1968, Cambridge, Massachusetts. Typescript.

Kapferer, Bruce. Untitled papers presented to departmental seminars, the Department of Sociology and Social Anthropology, Manchester University, 1966. Typescript.

Knight, John B. "Wages and Zambia's Economic Development." Paper prepared for the Institute of Economics and Statistics, Oxford University, 1968. Mimeographed. A revised version is forthcoming in *Constraints on Zambia's Economic Development,* edited by Charles Elliot. London: Oxford University Press.

Materials in the Phillip Emanuel Collection. Afrika Studiecentrum. Leiden, Holland.

Index

African advancement, 107. *See also* Zambianization
African labor force, size of, 81
African National Congress (ANC): origins of, 9–10; and Federation, 10; and Zambia African National Congress, 10; and UNIP, 11; as opposition, 11, 12, 236–37; and Mineworkers' Union, 126–30 passim, 141, 251–53. *See also* Opposition parties and government policy
Amalgamation, 8–9. *See also* Federation of Rhodesia and Nyasaland; European settler community
American Metals, 16
ANC. *See* African National Congress
Anglo-American Corporation, 16–17, 41, 111, 212
Annual Conference, Mineworkers' Union, 98, 99, 108, 154, 157
Annual Conference, UNIP, 173
Assistant ministers, 13

Balance of payments, 37, 70–72
Baluba Mine, 214
Bancroft Mine, 146, 168
Barotse Province, 118. *See also* United Party
Beatty, Alfred Chester, 16
Bevan Report, 20
Bledisloe Commission, 8
Boss Boy Committees, 20–21
Branches of Mineworkers' Union. *See* Local level of Mineworkers' Union; Mineworkers' Union
Branches of UNIP. *See* United National Independence Party
Branigan Commission, 223, 224, 252

British South Africa Company, 7–8, 15–16, 67
Broken Hill. *See* Zambia Broken Hill Development Company
Brown Commission of Inquiry, 42, 43, 46, 63, 112, 237–39
BSA. *See* British South Africa Company
Building and Woodworkers Union, 77
Bwana Mkubwa, 16–17, 213

Cabinet ministers, 13, 75–76
Capacity, 5, 204
Central Committee, UNIP, 12–15 passim, 118, 171, 237, 249–50. *See also* Elections; United National Independence Party
Chakulya, Wilson, 132, 146, 253
Chamber of Mines, 21, 26, 99, 137. *See also* Copper Industry Service Bureau
Chambishi, 17
Chapoloko, Jameson, 128, 251
Chibuluma, 17
Chibuluma branch, Mineworkers' Union, 102, 103, 108, 110, 155, 157
Chibuye, Peter, 152
Chima, George Bentley, 149
Chindele, Gordon, 128, 144, 251
Chisata, John, 91, 94, 103, 253
Chisunka, 101
Chitimukulu, paramount chief of the Bemba, 142
Chivunga, Jonathan, 132–34 passim, 253
CISB. *See* Copper Industry Service Bureau
Clerks' Associations, 21

spirit rising

spirit rising
my life, my music

angélique kidjo

WITH RACHEL WENRICK

FOREWORD BY DESMOND TUTU ❦ INTRODUCTION BY ALICIA KEYS

HARPER DESIGN
An Imprint of HarperCollins Publishers

HarperCollins books may be purchased for educational, business, or sales promotional use. For information, please e-mail the Special Markets Department at SPsales@harpercollins.com.

Published in 2014 by:
Harper Design
An Imprint of HarperCollins*Publishers*
10 East 53rd Street
New York, NY 10022
Tel (212) 207-7000
harperdesign@harpercollins.com
www.harpercollins.com

Distributed throughout the world by:
HarperCollins*Publishers*
10 East 53rd Street
New York, NY 10022

Design by Stislow Design

Library of Congress Control Number: 2012951249

ISBN: 978-0-06207179-8

Printed in China, 2013

PAGE 2: The photo used on the cover of *Ōÿö*. • OPPOSITE: My dad and I in 2004.

In memory of my father, who stood up and sent all his daughters to school.

contents

The road to Ouidah.

foreword

With Desmond Tutu in New York in 2003.

I lived in an apartheid ghetto. On one occasion with friends I went to see the film *Stormy Weather* with its all-black cast. It did wonders for our psyches to see people of the same skin color as ourselves performing on the silver screen. That was when I saw my first pinup girl, the stunningly beautiful Lena Horne, who sang like a nightingale. Much, much, later when I was an adult, I found my second pinup, Aung San Suu Kyi of Burma. I had imagined that that was it. But no—I have been bowled over by my third pinup, Angélique Kidjo of Benin.

She too is beautiful, yes. And can she sing? She has an amazing voice that takes possession of her whole being. She glides on the stage, and her song takes possession of her body, which twirls and turns amazingly, and it all makes her audience want to join her as they sway to the beat of her music. And often they do, or she joins them where they have been sitting. She is an international star who has appeared on the stage of Carnegie Hall. She has won a Grammy and international acclaim.

It is amazing all the glitter, glamour, and acclaim. She started her career almost accidentally. Her mother ran a traditional drama group in their hometown of Cotonou. Once when a child singer-actor was absent, ill, her mother grabbed her own child Angélique, dressed her in a costume and almost pushed her onto the stage and ordered her to sing. She did, and as they say, the rest is history.

Angélique was smuggled out of her home country ruled by a dictator and went to France. Things were tough but eventually she succeeded, and how! She embodies her creed that girls can succeed if given a chance, if they stay in school as long as possible and are not turned into child brides, that Africa is not just that continent of disasters and famine and drought, inducing donor fatigue. No, Africa has produced great musicians, thinkers, and leaders. Hard as it might be to believe, this Africa now producing so many refugees once gave refuge to others. Abraham and Sarah went to Africa to escape a famine in Canaan, as did Jacob, and the Holy Family, Joseph, Mary, and the infant Jesus, who fled to Egypt to escape the wrath of King Herod. It was a man from Cyrene, in Africa, who helped Jesus carry his cross on the first Good Friday. Some of Christianity's early thinkers came from Africa: St. Augustine of Hippo with his massive intellect; St. Athanasius of Alexandria; and St. Anthony of Egypt, the founder of the religious life. There have been leaders such as Julius Nyerere of Tanzania, and the universally acclaimed Nelson Mandela, the global icon of magnanimity and reconciliation.

Angélique was herself inspired by Miriam Makeba, Mother Africa, and she in her turn is now an inspiration to others with her message that, yes, the sky is the limit, and she urges them to reach for the stars. She has used her fame wonderfully to promote her ideals, which are universal ideals, and has often been a human rights advocate—spectacularly in a concert in Harare, Zimbabwe, when she electrified her audience by lambasting Robert Mugabe for bringing a great country to its knees.

So you can see why she is my pinup, if she will pardon the expression. I pray that she continues to inspire others to emulate her, and yes, to reach for the stars because the sky is the limit.

—*Desmond Tutu*

introduction

Singing with Alicia Keys at the first Keep A Child Alive benefit, in 2004.

I remember the very first time I saw Angélique Kidjo perform in Africa. I had made a trip to South Africa with Leigh Blake, who first helped me learn about the depth and complexity of the AIDS pandemic and with whom I had founded Keep a Child Alive. We did many things while we were there. We went to clinics. We visited with teenagers who were orphaned because they had lost their parents to AIDS. We met people who were working on the ground with organizations. And, one night, we went to see Angélique.

She was singing at Newton Music Centre, a club in Johannesburg. Leigh and I went to talk to her backstage before the show. She left me slightly in shock because Angélique is so powerful and blunt and loud and just stunning in all her queendom. She is funny and a firecracker, and at first, I was taken aback by her energy. It's almost aggressive in its nature. I thought, "What tornado did I just walk through?" This woman infuses electricity into every space she enters.

When she went onstage, that same kind of energy followed her. It was a transformative night for me because while I was there trying to help with the devastating impact of AIDS in Africa, here was this beautiful African artist who was so spectacular. She brought it all together for me, because within Angélique lies all of Africa, its triumph and its tragedy.

Years later, Angélique and I went together to Alexandria Township to visit the *gogos*, grandmothers whose children had died in the pandemic. These women are raising their grandchildren–little ones, sometimes five

in a family. There's this big generation gap, and saying it is not easy for them is a tremendous understatement. We sat with them under a tree and we sang together, and after a while, Angélique walked away. When I found her, she had tears in her eyes and she asked me, "How can we be letting this happen? What can we do?" She was very present in that moment, allowing herself to be swept away. We hugged each other, and it didn't matter where I grew up or where she grew up. It was beyond all that. It was beyond music, even. Nothing else mattered. Instead, it was about humanity: what can we do to help? That's the spirit of her energy. Sometimes you meet someone and you instantly understand each other. That was our case.

A few years later we performed together at Radio City Music Hall for Nelson Mandela's birthday celebration. At events like that, I think Angélique and I find ourselves experiencing similar feelings of disbelief. It's not that you don't deserve to be there. You've put in the time and the work, but looking up to a legend like Aretha Franklin and being surrounded by the legacy of Nelson Mandela, I think we both found ourselves wondering, "How did we get here?"

You know how it is when you're in a particular moment and you experience that feeling of awe, almost in a childlike sense? Like when it's only you and your sister in your room, and you're jumping up and down and giggling together? On that stage, that night, Angélique and I formed a bond of sisterhood. Not only did the music make us feel that way, but spiritually we connected too.

Angélique Kidjo embodies womanhood and bravery, as evident by her remarkable advocacy for children as a United Nations Ambassador. She pushes back against any stereotype that gets in her way. In reading her story, I am reminded that we're all human beings together in the struggle, and that we have the power to move forward under any circumstance. I like to tell people that if you don't know Angélique, you haven't lived because there's not one person who would be in her presence and not be changed.

She makes you feel more alive.

—Alicia Keys

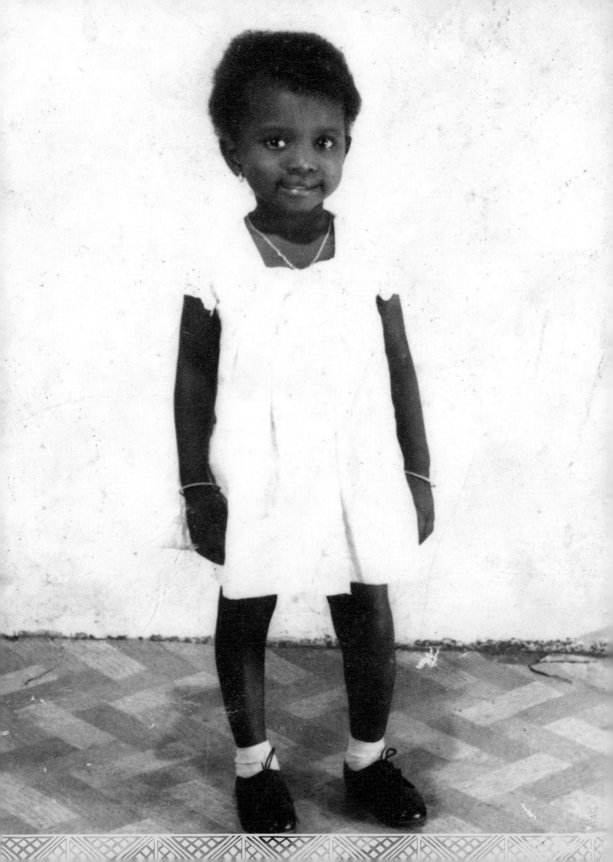

seeing new worlds

This is how it all began.

I was a little girl, always running and jumping around our courtyard on my skinny legs. The courtyard was at the center of our house and our house was in the center of our town, Cotonou, in Benin, my home on the west coast of Africa. My family's house was simple, built in a U-shape, with all of the rooms unfolding one after another: the kitchen where my mother cooked so many meals; the dining room where we sat together and talked and talked; bedrooms for my parents, my brothers and sisters, and our cousins from far away; and the tiny room where my mother stored costumes. At the front of the house, facing the street, was the white and blue facade of my father's photography studio.

Back then, most of those rooms were made with bamboo and the floor of the courtyard was sand.

There was a well in the courtyard and I would run around it in circles, stripped to the waist, under a blazing sun. "Slow down," my mother would tell me. "Be careful."

On the weekends, my mother would be busy directing all the singers and dancers of her theater company; they performed a

Yvonne, my mother. Her passion was theater.

traditional Beninese folktale. It was her beloved hobby and she did every-thing—rehearsing songs, designing costumes, drawing masks. I still remember all the colorful fabrics—brilliant orange and deep indigo studded with white cowries and sparkling with precious beads—and the powdery smell of the chalk they used for makeup.

....

OPPOSITE: **Me at age four.**

I wanted to learn everything. I would ask, "Why is she here? Why does he say that? Why isn't this there?" My mother would hush me. "Just be quiet, I'll explain later."

I listened to their songs and watched their moves, and I sang and danced along, even after they left the house. The play told the story of the famous Beninese king Akaba and his sister Naguézé. There was this one song I loved that a girl my age was singing. She was the daughter of one of the actresses and she had the role of the little princess. I was dying to be that girl and to sing her beautiful melody. It was a calling song, inviting people to join in a celebration. I'd sing it over and over. My mother said, "That's good. You know, that's really good. You sing well."

My membership card from Mom's theater company.

"Then why am I not singing in the show and why is she?" I complained.

"Because you're not the one playing the part," she said. "She's playing the part."

I wanted to know all about that, too, so I asked, "What's that mean, playing a part?"

My mother explained to me how you have to make a text your own. You have to really feel it so that you aren't just reciting it—so that it becomes a part of you.

One Saturday evening at the Palais des Congrès de Cotonou, the dusty concert hall whose facade was decorated with seashells, there was an important performance of my mother's play. I was backstage, trying on costumes and hiding away from the big scary masks. I remember one was a dragon and another one was Dan, the snake god that carries the earth. Back then, Benin was still called Dahomey, which means "in the belly of the snake."

My mom came back and grabbed me. "Get out, get out! You have to sing right now!"

"No! Why should I sing?" In that moment the thought of going onstage, in front of all those people, terrified me. "No way I'm going to sing!"

"Yes, you are," she said. She told me the girl playing the little princess was sick. "Put this costume on." Just like that, she slipped the girl's dress—a patchwork of green and orange African fabric—over me and pushed me onstage.

I was so stunned I couldn't move. The spotlight was in my face. It was so bright, but everything around it was dark. I knew the place was packed, but I couldn't see the audience. I could hear my whole skeleton shaking like in those old cartoons—*clack, clack, clack!* Then I heard people laughing, gently, and it reminded me of our house. In my family, I was the clown, always cracking people up. The audience thought it was part of the show for me to be so scared. When they laughed, I felt good. I felt home.

I started to sing "Atcha Houn."

O houn ye di sin houn de
O gbeto mindjomin we kple yeyi houn da la go ton. . . .

At the sound of our drums
The royal family and the people gathered to join us rejoice. . . .

I was six years old and I've not stopped singing since.

the beach club

When I was nine, my mother's theater company gave its last performance. She had put all of the money from her business of selling fabric into the theater; still, it was too costly to continue. But by now the family had taken on a new project. One day, I came home from school and our courtyard was filled with big boxes. The smell—sawdust mixed with varnish— was completely new to me. When everything was opened, I saw for the first time in my life those modern instruments—a guitar, a bass, drums, and percussion instruments. They didn't look anything like the traditional ones we used during all the ceremonies. It was like a different world coming into the house.

My father had taken out a loan and ordered everything from Albarica, the music store in town whose name meant "good fortune," so that my brothers could start a band like the Jackson 5. Their music, played on

Onstage in Benin.

imported vinyl brought back by students from abroad, was so popular. At
that time, everyone in Africa was copying their clothes and hairstyles. I
had so many brothers, each one with a name right out of the nineteenth
century: Oscar, Yves, Alfred, Victor, Christian, François, and Ernest. After
school, instead of going to do my homework, I would stand in front of the

kick drum with my arms crossed and listen in awe as they rehearsed "Get Ready" by the Temptations in our little lounge.

Every Saturday my brothers played at a discotheque called the Beach Club. It was a big whitewashed bungalow built on the sand near the Lagoon of Cotonou where the Nokoué River flows into the ocean. I wanted to go with them, but it was a nightclub and I was a little girl. Still, my parents knew I was determined. If I had it in my mind to do something, I was going to do it. The owner, Mr. Nikoué, was a friend of my father's and they worked it out so I could sing just two songs at the beginning of the second set.

Around midnight my father would come to the bedroom I shared with my older sister, Mireille, to wake me. I was too excited to sleep, but I would pretend, holding my songbook and lying very still so I wouldn't wrinkle my dress. I wore the

My brother Oscar playing the Farfisa organ.

same purple dress every time. I remember that vividly. My mother made it from fabric she used to sell. It was striped shiny then matte, with sleeves that ballooned out, and gathers all the way down. My father put his hand on my shoulder and gently shook me, telling me it was time to go.

Outside at night, beyond our rusted red front door, the world looked so different. I was used to seeing our little street during the day, with chickens and pigs and goats roaming around. Now I could see the closed mosque across the street and nearby the dark Cinéma le Bénin, the theater where we went on Sunday afternoons to see karate movies and Westerns.

Back then, my father had a huge white secondhand Citroën. I wasn't allowed to ride in the front seat—my parents didn't think it was safe—so I sat in the back and watched my father drive. He was a tall, handsome man, always

calm and elegant. He loved wearing hats and had a sleek moustache I could see in the rearview mirror when the lights from passing cars flashed by.

After a while, I would hang out the window and try to take in this new scene. During the day the streets were packed with people, but at night the vendors were out, cooking *tchatchanga*, a kind of lamb stew, by the flickering lights of their kerosene lamps. The air was filled with wood smoke. I thought, my friends don't have the chance to see this. I'm seeing it because I'm a singer.

That was the beginning of my discovery of new worlds through music.

As we got closer to the club, I could hear the spindrift coming from the sea. When my father pulled the car into the parking lot, I heard the music coming from inside and my posture changed. Suddenly I was wide awake and ready to go. He took me straight back into the kitchen where Mr. Nikoué was, then he went to tell my brothers I was ready. When it was time, he carried me through the crowd and set me right onstage.

The Beach Club was near the Hotel du Port on the Boulevard de la Marina. It was a stop for French and British tourists and for people visiting from Nigeria. This was the era of yé-yé–the French version of sixties rock 'n' roll with songs like Sylvie Vartan's "La plus belle pour aller danser . . ." and Sheila's "Samson et Dalila." I sang all of those in a high-pitched voice, and I liked them, but it was Bella Bellow, the angelic Togolese singer, whose songs I really loved.

The first time I went onstage at the Beach Club, my heart was pounding. Once I had done it two or three times, it was an addiction. At first, the crowd was really dumbstruck because I was so little, standing there in the middle of my tall brothers, but when I started dancing with such confidence under those colorful spotlights, people went crazy, shouting and cheering. It was almost a riot every weekend. The club was smoky and I had asthma, which meant that I would often come home with a wheezy chest, but nothing could prevent me from going back the next week.

As soon as I finished my two songs, I had to leave quickly because I was too young to be there. The cook would be on lookout to make sure the coast was clear, and my father would pluck me off the stage. He carried me through the club and quickly out to the car. I would fall asleep in the Citroën on our way back home, the strange nighttime world slowly turning back to day.

I continued singing with my brothers until the day I entered seventh grade. As a twelve-year-old girl, I still had my skinny legs. Everyone was calling me "mosquito legs." One day, I was coming home from school, Gbégamé Junior High, with lots of friends, boys and girls. It was very hot and we were all walking along the Boulevard Saint-Michel that crosses through Cotonou to the big Dantokpa market when I heard someone shout from behind me, "Whore! That one there, she sings! She's a whore." I thought, "They can't be talking about me." And then, all of a sudden, I was surrounded by a whole group of people. They yelled and spit on me, and I went running home alone, crying.

In Benin, traditional singers hold the symbol of their craft, made with horse hair.

Now on that particular day my grandmother, my mother's mother, was at our house sitting in the courtyard. I opened the creaky iron gate and told her, "I'm not singing anymore–I'm done with it! That's it!"

She came to me, asking, "What's going on? Why are you crying? Did someone hit you?" She was trying to calm me down, but when I told her what happened, she asked, "Why would you want to stop singing? Because there are people who are stupid and jealous enough to insult you? Are they the ones who will decide what you're going to do?"

That day she taught me something that I have always remembered: you cannot be loved and admired by everyone. My grandmother told me, "That's the way life is. There are people who'll love you and people who won't." What matters is what you do and how you do it. What matters is your family, how they see you and how they encourage you. She said, "Don't let other people draw you away from your own path." On that day I understood that jealousy drove those people. If you let people like

that influence who you are then they have won. I wiped away my tears and decided that from that moment forward, I wouldn't care what other people said, that I'd do what I want to do.

Of course, this isn't always easy. But that same year—when I was twelve—Aretha Franklin's album *Amazing Grace* arrived at our home. The way we heard new music was through my brothers' friends who would come back from Europe or the United States wearing flared trousers, sporting big Afros, and bringing precious vinyls. Everyone would come by to listen and dance, like in an old snapshot from Malick Sidibé, the great photographer who immortalized West African life in the sixties.

When *Amazing Grace* came, it was the first time I saw a black woman on an album cover. Aretha is sitting on the steps of a church, in front of an open doorway, and she's wearing a beautiful African dress the color of burnt sienna lined in pink. Just seeing an American singer wearing an African dress had a huge impact on me. She's looking right at the camera, giving a soft smile, and her eyes, they are so serene. Everything about the photo—the stairs leading to the open door, her open arms—suggests pathways and possibilities.

Until then, every album of soul music they put on the turntables had male artists. They were men with Afros or permed hair, and all sorts of Western accoutrements. They were standing up or taking the kind of odd pose that was popular in the seventies. So the first time I saw a black woman on the cover, the thrill inside me wasn't even about the sound of music. It was seeing her and knowing that there was a woman in the room that every man was listening to and grooving to. They were saying how good she sounded and they were singing along.

At that time I was wondering if it would be possible for me, as a girl, to become a singer. Another question was if it would be possible for me, as an African person. The response to these questions was Aretha.

Many, many years later, I was invited to perform at Radio City Music Hall in New York for "Mandela Day," a concert marking Nelson Mandela's ninety-first birthday. The show's organizers asked me to sing a duet with Alicia Keys right after Ms. Franklin performed. Radio City, with its lush red velvet chairs, golden roof, and Art Deco paintings was such a contrast

OPPOSITE: I was the favorite model at my dad's photo studio in Cotonou.

with my house in Cotonou where I first discovered her music. While I watched from the wings, Aretha performed, the black net of her gown floating around her. I couldn't believe my eyes. I felt the same way when I met Miriam Makeba. Those two women were so powerful that I always thought they could only be met in your dreams, not in real life.

At the end of "Make Them Hear You," as Aretha was starting to leave, she let out a "hallelujah" and began dancing and clapping. She was radiant. She was possessed. The thing is, when you sing, you know that the public is there, but you are with yourself, with the intimacy of the song. So for you to touch people's souls you have to open up yourself. It's like giving people a mirror to see into your soul. That's what it is. When you're singing, even when you're dancing or smiling, there's something about you at that moment that you don't control. It is something holy. It is something deep down. I could see it happening in her. She called out, "I feel like shouting!" and everyone in the audience danced and clapped with her. As she left the stage, everyone was on their feet; applause filled the hall.

My husband was right beside me at the show. Jean and I have been through so much together and when I looked at him, his mouth was set straight, but his eyes were wide. I could see right away how worried he was for me. I knew what he was thinking: This is the hardest scenario possible for a singer, performing right after Aretha Franklin! An impossible challenge! This wasn't the day for me to be short of voice.

But she had shown me that this life—the dream of singing and traveling, of being respected as a female singer—was possible. Without knowing it, she helped bring me to that stage, which is why it meant so much to share it with her. When I went onstage after Aretha, I thought, you started me on this journey, you gave me the baton and I'm gonna carry it. I was not scared at all. Her singing gave me the strength to perform.

My mom always told me that you have to be spiritually naked when you walk onstage. You have to have a hell of an ego to go out there, but from the moment you do, your ego becomes secondary. Out there, you are in service of something bigger than you. Each time I'm onstage, I'm brand new. Anything can happen during a show.

After Aretha left, Alicia Keys looked me in the eyes, smiling calmly, eyes aglow. She took my hand, and together we walked onstage singing my song, "Afirika."

Min bi fon do Africa gblé lo
Min wè na fon bo mon dèkpè ton
Min déssou sin alo min wè dé
Mindé ma nan lin dagbé min ton

Ashè é maman, ashè é maman Afirika
Ashè é maman, ashè é maman Afirika

This song is about blessings, blessings to Mother Africa. All too often when people talk about Africa, they say how awful it is, how many problems it has. They act as if it's another world, a terrible place. They forget that we are all African, that we are all part of the common memory of humankind.

If every day
the world just sees,
If every day
the world just talks
about misery
and trouble in Africa,
then who can see its beauty?
Who can see its strength?

If we stop criticizing, we can start working together to make Africa and our world different. We can begin a healing process.

Hallelujah.

The stage is a sacred place. The voice is part of your soul and the power of music is what links people together. The language doesn't matter. I get a lot of strength and love from the audience. They are experiencing emotions that they didn't expect to feel at the show, sometimes emotions they didn't know they had. When you feel the music, you forget your worries and discover truths about yourself. Music transcends in a way that makes all negative things seem to disappear.

Everything is possible. Everything is revealed.

ready for the revolution

My ancestors on my father's side came from the village of Ouidah, not far from the Atlantic Ocean, and just a few dozen miles from Cotonou. My family are descendants of the Pedah, a tribe of fishermen who cast their nets all along the magnificent, immaculate beach that goes on for miles and miles. Ouidah holds a tragic place in history. It was from there that so many slaves were forced to leave their continent for the Americas.

On the way to the sea, there is a red clay road that leaves the village and crosses a beautiful green salted backwater. The slaves were forced to take this path, and at the end to leave for an uncertain future. Before they got on the boats, they had to walk around a tree—seven times for women, nine times

FROM TOP LEFT: The Gate of No Return. ◦ The road the slaves had to take when they were forced onto the boats, leaving their loved ones behind. ◦ Fishermen pulling their net from the sea. ◦ Sitting on the beautiful and empty beach of Ouidah.

for men—it was believed that this would erase their memories, that it would make them forget where they came from. Now there is a tall arch called the Gate of No Return to commemorate this dark page of human history.

The beach at Ouidah is mystical, powerful, very peaceful—those three things together. It is empty today except for some fishermen. If you want to be with yourself and look for inner truth, inner peace, this is where you go.

A sculpture by the Beninese artist Cyprien Tokoudagba that depicts a slave who has been bound by chains.

You can see the fishermen going out in the long canoes that have been used for generations. At the edge of the pirogue there is a hole they thread with handmade hemp rope. They tie the rope to a tree because they have to head out to where the fish are—in deep waters beyond a reef of sand, beyond a whirlpool, beyond the sharks—and if you go too far you can't come back. They cast their net from the boat and spend the day fishing. Before sunset, people line the beach to begin pulling them back. It's teamwork. Family work. While they do this, they sing. Even though their clothes are now modern—yellow T-shirts and red baseball caps bob along the blue-green water—their rhythm is ancient. Like the waves of the sea, it is a call and response.

This was the daily life of my ancestors too.

My dad was a Fon, which is the main ethnic group in Benin, and my mom is a Yoruba, another important one with roots in Nigeria. The Fon and Yoruba have very similar gods, but with different names. Heviosso, the god of thunder for the Fon, is the famous Shango for the Yoruba. There is Ogun who is the Yoruba god of metal and Legba the Fon god who is the messenger for all of them. There is also Mami Wata, as she is called in Fon, the white and blue goddess of the sea whom the Yoruba call Yemandja. There are so many deities and together they create a pantheon as rich and beautiful as that of the Greeks and Romans.

The Fon and Yoruba share the same message of love, but the Fon religion has a very unfortunate name, Vodun. In the West, there is a sad misconception about voodoo. Most people think it's about sacrificing chickens and cows, casting spells, and getting revenge; all you see is blood and dolls stuck with pins. Voodoo from New Orleans and Haiti is very different from the Beninese traditional religion and has been vilified by Hollywood as the archetype of the scary African people ruling Haiti, the first black republic that dared to stand up against the West. In Benin, Vodun is not an evil form of witchcraft, but just one among a great many African animist religions that have existed for centuries.

Having a Fon dad and a Yoruba mom put me in a special place. It gave me access to so much culture and music. The songs and dances and the ceremonies are different, but they have coexisted for hundreds of years. Their beliefs are also never in contradiction with Christianity, which is a mainstay of Beninese culture. In my family, as in many Beninese families, we go to the Catholic church on Sunday morning and to the traditional Beninese ceremony in the afternoon. Each child born into our family has the right to two baptisms: a Catholic baptism and a traditional one, which is more about lineage. It is when we call to our ancestors to ask who will protect and watch over the child throughout his or her earthly life.

I learned the story of my baptism, like all of our family history, through its telling and retelling.

It isn't written.

In Benin, we don't have genealogy the way Westerners think of it. Our genealogy takes the form of a family tree in three dimensions that's kept in a special place called the *asen* room. In my family this room is like a small round hut built with red clay. It's inside the courtyard of our ancestral home, on a small street near the market of Ouidah where my father's family is from. The roof is corrugated metal and the ceiling is low, so you have to bend down to enter.

An *asen* is a little metal pedestal, used as a kind of altar. Every time someone dies, the person is represented by a small, delicate metal figure with a symbol connected to their name, or a proverb that defined them, or the profession he or she practiced. For example, my father's sister, who took over their mother's cloth business, is represented with scissors in her hands. The figures go back for generations and generations—ever

since our family's origin, at least three centuries ago—so the room is filled with them. The statues rust in the sea air and get coated with clay dust, but the room is never swept because the belief is that the dust is part of the asen, part of the spirit of the person. When the asen falls and shatters, the person's spirit will still live on forever.

My father calls it our little pantheon.

I was baptized when I was two months old. My mom and I stayed in the asen room for seven days. But first the *tanyin*, my aunties, had to prepare everything. They used a branch from a palm tree to sweep the rest of the house and the path to the asen room. Palm trees and their leaves are considered sacred in our culture. Through their deep roots, the trees are a link to our ancestors. Sweeping with the branch serves as a connection between the earth and the ones up there. It's like starting a conversation with them.

We both wore a necklace and bracelet of braided palm fronds. We do these things to clean and protect the mother and baby and to keep the ancestors close from the day of our birth until our death.

There is always one main tanyin and her voice is the link to the world of the spirits and gods. At my baptism, the main tanyin was the one we called the Nightingale because she had such a beautiful voice and an uplifting spirit. When I was a girl and I asked my mother why I sang all the time, she told me that when she was pregnant with me, this aunt used to come to the city to visit her and she would sing—right against her belly. She was the guardian of our family's songs.

It was the Nightingale's job to call to the ancestors and ask them for the traditional name that would link me to one particular ancestor. It was all joy, singing, and dancing, questioning the ancestors and celebrating.

The men had to stay outside, away from the door and the window—only the women could see my mother until the name was given. My father, my uncles, and our family friends were clapping their hands and beating their chests, and hitting glass bottles with spoons. Through this music, the men and women replied to each other. They danced, too, in celebration of what our ancestors have created—our family, which we love.

Wassi wassi wassi wassi Houeda nou vio: "We are so happy happy happy to welcome the child from the lineage of Houeda." Houeda is the python god, the tutelary deity of my family.

Me as a baby; same haircut and already an attitude.

Allou wa sio Owo Owo Owo Vi Do Le: "We are witnessing the gift of life of a child."

From inside the asen room, my mother heard the voices and she sang along in a whisper.

During the baptism, a necklace of cowries is thrown down like dice on a chalk-covered tray. Their arrangement provides the answer to the question asked of the spirits: Who will guide this child? The Fa priest calls to the spirits every day until they consent to respond. When an ancestor responds to the priest and accepts the role of protective spirit of a child, he comes with his own principles. These serve as guides for the child's life.

For my baptism, the legend goes that from the first of the seven days, and each day after, one spirit answered again and again: my ancestor Linhounhinto. At first they thought maybe it was a mistake. By the end they were in shock. "It's a male!" they kept repeating. I was the first girl in more than five generations who had a male protective ancestor.

NEXT SPREAD: The *asen* room. Each altar represents a scene that symbolizes the life of an ancestor.

In my family, we are named after our ancestors. Linhounhinto is a descendant of Hounsinou Kandjo Manta Zogbin, a warrior on my grandfather's side of the family. If you combine his name with Kpasselokohinto, who is from my grandmother's side of the family, you get my full given name, Angélique Hounsinou Kandjo Manta Zogbin-Kpasselokohinto Kidjo.

During his lifetime they say Linhounhinto lived according to very strict principles. I've been told that he advised me to be wary of my own anger. He also predicted that throughout my life I'd have to earn all my success and salary by the sweat of my brow. Nothing would be given to me effortlessly. Now, whenever I face a new challenge, I already know it's going to be hard work for me, and I just want to get started.

But the thing that everyone was really impressed with was that Linhounhinto was one of our most honest ancestors. He didn't know how to lie. My husband has said that this honesty of mine can be embarrassing at times, but he also tells me that I can speak to a reality—a simple truth—that people might not want to address. For me it's that I can't help speaking about the elephant in the room. When I make blunders or loudly say what everybody is silently thinking, people may be quiet for a moment, but then they usually laugh and it feels as if a tension has been released.

An *egun egun*: During traditional ceremonies, under this appearance, an ancestor speaks to the living.

My family told me that the Nightingale also reached out to the ancestors in order to give me the gift of singing. Her hope was that because I would be compelled to tell the truth throughout my life and because this would be a tough load to carry, I should also be able to use my voice to sing. She thought singing would help me to carry that load, to transcend those challenges.

Not far from my father's ancestral home, the Temple of the Python stands in the shadow of an immense Iroko tree. Having the python as our family's protective totem obliged us to have

The guardian of the Temple of the Python.

ten scarifications on our face. But my father paid a symbolic donation at the birth of every child to avoid the scars. "We don't know where you'll end up, where you'll be working," he said. "With scarifications you could run into problems. There are plenty of problems in the world as it is. We don't need to add to them if we can avoid it."

It so happens that the Temple of the Python in Ouidah is across the street from the first cathedral ever built in Benin. The story has it that the city's archbishop was unsuccessful in bringing the faithful to the cathedral and together with his priests he tried to do away with the animist religion but it didn't work. One day he went to see the priest of the Temple of the Python and said to him:

"I don't want your temple to stay open any longer. I want everybody to come to the church."

And the animist priest answered: "What is the most important message of your god? What makes you think that your god is better than ours?"

"The most important message of my god is: 'Let us love one another.'"

"We didn't have to wait for you to get that message. That's what our

gods tell us as well. Because our deities, our orishas, are the disciples of Mawou, the supreme god, and he, too, tells us to love one another."

From that day forward the priests were friends and constant supports for each other. It is said that they were often seen walking together on the busy streets of Ouidah.

Once a year, a special ceremony is held in honor of the pythons. On that day there are pythons everywhere. I hated snakes, but to taunt my brothers and sisters I said, "You guys think you're so modern. You don't even want to go to the village to see the ceremony." They said, "Go ahead. You'll see." So of course I went.

I found my cousins and we had fun, we kidded around, we ate, and went to sleep. Then in the morning I got up and wanted to make my bed. I lifted my pillow and there was a snake under it. A python. I screamed. I jumped up and down all over the place. They said, "What are you afraid of? He won't hurt you." And I said, "But I don't like snakes." I go into the shower. I wash myself. I look around and there's a snake. I came out and ran home to Cotonou and my brothers teased me, asking, "So,

....

The front door of our family house in Ouidah.

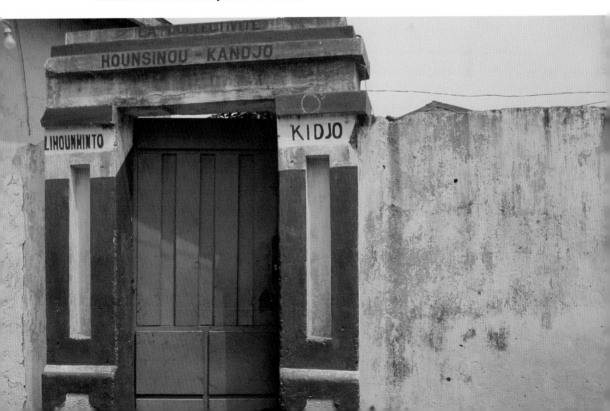

Standing next to my older sister, Mireille. I couldn't wait to remove my black patent-leather shoes and run barefoot.

how was the ceremony of the pythons? Did you like it?"

At home in Cotonou, which was a loud and lively African city at the time, there was such a sense of joy. My brothers and sisters were coming and going and my father had a very special deadpan sense of humor. We used to invite a lot of expatriate workers and friends to our house in the Maro-militaire district. The neighbors were always wondering what kind of people from all over the world would show up for our Saturday night dance parties. They began to say that the Kidjo house was the place to be. Everyone wanted to look like James Brown, but before they knew it their white suits would be stained with red dust from the dance floor.

What I remember most from my childhood is that I was always restless, a pain in the neck to my siblings. Since there were three of us girls, my mom took the greatest pleasure in dressing us up and making sure our hair was perfect. She was a fine seamstress and made clothes for us and for herself, but I hated it. I also loved running around bare-foot. She couldn't keep those black patent shoes on my feet. As soon as I arrived at school, I'd toss them and free my hair. She was completely desperate.

One of my grandaunts in Nigeria was of English origin and was very proper and strict. When I would visit her in Lagos with Mom, my grandaunt would dress us up like little dolls with flounced

Communion day with my brother Alfred and Mireille.

One of the rare photos of the whole family together. All the brothers and sisters born at the time are gathered around Mom and Dad.

socks and pink dresses. We even had to follow the ritual of five o'clock tea and sit quietly sipping our drink and eating cookies. This was more than I could bear so I would run around until the aunt told Mom, "Please don't ever bring her back, she is getting on everybody's nerves."

I grew up with seven brothers and I wanted to be like the boys: like Oscar, practicing his electric guitar, Yves, the champion of table tennis, Alfred the tall basketball player. François was always trying to take apart the engine of a moped. I would spend a lot of time playing soccer with my younger brothers, Victor, Christian, and Ernest, and their friends. They recruited me as a goalkeeper because I was fast and agile. That was another cause of desperation for Mom. I was never the model of the well-behaved little girl. I guess the blood of the Dahomey Amazons, the all-woman army created by King Agadja in the eighteenth century, was running in my veins.

We spent so much time braiding our hair, an opportunity for endless conversations.

At a young age I started to show my skills at dancing. My brothers got a crazy idea that would encourage my boyish tendencies. There was a carnival held around Christmas called Kaleta. It was organized in Ouidah by the Agouda, the descendants of slaves who had returned from Brazil. Boys would wear masks and dance to the rhythm of drums. If the dancers were any good, people would give them change. They could then take this money and buy little presents for their parents. I used to be so scared of the masks, but one day, my brothers dressed me in one. Nobody could guess I was a little girl. I danced like crazy and we got so much change. That may be why, many years later, I finally decided to cut my hair short, just like a boy. But that's another story. . . .

I remember thinking as a little girl that there were so many things I was told not to do. In Cotonou there was a mango tree in front of our house, but, of course, I wasn't allowed to climb trees because I was a girl. One day I couldn't hold myself back. I watched my brothers do it and then followed

their example, going high up into the tree. I discovered their hiding place, where the branches were intertwined. They made a kind of wonderful, natural armchair where you could sit down and relax in the cool of the shade. When I didn't feel like doing my homework, I'd quietly withdraw and go to my branch and eat mangoes until my stomach hurt. From there I could see the neighbor's house and the mosque across the street.

But one day, when it was terribly hot outside, I fell asleep there. Dinner-time came and no one could find me. I knew I'd get in trouble for getting up in that mango tree, but I also knew that I'd be in trouble for being late for dinner. This was a sacred hour at my house. My father and mother had decided that the house would be a free zone where no subject was taboo, where we could talk about anything, from sexuality to drugs and religion, and we often did this at dinner. I was angry with myself for missing this, but I was afraid to go home. I sat up in that tree until my brothers found me.

As I got older I realized how unusual it was that we spoke so openly in my home, because most of the time children don't have the right to speak up in Africa. Keeping quiet, not asking too many questions, is meant as a sign of respect for their elders, but it also prevents a dialogue with the adults. My family was very different.

Not only did we speak openly at home, but my mother also felt that each of us should be independent, not forced to rely on anyone else. When I was about eight years old she said to me, "Sit down so you can learn how to cook. One day I may leave the whole family in your hands, and you'll have to do the shopping and all the cooking." Of course I listened with only half an ear. I was so young, playing and singing were much more important to me than cooking.

One day she came home from the market and told me, "You're going to make dinner for everyone. If what you prepare is good we'll all eat it; if not, I'll cook for the others but you'll have to eat what you made."

I asked, "Why? What logic is there to this?"

"I'm trying to teach you, but you refuse to listen."

I thought it couldn't be all that complicated to feed people. I went off to the kitchen and made the food. I still remember the dish: smoked fish with tomato sauce. Half of it was raw and the rest was burned. My mom made me eat it and it was awful.

After that first disastrous experience I began to be very, very diligent in the kitchen. I'd sit down next to my mother and watch everything she did. I started to learn how to cook and what kinds of foods went together. My mother was always finding ways to use what was available. When it comes to food in Africa, you cook with what you have. This means you always have to adapt. She taught me how to prepare *poulet bicyclette*, the skinny chickens that roam the streets of Cotonou. I also began to invent new things, and see how I might create my own recipes. Seated on my small ebony stool, made by my grandfather, I'd stir the corn batter over the wood fire. We had no gas and used wood or charcoal. We didn't have a mixer, just a whisk for making cakes. When you're cooking under the African sun, it is so hot and your shin is the main spot that is exposed to the fire. I was constantly sprinkling my shins with water from a bucket by my feet because the heat would get unbearable. But it toughened me up. And then I learned how to prepare food for the twenty or so people who lived in our family home.

At home every one of us kids had a chore to do. We swept, did the dishes, and made our own beds. My brothers also learned to go to the market and to prepare food. In some ways my mother was a feminist. She always said she didn't want a woman to go through the nightmare she'd gone through: marrying a man who couldn't even boil water. Most of my brothers know how to cook and, trust me, that's very rare in Benin.

It was during this same time that I first heard the voice of South African singer and activist Miriam Makeba. After helping my mom cook and finishing my homework, I would go to my brothers' room and listen to their vinyls. One night, I found Miriam's *Pata Pata*. On the cover, her shoulders are bare. She wears big thin gold hoops and has her hair tucked up into a tall black hat with a satin band.

I pulled the record out of the sleeve and, with its edges pressed gently into my palms, I placed it on the turntable, and carefully laid the needle down. And that's when I began to dream while wide awake. Right away, the beat was magical, uplifting. You could not resist. You had to get on your feet. Her voice was so beautiful, so powerful and expressive, full of anticipation for a better world for South Africans. I didn't know what language she was singing, but her words felt revolutionary, hopeful, and I sang along.

My mom was very active socially. One of her endeavours was to create an association for children who had no siblings, something very rare in Africa.

When I was nine, her love song "Malaïka" was on the radio constantly. I'd listen to that song and whisper it, practically going into a trance. Gradually I began to learn it. "The Retreat Song" started with an a cappella cry, like a call to the people: "*Hindo gazamakwenkwe . . .*" When I first heard her sing that melody I was absolutely stunned. She was African, she was a woman, and she was a star. I wanted to be just like her.

The Beninese mothers who had created an association for women's rights picked up that song and created lyrics in Fon. All dressed up with their colorful headscarves, they would sing: *Min man so yonnoun le djiya nan o min.* "Don't hurt, don't abuse women. You must give them respect because a woman is a jewel." They sang of owing respect to a woman because she is the home and the beginning of humanity.

Madame Johnson, who was the president of the women's association, said to me: "Go ahead, sing with us. You have a pretty voice, little one." So, I did. The women were proudly dressed in sophisticated boubou with

colorful headwraps, and singing with, being with them, gave me strength. I thought: *Here I am with my mom and all the other mothers. We're going to change the country. We're going to do a lot of things.* I was completely naïve but, at the same time, it was such a deeply rooted feeling for me. Without understanding a thing, I was already supporting women's rights. I wasn't aware that it would shape my way of seeing the world, how I would come to associate music with social change and empowerment.

Just as my grandmother would instill in me the confidence to be true to myself, those women showed me I could go anywhere.

By the time I was a young teenager, I was always hanging out in places where I didn't belong. It was worse for my parents than when I was in the mango tree. As soon as something was happening, something different, I had to know what it was all about.

At school, from tenth grade on, we began to have group discussions. We'd sit outside near the vendors selling food from their little stores and talk about changing the world. There was Sylvain and Lazare, Avit, Mathilde, and Yolande. We discussed politics and philosophy endlessly. Sylvain talked about Marxism and Leninism. Then there was Marc, who was a fan of Camus. We spoke freely because there was no one around listening to us.

Learning about apartheid shattered my comfortable little world.

In 1972, twelve years after Benin gained independence from France, Mathieu Kérékou overthrew the government, seizing power with a military coup. His first rule lasted seventeen years. The paradox of that period was that we still had access to a good education. It was before Communism slowly destroyed the education system. In that way, we were the last lucky generation. But, at the same time, the political conditions of the dictatorship started to affect the well-being of the country. We began to lose our individuality, the ability to pursue our unique dreams and aspirations. It was increasingly difficult to find fulfillment in our lives.

My mom always made sure my stage outifits would be spectacular.

It wasn't until I was fifteen that I first heard about apartheid in South Africa. We had a small television set in the dining room but it was broadcasting just one or two hours a day—mainly propaganda. We would try to get TV channels from Nigeria by moving the antenna around in every direction. You need to know that in Africa there is no well-developed news network from one country to another to find out what's going on; you have to go through the French or English media to get news about the rest of the continent. It's like that even today.

Then one day, on the blinking TV set, I saw Winnie Mandela talking about her husband on a Nigerian channel and suddenly I was in shock. In the same way we would never hear about slavery at school, no one had told us about the situation in South Africa. Winnie Mandela's passion was burning, contagious, and listening to her I felt so much anguish and pain building in my soul; my whole world collapsed.

My parents had told me that you don't judge people by their color and that we're all born equal. Now I was discovering a new, harsh reality. The more I learned, the more my blood began to boil. This is what the feeling of injustice always leads me to—I lose my self-control. The only way for me to calm down was to sit on my little bed in the room I shared with my sister Mireille and write a song. Since I began performing with my mother's women's group, I had continued singing cover songs—Miriam's and my Bella Bellow's. I wrote my first song in 1973 when Bella died in a car crash. She was just twenty-seven, but she had already become a big star. Later, I understood how challenging her songs are, but when she sang it seemed so effortless. There was a sense of bliss.

That day, when I learned of apartheid, I wrote "Azan Nan Kpé," which means that the day will come when there won't be any oppressors or oppressed anymore. The first version of that song was very, very violent.

My father said to me, "Not in my house. No violence in my house. No hatred in my house. Music has nothing to do with hatred. I understand your frustration and I understand your anger, but you're going to revise your copy. You can't use your songs to add fuel to the fire. Music is supposed to bring people together and fight for peace, because it is art and beauty, not just politics." To this day, I always keep this in mind when I write a song.

When the Communist regime settled in Benin, they organized what they called *les cooperatives* in the high schools. Every Friday afternoon at five o'clock, the lessons would stop and the kids would have to work on something that was not academic, like sewing or farming. With a couple of friends I created a band called Les Sphinx.

At that time, modern local music was finally entering popular culture and it was a phenomenon among young people. At the cooperative, the band thing suddenly became a craze. The high school principal would organize competitions and challenges, and my band always won! From the little stage at the Gbagame High School, we started to play in bigger and bigger venues. I used to sing this one Miriam Makeba song called

With Nelson Mandela during the second 46664 concert, in Finland in 2005.

Singing with the famous Orchestre Poly Rythmo de Cotonou.

"Ushaka" that was about the fighting between the Zulu king Shaka and the British. On her albums Miriam would talk a little to explain the meanings of her songs. She spoke in such a soft, quiet voice, but what she was saying was so political and tough. So when I performed "Ushaka," I would quote Miriam: "The British referred to Shaka as the black Napoleon but I said Napoleon was a white Shaka!" That would make the audience go wild. I had fire inside me and performing gave me an outlet. I wanted to relate the South African struggle to the Beninese people. As I did, I saw the people in front of me get fired up too. I could see before my eyes the power of music.

By this time I had a boyfriend and we'd been together for a little while. He was tall and elegant, but he was also a player. One day, after he saw one of my concerts, he came by the house. I remember it vividly. It was a Sunday and I was reading under the *paillotte*, the big grass hut in the center of our courtyard. We sat down and then he said, "Your concert was really very good. You sing well, but once we're married you'll have to stop singing."

I was shocked. He'd already been getting on my nerves with his unfaithfulness, his running after every skirt, and this was the last straw. "If that's the way it is," I said, "you see that gate you came in through? You can go out through that same gate and get out of my life right now. I don't want anything to do with you anymore."

My mother was busy cooking, but she heard the conversation through the kitchen window. She was surprised by my reaction and after he left she asked, "Why were you so hard on him?"

I said, "Papa and you have always told us to choose our partners freely. For four years now I've been extremely patient but this is it. I'm not going to stop singing just to become Monsieur's sweet little housewife."

In that moment, I understood for the first time the depth of my passion for singing. Singing was a part of me that I could not simply do away with. That would be like cutting off a limb. I knew that to be a singer I needed to be free. It meant giving up a life that everyone expected of me. I would no longer be guaranteed a husband or a family. I wouldn't be following the paths that other girls took. But I didn't care. There was meaning and power in singing. I refused to be silenced.

Now I was starting to make a bit of money with my music. I was able to buy a year's registration for the swimming pool at the fancy new Sheraton

hotel near the sea on the way to the airport. It was an exciting, modern building with a marble floor in the hall. Hanging out on the deck by the pool, I really felt like a star. But just as I was getting settled in this role, things came crashing down. I was slapped by the realization of how people outside my country viewed me, by the harsh reality of postcolonial Africa.

At the time, the Sheraton was managed by the British. Most of the guests of the hotel were Westerners and Middle Eastern businessmen. I must have been eighteen or nineteen. I was lying out on my chair in the sun when one of these arrogant businessmen arrived, kicked my bag aside and said, "Hey you, get up!"

I couldn't understand why he was talking to me like that. "Why should I leave?"

"You have to get up so that my wife can sit on that chaise."

"And why should I get up for her?"

"Do you know who you're talking to?" he asked.

"I don't care who you are. You may have money, but you have no right to speak to anyone that way."

One of the Beninese waiters came over and said, "Miss, please don't make a scene. You have to get up."

"Get up? I was here first and I'm staying here. I've paid. I have the right to sit here and if this gentleman thinks I'm going to get up so his wife can sit down, well then he's seriously mistaken."

Then one of the British managers comes over.

"Did I pay or didn't I?" I asked. "If I leave this chair, are you going to reimburse me for the whole year?"

During this time the military, never far away during the dictatorship, came with their rifles. They demanded to know what was going on. But one of the soldiers recognized me. "This is our national star," he said. In the end, they left me alone because I was famous, which certainly is no legitimate reason. The dictatorship wanted us to think we were living in the People's Republic of Benin, but it seemed that foreign interests were still ruling the country. Twenty years of independence hadn't changed anything. At that moment I was so frustrated with the situation that I wanted only one thing, to get away.

Since the Communists had been in power, the cultural independence of the radio stations in Benin had disappeared. Before, they could broadcast

the music of Johnny Pacheco or
of Jimi Hendrix, the traditional
songs, or Congolese and Cameroonian bands. We would listen
to the intricate high-pitched
guitars of Franco Luambo and
Tabu Ley Rochereau, the masters
of soukous, and to the funky
sounds of Manu Dibango's
"Soul Makossa." There was such
a mixture of genres on the radio
we used to listen to. That freedom suddenly vanished after
the Marxist coup d'état of 1972
and gradually the radio in Benin
became propaganda radio. The
slogan of the revolution played
constantly, in a loop: "*Prêts pour
la revolution? La lutte continue!*"
"Ready for the revolution? The
fight goes on!" It's hard to

An afternoon at the Sheraton Hotel of Cotonou
for the starlet.

believe now, but after the coup it was compulsory to say those words
to every person you met in the street, even a stranger, before starting
any conversation.

Even at home I felt the pressure of the totalitarian regime. Maybe my
father was asked to be part of the government and he refused. I don't know,
but one day my father said that from then on we'd no longer talk politics
at home, and we lost that spontaneity of being able to talk about anything
and everything. The pressure was too great. All of a sudden our house,
which had always provided an open forum for any topic of discussion,
became a highly suspect place. It felt as if the government was watching
our every move.

Outside our home, the red symbols of Marxism-Leninism were
displayed everywhere. Africa had become the battlefield of the Cold War
and there were frequent military processions in the street. Little by little,
Beninese artists were forced to write songs about the revolution and for

the revolution. During one of the Les Sphinx concerts, I met Ekambi Brillant, a famous Cameroonian singer who was living in Benin. My parents invited him to the house to see if he might be able to produce my record. He said he could, as long as we paid the costs of the recording. At the time, we were naïve when it came to the music business. I took out a student loan with the national bank and wrote some of the songs with my brother Oscar.

One night I got to the studio at ten p.m. and recorded my album *Pretty*. My friends, the great Toto Guillaume on the guitar, Valery Laubé on drums, and Aladji Touré on bass, had already laid down their parts, and I finished

My first album brought me success in West Africa. My brother Alfred took the picture.

singing all the songs and all the backing vocals at two in the morning. We managed to pull off a whole album in less than a day. It sounds impossible, but back then, hundreds of African recordings were made that way.

That night I recorded the first song I wrote, my tribute to Bella Bellow, and there was even one last song, "Na n'de," that wasn't scheduled, and I had to learn it on the spot. During that session, I also recorded a song in Douala, a Cameroonian dialect, called "Ninive." It's an upbeat makosa with a lively bass that would make me famous overnight all over West Africa.

My brother Alfred took the cover photo of *Pretty* in my dad's studio and my mom designed the dress: it was a family affair. I had a big smile and my hair was beautifully braided. Today, people always laugh when they see all that hair. After the record was made, we sent it to radio stations and a promoter my dad knew. This guy had become big in the musical world on the west coast, bringing Celia Cruz, Johnny Pacheco, and Miriam Makeba there. For every act that toured Africa, he was the one who brought them to Benin.

After hearing my record, he agreed to help us do a concert in Togo. I already had a following in Benin, so we thought going to a neighboring country might jump-start my career. We booked the venue, put the band together, and started publicizing the show. Then, two weeks before it, the promoter came to my father and said, "I love your daughter's music, but she's too little to perform. Nobody's going to see her onstage."

"Is that how you measure talent?" my father asked. "Do you hear how stupid you sound?"

My father was so mad that he decided to produce the show himself, but when the promoter pulled the plug on the radio and TV ads, everything collapsed. Even the band I was rehearsing with backed out. They couldn't risk upsetting the promoter. In their place, we found a band of Zairian immigrants living in Togo who could learn fast. My sister Paulette had moved to Togo, so I went to stay with her and began rehearsing from scratch.

As a result of all the problems, we had to change the date of the performance. The posters had already been printed, so my father took a black marker and changed the date on each one by hand. Putting a concert together like that, especially with no radio or TV promotion, makes it hard to get a large crowd. My father was a postman; what did he know about music promotion? But the whole family had committed to making

The original poster for my first concert in Togo. The date and ticket price had to be edited with a Sharpie at the last minute.

the show happen, even though it meant making sacrifices because my father had to cover the costs. For a good while afterward, we had only tea and bread for breakfast, lunch, and dinner.

The concert changed my career. It's why my name began to be widely known. After it, I went on tour with Ekambi Brillant. His music was inspired by the artists of Stax Records and by James Brown–he even wore a cape like Brown. We performed to packed houses all over West Africa. Before this, I was well known in my own country, but now, with my success as a singer growing beyond Benin, I was approached to play for the government.

There was no serious record company in Benin and

I N V I T A T I O N
——•——

FRANCESKIE INTERNATIONAL ORGANISATION

a le plaisir d'inviter ℳ...................

à assister au Show Musical de la Vedette Béninoise Angélique Kidjo qui aura lieu le Samedi 31 Mai 1980 à 21 h. 00 à la Maison du R. P. T.

Places Réservées.

An invitation to my concert in Togo made by my father.

this meant no steady income for an artist. The only way to make a living for many African singers in those days was to hold concerts, but to do so you'd have to praise your leader in your songs and onstage. The careers of many wonderful African singers came to a halt at that time, for they were asked to compose nothing but ideological songs, or else exaggerated praises about the dictator in power. There are so many forgotten songs applauding Mobutu Sese Seko, the dictator who ruled Zaire (now the Democratic Republic of the Congo). Who could sing them now?

Thanks to my tours, every now and then I was able to escape from the frenzy of "for the revolution, the fight goes on!" Each time they asked me to sing at an official event I would try my best not to be around, but one day I was summoned to sing at a meeting of the ECOWAS, the Economic Community of West African States, and this time I couldn't make an excuse. I saw all of these presidents–men my father's age–looking at me as if I was a piece of meat, with disdain, without any respect. Like I was a call girl because I was performing. I remember standing onstage in a black and golden dress and feeling so humiliated. I knew then that I could never go on singing in these conditions.

Onstage in Benin.

The only respectful person there was the leader of Ghana at that time, Jerry Rawlings. Later he would become the first elected president, but at that time he had come to power in a coup d'état. After the performance, he insisted on thanking all the artists. He wanted us to understand how important we were for our countries as ambassadors of our culture, and how music and culture go beyond simple entertainment. They speak for a people, for a continent. He came to me and said, "Your voice doesn't belong to you. You have the responsibility to care for it and use it for those who are voiceless."

Those words gave me wings, and have always stayed with me. It was at that moment that I decided to leave Benin. I knew I had to if I wanted to keep singing, and if I wanted to keep my freedom and my inspiration.

I told my father, "I can't stay and do my music here. I'm not spending my life singing 'Ready for the revolution, the fight goes on!'" What choice do you have left when you are an artist living under a dictatorship?

My brother Yves, who had left a few years before to study in Paris, told my parents, "If you let her leave she'll have a better chance than in Cotonou. If her music doesn't work out she can at least continue her studies." But because I was so famous in Benin after the success of *Pretty*, I had to do it secretly. The authorities would not have let me move because I had become a symbol of the people. I would never have been granted an authorized laissez-passer.

As a family we made the decision that I should leave. It was the right thing to do, but we had to find an opportunity. No one could know what we were planning.

I had a cousin getting married in a different neighborhood, very close to the airport. My parents were to be the witnesses at her wedding, so we decided to use the hustle and bustle it to conceal my departure. Knowing I was leaving my country and traditions behind broke my heart, and I was worried what would happen to my parents if I did this. But I also had so much hope for what life in France could be like. It was the country of freedom and the arts.

The ceremony took place during the day and in the evening I put on a fancy white dress as if I was going to the party. We closed all the doors of the house. We shut the garage and we put my suitcase in the trunk of my father's car, the same old Citroën that used to bring me to the Beach Club. Then we left to go to the wedding dinner. At my cousin's house I changed clothes for the plane.

I was planning on taking the late-night flight to Paris at the very last minute. In those days we didn't need a visa to visit France, which is hard to fathom now. It was almost midnight. The airport was empty. On my way through, a lonely customs officer stood looking at me, confused. My heart stopped. All the anger and sadness inside of me turned into fear. I knew I couldn't stay, but I didn't know what would happen to me if the government found out what I was trying to do. But when I approached him, he didn't ask questions. He said he was a fan, and by looking into my eyes, he understood immediately.

The passport that brought me to France on September 11, 1983.

He told me the second officer had just stepped away for a moment.

He whispered, "I won't stamp your passport. I won't say anything. I didn't see you. Just leave," he said.

"Disappear."

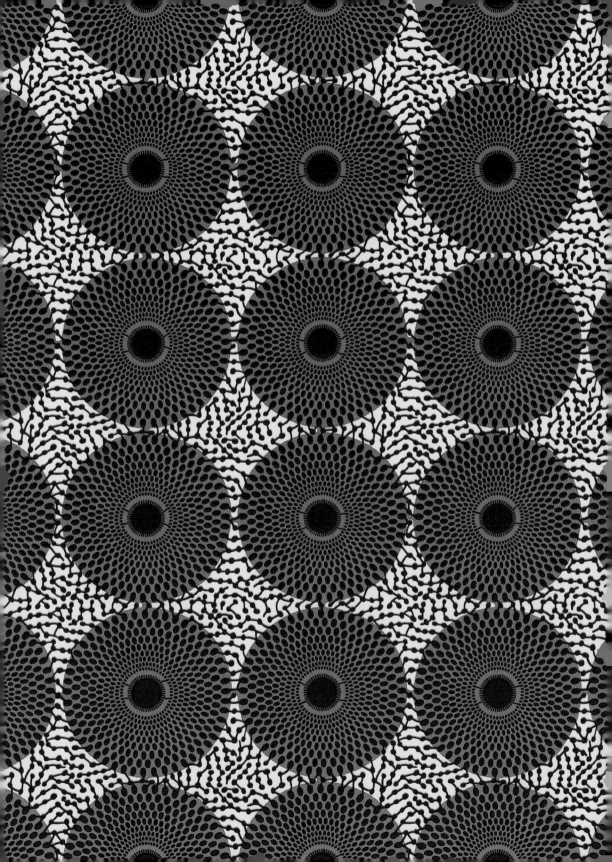

CHAPTER TWO

the musician's life

I arrived in Paris on September 11, 1983. Going through Charles de Gaulle airport with its sloping sidewalks carrying people through the white hollow building was like an eerie sci-fi film. An escalator is a scary proposition for an African person coming to Europe for the first time. Even today you will still see people stopping short before them, not quite sure how to embark on this next leg of their journey.

Outside, it was a beautiful sunny day. I thought it was summertime because to me sunshine means heat. When you've spent your whole life in a tropical country, it's impossible to imagine what being cold really means. And growing up in warm weather means you can go out in colorful

skirts and dresses all year long. There is a freedom with heat. The next morning, I put on a light dress—I still remember it was beige with stripes and short sleeves—but when I headed outside, it was a cool fall day. I was freezing. Catching a terrible cold, that was my arrival in France.

I was twenty-three and staying with my brother Yves in his one-bedroom apartment in Nogent-sur-Marne, southeast of Paris. Yves was a college student and still competing as a champion table tennis player. To make a living, he taught English to high school kids. When people think of Nogent-sur-Marne they often think of the *guinguettes* of Nogent in the paintings of Cezanne and Renoir: the scenes of people drinking wine at terraces by the river. But that's the fairy tale. I realized what the reality of France was. Seen from far away in Africa, France looked full of happy, generous people, smiling and welcoming you. We thought of France as the symbol of freedom and equality because it was in France that the Universal Declaration of Human Rights was adopted. The idea of France we had in Africa was so different from the reality of the country.

We lived on the second floor of an apartment building. Every time I'd go down and run into a neighbor I'd always say hello, and every time people would look at me with annoyance. They'd turn their gaze to the wall and I could almost hear them ask, "What does that girl want from me?" Their suspicion killed me. This was one of the most difficult things to adjust to because when I lived in Cotonou, I had learned to say hello to everybody. Everyone knew each other and everyone greeted each other.

My brother had already been in Paris for four years. He watched me change, little by little, and he'd say, "In the end you'll understand."

"Just saying hello is supposed to be a bad thing?"

"You'll see," he said.

It took me a long time to understand that some French people have a hard time grasping that a person of color could be French. I was born two weeks before Benin became independent of France, so technically I was as French as they were! This coolness toward African immigrants is such a waste of goodwill and humanity.

OPPOSITE: I had just arrived in Paris. My smile was still so wide. But I was not dressed for September weather and got a cold on my first day out.

Through all of this I couldn't even talk to my parents. After years of living under the regime, our political paranoia drove us to believe, rightly or wrongly, that our phone was tapped. People would show up at our house and ask my parents if they had news from me. They would only say that I was on tour. My mother and father were both so worried. And all the while I was dreaming of them: the echoes of their laughter in thc courtyard, and the spirit and warmth of our family and friends gathered under the paillote.

Yves introduced me to an Afropop band called Alafia put together by one of our friends from Benin. They needed to replace a backup singer. I'd never been in a chorus before and I thought it would be good to learn what happens behind the solo artist. To make some money we played concerts just about anywhere. Sometimes we played at the Phil One, an African club in La Défense, the futuristic-looking business center west of

My first recording with the band Alafia, which means good health, in Paris.

Paris. After the workers left at the end of the day, the area got very deserted. Phil One was a warm little island of African music in the middle of the cold, empty skyscrapers.

The metro stopped running around midnight, so I'd get a ride home from someone in the band. One night the guy who was supposed to take me home had an argument with his girlfriend and he just left me there. I didn't have enough money for a cab. I spent the night in the La Défense metro station with its high ceiling and empty corridors, wedged in a corner trying to be invisible and hoping that nothing would happen to me. I couldn't sleep. The station filled with homeless people and I saw another side of Paris, so far from my dreams. I went home with the first RER train to Nogent-sur-Marne in the morning.

There was never a time that I felt France or Europe was waiting for me with open arms just because I was a star in my own country. This illusion has broken so many African artists. They had recognition in their own countries, but when they arrived in France nobody cared about them. They'd start to sink into depression, but pride prevents them from going home empty-handed. The challenge of having to start again from scratch was something that churned inside me because there was no Papa anymore,

there was no Mama anymore. I wanted, needed, to make it on my own. These early days in Paris were trying, but also thrilling.

I planned to keep singing, to use my voice as I saw fit, that was my impetus for going to France, but I also had this crazy dream of becoming a human rights lawyer. I was always obsessed with justice and fairness. I got in so many fights over this as a child, and once I'd learned about apartheid and the history of slavery I couldn't shrug off the injustice of it. I wanted to get people to understand, to live with as little hatred as possible.

At that time, I thought being a human rights lawyer was the best way to do this. I didn't know much about what being a human rights lawyer actually meant, but it seemed like a way to be taken seriously. When I got settled in Paris, the academic year had already begun, but I had a friend from high school who was studying law at Villetaneuse, a university north of Paris. The campus had that rough concrete architecture that was common in the seventies. It was so gray, and depressing. Still, I asked if I could sit in on some classes. There was one particular professor who moved me. He was smart and worldly, and he passionately debated with his students. He would go around the room and look each student in the eye, "What would you like to do? What motivates you?"

After everyone spoke, I stood up and said, "I want to be a human rights lawyer." I described what I'd learned about slavery and apartheid and what it had sparked in me, and that for me the individual can't be defined by skin color, but that a person must be respected for being a person. It doesn't matter what language he speaks or the religion he is or the culture he's from. It doesn't matter how much money he has or what kind of society he is a part of. An individual must be respected by the law that's been given to us. We all should be treated with dignity, and we all should be allowed to speak and move freely.

"Okay, I agree," he said. He could feel my conviction. "But you ought to study politics."

I had just left my home, my family, because of politics. I told him, "Politics is out of the question!"

"I'm going to ask you a simple question," he said. "You're defending an individual and your preliminary investigation has proven his innocence, but his country's government can't be brought to trial. Someone must take the blame to placate the relationship with that country. What will you do?"

"But that government must be brought to trial," I said.

"You can't," he said. "When human rights are attacked there are a lot of politics involved, there's a lot of diplomacy needed, and often justice comes after diplomacy."

Suddenly, studying to become a lawyer seemed pointless. It was at that moment that music became my sole vocation. My understanding of human rights and world problems had come through music, through the discovery of the activism of Miriam Makeba and her struggle against apartheid. I wondered what I could do with music, if I could use it the way Miriam Makeba had.

I registered at Les Ateliers Chansons de Paris et d'Île-de-France—a little school for singing located on the hills of Ménilmontant. There I learned classical voice technique. In Benin, there are no music schools or teachers. You sing from the time you can speak, and, since there are no microphones and you are surrounded by powerful drums, you sing loudly. It can be dangerous for your voice. Eventually, my mom lost her singing voice. Suddenly, in France I began to think of my voice as an instrument, one that I needed to take care of. I had to learn how to sing with more control and to use a microphone to carry the same energy.

I also learned all the music from after the yé-yé era. After the revolution, when music began being censored in Benin, French music stopped arriving. Now, I was catching up on everything I'd missed. I discovered Maxime Le Forestier and Alain Bashung, singers who are famous for singing what they call "*la chanson à texte.*" In these songs, there is a story, and the way in which it is told, is so important.

Reading Baudelaire and all the classics had been a part of my early education in Benin, and since then I had always loved the French language. For me, Serge Gainsbourg perfectly brought this beauty into songs. In France, popular music isn't so much about the quality of the voice, but about the poetic use of language. Gainsbourg understood that words have their own musicality and that to make a piece of art you have to combine words in a way that doesn't only rely on their meaning. You can enjoy his songs even if you don't understand French. In my music, I wanted to show the beauty of the Beninese languages.

Classical music also began to speak to me. I had never heard classical music before. It was so different from what I was used to. I'd always

thought that emotion was carried by the voice of the singer, but now I discovered that instruments like the piano and violin could speak to the soul like a voice. I didn't understand what was happening to me when I listened to classical music. I felt as if I was opening up—I was breathing differently. My only contact with it in Benin had been the disco arrangement of Beethoven's Fifth from the *Saturday Night Fever* soundtrack. Traditional music in southern Benin doesn't have harmonies. We sing in unison and all the complexity comes from the rhythms. This was another world to learn about, and I would need to start at the beginning. Listening to the harmonies of classical music felt to me like entering a new dimension.

After two years at the small singing school, I moved on to the school for jazz, le CIM. The school is near Boulevard Barbès in the northern eighteenth arrondissement of Paris—known for its discount stores and record shops, but also for its immigrant population, its fish market, and its African grocery store. It's full of color and energy—exactly what the extreme right wing hates about Paris. Walking up rue Doudeauville, you could pass right by the building and never see it. Glass block windows and a little metal plaque next to the door quietly signal what happens inside: musicians cramped together in little rooms, learning the standards, working to absorb the history of jazz through their fingertips.

My membership card at the CIM, the jazz school where I met Jean. I still had my braids, but not for long.

I remember going up the stairs for the first time, two girls were coming down—a blonde and a brunette. They were the school's star singers, but I didn't know that then. I asked where the administrative office was and they said, "Upstairs, second stairs, turn left." But then they asked, "What are you doing here, anyway?"

"I've come to register."

"Are you African?" They were both looking hard at me. Neither girl had even a trace of a smile.

Rehearsing in the jazz school.

"Yes," I answered, wondering what would come next.

"Jazz isn't for Africans." It was clear they thought jazz was too sophisticated for primitive Africans.

My father studied in Paris when he was a young man. He was there for a few months just after World War II. No one in my family knows much about his time there, but it must have made a deep impression on him.

When he came back to Benin he bought a green Vespa—he used to pick my mom up in it when they were dating—and for years after that he drove his beloved Citroën. He also returned with an enduring love of jazz, especially for Sidney Bechet and Louis Armstrong. I wonder now what my father would have said to those girls. Their words hurt, of course, but they also gave me motivation: I wanted to prove them wrong.

As you might imagine, my start at CIM was tough. Every time I opened my mouth to speak I'd hear, "What kind of French is that supposed to be? You have to check a dictionary to understand what she's saying!" In Benin we had learned a very academic French. It's hard to believe, but in a certain sense we Africans speak better than the average Parisian. I never used to curse and my grammar was impeccable, but by the end of the year I'd learned to use bad language just so they would accept me. I embraced this a little too much because even today I tend to swear a lot.

I loved jazz because it helped me understand the connections between classical music, pop, and African rhythms. I studied the way the musical notes flowed together. I also studied its history and influence on popular culture. I learned how jazzmen like Coltrane revered their African roots, and how a whole group of jazz musicians used African modes and signatures. Coltrane even had a song called "Dahomey Dance."

Around this time Yves was hired by a table tennis club, so we moved from our place in Nogent-sur-Marne to Gouvieux, north of Paris. My only income came from my concerts with Alafia and that went to my schooling. I needed to find small jobs to pay for rent and food, and that wasn't easy. I looked for work near Château Rouge, the neighborhood known as Little Africa.

Here, the African community gathers for the market on rue Myrha. The street is packed with vendors selling colorful fabrics, fish, fruits and vegetables, and spices—all the ingredients for traditional dishes. On the way to the CIM, I would go to the African grocery store. I'd buy *garri*, cassava flour, hot peppers, and plantains. The vendors came from all over the African continent. Many were Malian or Senegalese. I'd pass women from every African country wearing traditional dresses, carrying huge, stripped nylon bags, and calling loudly to each other from across the street. I found everything as if I were at the market in Cotonou.

For work I did babysitting and sometimes cleaned rooms in one of the Ibis hotels right next to the Périphérique, the highway ringing Paris. But

mostly I worked in a hair salon specialized for people from Africa and the West Indies on the Boulevard de Sébastopol. At home, in Benin, doing our hair was a social thing. We would all line up in a row. I would be doing my sister's hair, and someone else would be doing mine. It took hours and we talked the whole time. At the salon, I'd be on my feet, often for twelve hours without stopping, and I only earned a few miserable francs a day. The owners of those salons take advantage of naïve, often desperate immigrants who are ready to work. I didn't realize it then. I was just happy to make some money.

Usually I made enough to pay my tuition and to help my brother pay the rent. But there were other times when I had no money for food, so I'd soak a crust of bread in hot water. I could make the bread last for a week. I grew up in a crowded house and food was not always plentiful, but my mom used to say you can have one meal a day and keep your dignity. I had learned how to survive hunger.

One night, during my first winter in Paris and after a late concert at the CIM, I'd taken the last train for Chantilly from the Gare du Nord. There weren't many people in my car. There was an older gentleman whose hair had gone gray at the temples. He wore an expensive-looking beige suit, the trousers sharply creased. When he asked where I was going, I told him Gouvieux, which is far from Paris. After I got off the train, I would need to walk more than two miles and cross a cemetery to get home.

"I can give you a ride," he said, and I accepted.

As we drove, he started to touch my leg and he wouldn't stop. After my night spent in the RER metro station, I always kept a box cutter on me. When I took it out and he saw that I wouldn't let him push me around, he stopped.

"Out," he said. "Get out of the car."

When I finally got home and told Yves, he was so mad.

"Why didn't you call me?" he asked. "I would've come." But I didn't even have money to make the call. Yves is six years older than me and he was always so protective, but, both because of my desire to be independent and because I was naïve, I wouldn't always tell him my plans.

After that, we knew I needed to find a way to stay in Paris. Jean-Marc, the manager of the group Alafia, and his girlfriend, helped me. She said, "Listen. I have a friend who works in construction and he's always on a

job. He's never at home, but he keeps a place in Antony. If you want you can live there." So I moved my belongings there little by little. The place, in the southern suburbs of Paris, was so rundown and damp. The walls were covered with mold. I slept in the living room. There was no heat, so I'd light the kitchen stove to keep warm. A few years later, when Jean came to help me move boxes I had left behind there, he got tears in his eyes when he saw the conditions I had lived in.

But I must have had a guardian angel looking after me, because one day I received a phone call from Philippe Nossin who was the program planner at the Phil One. Nicolas Fiszman, a Belgian bassist, had told him he was looking for an African singer who had some knowledge of jazz and who knew traditional music to go on tour with the group Pili Pili, put together by the famous Dutch pianist Jasper van't Hof.

"Nicolas will call you," Philippe said. Soon after, I took a train from Paris to Brussels to Rotterdam to meet them. Looking back on it now, I realize I was the only girl with six or seven guys in the band, but I wasn't scared. I never thought twice of it. It was the musician's life I had dreamed of.

Jasper van't Hof and me. Jasper is a genius jazz pianist who fell in love with African music.

The first time I met Jasper, he told me, "I can't do free jazz anymore." He had recorded the album *Mama Rose* with Archie Shepp, a prominent saxophonist from the free jazz movement. Then he'd taken a trip to Zaire in Central Africa with guitarist Philip Catherine and he returned to Europe entirely transformed. "We Westerners have a chip on our shoulders," he said. "We think we're musical experts, but we've invented nothing. Everything comes from Africa." I thought, "This guy looks so Dutch with his red hair and his Viking mustache but he has an African character. He talks so loud!"

Then he says, "I want to mix my experience as a jazz player with African music."

Pili Pili was modern jazz with African lyrics and rhythms, and Jasper was a genius at improvisation. The first time I went to the studio, I asked him to play me the song we were recording. He looks at me and says, "What song?" I thought he was kidding. We were there to make an album. It was the first time I wrote something on the spot like that. He'd sit down at the piano and melodies and rhythms would magically appear. I've never seen a piano player like him. It's like he has four hands.

Seeing the respect that African music inspired in him made me so proud. When society looks down on African people, true artists know better. They can see the beauty of our art. Later on, this music also had a great influence on my own jazz rhythms. I understood that you can blend traditional melodies with jazz chords and modern rhythms. The sound can be complex and entrancing. It was my first glimpse of how to create something new out of the magic of traditional African music.

I worked on and off with Pili Pili for four years, both in the studio and onstage. My first trip to the Montreux Jazz Festival was with Pili Pili. But most often we played in Germany, where the group had a lot of fans. In January, I would skip out of jazz school to do our yearly tour in the cold of Germany and Austria. We visited every little town and our audience was a mix of jazz fans and hippies. In Benin, music is always part of a bigger picture. We have a ceremony, so we dress in elaborate costumes. Because we're singing in unison and our bodies move to the beat of the drums, an excitement builds under the skin. The drums call us into the celebration.

The concerts with Pili Pili would always start with an insistent rhythm on the cowbell: the clave pattern, so important in Africa, and everyone in the audience would fall into a kind of trance. It amazed me to see all these

pale, quiet Germans losing their minds to our drums and chants. Their moves weren't part of our canon of traditional dance, but they surely looked possessed. Then, the instant the concert was over, they were back to their reserved selves. It made me realize the power of our music over the audience.

In France, June 21, the summer solstice, is Fête de la Musique, a holiday in celebration of music and summer. It's always a crazy day in Paris. All day and night, all over the

One of the singles of Pili Pili.

city, you see people performing in clubs and on street corners. Alain Guerrini, the founder of the jazz school, wanted to organize a small concert at the bar on rue Doudeauville, Au Petit Château.

That first day I came to CIM, I didn't know it, but Alain had heard the greeting I'd gotten from the star singers. At one point he came to me and said, "I heard what those women said to you, and I've heard you sing. Prepare something that will nail them to the wall. That's the only answer you can give them."

So when he put together the show for Fête de la Musique, he had an idea: Why not introduce the slender young African singer to one of the groups that keeps on trotting out the standards in the school's rehearsal rooms? Jean, who would later become my husband, remembers how I came rushing into the rehearsal room the day before the performance, and, when I saw the cloud of smoke hovering just under the ceiling, I didn't even stop to say hello. Instead, I snapped, "From now on, no one is to smoke in here! I've got to protect my vocal cords." Now, this line seems harmless, but at the time it caused an uproar. I was demanding that a roomful of French jazz musicians put out their cigarettes. Jean says he thought I was so arrogant. He wanted to know, "Who does she think she is?"

It sounds like a cheap romance novel the young girl and guy getting off to a rocky start before falling in love. But that's how we first met.

The next day, at the glorious Fête de la Musique celebration, at the bar on rue Doudeauville, I was again in a smoke-filled room. We were playing side by side—my voice floating out over Jean's gently insistent bass line on "Cry Me a River," "Green Dolphin Street," and "God Bless the Child." At the end of the concert, our eyes met. Everyone around us was tipsy, shouting and laughing in their own little world. We felt for a moment that we were on the exact same wavelength. We were seeing the world and this particular scene through the same pair of eyes, even though our cultures were miles apart.

Twenty years later, after traveling around the world several times and finally settling down in New York, we would have dinner with Jack Lang—the French minister of culture who created the Fête de la Musique—on the famous promenade in Brooklyn Heights, looking across the river to downtown Manhattan. He was in the city for the first performance of the Fête there. When he told us that through the years many couples had met on this day, Jean and I smiled at the memory of our own day back in 1985.

It took two more years before Jean and I were onstage together again. We lost track of each other in '86, but in '87 we began to play together in clubs. We found ourselves connecting intellectually and musically. He listened to everything I'd done in the past, things like my album *Pretty* and the albums with Pili Pili. What especially excited him was the traditional music of Benin. It was the ancestral rhythms that interested him—not the *kwassa kwassa*, the Congolese dance music of those days, which sounded modern to him.

Our traditional melodies are so unusual to Western ears. They sound mysterious. And when you put a modern chord behind an ancient melody a new color emerges, giving new life to traditional music. This is what Chopin, Bartók, and Liszt did with European folk songs. And the rhythm? You have to study like a scientist to understand our polyrhythms. In West Africa, the beat isn't perceived the same way it is in the West. It's not a step on which you lean, but an accent that the dancer can shift at will. As a bass player, a student of grooves, Jean was confronted with something that was moving him, but that he couldn't understand. Before studying jazz he had studied philosophy at the Sorbonne and the philosopher in him saw this as a challenge. He would try to write down the patterns, but he couldn't find the downbeat and so he was always asking me, "But where is one? Where is one?"

OPPOSITE: In the arms of Jean.

We moved in together in '87 and six months later we were married. Our passion for each other and our passion for music were intertwined. We would spend hours listening to Coltrane, Miles Davis, and Weather Report. The album *Tutu* by Miles was the main soundtrack of our life. It was jazz, but had a cutting-edge sound. It was both funky and complex.

Our first date was when I asked friends to help me move from the apartment in Antony to a tiny place I had found on boulevard Ornano in Barbès. Everybody said yes, but Jean was the only one who showed up. He was shocked by the insalubrity of the place. He also couldn't believe it when I carried my huge moving boxes on my head as we do on Africa—for seven floors!

The first time Jean brought me to meet Yves and Claudine, his parents, it was to their house in a nice suburb of Paris for Sunday lunch with some of the extended family. They had never really talked with an African person before, but they were liberal and anti-racist and so they welcomed me warmly. I was anxious and didn't know what to expect, so when someone offered me a coffee, I didn't dare refuse out of politeness. You have to know that coffee and I don't get along. I'm already too hyped up naturally. So then, in front of a silent group of French people, I did a thirty-minute monologue on how bad white people were in South Africa—this was during the days of apartheid—and how we had to have a revolution to free Mandela. Everyone must have thought Jean was dating Angela Davis. It was an odd first meeting, to say the least, but over the years Yves and Claudine have adopted me as a daughter.

Jean and I had been playing as part of a small jazz combo in restaurants in Paris and on the coast of Normandy, but once we were married we wanted to play our own music. We decided to put our own group together and found musicians from the school. If we really wanted to make a name for ourselves, we needed to write our own songs. At that time, our repertoire consisted of a mixture of songs by Sade, Stevie Wonder, and my African pop songs. I wanted our music to reflect the person I was, but this wasn't easy. Beninese music was fresh to Western ears and I had so many modern influences that had become just as much a part of me. I would never abandon my African rhythms, but I also didn't want to be representing the past, singing tribal music and wearing a boubou. I thought, if Paul Simon and Peter Gabriel were using African elements in their music, why couldn't I use Western elements in mine?

ABOVE: Our wedding in the city hall of Paris. The mayor seemed to think this was a *mariage blanc*, a sham marriage. • **RIGHT:** As students we could not afford a fancy dress or suit. But it was still a beautiful day.

The crucial moment, the big break for both of us, was when we had our first engagement at le Baiser Salé–the salted kiss–a club on rue des Lombards near the Châtelet in Paris. Rue des Lombards was a tiny street hidden between the fancy Théâtre de la Ville and Les Halles, and it was famous for its jazz clubs. It was the center of the musical nightlife of Paris in the late eighties and le Baiser Salé was the cult club. If you were a musician, you absolutely had to pass through there. It was a dream if you got to play there. That was where the cream of the crop of African and Brazilian musicians and the Paris jazzmen would come together at the end of the night after their concerts.

We were so nervous at our audition, and once we were done, my heart almost stopped. Maria, the formidable and loud proprietress who has discovered many artists in Paris, took out her large black notebook and signed us up for a week. She said to me, "You know, you don't need to sing English cover songs. It's when you sing the African rhythms that we really see your personality and energy."

We were floating through the air when we went home. Since then, I've played the finest halls in the world and received many honors, but the moment that Maria picked up her notebook is still so clear in my mind. It was the start of my conquest of Paris.

Many musical things were going on at night in the rue des Lombards neighborhood. We'd play at le Baiser Salé until dawn and then we'd go to eat at le Caf' Conc', an African restaurant upstairs from the club. Mamayo, a female chef from Zaire, ran the place. She had such a warm heart and she'd make us her delicious *yassa* chicken. Food has a special taste at six in the morning. We'd stuff ourselves and then go home to our little apartment.

By then, Jean and I were living at 9 rue des Gravilliers, right in the heart of the Marais, in a tiny 270-square-foot studio. That's where we did everything. We wrote music on the Fender Rhodes piano, cooked, and invited musician friends for dinner. Once, we packed in thirteen guests, but I still managed to cook *amiwo* and *colombo* in our closet of a kitchen.

We'd sleep all day and start all over again at night. We'd managed to finish music school, and now we were actually playing and living off our music—even if it was very modestly. Our music was like an obsession for us both. When we weren't playing it, we were talking about it. Our set at le Baiser Salé went from ten until four, so we were together around the clock, breathing the same air. Onstage, we each knew what the other would do next. In a way, it was a continuation of my musical life in Benin: making music as a family. The most important thing for us was that we were playing for an audience, trying to find our own voice, and seeing if we could make careers out of it.

That's when I met the well-known musicians of the Paris stage—André Ceccarelli, Thierry Vaton, Jaco Largent, Louis Winsberg. Right next door to le Baiser Salé on rue des Lombards was the Sunset, where all the jazzmen played. The fusion group Sixun played there from time to time. Sixun had the finest Afro-Caribbean rhythm in Paris: Paco Sery, the Charlie Parker of African drummers, and Michel Alibo, the Caribbean bassist who had played on more than a thousand records. He mixed the *makossa* style from Cameroon with the Caribbean *kompa* and *zouk* music.

It was the magical period when what they called world music was born: the encounters of the great Parisian studio sharks with the virtuosos of African and Caribbean music who came to Paris in the hope of making

Onstage with Jean in Japan.

a living. People began to talk about Guinean singer Mory Kanté and Senegalese performer Youssou N'Dour. Salif Keita had just arrived in Paris from Mali with his amazing album *Soro*. Zaire's Ray Lema was the guru of the new African music.

Jean-François Bizot, who had a contagious passion for discovering the world and its unheard music, created the Parisian station Radio Nova. He had coined the phrase "*la sono mondiale*," broadcasting all the sounds of the world, and Radio Nova played an eclectic array of music unlike anything you would hear elsewhere on the dial. The station was near Bastille, which was a little rough at the time. It was situated in the courtyard of an old, graffiti-covered building. Artists were constantly performing at the station. MC Solaar and his contemporaries were creating French rap there. Bizot was a great bourgeois and a converted hippie. At night he would go back to his castle in the suburb of Saint-Maur, where Jean's parents lived.

After one of our concerts, Alain Guerrini, the founder of the CIM, came to see us. Alain was an important person in our lives. He was there when I first met Jean and had been one of the dozen people at our wedding. He was a great man who would die young because of his passion for Parisian nightlife and music and its excess. That night, the energy of our show had gotten him quite excited and he offered to produce my next record. He had a small jazz label called Open. He had produced Sixun, and though my music was far from being jazz he found it refreshing. Jazz has its many purists—people eager to define what it is and is not—but it has always recreated itself by absorbing outside influences: Stan Getz and his Brazilian music, Miles Davis and rock.

What was unbelievable at the time was that Alain gave us a completely blank slate. It was the first time that Jean set foot inside a studio. He had no idea how a mixing desk worked, but he had to learn fast. We invited all the musicians we had known at le Baiser Salé to the studio. Jasper van't Hof came to play the keyboard on an old song by Bella Bellow, my Togolese idol. Back when I was a teenager in Benin I would watch her on TV and wonder how someone could be so beautiful. Looking at the camera with her lids lowered and a warm smile, it had seemed like she was singing just to me and now I was recording her song "Blewu" with a modern arrangement.

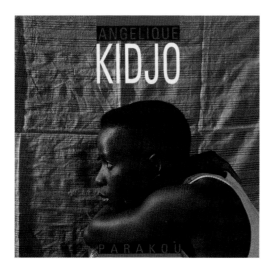

Mamadou Konte sent my album *Parakou* to Island Records founder Chris Blackwell.

We'd prepared the sessions with Christian Lachenal, another musician who had been at my first music school and would work with us for many years. He had a small studio in Pantin just on the other side of the boulevard Périphérique. The studio was in an apartment upstairs and

while we were recording the samples of the album that was to become *Parakou*, there was a group of Senegalese women in the courtyard below. They were laughing and talking while preparing food. It was like my courtyard at home in Cotonou. Through the window we had a little piece of Africa to inspire us.

Parakou is the biggest city in the north of Benin, but having grown up in the south, I had never set foot in the north of my country. In order to maintain power, the colonizers made sure that we stayed divided. When Benin gained independence, tensions grew between the south and the north. Just as in many other African countries where one ethnic group has been favored, the people in the north didn't have political power, so their interests weren't taken into account.

For a child born in north Benin to go to high school and university, the student must have exceptional grades and then be transferred to the south. These children are typically no older than thirteen, and the transfer happens in the middle of the school year. It is hard for these kids. Students make fun of them because they don't have much money and don't speak the languages of the south—only French. I always asked, "Why are you doing this? We're all members of the same country. Why do you pick on them?" After moving to France, I understood what it must have been like for these kids. I understood how hard it is to leave your home for a chance to have a new life—and then to be met not with understanding, but with ridicule. I called the album *Parakou* as a tribute to their resilience.

In May of 1989, we were home in our little apartment when I got a call from Jean-Michel Boris, director of the legendary Olympia where Jacques Brel, Edith Piaf, and so many great artists have performed. He asked if I would open for Miriam Makeba. I turned to Jean to tell him and even though the words were coming out of my mouth, I couldn't believe them. I never dreamed I'd get to meet the woman who made me believe I could be an African singer and not feel like a prostitute.

A few weeks later, I was standing on that famous stage, looking out over endless rows of red velvet, and finishing my sound check when I saw Miriam come in. Even surrounded by her entourage of musicians, she had an amazing presence—a mix of a gentle girl and a fierce warrior. When she saw I was nervous, she walked over to me, took my hand, and said, "Don't worry. Everything will be fine." I had never even had the

chance to see one of her concerts, but now here she was, right in front of me. She thanked me for being there and her spirit was so warm and generous, like a mother.

My set went by in a blur that night, but I remember that the drummer took his usual thirty-second solo and extended it for several minutes. I was fuming, but I also understood his desire to show off for Miriam. For me, this was a moment of pride, joy, and enormous stress. I danced like a madwoman and pushed my voice as hard as I could. Afterward, walking off stage, I was so overwhelmed I was physically sick. I had a fever and couldn't stop shaking. Even so, I was so happy to be standing in the wings, watching her sing.

We finished *Parakou* and after it came out Alain told us he couldn't afford a budget for promotion. We'd have to do it ourselves. He said he'd give us one hundred of the five hundred records he'd pressed for us to send to journalists. He put the rest in the music section at Fnac, the largest music store in Paris. "We'll see what happens," he said.

With the album's release Jean put his bass aside and became my press agent. Muriel, a friend who was working for the famous jazz club the New Morning gave us a long list of journalists whom Jean, who is essentially a shy man, began to phone, one at a time, without mentioning the fact that he was my husband and the coauthor of the songs. At last one day the phone rang and it was Patrick Labesse, the first French journalist to want to interview me. That is how we started getting small articles in *Libération*, then in *Le Monde*. Gradually a buzz started growing.

The attention allowed me to meet an eccentric, and important, member of the Paris music world, Mamadou Konte. At the time, Mory Kanté's "Yé ké yé ké" was a hit on the radio. It used a *kora*, a very traditional string instrument made from a gourd, and was in the top 40. I knew Mory's manager, Otis M'Baye, and Otis introduced us to Mamadou.

Mamadou had enormous hands and wore a fedora that covered his dreadlocks. Knowing him was a *passage obligé* for anyone involved in African music in those days. In 1965, when he was twenty, he'd left Mali with two sheep to help him navigate his journey. He sailed to Marseille illegally in the hold of a cargo ship. He didn't know how to read or write but he was exceedingly intelligent and had a generous spirit. He spent years as an activist lobbying for immigrants, and after, he devoted himself

to his passion: promoting African music. By the time I met him he'd become a legend. He seemed to spend all day, every day, trying to find the best way to have the intractable French learn to love Africa and her culture.

Mamadou was a man of few words, but he was like a wise guru people came to seek advice from. His home was on the ground floor of a small hotel. In fact, he would live his whole life in hotels between Paris and Dakar. This one was situated on a quiet little street and you had to climb up a steep hill from Place Pigalle, the corner of the red-light district, to reach it. His office, just next to the lobby, was always filling up with smoke as musicians and managers poured through. The vibe was so laid-back, but with the success of both his protégé Salif Keita and Mory Kanté reaching toward the Top Ten on the European charts, excitement was building.

Mamadou would listen to all of our demos and then, with the smile of a wise man, say, "Right. You have some good ideas." One afternoon he put my record in a large white envelope and sent it to Chris Blackwell's private address in Jamaica. Chris Blackwell was the founder of Island Records. Just his name would evoke for every musician the coolest music imaginable. He was the man who discovered Bob Marley, U2, Grace Jones, and so many more powerful artists.

The day after he received my album, Chris Blackwell sent a fax to Jumbo Vanrenen, the artistic director of the record company in England. He wrote, "You must sign this girl up at all costs and as quickly as possible." No one in the Parisian record companies had taken the trouble to listen to my record or come to see me while I was performing, but suddenly the owner of the coolest of the international labels wanted to sign me up. When Mamadou told me about this, I was incredulous. I had to see those words myself! Jumbo faxed his copy over to Mamadou.

When I read it, I started to dream. We had spent that time in Paris fighting so hard for success, always meeting people—journalists, agents, other musicians trying to make it. We experienced a lot of disappointment, of course, so when good news came we tried not to get too excited. This time we tried to resist, but the feeling was overwhelming. We gave up and talked about it constantly in the streets of the Marais, hanging out near Châtelet-Les Halles.

I saved that sheet of paper as a lucky charm. Over the years the letters have gradually faded, but the record deal was real.

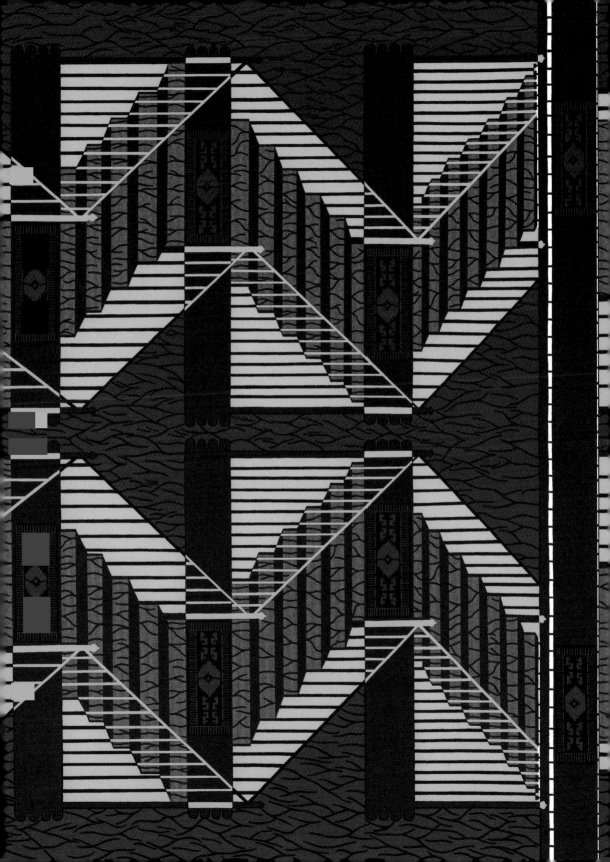

say it loud

Not far from Gare de l'Est, near the metro station called Château d'Eau–where you can see crowds of people from Africa and the West Indies chatting in front of stores–is the most famous jazz club in Paris, the New Morning. It was run by Madame Farhi, an elegant old Egyptian woman. Even in her eighties, she would be there at one in the morning to close the club. So many great musicians have come through there. We saw Chet Baker perform just a few days before he died. Ravaged by excess, he showed up just for the second set and his playing was so fragile and touching. We used to go to see Dee Dee Bridgewater, Monty Alexander, and other artists who came from the United States, but also African

musicians like Manu Dibango. Now I was performing here, not far from the Afro hair salons where I used to work for fifty francs a day. It wasn't fancy like the Blue Note club in New York. The ceiling was low and there was a long corridor leading toward a small dancehall filled with tables and cigarette smoke. The yellow dressing room was minuscule. One night, in between sets, I went back and there were the big bosses of Island Records from London and Paris–Jumbo Vanrenen, Suzette Newman, and Jean-Pierre Weiller and his staff. They were all packed in that little room, waiting to ask if I wanted to sign with them.

I'll always remember the meeting I had with Chris Blackwell a few weeks later at the Island Records office on rue Tiquetonne next to Les Halles. Chris is a handsome man with blue eyes. He was dressed very simply, just in a casual shirt, jeans, and sandals. If you passed him on the street, you would have no idea how rich and powerful he was. Even though this deal was what I had always dreamed of, I was still hesitant to sign. I looked at the contract and then I looked at Jean. Chris was relaxed, leaning back against the edge of the desk. He smiled and asked what was worrying me. "Island is like a home. I want you to feel at ease," he said.

I told him, "I need to have the artistic freedom to sing what I want to sing, and make the music I want to make."

"That will never be a question," he said, and my instinct told me to believe him. I could tell he was a man of his word. "At Island we are responsible for selling what you give us. You are entirely free to do what you want to do."

I signed the contract and he kept his promise. He never treated me like a second-class artist just because I was coming from Africa. He recognized that I had to be true to myself. That I knew when and how my music worked.

That night, Jean-Pierre Weiller invited us to Charlot, a fancy seafood restaurant on the always-crowded Place de Clichy to celebrate. When we arrived, Jean-Pierre offered me a drink. Alcohol is worse for me than coffee. I don't drink. Ever. I don't handle it well. When Jean started to tell him this, Jean-Pierre interrupted, saying, "C'mon, Jean, don't spoil the party. This is a big day for Angélique." So I ordered Cointreau–that was my fantasy drink. And then I didn't stop talking–or laughing–for hours. At the end of the night the lights of Place de Clichy were spinning all

around me. Jean told me later that at the end of the night I turned to Jean-Pierre and said, "You! Tell me who you are. Do I know you?" I can imagine Jean's face getting whiter than he already is. From that day on, word spread at Island Records: Don't encourage Angélique to drink.

In our little apartment at 9 rue des Gravilliers we began working on the songs that would become *Logozo*. It was a sixth-floor walkup, and from our window we could see the gray rooftops of Paris lining up in front of us all the way to the Sacré Coeur. We continued our routine of writing music, cooking, and inviting friends for dinner. In a way, even in that tiny apartment, with people coming and going, we were recreating the busy, vibrant life I missed so much from home. Yves was married now and starting a family in the suburbs of Paris. Mireille was in the West Indies with her daughters. My sister Paulette was now a widow in Togo.

At our parents' house in Cotonou, they'd had a rule: the front door was never to be locked during the day. This created a sort of perpetual mayhem that still goes on to this day. Once my dad tried to put a bell on the door, but so many people were used to coming and going at all times that the bell would ring the whole day. It was soon removed.

It was around this time that I first brought Jean to Benin. When my mom met Jean, she took me aside in our little courtyard and told me, "Your husband needs to stay in the shade all day." Then she said, completely deadpan, "Of all the white men in the world, you picked the whitest."

It took time for Jean to adjust to the activity of the Kidjo house. From seven in the morning until eleven at night he would meet all these people who were coming and going. He was so sweet, trying to figure out who they were and to remember their names. One day he came to my mom and asked her, "Can you tell me the name of that person sitting on the couch?" She looked and, to his surprise, answered, "Well, I don't know him!"

I had missed this sense of continual excitement and human warmth when I landed in France. One day, I was riding the metro and I saw a young woman weeping. No one stopped. Everyone was completely ignoring her. I went over to her to ask what was wrong and we got off the train together at Place d'Italie. I gave her a handkerchief and we sat together while she told me her story–a love story, a broken heart. As we separated, each going our own way, she said to me, "You know, no one ever stops for anyone else in this country. You must have just arrived from Africa."

Even though my brother had warned me, I never lost my love of talking to and connecting with people—all people. And back in those days in Paris I felt that everybody was living in a kind of shell, like a tortoise. So, a few years later, in our little studio, I wrote the song "Logozo," which means tortoise in my language, to express this feeling of loneliness I felt in France.

Listen to the song of the tortoise. She lives alone,
Folded up in her shell with no one to confide in.
Don't laugh at her solitude because death and exile
Have taken away her family and friends.

Our space in Paris kept growing smaller because of all the clothes and shoes I was accumulating to wear onstage. We had a second-hand Fender Rhodes piano and every inch on top of and below the piano was filled with cardboard boxes. It was on that piano that we composed "We We" and "Batonga." I would sing African melodies with their intricate rhythms and Jean would write them down, analyze them, and try out modern chords on the Rhodes. He loved the rhythm of Tchinkoumé from Savalou, a city about one hundred miles north of Cotonou. It is very close to funk music and somehow found its way from Benin to America. The melody is very syncopated and it drives the groove. We also used a rhythm from my beloved village of Ouidah: the *gogbahoun*, which I'd named a song after on *Parakou*. It's based on a complex polyrhythmic cowbell pattern. No musician in Paris could agree on how to transcribe it.

Our biggest influence then was Salif Keita's *Soro*. Salif is a musician's musician and this album, which would become known as a breakthrough record, was just becoming popular among world music fans. The cover is wonderful: Salif is leaning against a conga drum looking as if he's dreaming, his albino face in contrast with the dark stage behind him. The arrangers, François Bréant and Jean-Philippe Rykiel, the blind son of fashion designer Sonia Rykiel, created layers of synth behind his griot's voice. An essential part of the oral tradition of Africa, griots were part of a special caste of professional musicians who sang the histories of the dynasties. The tradition was passed down from father to son, mother to daughter, and Salif was inspired by it. This gave him an epic tone that paired perfectly with the irresistible rhythm section of drummer Paco Sery and

bassist Michel Alibo, the forces behind his lyrical melodies. With my headphones on I would listen to his voice rising above layers of chords, dreaming that one day I would be able to push my voice to its limit on top of music as lush as this was.

Once we'd written all the songs for *Logozo*, we had to find a producer to make the album happen. Chris Blackwell chose Joe Galdo, an American who'd worked with Latin superstar Gloria Estefan and Miami Sound Machine. Joe was a former drummer of Cuban origin with a passion for Latin beats and drum machines. Going to Miami to work with him was the first time I set foot in America. I liked it because it was so warm. I thought everywhere in America was warm like that. I also discovered smoked swordfish. We would pull off the highway and drive down a small dusty road until we passed under a bridge. There we met an old fisherman with a wrinkled, bearded face straight out of Hemingway. He kept a shack there where he smoked the fish himself and sold it for just a few dollars.

At night we would hang out in the art deco hotels in South Beach that Chris Blackwell owned. A mix of Latin and house music was everywhere. I remember one morning Joe told us that some musicians carried guns in their bags. This culture of guns is a shocking reality for people coming to America. For us Africans, guns are associated with war. The last time I'd heard gunshots was in '77, when the French mercenary Bob Denard tried to overthrow Kérékou. The streets of Cotonou were filled with military fighting and people fleeing. The thought of someone carrying a gun in a time of peace is unreal to me. I had no idea what was going on in Miami back then. I kept thinking, Don't pull out those guns while I'm here. I don't want to see any guns.

Because our budget was small, we lived at Joe's place. There was a patio in the center of his house, with a greenhouse filled with tropical plants that reminded me a little of my mother's flower garden in our courtyard back home. We would sit in Joe's living room, next to his large music collection, and talk late at night, the lights from inside reflecting off the greenhouse glass. I told him how the percussion is the foundation of a song for me. Everything has to start from there. This is because Beninese music is not based on melody and harmonies—in the south we don't have a harmonic instrument like the guitar. Rhythm inspires the dancer who in

turn inspires the singers. The movements of the body are transformed into riffs of percussion on which the lyrics begin to dance. Dance and music are inseparable: you simply cannot imagine one without the other. During these talks with Joe, we realized how close Cuban music is to its African roots. The essence is percussion.

The whole team behind Miami Sound Machine was part of the extensive community of Cubans living in exile. We did the preproduction work for *Logozo* in a suite in one of their offices. Everyone was speaking Cuban Spanish with its dropped and soft consonants. It was the opposite of the Fon language. Its sonorities are so rough and course with all kinds of percussive consonants. It drives Jean crazy when we write songs. We have to work really hard–and sometimes take poetic license–to make it musical, melodic.

The first thing we did was lay down the percussion tracks we'd done back in Paris with Djanuna Dabo, a musician from Guinea-Bissau who toured Europe with me. Then, to get a new sound, Joe would program some drums. In a way, the production was at the forefront of what was being done in world music. One day he brought a very young and shy keyboard player who had just finished touring with Julio Iglesias. He was so knowledgeable about all kinds of music and he started to pile up keyboard tracks. His name was Lester Mendez and he was to become a famous producer. He would later work with Shakira and Carlos Santana.

Because I had insisted from the start that we record African musicians in Paris, we returned there to finish the record. We set ourselves up at Studio Davout. Davout was once a movie palace and the building has endless little corners, from the attic all the way down to a hidden set of steps leading to the metro. From the studio you could walk to the flea market of Montreuil, which was filled with people from Mali and Senegal. It was the first time I recorded in such a great studio, but for me the best feature was the kitchen! I would cook maffé, a stew made with ground peanuts and tomatoes, in between sets for the whole crew–Cuban sound engineers and African musicians.

OPPOSITE: In the studio with producer Joe Galdo, young keyboard player Lester Mendes, and my friend Branford Marsalis.

One day while we were recording, Manu Dibango walked into the studio. It was the most beautiful blessing. He was from the first generation of African musicians to arrive in Paris and mingle with French artists. Since the sixties, decades before Michael Jackson used his song "Soul Makossa" in *Thriller*, Dibango has been the ambassador of African music, and his knowledge of it is infinite. With his deep voice, bald head, and dark glasses, he had come to define African style in Paris. To this day he remains the godfather of *la sono mondiale*.

While I was growing up, I learned about music through the traditional ceremonies. It was all in the performance. There was no record. You live the music in the moment—nothing is left after the dance has stopped. From Joe Galdo I learned that at the end of recording you have to be truly proud of what you have on the tape because once the song is out there, it is heard over and over again and you can't go back to correct anything. Any conflicts you may have with the record company or the managers, or other performers, any feelings you have about the negotiations that made it possible for the song to exist, and all the hours that were spent in the studio—all of that is forgotten. What remains is the thing you can hold in your hand. That's all that counts.

For *Logozo*, the cover signifies what the record came to be—a blend of traditional and modern. The zebra-striped catsuit I'm wearing symbolizes Africa with its modern and energetic design. It was made by Yvan & Marzia, designers who had a shop around the corner from le Baiser Salé. The stylist for the shoot, Emmanuelle Alt, would go on to become the editor-in-chief of French *Vogue*. At that photo shoot, I also wore basketball sneakers like rappers, but with a little skirt made of raffia palms from Africa. Like pop art, we were using a cliché to subvert the stereotype of exoticism. One of the things I learned from Chris Blackwell is that music is not just the songs. It's also the way you present it to the public. A great album cover—and Island Records had many—is like a pair of colored spectacles that illuminates your music.

We carried that idea through when we made the video for the song "Batonga" by filming the Beninese choreography and African masks with a black light. The spirit and the strength of Benin are clear, but it is a modern and self-assured Africa ready to conquer the world. I realized many years later that this video really made an impact on the continent

It's not a hit until it's a hit in

Billboard

A full page in *Billboard* magazine celebrating my first number one album on its world music chart.

Artwork from the album *Logozo*.

showcasing a proud, modern African woman with very short hair who didn't seem afraid of anything.

Logozo was wildly successful in the United States and around the world, going to number one on *Billboard*'s world music charts. When I learned this I was in my tiny kitchen in Paris cooking *gambo*, an okra-based stew that's another traditional dish from Benin. The magazine ran a story about *Logozo* under the headline "Living Proof: Dreams into Reality." It was because of *Logozo* that Timothy White, *Billboard*'s editor-in-chief, began following my career. One day, he called me up and asked me so many questions. He wanted to know where I came from, who my influences were. He would become my mentor and a huge supporter of my work, but from that first moment we spoke he also became my dear friend.

Timothy knew how much I loved James Brown and how when I was a kid I would make up lyrics and pretend to be him. So when *Logozo* came out and I was doing an interview at the *Billboard* offices, he arranged to have James Brown call

Invitation to a cocktail party celebrating *Logozo*.

in. When they told me Mr. Brown wanted to talk to me, I said, "Yeah, right. And I'm the Mother Mary." But then I heard that voice come through the speakerphone. "Angélique," he said. "This is James Brown." I almost fainted! We talked about my home country and he told me about his experience playing in neighboring Nigeria once and meeting Fela

Kuti. He congratulated me on the record, and we talked about what it meant to be a representative of Africa. Then suddenly he shouted,

"Say it loud!"

I answered,

"I'm black and proud!"

Then he screamed,

"Soul power!"

I started to sing the horns part of the song and again he hollered,

"Soul power!"

I was doing call and response with the man who had inspired millions of Africans. My whole body was vibrating that night. I couldn't sleep. The people at the magazine had recorded our conversation and the following week *Billboard* published the transcript.

The success of *Logozo* brought many things, but more than anything else it meant Jean and I could now have a child. We were starting to make a real living, doing what we'd only hoped was possible back when we were a couple of struggling jazz students. And so, in June of 1992, we decided it was time. Before, we couldn't afford to have a kid, but now we made a plan. We were so naïve. Our doctor told us that, at five months in utero, a baby's hearing would be damaged by the loud music of rehearsing and performing. Since we had committed to tour dates through November, I had to get pregnant in July. That way I could finish the tour and then we would spend the remaining months writing. Once the baby was born, we would record the next album. Mind you, people told me I couldn't get

Artwork from the album *Logozo* was used on posters in the Paris metro to promote my show at the Olympia music hall.

pregnant like that, on a schedule, but I would remind them, "You know where I come from?" When it worked, everyone asked how we did it. I said, "Benin magic!"

One night soon after, the phone rang at Jean's parents house. It was my mom on the line. I had intended to call her after dinner. I took it as a sign and gave her the news, but she wasn't surprised at all. The legend goes that during a ceremony, the spirit of our child, an old soul, had announced her imminent arrival into the world.

But Jean and I are still amazed that everything worked out exactly as planned.

On October 31, 1992, I was back at the Olympia in Paris. This time I was headlining. Seeing my name on that famous marquee in tall red neon letters signaled that I really had arrived in Paris. To promote the show, they had taken the image from the *Logozo* shoot of me dancing in a raffia skirt and sneakers and plastered it throughout the Paris metro. By the night of the performance, I was four months pregnant–and it showed! I was wearing one of those impossibly tight catsuits so there was no hiding my little round belly. I was so happy and proud. They built a special stage with a staircase for the event, like the set of a Broadway show. I didn't want to hurt the baby–I was just beginning to feel the first flutters of movement–so I was trying not to dance too hard. I saw the worried faces of my family in the audience–Yves and Mireille attended, Alfred had traveled to Paris just for the show, and Jean's parents and his brother, Georges, were there–but even they couldn't keep me sitting. When I finished the show, a long line of friends and journalists formed in front of this dressing room that had seen so many legendary artists, including my dear James Brown. Success and expecting a baby–everything was coming to me at once.

I learned later that some images from the show were broadcast on the evening news in Benin. My mother told me that people rushed to the house to congratulate her on my pregnancy. When everybody was gone, she went to her bedroom and started to cry. When she found out that I was going to be a mother, she had told all her friends and relatives about it, but nobody believed her until they saw it on TV. They'd said I couldn't possibly get pregnant after all the hundreds of men they imagined I had slept with.

In Africa, it was—and still is—very hard for a woman to be a singer and be respected. Because music is part of daily life, people don't understand what it means to make a career out of it. Here I had sold out the most prestigious theater in Paris, but the same rumor that began when I was just a girl running home from school to cry to my grandmother was still following me.

CHAPTER FOUR

motherhood and mother earth

After the concert at the Olympia, I continued touring but my mom was worried, always reminding me to "Be careful." Then in Zurich, after a performance, I had to lie down on a couch in my dressing room. I was so weak I couldn't move. Tommy Sokoll, the Swiss label manager, brought me to the emergency room at two a.m. I was having contractions and my cervix had started to dilate. At five in the morning, the doctor finally asked me, "Do you want the baby, or do you want to tour?"

That was it. I wasn't taking chances. I had wanted this baby for so long. We cancelled the rest of the tour right away, packed our car to the roof, and drove to Jean's parents' house at the seaside. We arrived in Vaux-sur-Mer,

a little town near Royan on the Atlantic Ocean not far from Bordeaux. In winter, the town was deserted and quiet. I felt so free out there. Jean and I were finally alone, without all the noise of the outside world. For two years we had been traveling constantly, but now we were spending days enjoying each other as a couple, as future parents, as musicians.

Every day we would walk on the beach together, until finally my belly grew so big and heavy that I could no longer keep up with Jean's long legs. Jean always loves to go for long walks–he finds it peaceful. But walking with no purpose is something that seems to me so completely Western. What do you do that for? When we were out there, I wanted to walk because I had a purpose. Looking out over the waves on those walks along le Chemin des Douaniers, the path bordering the sea, brought me memories of home.

Six months into my pregnancy, I was so big I couldn't even tie my shoes. Jean helped me with everything. He was also overprotective. If I said, "I want to do this," he'd say, "No, you can't." I'd ask why. He'd say, "Because you're pregnant." I'm so fiercely independent that there were many times when it drove me crazy. But I knew it was his way of showing love and caring for me and our family. Jean's father is the same way with his mother. And my father was always protecting his wife and his children. When you start your own family, you bring your history with you.

During those days, we set up a little studio in the living room to work on some songs. My voice had a special tone then. They say pregnancy changes it, and it did. I was singing like a bird–that's the expression. When I touched a high note, the baby would shift in my belly. She followed along with the song, listening for the sound of my voice or her father's bass. I felt centered. Absolutely centered. There was nothing threatening at all. Nothing over-whelming. The sense of security, safety, and love was just perfect. I felt as if I had waited centuries for this. Just describing it now, I go to that place.

It was pure bliss in so many ways, and yet only a few weeks into our stay, there was also a consciousness, an awareness that I think every mother experiences. I went to take out the garbage one day and I realized that we had just taken it out a day or two before. I thought, "Here we are complaining about pollution and blaming the government, but we have control over what we consume." As I was becoming a mother, my perspective was changing. The future didn't look the same as it once did.

In Africa, countries that weren't even industrialized were already affected by climate change because Europe was exporting industrial waste to Ivory Coast and neighboring African nations. The trash needed to go somewhere and this was their solution. It struck me that I, all of us, were silently watching our planet suffering. I wondered what would be left for my child, for my grandchild, if we were destroying our world.

The songs I wrote during this period reflect the way my view of the world began shifting. I wrote "Agolo" to ask each of us to please pay attention to Mother Earth. *Agolo* means "please" in Fon. When you walk through a Beninese market, there is always a woman carrying a heavy load on her head. As she moves through the crowd, she'll warn the people around her,

BELOW LEFT: The doctor advised me to sit during my concerts because of my pregnancy. This was hard for me. • RIGHT: Six months into my pregnancy, working on the songs that would form the album *Ayé*.

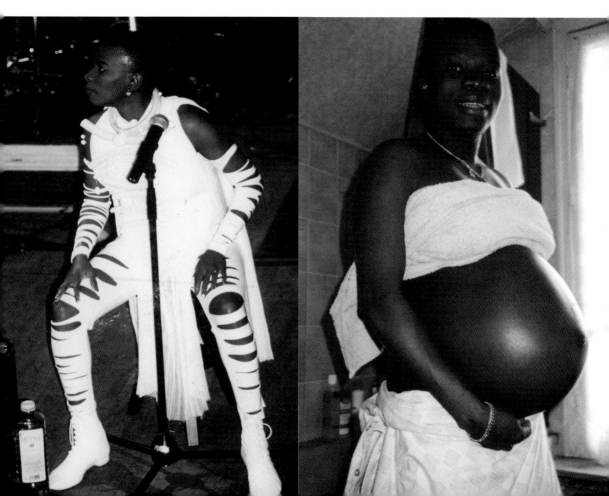

loudly repeating, "*agolo, agolo.*" Please, please excuse me. Mother Earth has been nurturing and nourishing us and we haven't been giving back.

Morio orio
Ola djou monké n'lo
Ola djou monké
Ola djou monké n'lo

I just saw the face of the God of love and tenderness passing my window. At this moment don't despair, let's think of the love that Mother Earth offers us.

I didn't know it then, but this song would become my biggest hit and earn my first Grammy nomination.

As we got closer to my due date, we returned to Paris. With the baby coming, we needed a bigger place. Our little apartment with all of my clothes and shoes and our musical equipment had become too small. We were desperate and went on a house hunt in the suburbs, but I was getting late into my pregnancy and it was tiring. One day, I woke up and felt I'd had enough. Something had to happen. I prayed to my beloved Virgin Mary—she is so popular in West Africa—and picked up the real estate listings. I saw an ad with a photo of a house and thought, *This is it.*

Like many women about to give birth, I was busy unpacking, moving things here and there, and getting the nursery ready. The day after we moved in we had a housewarming party that went late into the night. I needed to rest, but I could barely climb the stairs. Once I got in bed, I just kept turning left and right. I called a friend who was a midwife. She told me to drink a cup of very sweet tea and no more. The next thing we knew, it was time to go to the hospital.

I had a difficult time giving birth. After ten hours in labor, I almost couldn't breathe anymore. My sister Mireille was there. Mimi is always there for me. She was holding the oxygen mask over my nose and mouth, and by the end I had almost nothing left. Jean was so nervous. I remember he tried to pass the time by putting all of his contacts into his first cell phone. I can't help but think how lucky I was to give birth in a hospital, with so much equipment and comfort. I often wonder what would have happened if I'd been in Benin.

When I was eight years old, my mom was pregnant again and when the time came she almost died giving birth. Somehow, when she was laboring, she was given a wrong injection. We never found out for sure what happened, but it took her a year to recover. She was in and out of the hospital. It was devastating for our family and especially for my father because we weren't sure if she would survive. In these types of situations, there's no need for a miracle cure or an expensive drug–just access to proper knowledge and basic health care. Even today my country still has one of the highest rates of infant and maternal mortality. That the world is so unbalanced is outrageous to me. It's something I can't get past.

When I was giving birth, a memory from Benin came to my mind. I must have been fifteen years old. I was in the kitchen and from the other side of the courtyard wall I heard someone yelling. It was Germaine's mother, our neighbor, calling for help. I ran to my mother and told her. We hurried over and saw that Germaine was about to have her baby.

My father had left with the car and there was no ambulance, but it was too late to take her to the hospital anyway. My mother told me, "Go wash your hands and heat some water." Germaine's mother got towels ready. I was so shaken because Germaine, who was usually so quiet, was screaming and I could see the fear in her eyes.

As the baby started to come out, Germaine's mother was standing next to her daughter, stroking her head. Mama said to me, "Pull very gently. It's very delicate. Then, as soon as the baby is out, hold it and put your fingers in its ears. I'll cut the umbilical cord. Be careful because the baby can slip through your hands." It was the first time that I saw my mother play at being a midwife. Where had she learned this? God only knows. Still, in this century, no woman should fear for her life when giving birth. Only when my father finally arrived could we get Germaine to the hospital so the doctor could examine her and the baby.

In the back of my mind, I'm always thinking of what women in Benin have to go through to give birth. When it was my turn to do so, I was lucky to be in a fancy hospital with a nice doctor. He put his hands on my belly and said, "You push and I'll push," and, finally, our daughter was born. There had been four of us in the delivery room and suddenly we were five.

....

NEXT SPREAD: Naïma on the first day of her life.

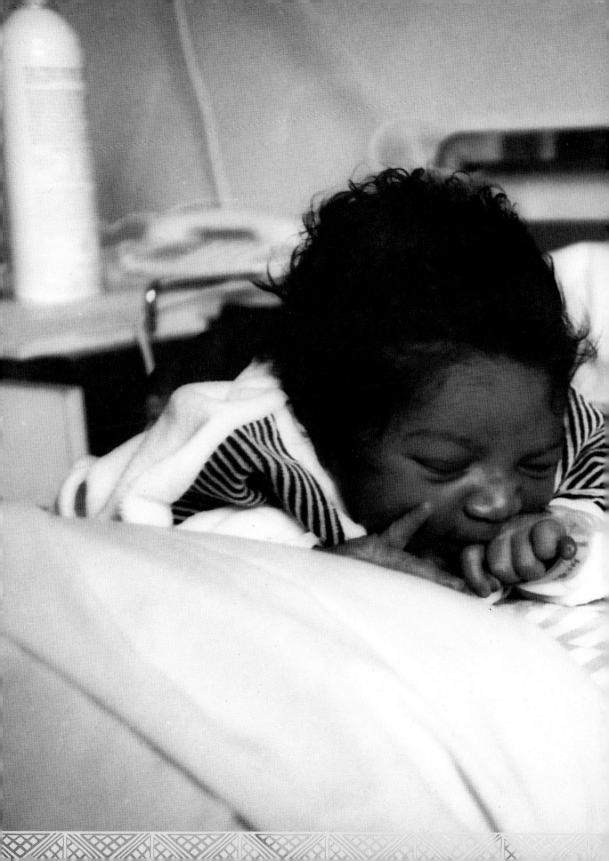

Giving birth is a joyful and grave moment. It's a moment where you witness the beauty of God's work. For me, God can't be compared to. God is a love with no frontiers. When a child is born you witness the presence of something bigger than you. When I first saw Naïma, right away she looked around with a face that said, *Hello, here I am.* And she had so much hair!

Then Jean said, "Oh, we have the best guitar player in the world." He saw that Naïma was born with six fingers on each hand. My father's mother had been born with six fingers, too. Once, years before, she told me that no man would want to marry me because I was a singer. Now, it felt like she was coming through, trying to make amends and telling me that she had been wrong. The doctor said it was quite common at birth. He said if you tie an extra finger, it will often fall off on its own.

We chose Naïma's name because it has a special meaning for us. It's the title of a John Coltrane song. The jazz legend was one of our favorite saxophonists back when we met at school. His wife was named Naïma and he composed for her the most beautiful ballad with a gentle melody climbing down over an ostinato bass line.

Baby Naïma.

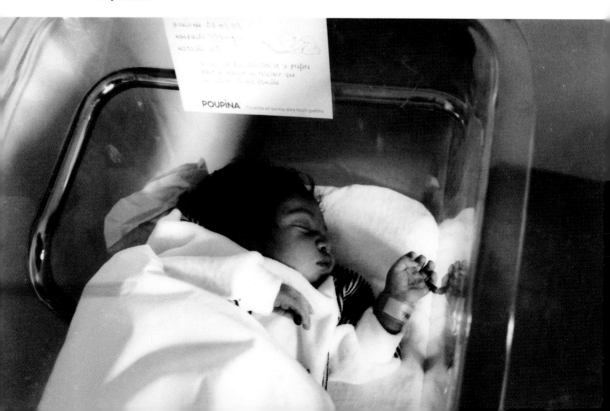

My mother arrived the next day from Benin. Up to this point, Jean and I couldn't afford to make regular trips back so it had been two years since I'd seen her. When she walked into the room and saw me holding my baby, we didn't need to speak. We both knew how hard it had been to get to that moment. We exchanged a look that said, 'This is a miracle.' With all the power men have, they can't have this. I think the strength and power this gives women sometimes threatens men. They are part of the process of making a baby, but the relationship a woman has with her child from the moment that child is conceived to the delivery is between the two of them—men are on the outside. I think the explanation of male insecurity, of the need of some men or some patriarchal cultures to deny women the right to do what they want, lies there. They want to break down what they don't have, but they will never be able to break this.

Once my mom arrived, I knew everything was going to be fine. She washed Naïma the way we do at home, massaging every muscle of the baby, feeling to make sure that the baby is healthy and to adjust the shape of the body. Then, the baby is tossed very gently in the air, just three times, and we watch its reflexes. It is a science taught from mothers to daughters in Benin. After that, she put Naïma to my breast where she slept for two hours.

For me, she brought dried bark from a special kind of tree in Benin called *calcedra*. When you boil it, the water becomes a deep burgundy color, like red wine. She made a tea with it for me to drink to help my milk come in and some for me to wash with to help heal my body. Afterward, I felt like I could run a marathon, which was just what I needed because only ten days after her birth, Jean, Naïma, and I had to catch a plane to Minneapolis. It had been arranged for us to go to Prince's Paisley Park Studio to begin recording the next album—*Ayé*, the Yoruba word meaning life.

David Z, one of the album's two producers, was a very busy man and he had only a few days open for our first sessions. We were on our incessant run to create and perform and make something new happen. We rushed around Paris to get a passport for our newborn. Those days are blurry because I was taking care of our little baby and sleeping so little. We planned the recording so that I could spend as much time as possible with her. When Jean and I had to go to the studio, Jumbo Vanrenen

Shooting the music video for the song "Agolo." It will become my most famous one.

would play babysitter while I sang. He was such a big, tall guy and he loved taking care of this tiny baby.

Life was changing so fast, and my music was too. I was using the latest sounds and technology and applying it to the deep roots of my tradition. I recorded at night because the voice sounds better at night–and the musicians were all so supportive. David Z had mixed Prince's *Purple Rain* and in the rehearsal space we could see the members of the group New Power Generation playing their incredible funk. That was so inspiring for me. The energy of the African rhythms had stayed intact through centuries of exile. At Paisley Park we would sometimes witness an impromptu concert by Prince in the studio lounge. But he wouldn't talk to anyone. He carried a cane and we would watch his dandy silhouette quickly disappear in the night.

We recorded the second half of *Ayé* at the Soul II Soul studio near the bohemian Camden Town district of London. Jazzie B, a Londoner of West Indies origin had reinvented R & B with drum loops and hypnotic bass lines. In his studio we mixed those with African percussions and a Minimoog synthesizer played by Soul II Soul's keyboardist Will Mowat who was the second producer. I knew the purists of African music would not be happy with us introducing such modern equipment, but how fun it was to create something fresh by mixing two musical worlds that had never before met. I hoped the tone of my voice would carry the spirit of Africa and unify the sounds. I wanted to bring Beninese tradition to the modern world.

On the cover of the album *Ayé*, I am surrounded by Aïdo Houédo, the rainbow snake.

We worked furiously on the song "Agolo," mixing Andy Gangadeen, Massive Attack's drummer, with Jamiroquai's horn section, and the Gap Band's guitar player Glen Nightingale, one of the funkiest musicians I've ever met. But right up until the last minute, I felt like something was

missing. When you want that inspiration, sometimes it comes right away, but sometimes it's on the periphery. Finally, just before sending the tape to mastering, I did a vocal overdub. That scream, "Agolo!", right at the start of the song, is my pleading for the well-being of our motherland. I hit a high E and as soon as I sang it, I knew the song was complete. But I didn't know that scream would become my trademark.

The music video for "Agolo" was created with the same spirit, the same energy. It fuses the visual elements and dances from the Beninese purest tradition with modern special effects to convey their power. In the video you see three-dimensional golden images of the Aïdo Houédo rainbow snakes turning slowly around a group of dancers lifting me while a green Zangbeto ghost, a voodoo spirit, is gyrating in the background. The video was very popular in Africa. To this day, every time I arrive at the gate of an African airport the custom officers start to sing: *Agolo, Agolo. . . .*

My maternal grandmother, Mama Congo.

We finished recording *Ayé* when Naïma was two months old. I had committed to shooting a documentary in Benin, but had to postpone it when I was pregnant. Now was the perfect time to take her to Benin to introduce her to my family. The first thing we did was go see my grandmother, my mother's mother. I loved her so much. She was wise and strong. She had followed her husband to Congo but was widowed at an early age. When she came back she decided not to remarry and worked hard in her little deli store while raising my mom and sending her to school. She sold beignets made of beans, sugar, and milk. In fact, both of my grandmothers were widowed at thirty-five and both refused to remarry, choosing to build their own businesses instead. This was unheard of in their day.

Four generations of women: Mama Congo, my mom, Naïma, and me.

Mama Congo, as we called her, was shy but very caring. She worried a lot for me when I was a teenager because people said I would never have a child. And after my boyfriend had told me he wanted me to stop performing and stay at home as a housewife, I said that I never wanted to get married. I used to say it every day. That's why, when I married, everyone said they had to see this man. When they meet Jean, people say, "I understand. He's so calm. That's a good balance. What they don't realize is that he's like a duck swimming in a pond: calm and relaxed above the surface, but paddling furiously underneath."

Mama Congo always told me, "I know for you to complete your life, you will need to have a child." When we brought our daughter to her, the first thing she said was, "Give me the child!" She held Naïma and told me, "Now I can die in peace. I couldn't leave this earth without seeing you as a mother." She knew all the pain I had been through and now I had a child.

When my grandmother passed away a few years later, I was not able to go to the funeral. I remember we called Benin that day. I was crying so

At the Summerstage festival in Central Park. I performed with Peter Gabriel and Branford Marsalis.

much. My mom said, "Don't cry, listen." She held the phone out and I heard singing and dancing at Mama Congo's funeral. My mom said, "I didn't know how good my mother was to people. To people I didn't know." As soon as the news broke that Mama Congo had died, people came and asked my mother to let them take care of the funeral. They paid for everything. They carried her coffin. She did so much for people. My mother never knew and I never knew because my grandmother never talked about it.

The day I brought my daughter to her, we were four generations of women—my grandmother, my mother, Naïma, and me. Jean took a picture while my grandmother held her. He said, "We can't miss this." I will always remember that moment, a rare instance of standing still, introducing Naïma to her African lineage.

But then, very quickly, it was time to get back on the road. The success of "Agolo" had me touring all over the world. With my baby on my hip and

the help of a wonderful sitter, we traveled from Australia to Scandinavia. For *Ayé* I had won a Danish Grammy for best singer, competing against Whitney Houston and Mariah Carey. The award is a heavy piece of brass with a singing bird on top. It still sits in my living room today. In a country like Denmark, my music was considered mainstream. I would meet kids in the street singing my songs and college students filled the concert halls.

Finally, we returned to America, finishing the tour with an unforgettable concert in Central Park for the SummerStage Festival. Mamadou Konte had wanted to create a whole movement to promote African culture and so he created *Africa Fête*, which means African party in French. It was a music festival travelling from coast to coast, bringing not only African music but also food and fabrics to the American public.

The concert was free and twenty thousand people stood under a blazing sun in Central Park on July 25, 1993. They were ecstatic, even in the ninety-degree heat. The audience was mixed, which was unusual at the time, and the show was a turning point for the success of world music in the US. Through the years, I've met so many people who've told me that show was the first time they listened to African music. From the stage, I could see that the audience understood how the power of African music goes beyond singing and dancing, that it carries a message of bonding between people.

Peter Gabriel, a hero in our eyes who had done so much for African music, came to the show wearing shorts and a Hawaiian shirt. I summoned him onstage–I didn't leave him a choice–to sing "We We" with me. Branford Marsalis, dressed like a rapper, joined us on the saxophone. Adam Clayton, the bass player from U2, Chris Blackwell, and Mamadou were all watching from backstage. That day, Jean and I showed our daughter to Chris and asked him, "Who does she look like more?" He laughed and said, "She looks tough–like both of you." Coming from a Jamaican man, we considered that the best compliment.

What I remember most from being onstage that day was feeling Jean behind me playing syncopated bass lines on his shiny white Fender Jazz and knowing that after the last encore I could go back to the dressing room where Naïma was waiting, remove my sodden clothes, and wrap my baby around my back in true African fashion so she could feel my heart beating, still a little too fast, from the adrenaline rush of a New York City show.

CHAPTER FIVE

back to benin

In Benin, drums are at the center of the music. Everything revolves around them. Their impact on your body is like a heartbeat. Sometimes, the rhythms are so powerful, they can create a trance state. You can see it during ceremonies held in the center of a village or on the beach in Ouidah when an orisha's follower dances until he is lost in himself, moving erratically, and then nearly collapsing. His family members hold him up and then, according to traditional beliefs, the orisha speaks through him.

These rhythms are so vital to my music, but some are so complex that no one outside my country is able to play them. In 1995, after several years of touring, we began the *Fifa* project. The idea was to go back to Benin

and record these rhythms of my homeland to use them as the inspiration for and basis of my next album. Since the night I left Benin, I'd only been able to return for a few short visits. It had been more than a decade since I'd been able to listen to the traditional drums. I needed to go back and meet up with those drums again, to reassure myself of the power they still have in my life. The *Fifa* album opened with this confession.

> **I've been away for so long**
> **That I wonder,**
> **If the sound of the drum**
> **Still has his power.**

Of course, being at home and getting to spend time with my mom and dad and my siblings was like being a child again. In Benin, hospitality is sacred. Cooking for family and friends is essential and my mom was busy at work in her kitchen. Our friend and sound engineer Christian Lachenal had come with us and he quickly learned that he couldn't say no to her. *"Mange tout!"* she'd order, making him eat double what was on his plate. I know I took that from my mom. For my own guests, I always cook more than we need. In Benin, the ultimate shame for a host is not having enough for his guests to eat. You would rather cook too much than too little.

We spent two weeks in Cotonou. We'd hang out at home, in the room where I'd listened to so many vinyl records growing up. At night we recorded dozens of musicians. We listened to the *atcha*, a rhythm played on the chest by a group of men. Standing with them, I felt happy, secure. The dictatorship had tried to suppress our traditions, but we were still here. We also heard the *kaakaa* with its long bamboo sticks, and the *zinlin*, the slow dance of the Amazons, the women warriors from the ancient capital of Abomey. The sound of a lonely cowbell drives their elegant moves.

Then, with our eight-track tape recorder and all our equipment, we packed our bags and traveled to the north, heading in the direction of Natitingou, the main city in the northwest. Going from village to village, we talked to anyone we could—school teachers, elders—to tell them we were scouting for musicians. This was a true adventure, both for me and for Jean. Music in the south was familiar, like a part of me. I wanted to

discover places I didn't know and languages I'd never heard before. All in my own little country, the richness and diversity of the music and culture was unlike anything we had experienced. You drive twenty miles and encounter a new language, new instruments, new songs.

We'd rented an old brown Peugeot 504 and hired Adam, an unemployed Beninese college graduate, to help us drive. We traveled for miles along those little dusty red roads having endless philosophical discussions about Camus and Sartre. Since we had no air-conditioning, we opened all the windows but whenever we passed another car, usually the same model Peugeot with at least ten people on board, we'd have to frantically crank the handle so we wouldn't choke on the dust.

One day we arrived in a village called Manigri, which to me was one of the most astonishing places in northern Benin. The first thing we saw was a giant old Shea tree; its branches reaching up and out to the sky. It looked like a mythical place. The women were gathered in the shade of the tree, waiting to welcome me.

In the southern part of Benin, the drums are played mostly by the men. For celebrations like weddings and traditional ceremonies and even during impromptu occasions, men and women mingle to make music, taking turns to sing and dance. In the north the Bariba women have their own music and the men have theirs. In that village, the polyphony of the women's voices was unbelievable. It sounded like gospel music, though they had never heard of it. These women created strange harmonies that would crisscross, come together, and endlessly divide.

They welcomed me with open arms, with such warmth, and then they sang for me. Their language is a mixture of Yoruba and the local northern tongue. I was able to understand it a little because they sang in Nago, which is very close to the Yoruba of my mother's family.

Assé assalam alé
Eolo Ouidah a assé
Assalam alekouo, ahé

We say Salaam Alaikum
To the child from Ouidah
Who has come from far away to visit us

In Benin, traditional singers don't sing for an abstract audience, as a Western singer is able to do. They direct themselves to you, the person in front of them, in the present moment. They look you in the eye and the intensity of their gaze always surprises visitors. Can you imagine Ella Fitzgerald looking right into your eyes as she sings just for you? What they offer is a marvelous gift, a bonding, an immediate familiarity. It's a feeling like they are accepting you as a member of their family.

I was overcome by the need to carry the words of these women and the beauty of their songs beyond the borders of Africa, to tell the world about them and to give the gift of their voices–the energy and raw emotion it carries, to the world. Christian was there with his tape recorder and his sound-mixing board, both of them connected to a car battery that we had to charge each night at garages along the road. That's how he was able to capture this music. I used the recording of their voices as an introduction to my song "Welcome":

> This trip is so long, I can't rest.
> Red dust is covering my body, dyeing my hair.
> A child rushes up to me, a smile on his face
> I know I will arrive before nightfall.
>
> People say "welcome,"
> People say "my house is your house"
> I can't tell you how I feel to finally be home.
> I want my song to express
> This warm feeling you're giving me

OPPOSITE: During the recording of *Fifa*, we travelled all over Benin to capture the musicians' performances. • CLOCKWISE FROM TOP LEFT: A drummer from the village of Kandi. • We often recorded the musicians in empty classrooms. • The trumpets of Kandi are only allowed to be played to honor the king, but an exception was made for me. • The rhythm of the Tipenti is made using only handbells and chanting. • Everywhere we went, the music and dance was unique, but the people were always welcoming. • Watching the women dance and sing was entrancing.

Nearly twenty years later, I will return to Manigri and record these same women again. Their voices, as well as those of other traditional women's singing groups from Kenya and Benin, will become essential to *Eva*, an album celebrating the power of women and named for the first of us. Usually, I hire professional back-up singers because I want those vocals to be done perfectly. But this time, it isn't about that. It's about gathering. It's about smiling and dancing, joking and laughing. You hear it in the sound of our voices together–the harmony. In this way, it's perfect.

When I tell these women about some of the songs I've written–about early marriage, forced marriage, violence–I see in their eyes that they've known these things. They know them. But they also know the other themes: the leadership of women, the friendship of women. No matter the problem, women always regroup. They always come back. For themselves and for their daughters.

On this trip, everywhere I go throughout my country feels like home. Not just in Cotonou, where the women decorate their chests with makeup like the actors in my mother's theater group used to do. But also in Porto-Novo, where the woman who buys glass bottles comes through town calling out and her song is one I remember from when I was a girl collecting bottles for a few coins. And in Manigri, when I pick up a mango that's fallen to the ground it's as ripe and delicious as the ones I used to eat and eat as a kid, until I was nearly sick. Going back there, I see how everyone has aged beautifully. This time they sing, "Welcome again to the girl from Ouidah, to the one who has not forgotten us." There is so much light and love and joy in being together again.

Traveling through the villages on that first trip years ago, we often set up our equipment in classrooms after school had let out for the day. In Africa, the sun is so strong that the school day ends by early afternoon, before the heat gets too intense. In Korontière we recorded the rhythm of the *tipenti*, played with a bell and an iron ring. A parade of men came through, about ten or fifteen of them in total, all of them dancing in traditional dress: bare-chested, with white wool arm and ankle bands. They were each holding an animal tail in one hand. On the other they had the ring on their thumb and the little bell on their index finger. The effect is a very sharp, almost supernatural ring. The men perform the *tipenti* in unison,

creating an impenetrable wall of music. We watched the meters of the recording equipment soar with each beat.

A few days later there was another group of men whom we wanted to record, but we had to wait all day for the horn player, a shepherd, to come down from the mountains. The horn was a pierced ram's horn and this man was the only one who still knew how to play it. When he arrived I understood why we'd been waiting for him. The sound is like a cello mixed with a hunting trumpet, and the way he played added another layer of life to the music. You can hear it in the beginning of the song "Bitchifi."

When I asked him why he was the only ram's-horn player left, he explained that his children, and the other village children, don't want to play traditional music anymore. He told me, "They'd rather go to the city, sell things at the market, lead a wretched life down there than stay here and learn the regional traditions." It's always the same story: going to the city, dreaming of a better life. But the reality is very different. African cities are so crowed and health conditions are precarious. Young people find themselves alone, without the support of their family and community.

From him I began to understand how many traditional instruments in Benin, as everywhere else in Africa, are in the process of disappearing because of urbanization and globalization. With these instruments vanishing, how can we hold on to the memory of these sounds and dances? This is the dilemma we face: How to raise the standard of life of a people and help them integrate into the modern world without killing the beauty of their traditional culture? Without causing a cultural wealth to disappear forever?

I have faced this dilemma throughout my entire career. The *Fifa* project was an experiment in trying to combine modernity and tradition. The trip was about confronting the rhythms of my life and keeping the legacy of the traditional drums alive. I also saw that music was a weapon against the trials of poverty. If the drums were to disappear, the suffering would be immense.

From Korontière we went to Kandi, the kingdom of the Baribas, right up in the hills that border Nigeria and Niger. We had been told about the famous royal trumpets that are heard only when a king, queen,

prince, or princess has died. We wanted so badly to hear and record those, and maybe because they wanted to honor me, they didn't dare say no. These golden trumpets are very long and lean and they come in different sizes, each with a very rich timbre. First the drummers begin to play while the player assembles the trumpet. Then, with a two-note melody, the trumpet begins to answer the call of the drums. When the men began to play there was a great panic. Everyone started running in all directions before they realized that it was just for me that they were playing the trumpet.

While we were in Kandi, it hit me that this was where my parents lived as a young couple. When my parents wanted to get married, my father's mother tried to stop them. She didn't approve of my mother because she was Yoruba, not Fon, and so she used her influence to keep them from getting a license in Cotonou.

From the time my father's mother was widowed, she focused her life on accruing money, and, with it, power. She did it by building a fabric business. Before her, women would trade fabric house to house, but she said, "Let's take it to the market." Even today, when I go to the market in Cotonou to buy fabric, women recognize me as her granddaughter.

When I was a teenager, she was always trying to teach me how to sell. "All you can do is sing," she would say. "You can't be at the mercy of men. You need a job." But near the end of her life, she

Relaxing under the *paillotte* in the courtyard of our house with Mom and Mireille.

told me, "If I have any advice for you, it's that when you have the choice between having friends and having money, choose friends. I've chased away everyone who cared about me in the name of trade and power, and now I have nothing."

OPPOSITE: Nana, my paternal grandmother, was a widow at an early age, and decided to be an entrepreneur.

The day after she died, in front of our stunned family, my father opened the armoire where his mother had been saving her money for years, and all the bills had crumbled to dust. The absurdity of that moment imprinted itself on me. With the image of those crumbling bills always in the back of my mind, I've tried to live my life according to her advice.

When my parents were trying to marry, my grandmother would do anything she could to keep them from each other. At the same time, my father was ready for a raise and to move forward with his career, but he knew he would have to change jobs for this. There had been talk about opening a post office in the north and that there would be new jobs. But no one wanted to go because they said it was full of forests with deadly snakes and scorpions. But my parents knew that if they were to live there, they would be beyond the reach of his mother's power. It was the only chance they had to get married. It also brought them even closer together, building a solid base for their marriage.

During this time, my mother had her first child, my brother Frejus. The family legend said that even as a baby, he was known to have a sixth sense about danger. They would be sleeping in the middle of the night—they had no electricity, just petrol lamps—and Frejus would scream, "Bibi! Bibi!" They woke up to see a black spider ready to bite. Other times he would point behind a door and there would be a horned viper snake. When he was four, Frejus died of a high fever that wouldn't go down. His death was senseless. It could have been prevented if only the proper medication had been available.

In Africa, the firstborn son is really the center of a family. He is worshipped like no other. When Frejus died, my parents almost didn't survive it. It is something that still haunts my mom and haunted my father until his death. My mom always said she never wanted any of us to witness the death of a child.

My brother Oscar was two years old at the time. To this day, he is a quiet man. It was only after my father died that Oscar spoke to us about what had happened. "You don't know what I went through after the death of our brother. Words can hurt so much. Words hurt mom and dad deeply. Knowing this makes me keep my mouth shut, so I don't hurt anybody." There's a saying in my country: Words are like eggs. Once they fall and break, you can't put them back together. That's why in Africa, what you

say means much more than in any other society I've been in. You can destroy a part of someone, change them for life, if you don't pay attention to what comes out of your mouth.

Leaving those sad memories behind, right after recording the royal trumpets of Kandi, we headed for Natitingou. Sitting on gentle green hills, Natitingou feels like a new world. There we taped young people performing the dance *sinsinnou,* a percussive rhythm they made with their feet. The dancers put a kind of straw ring filled with seeds around their foot and it runs from the ankle up the calf, producing an enormous noise. I think of it as the ancestor of tap dancing. On that night we admired so many great dancers: unknown James Browns, unknown Michael Jacksons that the rest of the world will never learn about.

The sounds differ, depending on whether the dance is performed during a funeral ceremony or a celebration. They're also coded, with meanings only those who are playing can understand. This is an interesting hidden truth about African drum patterns. Usually a poem, an incantation, or a prayer is associated with a drum phrase and the player recites the lines to himself while playing. The musical phrase takes its shape from the spoken phrase. They are a reflection of each other. Just as the meter of the rhythm reflects the shape of the body–there are generally four beats because we have two arms and two legs–music is the intersection of body and mind. And in Benin, the dancer is the leader of the drums, like the conductor of a symphonic orchestra. With his body, he slows down or speeds up the tempo and drives the crescendo. With a sudden swing of his hips, he gives the cue to end the song on a loud final note.

In this village we also recorded the *teke,* which is one of the great rhythms of the north. It is made by about twenty young girls. We watched as these girls, around fifteen or sixteen years old, stood in a single-file line. They wore indigo *sirwals,* loose, flowing pants, with matching head wraps. Each held a small stick in her hand shaped like a phallus and they danced to a slow, hypnotic beat. To witness it firsthand, it's like experiencing magic. It takes hold of you; you are entranced by it. Then the rhythm doubles with a frantic percussion solo and the girls begin to bend and turn. Suddenly, in a perfectly synchronized way, they all turned and beat their sticks together. Even though there are more than twenty people doing this, you hear a single sound.

It's extremely hard for musicians to play as one, in perfect sync. I often wondered how these young girls do it with such precision. My musician friend Lokua Kanza provided me with the answer one day. These girls belong to the same village, sometimes even the same family. They've grown up together, and this community life is expressed in their gestures and their dance. It's almost like the Rolling Stones in that they've been playing together for so long that their connection allows them to play on the same wavelength. It makes a sound that no one else can reproduce. Because they live and breathe the same rhythm, they become one through music and dance.

Everywhere we went, even though we were just recording the sounds, we noticed that the musicians always arrived in their costumes. People always dress up when they play because it is part of the music itself. African music is never really separate from the dance or from the ceremony that gives it its meaning. It's a little like a Broadway show. You need sound, costumes, lyrics, and dance, and only then is it a complete art.

I first learned this as a girl, watching my mother's theater company rehearsals, and I felt it when she slipped that first costume over my head when I was six. The costume gives you the sense that what you're doing is important. Presenting ourselves elegantly is a way of living all over Africa. (Even today this is true: I recently came back from a visit to the Samburu region in Kenya, and there the poorest of the poor were the most elegant people.) Maybe that is why our poverty is so photogenic. It fills the pages of news magazines, endlessly perpetuating the stereotype of a broken Africa.

While we were recording in a small, remote village, a young man of about twenty, wearing a coat although the heat was unbearable, came toward us and, through an interpreter, asked Jean, "What are you doing with all this machinery?" When Jean told him we were recording, the young man asked, "What is that red light there?" And "Why does it turn green?" He didn't know what a recording was. Jean explained that when it was red they were in the middle of recording, the music would be preserved by the box, and when the light was green, you could listen to it again.

The young man turned to Jean and laughed in disbelief, "But why record the music? If you want to listen to it all you have to do is pick up the instruments and play it again."

Music is often that spontaneous in Africa. It exists in the present moment and everyone participates. There is no separation between musician and audience. That's what's so difficult with traditional African music—to really understand its power you have to experience it. You have to see it. You have to be present in the moment that it's made. That's why I always go out into the crowd during my shows, and it's why I have the audience come onstage. I want them to feel that experience.

When we were finished recording in the north, we went down south to Adjara—a village near Porto-Novo—where practically all the drums in Benin are made, especially the drum that I love most, the *gozin*. It's made of red clay and shaped like a vase. The goat skin is stretched across the top very tight and you play it with one bare hand and one stick. The variety of drums in Benin is unbelievable. There are the Yoruba *batá* drums, which are found unchanged in Cuba. There are the talking drums like those played in Mali and Senegal, although in Benin we put them on our thigh. There are drums of every size to play *juju*, the music of King Sunny Adé. This is a royal, courtly music with a very special cadence. Because it's parade music, and celebratory, it conveys happiness, light-heartedness.

While we were traveling, we had left Naïma with my parents. The trip was too harsh for a two-year-old: we were sleeping in poor conditions with no electricity and scarce access to water. The whole time we were traveling, I wished she could enjoy the beauty of the culture, hear the enchanting sounds of the music. So "Fifa" was written for her while we were on the road. The powerful yodeling of an old woman we recorded in a village inspired it. *Fifa* means peace in Fon. I wish that for her.

> *Sousou towé nin yon looo*
> *O djidido wè n'bio nou wé*
> *Afotowé didé nin yon loooo*
> *Bonou wiwa towé ninon té*
>
> *Wherever your feet take you,*
> *I always pray that in the face of danger,*
> *My love and guidance will save you from harm.*

TOP: The album cover
of *Fifa*. *Fifa* means
peace. • LEFT: A single of
Fifa's "Wombo Lombo."

After a month, when we came back to Ouidah, my ancestral village; it was a chance to reconnect with my family's traditions. It's complicated to do this because the protocol is rigid. We have to follow all the rules of the elders, and it is sometimes hard to bear. The vibe in Ouidah is much different from that of Cotonou where I grew up, with its city noise and traffic. Ouidah is a much smaller, quieter, more dusty city. It feels like a provincial town. Each time I go I feel as if I cross into a different time zone, one in which I'm still a little kid linked to its long lineage.

There we recorded the *gogbahoun*, the rhythm from my village that Jean was trying to understand back in our little apartment in Paris. It's played with drums and the body. The men beat their chests and the women hit their legs. You also need an empty bottle and a spoon. There are many musical sounds that derive from the *gogbahoun*. It's such an intricate beat that it is difficult to manipulate, to use it differently from what it was created for. The only music into which the *gogbahoun* is easily integrated is reggae. It is to this beat that I would later record my duet with Ziggy Marley.

Not far from Ouidah is Azizakoué, a village situated on a small island in the lagoon. My grandmother's first cousin was the chief there. I had seen some young people from the village playing on the beach and knew I had to record them. To get there, you have to cross the lagoon in a pirogue, a fishing boat with a flat bottom. We took a big one because my mom and dad insisted on coming along with Jean, Christian, me, and all of our weighty equipment.

In the middle of the lake, we discovered there was a hole in the hull. Water was slowly filling the boat. Jean asked my parents if they knew how to swim. When they told him they didn't, I was surprised to see he kept his calm. Maybe the resignation one needs to survive in Africa was rubbing off on him.

We made it to shore and we recorded an amazing rhythm. Ten cowbells of different sizes were playing polyrhythmic patterns while two drums played a long chant in unison. With the cowbells changing cadence and the heat of the sun, your head spins and you start to get into that trance—especially after drinking the traditional gin that the village chief offers when you arrive. You pour a few drops on the floor to honor the ancestors before having to finish the whole thing. We captured the rhythm on tape and used it in the breakdown of "The Sound of the Drum."

In some ways, what is considered traditional music is actually quite modern, for over the course of the years it has adapted and has been enriched. If it hadn't modernized in this way, it would have disappeared. I always have a problem with people who see themselves as purists of African music, ones who talk to me of traditional music without having a clue about its evolution. They have a vision of some original, fossilized thing that needs to be preserved like a museum piece. It's a rather sectarian, rigid bias, as if Africa is some exotic thing that can't, or shouldn't, evolve. It's a Western fantasy—a belief in an imaginary primitive land that hasn't changed since Homo sapiens left Africa.

With the recordings in hand we traveled to the United States to mix the album, and then something very exciting happened. I got a call from Island Records, telling me that Carlos Santana wanted me to be the opening act on his tour with Jeff Beck. We weren't finished in the studio, but Jean said to me, "You really can't say no to this."

I had never met Santana, so I had no idea why he picked me for the tour. One day, before a performance, I went to see him. I had to ask him why.

He said, "Chris Blackwell gave me your record and when I listened to your voice for the first time, it was like someone plunged a knife into my heart. That's the effect your voice had on me."

In the end, he played a solo on "Naïma," the lullaby I had written for my daughter. We recorded him at the Record Plant in Sausalito, a small city north of San Francisco, on the other side of the Golden Gate Bridge. His guitar holds as much emotion as the human voice. He asked us not to change his sound during the mix. "The sound of a guitar is like a human body," he told us. "The low end is the legs and the high notes are the head, the mediums, the heart. A well-balanced sound has to have all its body parts." That's so true, not just for the guitar but for all music.

We finished the album in late 1995 and started a world tour the next spring. At the end of that year, we toured all of West Africa, beginning in Mali, then Niger and Togo, before arriving in Benin in December 1996. When we got off the plane we found the country in a state of transition. Mathieu Kérékou had managed to stay in power from 1972 to 1991. By the late eighties, the country had become isolated, the national bank was

OPPOSITE: Onstage with Carlos Santana, who gives me so much support.

bankrupt, and rioting had begun in Cotonou. In those days, Western groups were lobbying African leaders, pressuring them to instate democracies in which the people could elect candidates with their countries' best interests at heart. It was in response to this and the growing demoralization of the people that Kérékou announced in 1989 that Marxist-Leninist policy would no longer be the official state ideology: Benin was to become a democratic state. This was unheard of in Africa.

I remember doing an interview at the end of '89 for Radio France Internationale, the French equivalent of Voice of America. When the journalist asked what my wish for 1990 was, I told him I was dreaming of a peaceful transition to democracy in my country. Thankfully, under the supervision of Archbishop Isidore de Souza, it was. It was a surreal time. In 1991, in the country's first democratic election, Nicéphore Soglo, a former cabinet member, was elected. But just nine months before I arrived in Benin, another election had taken place. Kérékou had made a big show out of apologizing to the country for all the problems it had faced and promising a better future. He defeated Soglo in the March election of '96.

The Benin concert was intense. Not only because it was my first concert in a Democratic Benin, but also because while I'd been back to visit my country, I hadn't played in my hometown, Cotonou, since I'd left. It was arranged that I would play at Stade de l'Amitié, the stadium that has a twenty-thousand-seat capacity. Every Beninois had followed my career and its growth abroad every step of the way with surprise but also with skepticism. In one way they were extremely proud of the fact that people were talking about me, but they were also wondering whether I was really up to it. People were saying that I wasn't real. That it was just hype or a smoke screen. I knew this concert would be a test in front of a crowd of extremely demanding judges.

The night before, when I was playing in Togo, I'd had food poisoning. I was throwing up constantly and very dehydrated. When they came to pick me up I was barely walking. My whole body was weak and I couldn't breathe, but I refused to cancel. I was fueled by the pressure to show the African people what I was capable of. Afterward, when we got back to the hotel, I was wiped out but I couldn't sleep. Jean didn't sleep either. I was still running on the need to prove myself, and I needed more than anything to prove myself to Benin.

When I got to my parents' house, it was full of activity, with friends and cousins coming and going like always, but this time there was a big drama brewing. My mother had been crying all morning, her eyes were red and puffy. There was a rumor coming from Porto-Novo, the capital city, that if I sang that evening, I would die onstage. My father was trying to act as if he wasn't worried, but I could tell he was tense. I had to explain the whole situation to Pascal Signolet who was there to shoot a documentary for ARTE, the European cultural channel.

I turned to my parents and said, "If it is my destiny to die this evening, I will die because it will be my fate as a singer." In Africa, fatality is part of our daily life. How can people dare to live happily when they know that health care is so bad and you don't have retirement when you grow old? You have to be a little bit fatalistic. I wanted to reassure my parents, and I'd also become a lot less superstitious through the years. Superstition in West Africa is engraved in our culture and at times it restrains our full potential. My mother asked how I could talk like that, but in a few hours I was to go onstage in front of so many people and I couldn't let myself get upset. I told her, "You both taught me never to get in a state about these kinds of paranoid things. We've never believed in them, and we're not going to start believing them today."

The phone rang and it was my great-uncle, who was the traditional chief of Ouidah. He had heard the rumors and he told my father, "Just drop it, Franck. Nothing is going to happen to your daughter." He had decided to come from Ouidah to attend the concert even though traditional chiefs who hold a position like his are not supposed to go out at night like that. He said, "Find me a seat facing the center of the stage and that's where I'll sit."

Jean was so stressed that day. There was the drama at home, the TV crew was following us, and, on top of it all, nothing was ready at the stadium. It had been built by the Chinese in the seventies during the Cold War when Africa was the silent battlefield between capitalism and Communism. As soon as a country would embrace Marxism, there was an influx of Chinese who built the palaces and stadiums. What this meant for us was that all the instructions we had to operate the systems were written in Mandarin. In order to turn on the electricity, you had to get this one elusive guy to do it.

The opening act was set to go on at eight o'clock and at six, athletes were still running around the track. There was no stage, no sound equipment. The setup crew didn't come until two hours before the concert when the public was already waiting outside. It was nerve-racking, but that's how it was with concerts in Africa. I've always told people, "When you're going to Africa, just forget your watch, forget your sense of time, and you'll adapt right away. Otherwise, you'll go crazy." I try to fight this cliché about African people by always being on time.

Finally, it was time for me to head out for the stadium. We were in a dark–green town car, riding along the same roads my father had driven to take me to the Beach Club, Avenue de la Marina then rue de Lomé.

Me with my great-uncle, Daagbo Hounon.

But this time, the car was surrounded by police on motorcycles. I had asked them to be discreet, but they all had their sirens on like a politician's motorcade. When we approached the stadium and people heard the sirens, the whole place rose to its feet. It was filled to max capacity and twenty thousand people were all yelling in Fon, "*Éwa, éwa!*" "There she is, there she is!" They were proud of their *vedette internationale de la chanson*, as they called me, their star international singer.

I thought, *This huge crowd can't be there just for me.* But I kept my calm. I'd decided to give the finest concert I had ever done in my life. If it was going to be my last one, I was certainly going to give it my all. I was set on this. By the time we got behind the stage, I was already preparing myself. I stretched, practiced my scales, and did warm-ups with the members of my chorus. These things are an important part of my routine. There's also one ritual I always do: I iron my outfit for the stage myself, like a skydiver who has to fold his own parachute.

As difficult and emotional as that concert was for me, I was also in heaven doing it, because I was home. When I went onstage for the first song, it felt as if angel wings were carrying me. My feet weren't touching the ground. I jumped and spun in every direction. The threat added to my adrenaline, giving me a sense of invincibility. I remember thinking, *You may knock me down, but before you do I'm gonna sing you to death.* I knew that if something was to happen, I had my family there. I wasn't alone.

Jean's eyes were on me the whole time I was onstage. He knew the importance of that show and he was completely focused. He was driving the musicians, being the musical director, bass player, husband of the singer, and Naïma's dad. It's too much for one person to bear. When this tour ended, he quit performing with the band. But that night, he gave his all for me. Wherever I chose to be, he was there with me. He was completely in the show. I could see his head bobbing. Every time I turned, I saw his eyes. He wanted to make me understand that he was there. Later he would tell me that he was so worried, he played his bass automatically, without thinking. He said, "I wasn't driving my body."

The crowd was out in the bleachers, but the VIP section was rows of chairs set up on the grass just in front of the stage. I saw my great-uncle in the first row, so proud, with his big hat and big smile. My brother Oscar was tapping his feet to the beat. My mother, her head wrapped

in black and white fabric woven in Nigeria, was standing on her chair and dancing.

Later, my mother told me that my father had looked at her during the show and said,

"She's good."

"Of course she's good,"
she said.

"She's my daughter."

She knew because she watched me growing up in the theater, always asking questions, mimicking the actors. My mother's voice is always in my head. The beginning of my singing really was my mother. She told me, "Not like that, you're screaming. Watch your body. Watch your breathing." She had so much insight. She would say, "You don't need too much make-up" and "You can be sexy without being naked." She also taught me how to choose the fabrics for my costumes and what suited me. Because of her, I stood out from the other performers.

But my father sat, frozen. He hadn't seen me onstage since 1983. When I left my country, I couldn't speak to him for six years. When he was finally able to come to Paris and saw me as a student, I was so skinny. It was so painful for him, he was crying. He said, "You have to go back home." But I couldn't. If I went home with him then, I would never leave again.

After all those years of exile, all those doubts and uncertainties, I was communicating with the audience that was most dear to my heart. I was telling them that they are the source of my inspiration–that everything I did, I did for them. I asked them to sing along with me and at first they were shy. But almost all of my songs are for them, in their language. It's spoken by just seven million people and this was the one place in the world where the audience could sing along and understand every word in the songs–not just the feelings. I shouted, "I'm in the only place where people speak my language and understand my lyrics!" The

audience went hysterical, screaming and cheering. And then they began to sing.

How to leave the stadium once the concert was over? Impossible. The car had been waiting right next to the stage, but as soon as I was in it, the crowd pushed the barriers aside and surrounded the car on the field. I felt a moment of fear before I understood that it came from pure enthusiasm—and pride. There was no violence whatsoever. It was nothing but love. The policemen couldn't get me out of there, so we made our way back to the dressing room. Together with my parents, we stayed at least an hour before the crowd began to leave and I could go back to our house, the one I'd left to go into exile fourteen years before.

After everything it had taken to get to that day, what mattered most to me was what my father had to say. When I asked him why he'd been sitting so quiet, he said, "When we started, I never knew it would be like this. God gave you a talent and you used it. But I was afraid for you. The power you have on that stage, I've never seen it anywhere. As a father, I was afraid that someone might want to break down that power because you are fearless."

CHAPTER SIX

voodoo child

One day, when I was nine and he was nineteen, my brother Oscar came into the rehearsal room wearing a huge Afro wig. I thought maybe it was a lucky charm for him, but he always played the guitar brilliantly, so I asked him why he needed it.

"I want to be like Jimi Hendrix!" he said. He said Hendrix was one of the coolest American musicians and showed me the cover of *Axis: Bold as Love.* I still remember the psychedelic colors, the Hindu imagery, the snakes hovering over his head.

"He's not American," I said. "He looks like us. He's African."

"No, he's African American."

"I'm a kid, but I'm not stupid," I told him. "You're either African or American. You can't be both."

"He's a slave descendant," Oscar said.

"What's a slave?" I'd never heard that word before–not at school, not at home.

Oscar gave me a hard, quizzical look. Then he said, "I don't have time for this now. I need to practice," and walked out of the room.

You know me by now, so you know I ran around and asked everyone what a slave was. No one seemed willing to explain it to me. It was only later that I understood it was because slavery is still, even now, a very sensitive subject in Benin. Among today's Beninese families, there are both descendants of slave traders who helped the colonizers and of families who fought them. These people live side by side.

It was my grandmother, Mama Congo, who finally explained slavery to me. She said Westerners came in and bought people, like merchandise, to be sent far away. I couldn't fathom how or why this would happen, and what it would mean to "own" someone else. The Benin that I knew was so colorful, so rich with laughter and tradition. If there was one humanity like my father said, how did slavery fit into that picture?

So many slaves forced out of Africa to go the Americas were made to leave from Benin. A lot of them left from where my family lives, from Ouidah. Beninese religions and music have spread around the world because of this. You have the Candomblé religion in Brazil that embraces our orishas. Same thing in Cuba with the Santería religion. In Haiti "Vodun" was translated into "Voodoo." After the slave revolution gave Haiti independence, a mass exodus brought voodoo to New Orleans.

It is impossible for me to think about slavery without feeling anger. African people were treated like cattle and their status as human beings was denied. But what is astonishing is how they safeguarded their culture, in spite of this. They brought their religion with them, they also brought their music, and they used their music to invent new and sophisticated art forms. In Brazil, African music was transformed into the samba. In Cuba it became *son*. In North America the slavers saw the drums as a powerful tool, a dangerous method of communication. They thought that by removing the drums, they would wipe out the memory of the motherland in the mind of the slaves. So African tradition continued mainly through

the voice. The blues is how African Americans sustained the African tradition through singing because they didn't have access to drums.

When this music arrived in the United States, it created new scales that had never been heard before. In classical music, you are either in minor or major scales. They're two different things. But the slaves would start singing their African five-tone minor scales on the major chords of the master's guitar. This created blue notes–tensions. Because they didn't have their original instruments, they forced African melodies on the American harmonies and that is how this happened. The power and beauty of their music enabled them to keep their dignity. They refused to become beasts of burden.

In New Orleans this led to ragtime, which later led to jazz. George Gershwin and Leonard Bernstein both proclaimed that Afro-American music was the most innovative form of twentieth–century classical music. It's amazing that the lowest class of society was able to shape the art of the upper class. But, if you can believe this, it has been that way since J.S. Bach used the sarabande, a dance of the African slaves from Panama, to compose some of his music. It's primarily through music that we can create a dialogue between peoples. People don't always speak the same language, but everyone can understand rhythm. You understand the meaning of a song through your body, not just through your brain.

Africa is often regarded as being superfluous, a continent of savages–not part of the modern "enlightened world." I've always wanted to recreate that lost link with the diaspora to prove that my continent has made immense contributions to contemporary culture. In the late nineties, as I began thinking about what I wanted my next recordings to be, I kept coming back to how the music of slaves transcends borders. I thought that if people understood this, they would understand Africa differently. After focusing the last album on the rhythms of my homeland, it seemed the natural next step was to trace the routes they'd taken with the slaves. And so I began to think of my next album as a trilogy. I could collect music from each part of the Americas, North America, South America, and the Caribbean, and show people how the music all has the same African roots.

I decided then that it was time to leave Paris. In America you have all those black and white, Native American, and Latino communities. People

of all colors and backgrounds live there. I'd always imagined singing with Cuban singer Celia Cruz and American legend James Brown, and they symbolized the Americas in many ways. But I also wanted to meet other American artists, no matter what ethnicity they belonged to. I wanted to write music with them, to share with them the idea of a common humanity so that a musical dialogue with Africa could begin.

I moved to New York with Jean and our little Naïma, and I was welcomed with open arms by my friend Branford Marsalis, whom I had met in Paris. Our first meeting, in 1991, was just ridiculous. He had no idea who I was, and I had no idea he was already a legend born from a very musical family in New Orleans. I had just been signed by Island Records so I was on a cloud and then here comes a guy who has been doing music forever. I was doing an interview at Radio Nova in Paris and my journalist friend Bintou Simporé said, "This is Branford. He's a saxophone player."

I said, "Oh yeah? You play good?" He laughed and we were friends from that moment on. His open spirit, both musical and human, is truly amazing. I also sensed in him a genuine admiration for African culture, which was quite a change from the condescension I was used to feeling from people who didn't know much about Africa. Branford and I exist in the same world.

There isn't always an easy relationship between Africans and African Americans. There can be a distance, because of what many people have been taught about their African roots. The first person who opened my eyes to this was Scorpio, one of the rappers from Grandmaster Flash. We did a project together in Germany, rap meets African music, and after we finished some interviews he looked at me with surprise and asked, "How is it that you come from Africa, but you're so educated and eloquent?"

When I asked him what he meant, he told me that when he was in school he was shown history books with images of savages, pictures of people with bones in their noses. This, he was told, was Africa. He said, "We all said we didn't want to look like that. We thought our lives were better because we had been saved." He started realizing his generation has been fooled. When you justify slavery by belittling the African people—*Look, we saved you from being like these savages*—for me that is double slavery.

With Branford, talking about slavery was different. Because he comes from New Orleans, he has a different understanding of it than most people.

New Orleans is the only place in America where the African tradition and roots are really deep down in the music The French and Spanish masters had allowed drumming on Sundays in Congo Square. When I hear a drummer from New Orleans, I know. The feel is completely different: it is the mixture of the African music and Native American dance. Trying to explain it is like trying to tell you how my heart beats. You just have to feel it. The drummer who really embodies this is Zigaboo Modeliste from The Meters. When I hear him play the drums, I hear the timbre, the rhythm, and the time. You dance just listening to him drumming.

Before I went to America, I called Branford and told him I wanted to do this trilogy. He said, "Come and stay at my place." Jean, Naïma, and I lived at his house in New Rochelle, a few miles north of New York City, for more than a month. His house had a field and garden, and Branford had this old-fashioned study that looked out over a garden. I sat in that room and listened to his collection of African music from every corner of the continent.

Naïma was still so young then and when she didn't want to go to bed, Branford put on Mahler's Fifth Symphony to lull her to asleep. Later on, when she started playing piano, I would watch her fingers reach so far across the keys and think back to those nights. I say to Jean all the time, you don't raise your child alone. The friends you surround yourself with are part of it too.

We spent our first Thanksgiving at Branford's house. We knew nothing about the holiday. I said, "It's a party of binge eating. I don't understand the point of it." When he explained the story of the Indians to me, I asked him if I understood it right. "The Indians saved the British, but then the British ended up killing the Indians?"

"That's right," he said.

At the time, it seemed to me like a crazy thing to celebrate. Later I understood the spirit of redemption it carries.

At Branford's house we started working on *Oremi,* the first album in the trilogy. Together we wrote "Itche Koutche," an Afrobeat hymn whose insistent brass riff Branford composed. I swear that on the day he recorded his solo for this piece he wasn't in the studio for more than fifteen minutes. He gets out of the elevator, opens the case of his soprano saxophone, goes behind the microphone, and the tape begins to roll. Then, just as

The cover of the album *Oremi*, the first part of my trilogy.

quick, his instrument is packed up again and he's out the door, and the recording was perfect.

One day, while we were at a party in New York, I ran into our friend Isaach de Bankolé, the famous African actor whom we knew from our Paris days. He introduced me to Cassandra Wilson, the wonderful southern jazz singer with a deep, bluesy voice. They were married at that time and he was doing his documentary about her, *Traveling Miles*. They invited us

to their apartment in Harlem, in the same building where Duke Ellington used to live, and we talked about her interest in African culture.

One night Cassandra came to sing with me at Quad, the recording studio near Times Square where Tupac Shakur was shot. With windows overlooking a rainy New York, it was the perfect mood for making jazz. On the song "Never Know," her warm voice was the ideal counterpoint to my African timbre. Our personalities are reflected in our voices, too. She's reserved and laidback and I'm more of an extrovert, exuberant tomboy.

Recording at Quad was a big deal for me. The famed studio was now witness to a procession of Paul Simon's African musicians as well as African American musicians like Questlove, the great drummer of the Roots, and TM Stevens, James Brown's bassist. We were starting to build back a bridge between our cultures, like Harry Belafonte had done by singing with Miriam Makeba in the sixties. One day, Harry Belafonte even invited me to lunch. He told me stories about Miriam coming to America and about his own relationship with Africa. He explained that it began in 1932, when he was five. He went to the theater with his mother to see the movie *Tarzan*. The way African people were depicted was so repulsive he didn't want to be associated with them. Then, slowly, he learned to embrace his Africanism through the teachings of the Jamaican politician Marcus Garvey, who had been born in the same town as his mom. It drove him to financially support the civil rights movement and Martin Luther King at a time when he himself was selling millions of records and very few people knew of MLK. Not only is Harry Belafonte wise, he's also very funny. Most people don't know this. During lunch, as he's

Harry Belafonte has taught me so much about how American history portrays the diaspora.

dipping his bread in olive oil, I tell him that it isn't good to eat so much oil. He says, "You see how good my health is, right? Through the years, I've learned it isn't good to listen too much to African women's advice!"

On the last day of the recording, jazz pianist Kenny Kirkland played on my version of "Voodoo Chile," in homage to Jimi Hendrix. All these years I had wanted to pay tribute to my first encounter with Hendrix's music. It was he who had unknowingly opened the eyes of a little West African girl to the immensity of the diaspora. I recorded my own version of "Voodoo Chile" because Jimi was proud of his African ancestry and he claimed it in this song. Also, who could better claim to be a "Voodoo Child" than me?

The *Voodoo Child* single. It took me years to find an original way to cover this Jimi Hendrix song.

From the moment I decided I would cover it, the song was always in my head. Since I couldn't very well ask any musician to compete with Hendrix's virtuosity, I had to find something to sing in place of the guitar riff. Until I figured out that piece, I wouldn't record it. It took years of that song floating around in my head until one day I woke up and said, "Jean, here it is." I replaced Jimi's guitar riffs with Beninese chanting, and then we slowed down the tempo to make it more hypnotic and haunting.

Amon Min keledje
Vodoo vi amon
Amon min keledje
Vodoo amon

You think I'm worthless
but you're looking at
the real
Voodoo child

Every time you talk about voodoo, the conversation goes to a dark place. With this song, I was trying to rehabilitate the reputation of Vodun, the rich animist culture I'd grown up with. I surely don't practice what people call voodoo. I'm not sacrificing chickens in my kitchen and piercing dolls at night! I'm a baptized Catholic girl from the city. I am also very critical of the superstition and obscurantism that slow down the development of humanity. But I want to acknowledge the importance of this culture and its beautiful and loving sides.

Once, in the gothic Cathedral of Saint John the Divine, on the edge of Harlem, I was singing at a fundraiser for Bill Clinton's foundation. When he was introducing me, he said:

"Angélique is from Benin, which for hundreds of years was known as Dahomey. And so I asked her … if she was a Fon from Dahomey and she said "Yes, my father was." Three hundred years ago, the Fon people were taken out of their home in West Africa to become the slaves in Haiti and they developed a spirit-based religion called Voodoo, which has been twisted, distorted, and misrepresented by many people. [This is unfortunate as] they are a beautiful people."

Onstage with Eric Clapton, Bill Clinton, and Jon Bon Jovi.

I had been living outside of my country for so long and had gotten used to drawing a map of where it was and teaching people about it because most people know very little about Benin. For a head of state to know not only where I come from, but also the history of my country, was really moving for me.

All of the songs on *Oremi* have a special meaning for me. "Babalawo" speaks of the role of the traditional Yoruba priest, who exists in Brazil as well. In our societies, the *babalawo* was a sort of psychoanalyst. Often when young people were looking for a neutral person because they had done something foolish or because they found themselves in some impossible situation not knowing whom to turn to, and especially not wanting to turn to their parents, the babalawo played that role. They would talk to him and he'd help find a solution. If it wasn't the babalawo, it would be an uncle, an aunt, or a grandmother. African society has no expensive psychiatric system because it was enough to talk to one another to be able to find a solution.

"Loloyé" is a love song that I wrote based on one of my father's sayings. When my mother began to do theater in Benin, she was traveling alone with her group a lot. A woman came to see my father and said, "Really now, Franck, how can you let your wife go so far away by herself? Aren't you afraid she'll cheat on you?"

My father told her, "Love should never be a prison. When you love someone, you've got to let them be free."

After we wrote the song, we did a demo version, then we took a break to have lunch. All of the sudden we realized our four-year-old girl wasn't with us. We called her name, but she didn't answer. She was lying on the bed listening to the song with headphones on, so she hadn't heard us calling her. She was looking at my lyrics, even though she couldn't read yet. I said, "What are you doing? We've been looking for you all over the place."

A publicity shot from the album *Oremi*.

My daughter, jamming out.

She said,

"I really love this song, Mama. I have to sing it with you!"

When we were recording in New York a few months later, our little daughter asks, "So, when do I get to sing the song?" She hadn't forgotten. They had to give her a high stool to get her mouth near the microphone. But after they did, in a matter of seconds, she quickly changed into a diva. I'll never forget it. She says to us, "Could you please lower the light a little? I can only sing when the light is dim." You can hear her little voice, so sweet and tender, in the song's final refrain.

The last song on *Oremi*, "No Worry," a minimalistic hip hop beat intertwined with African chanting, talks about how you can overcome sorrow, loneliness, and despair. You need to accept them as a way of life because sorrow goes hand in hand with joy, just as life goes hand in hand with death. It is like this for all of us. You also can't know love if you haven't known sorrow. Ishmael Beah, the former child soldier from Sierra Leone who became a famous writer, once told me that this song had kept him going in his moments of hardship.

Through the years, I've learned that when you write a song, it doesn't really matter if it reaches number one on the charts. You write in the hope that just one person will feel what Ishmael felt.

the messenger

The second part of the trilogy took us to Salvador de Bahia in Brazil. Years before, I had met the old writer Jorge Amado at the Brazilian embassy in Paris, near the Champs-Elysées. He had this amazing head of white hair and an aura of such kindness. That night, he told me how the orishas of my country are revered in Bahia, and how their mythology had been brought to Brazil by the slaves. I knew one day I would have to make a trip there. The first time I arrived in Salvador was a shock for me because it had the same smell as it does at home. The vegetation is the same: sea grass, trees wet at the root. It's a spicy smell. Like a perfume scented with earth. With the very first whiff of air I breathed, I thought,

This isn't possible. I can't be home. But, in some ways, I was.

We were living in the old neighborhood of Santo Antônio, at the house of Dimitri, a Frenchman born in Morocco. He owned an art gallery and a bed and breakfast overlooking the bay of Todos os Santos and he knew everything about culture and art in Salvador. The house was not far from the Pelourinho, the historic center of Salvador, where famous percussion ensembles like Olodum and Ilê Aiyê often play. I loved the old Portuguese architecture, the walls alternating between pastels and whitewash. Walking up and down the hard slopes, my feet on the pavement echoed the sound of the drumming always playing somewhere in the distance. One day I was walking toward the market on the seashore when a young kid–he must have been eight or nine–approached me with a sassy look and asked, "Where are you from?"

I said, "I'm African."

He opened his mouth wide and asked, "You're African?" My continent is so often looked down on, but this boy's eyes were shining–it was as if he'd just seen a goddess. "Then you're an African princess," he said. And he followed me, grinning, with his eyes popping out of his head. This affected me so much because I'm no princess, but for that child, as for all the inhabitants of Bahia, Africa represents the full pride of their roots. It's one of the rare cities outside of Africa where 85 percent of the population is of African origin, which is something you can feel in the music, in the dance, and in the food.

In North America slavers were afraid that access to drums would strengthen the slaves, and so they refused to let them have them. But in South America, it's the exact opposite. Having realized how greatly they were outnumbered, the Portuguese slave traders encouraged the slaves to nurture their cultural differences so that their internal rivalries would prevent them from uniting against their masters. Divide and conquer, as the saying goes. They were allowed to gather every Sunday by ethnic groups to sing and dance together.

To me, Brazilian music is the true fusion of what's best in the world: African music and classical music. Chopin meets Benin. This is what the work of Antônio Carlos Jobim, the composer of "The Girl from Ipanema," is about: lyrical melodies inspired by the Romantic era sung on top of irresistible Afro-Brazilian grooves. In Salvador, I wrote songs with the

genius percussionist Carlinhos Brown at his house on the Rio Vermelho. The first time I heard him was on *Brasileiro*, his great first recording with Sergio Mendes. Then we met while we were both touring. Carlinhos was born in a favela called Candyall and, once he became famous, he built a music school for the street children of his area with the help of UNESCO. He invested in that specific district to bring it out of poverty. He's an amazing writer and his songs are so popular that you hear them constantly throughout Carnival. He has the talent to create little riffs that stay in your head forever. We spent a crazy afternoon writing together. I wasn't speaking much Portuguese then, but we spoke through music. He works so fast that he wrote ten songs in just a few hours. I recorded everything and then went back to Dimitri's to write my parts. I had to go back through the recordings to find the riff, the hook, a verse, a chorus, and a bridge—all while still keeping the inspiration of the moment.

With Carlinhos's group Timbalada, there's no need for guitar or bass. There are more than a hundred members, so the percussion alone is enough to create a tremendous energy. It can make me dance for hours. The key of a song is determined by the root note of the low drums. The music carries you because you have the full register of the sounds from the bass to the very high *repique* drum. You're caught in a kind of grid that dictates the movement of your body. You can't escape the Afro-Brazilian rhythms. They are like the traditional music from Benin, but the beats are simpler. We played our song "Tumba" together for the first time during Carnival. It was heaven on earth.

> *Tumba, tumba, tumba, tumba yo*
> *Tumba, tumba, tumba wa*
> *Tumba é tumba éa, tumba é tumba éo*

Carnival was an extraordinary experience. The Carnival of Bahia has nothing in common with the Carnival of Rio and all its glitter. In Salvador everyone is out in the street dancing. The *trio eléctricos*, gigantic trucks with enormous PA systems and musicians playing on their roofs, drive through the streets all night long. The public surrounds the trucks and they move on little by little. The dense mass of people swaying to the rhythm, to your right and your left, creates a strong sense of unity. You

Naïma getting ready for the Carnival of Bahia.

have this big drumming and the people, they aren't dancing as much as pulsating together. It's like little currents inside a vast ocean of people, and you can't swim against them. I was happily stuck in the middle of the crowd, in the heat and the rain.

Many of the great Brazilian singers I admire come from Salvador. During Carnival I got to meet Gilberto Gil who came to sing on my Benin-inspired version of his song "Refavela." His voice is like the most musical thing you can imagine. Rhythm and melody just become one when he sings. I also met my hero Caetano Veloso in the backstage VIP rooms that run along the *camarotes*, the truck routes. He taught me how to dance the elegant old form of samba. Daniela Mercury, who had covered my song "Batonga" a few years before, recognized me from the top of her trio eléctrico and invited me up to sing with her. Naïma and Jean stayed with the crowd. Naïma was on Jean's shoulders and, as they followed the truck, they kept slipping in the mud. She held on by grabbing the hair on top of Jean's head.

Singing and holding a microphone and moving–not only my body, but the whole stage–was something that I'd never experienced. The sense of gravity is completely different. As you move, you see all these excited faces. But you can only keep eye contact for a couple of seconds, and when you look again the faces have changed. It was amazing because there were so many people excited to see us, but it was also disconcerting because I am used to focusing on people when I sing. At one point, you just see tons of heads. We were on a floating island in the middle of a sea of people lost in the music.

Bahia is surrounded by hills, and as we approached them, I realized the trio eléctricos are designed not just for the crowds that surround them, but also for the people who are listening off in the distance. With the music being blasted out of those huge speakers, I could almost see the sound floating up and over, into the hills in waves.

One night, we went to a Candomblé ceremony. Dimitri had a friend, an ethnologist, who agreed to take us with him. Candomblé is a Brazilian religion with roots in Africa that celebrates the Yoruba orishas. The ceremony took place on a hill outside a large white house. Under an arbor was a dance floor stamped out in the dirt. Women wore big white dresses with patches of color that indicated their orishas–white and blue

for Yemandja, red and black for Shango. They were dancing in a trance, twirling with their eyes closed, but they didn't bump into one another. I don't know how they did it.

As I watched, I found myself surrounded by Brazilians who spoke Portuguese, which was foreign to me, but when the ceremony began, I recognized all their songs! I had the feeling there were two of me, one who was there listening to the people around me speak Portuguese, and, at the same time, one who was hearing the traditional songs in Yoruba and following the entire sequence of the procession and the trance, just as if I was at home. It was surreal. On the back cover of *Black Ivory Soul*, the album born out of this trip and the second part of the trilogy, I put a quote from the French writer Roger Bastide that captures what I felt that day: "*In the sacred ground of Bahia, I saw a tree whose trunk was covered with seashells and whose roots were pushing beyond the ocean as far as the African land.*"

Translating Yoruba lyrics to a babalawo in Salvador.

Later I met a babalawo, a priest, whom they call "saint's father" because Bahia is known as the Bay of All Saints and the babalawo are the spiritual protectors of it. I remember he had a relaxed way about him, and his smile was framed by a beard. We began to talk about the Candomblé religion. He said, "I'm going to sing you a song that one of the best-known and most powerful of the saint's mothers of Bahia used to sing. She sang it all the time, but we don't understand what it's about."

For all these years he had been singing in a language he didn't understand, just like a country priest does when reciting Latin. But when he sang for me, I understood the song's meaning completely. The saint's mother was meant to transmit the words of a god through her songs, but the Eshun, the messenger of the gods, speaks through her instead because he feels comfortable there. And the saint's mother, halfway in a trance, sings his praises, flattering him, saying, "But you really must leave, Eshun,

to allow my god to have his rightful place." When the babalawo heard me translate the song, whose meaning had been lost for generations, he was brought to tears. It was incredible that the song has survived centuries out of Africa, intact through history.

In Bahia we also went to visit the house of Pierre Verger. Born in 1902, Pierre Verger was a French photographer who devoted his life to studying the African diaspora. It was his work that first introduced me to the relationship between the Afro-Brazilian and Beninese religions. After having been all across the globe and settling in Salvador, he discovered Benin, and studied all its cultural forms. He was even initiated as a babalawo.

Verger's black-and-white photos show regular people from the street and display how they are transformed by the traditional costumes, the ceremonies, and the dances. He chose to live for years right in the heart of the Salvador favelas, in the house that became the home of the Pierre Verger Foundation after his death. They call the house Casa Vermelha because it's painted a vibrant red. Inside, it's stripped to a bare minimum.

His work was extensive—there are more than sixty thousand negatives—and the collection of his photos taken in Benin in the fifties is fantastic. It shows the beauty of the people and their costumes, and the intensity of their dances and ceremonies. He had taken the pictures before I was born and the places had changed, but sometimes a building seemed familiar to me.

After hours of going through the archives, I was suddenly blown away by one picture. It was a photograph that Verger had taken on the square of Ouidah, sometime after World War II. It showed a woman at the marketplace. I recognized her face first, then the village second. It was my aunt, on my dad's side, now long gone. We didn't have any photos of her anymore. She had died when I was ten, but I recognized her face right away. She was the one always telling me stories and legends. She was one of the few people willing to answer my questions.

The photo is candid. In it my aunt is wearing wax clothes and a short, flowered boubou. She is standing in front of the market, looking in the direction of the camera. With her mouth open slightly, she looks like she is calling to someone across the way. In Benin, we always speak so loud, talking from afar. The picture made me feel that if Pierre Verger hadn't

captured her at that exact moment, she would have moved out of the frame, and the beauty of her expression, with all the noise behind her, would have been lost.

The market in the photo is very close to my ancestral house in Ouidah. I would walk to it ten times a day when I was there. I spent so much time in the market with my aunties. That's where they sell everything, fabric, salt. I used to sit with them, talking about everything and nothing.

Standing in this home in the heart of the Salvador favelas with my husband and daughter only a few feet away, I began to wonder how it happened that I had to come digging so far away from home, to find a portrait of my long-lost aunt. It was like Pierre Verger had left a message, just for me, through the photo: a reminder of how my family is always watching over me, and how our world is so interconnected.

Everywhere we went, we brought Naïma with us. We took her to see the Bagunçaco, the center for street children that encourages them to make music to keep them out of trouble. Poverty in Brazil affects the young people the most and they can quickly end up living in the streets. Playing together in a group, sharing those moments, recreates for them the family they've never had. That day, it was the birthday of one of the girls. She was turning fifteen and had never celebrated her birthday before, so we quickly organized a party and I sang for her. When we brought out her cake, she started to cry.

Naïma must have been about six years old at the time. She came over to me and asked, "Mama, why is she crying?" It would later be the same when we went back to Africa together. Naïma asking questions about the children and why they didn't attend school, and why some children her own age had to work. I explained that the girl had never had a birthday cake. Naïma was like me as a child, always asking questions.

When she went back to school in Brooklyn and her teacher asked her to tell about her trip to Brazil, she didn't talk about Carnival and the unbelievable costumes, or the music and the dancing, she only told the story of that young girl. I was so proud to see that my daughter had realized there was another reality in the world, and that, even at such a young age, she too understood the injustice of it.

OPPOSITE: Being near the ocean always calms me.

In the studio with Ahmir "Questlove" Thompson.

Coming back to New York, our new home, after the exuberance of Brazil, was harder, in a way, than my move to France had been. Compared with Europe, America was far away from my reality. Even though American music was close to me, and the story of the African American was close to me, I never thought I would be here, living this life.

In the beginning, it was hard for me to trust people, just like it had been in France. One person who helped change that was Timothy White. He was both very serious and very funny, always wearing a dotted bow tie, and when I moved to New York, he took me under his wing. As editor of *Billboard*, his knowledge of the music world was unsurpassed and he was one of those rare journalists with integrity. He also saw beyond clichés of blacks and whites, which was impressive at that time because segregation was still so ingrained in the music business—and in the broader society. Naïma's first public school in Hell's Kitchen, where we lived at the time, had only African American and Latino students. I could not believe it. As a mixed couple, Jean and I were an oddity, though in a way our African and French accents made us nonthreatening because it meant that we were both different from everyone else. In the music business, black artists had to do hip hop and R&B, white artists did rock and folk. Timothy was not about that at all. He was color blind in his love for music and people.

Since *Logozo*, he had become so important in my life. He understood the person I am. And how music, not only black African American music, but all music, shapes my work. Sometimes, when Jean and I would write new songs, we asked Timothy to listen to them even before Chris Blackwell, and he told us what he thought, honestly, out of his heart.

In 2001, I had just signed with the prestigious Columbia Records. They liked my Brazilian album, but because I was not a mainstream

ANGÉLIQUE KIDJO *Black Ivory Soul*

TOP: Photos from *Black Ivory Soul*. • **BOTTOM:** The cover of the *Black Ivory Soul* album.

artist, the executives there didn't really understand who I was. When I spoke with Timothy about this, he asked, "Do you really want to impress them? Organize a dinner at your apartment and I'll come." So we invite everyone and I spend the whole day cooking all my specialties. In the evening, everyone from Columbia arrives at my new apartment in Brooklyn, but there's no Timothy White. We're all waiting, trying to make small talk, but Jean and I keep exchanging nervous looks and sneaking glances out the window. We could tell they didn't believe someone as powerful as Timothy White would think a little dinner at my place was important.

Finally, after what seemed like forever, the bell rings and he's standing in our doorway. He had been coming over the Brooklyn Bridge when his cab had run out of gas. He had to get out right there in the middle of the bridge and walk the rest of the way into Brooklyn until he found another cab. I'll never forget the look on those record executives' faces when they realized the length to which Timothy White had gone to get there that night.

We finished *Black Ivory Soul* when Dave Matthews put his beautiful voice on my song "Iwoya" in a small Soho studio called the Magic Shop. On my way there one day, I stopped at a street vendor's stand and I found an old Manu DiBango vinyl. In the liner notes, he wrote: "I call my music makossa, but American people call it black ivory soul." When my album came out, Timothy loved it so much that he put it on the cover of the weekly issue of *Billboard*. The headline in big bold letters read: "Columbia's Kidjo Bares Her Black Ivory Soul." The seeds of my African roots were starting to grow in America!

But life taught me a hard lesson. I was scheduled to give a performance at Virgin Megastore in Union Square. The day before the appearance, Timothy called. It had been a while since we'd talked and I was so happy to hear from him, but the connection was bad. Jean was able to get through just long enough to ask him to come to the show. "Okay," Timothy told him. "I'm feeling a little tired, but I'll see you tomorrow."

The next afternoon, while Jean, Naïma, and I were in the car on our way to Union Square, Jean got a call from my manager. Timothy had a heart attack in the elevator at the *Billboard* offices. He was dead. When someone close to us dies suddenly, we often say, "I can't believe it." We cannot allow ourselves to know what's real. That was how I responded.

While we slowly made our way through downtown traffic, I didn't just cry, I screamed. It seemed like as long as I made that sound, the news would not be true. We would walk through the doors and Timothy would be standing there. But then I looked in the backseat and I saw Naïma watching me. "Mom, stop," she kept saying, over and over. I knew she was scared, so I forced myself to calm down, to go quiet. In a few moments we would arrive at the store and I would have to perform.

Afterward, when I called my father to tell him what had happened, he had no philosophical response for me. Instead, he, who never swore, could only say, "Sometimes, life's a bitch." I was so surprised to hear that word come out of his mouth. He made me laugh through my tears.

I knew he was right, of course. And I also knew that with Timothy White's death, I had suffered a loss from which I would never recover. Even though he wasn't much older than me, he was like a spiritual father. He was always there. He had played a role that my own father, because he was so far away, at times could not.

mutoto kwanza

As a child, one of my nightmares was the UNICEF truck. As soon as I saw that blue and white van parked on Boulevard Saint-Michel, just a block from our house, I knew I'd have to get my booster shot. I've always been scared of needles. I tried hiding in Paulette's closet or the dark room of the photo studio, but little by little my mother found every one of my spots. When she came to get me, I asked her why we had to get vaccinated. The kids at school teased us because of it and said we were acting like European children. She told me, "I don't care. You need to be in good health at school. If you're not healthy, you can't learn well."

In May of 2002, under the direction of Secretary-General Kofi Annan, the United Nations Special Session on Children was organized in New York with more than seventy heads of state, and Nelson Mandela, Bill Gates, Harry Belafonte, and Roger Moore. I was invited to sing at the closing ceremony, which took place in a large tent in the shadow of the white, futuristic UN headquarters building on the bank of the East River. It was the first time I had been approached by the United Nations. I had met Kofi Annan's secretary at a party a little while before, and she told me that he had been following my career for a while and would be in touch.

Michael Douglas hosted the closing ceremony, and at it I was surrounded by people who had come from all over the world and spoke every language imaginable. It was like a Tower of Babel and I felt completely at ease. It reminded me so much of our family home in Cotonou where, one after another, people of every nationality paraded through the courtyard.

When I went to sit in the audience before my performance, I turned and saw Mathieu Kérékou, the dictator of Benin who had since come back to power through democratic elections. I'm still shocked by this. History takes strange turns sometimes. The last time I had seen him was when I was made to do a show for the heads of state, just before I left Benin. All these years later, here we were sitting across the aisle from each other at the UN. Suddenly, the fear he had inspired in me had disappeared. He was just human.

Then it was time to go onstage. *Black Ivory Soul* was just out and I decided to sing my song "Afirika" in public for the first time. Jean and I had written that song sitting on our bed in our rented apartment on Ninth Street in Brooklyn in about fifteen minutes. It is a tribute not only to Africa, but also to Miriam Makeba whom everyone called Mama Africa. The verse is very Beninese, but the chord progression in the chorus is classic South African. The song poured out of me. It was one of the fastest ones I've ever written. Sometimes you trigger something that was already there, waiting.

That night at the UN, I sang with a children's choir from Harlem and a symphony orchestra of young Venezuelans. The sound was bouncing back and forth inside the tent and the energy and sense of togetherness was so strong. That's when I realized the power of its simple chorus to lift people's spirits. The audience joined in. I didn't have to ask. It became

My first collaboration with UNICEF was to sing for the United Nations Special Session on Children.

an anthem for me that night and has remained part of all my performances. Since then, I have played this song all over the world with every possible lineup you can imagine: from the solo upright bass of Christian McBride to the Red Army Choir; from the street percussion of Nairobi to the Luxembourg Philharmonic Orchestra. I've sung it with iconic singers Peter Gabriel and Annie Lennox, and presidents Jimmy Carter and Bill Clinton. I've sung it with Nelson Mandela and Desmond Tutu, with the royal families of Norway and Monaco, Queen Rania of Jordon, and also young Beninese girls.

The day after this concert, I received an unexpected phone call that would change my life. It was from Maria Zanca, the head of UNICEF Celebrity Relations, inviting me to their headquarters at the UN Plaza. At the time, I wasn't very involved in advocacy and humanitarian work so it was something new to me. But I saw it as a way to reconcile my passion for music and the obsessive question that kept coming to mind: What can I do to give back to the continent that has given me so much? An African

artist, as opposed to a Western one, is always confronted by this question because while you are pursuing your dreams, you come from a continent that still bears so much suffering.

I thought of my own childhood, of the large UNICEF truck, of my mother's obsession with the health and education of her children. Since I had become a mother myself, the situation of the disadvantaged children on my continent bothered me more and more. Motherhood gives you another sense of responsibility and seeing children Naïma's age working instead of going to school and enjoying their childhood pulled at me.

The tradition of *vidomegon*, the little child servant, is still widespread there and when I go back to Benin, a small voice inside me always whispers *that child who's suffering could be your own daughter.* It's a silent crisis. In Europe you had the same practice. Westerners think of it and they may picture the little girl in *Les Misérables*–they don't grasp the reality of it. Children from the countryside are sent by their parents to the city to work as servants in the family of some distant relatives. The hope of people from these small villages is that their kids won't live in the same misery they do and that the family from the city has a good heart. Maybe they will decide to send the children to school. But if the family is not responsible and lacks compassion, you have little kids seven or eight years of age working all day long.

The last decades have brought an even more sinister twist. International traffickers convince ignorant villagers that their child is going to the city to learn when in reality he or she is sent to another country to work in a mine or in a factory. The issue is complex as the tradition is common at all levels of society. In a way, everyone is closing their eyes. Not only does the legislation have to change, but so does the mentality. I would learn from UNICEF that the first step is birth registration: a simple act that makes the precious life of a child a traceable existence in our modern world.

From her office overlooking the East River, Maria asked me in a very serious voice if I would do them the honor of being one of their international goodwill ambassadors in the struggle to protect the young. So without any hesitation I told Maria, "Yes, of course! Why not?" I didn't realize at the time I was entering a new family with Mary, Fran, Dheepa, Marissa, Gloria, Malene and many more UNICEF workers around the world.

When I asked Maria what the role of an itinerant ambassador is, she told me, "That depends on the ambassador—what he or she chooses to do." What interested me then, as it still does, is not being an ambassador who spends her time going from one cocktail party to another. I understand that cocktail parties can be important for lobbying the politicians, but what I really wanted was to meet the children and the women of my continent. I wanted to see what their real needs are and to have a more concrete idea of what UNICEF accomplishes.

A few weeks after our meeting at the headquarters, I received my UN passport—light blue with the UN logo on the front. I was so proud. You know I'm not a politician because I always speak my mind—thanks to my ancestor Linhounhinto—and here I had become an ambassador! I would be asked to speak on behalf of UNICEF at meetings with politicians, perform at rallies, and give interviews at UNICEF program sites. I had to be sure I behaved myself. I could see Jean was worried.

The mainstream news generally talks about my continent in a way that diminishes its importance. Such coverage is justified with political and economic reasons, as if Africa can't keep up with the rest of the world. This goes back to slavery and colonization, ignoring and denying the equality and contributions of the people. If you recognize this, you have to question what you've done to promote change.

But this problem is not just a Western one. We Africans also don't know enough about Africa, and we certainly don't do enough to improve its reputation. We grow up with certain prejudices, and we don't travel inside Africa to disprove them or meet people we know nothing about. We stay in our corner and we know our corner better than anyone else— we don't want to question what is going on around us. Before my work with UNICEF, my own understanding was also insufficient. I sang about Mother Africa and how we are all African, and I had traveled through West Africa, but my knowledge of the rest of the continent was limited to books and storytelling. UNICEF gave me a chance to discover where I came from, where all of us come from.

My first trip, in November 2002, took me to Tanzania. It was my first time to East Africa—a whole different world from West Africa. People seemed to be more reserved, less exuberant. In the suburb of Dar es Salaam we visited a community that was seriously affected by goiter, a

swelling of the thyroid gland that seriously impairs organ and muscle functions. It was the first time I learned about the problem. People used to think it was a genetic condition, but it's caused by iodine deficiency.

In the United States we use iodized salt so you don't have this problem. But in Tanzania and other countries where this deficiency is prevalent, a salt tester that costs one dollar has unbelievably positive results. With it, women can go to the market and test the salt before they buy it. If it's been iodized, the salt will change color, and they will know whether to buy it from that vendor or from someone else. A very simple, inexpensive act can have an exponentially positive effect. I was with Carol Bellamy, then executive director of UNICEF, and she knew this program inside and out. We sat with the generation of women who had goiter, and then with the next generation who didn't.

These testers changed the entire life of the community. I saw the women's engagement, but also the participation of the men selling in the market.

PREVIOUS SPREAD: Visiting a UNICEF assisted pediatric AIDS clinic in Githorogo, a settlement near Nairobi, in Kenya. • BELOW: Reading to children at the Tesfa Gebrehane kindergarten in Awasa, Ethiopia.

They too wanted the testers so they could show their salt had iodine. With these people I witnessed how UNICEF works hands-on to improve the quality of life in suffering communities. They work to make the people responsible for their own lives, so that once the organization leaves, the programs they helped set up continue, and the knowledge that has been transferred will endure.

One thing I realized is that you have to be careful when you're trying to help people. This is always a double-edged sword. When you're providing a community with goods or services, there is always the risk of crippling their potential if the people see that the solution comes from the outside and they don't feel involved. People are very proud and if they lose this pride, the fight is lost.

While we were in Dar es Salaam, I visited an orphanage where some of the children are HIV-positive. The disease was still shrouded in silence, and when Carol first asked me to go, I was scared. I dreaded that visit because I knew it would be beyond difficult, and I knew it would take its toll. We walked through a building that was filled with bunk beds for the kids. Outside, in the courtyard where they played, the ground was dark sand, the color of charcoal. The shock of seeing so many children without parents in one place took my breath away. Most were so frail you could see their ribs, but they were still running around being kids. And they had cooked lunch for me.

From the moment I arrived, this one little boy followed me everywhere. He was five or six years old, but he looked younger. It seemed as if he would break if you held him too tight. He sat in my lap and told me, very seriously, that he had a message for me. He told me I needed to make the world understand that children ought to be the priority for all adults.

When you have a little boy, an orphan, tell you this, it melts your heart because it is a reality, a real truth. We forget this truth all the time in our everyday lives. In the course of our daily routine we don't always think of children, of how their future is endangered by our unbridled consumption and our indifference.

He said, "You're not going to cry, right? We waited for you all day. You have to sing." But I just couldn't. "If you sing," he said, "we'll teach you something." They had a rallying cry at the orphanage: "*Mutoto Kwanza oyé oyé!*"–which means "children first!" in Swahili.

Mutoto Kwanza oyé oyé! Mutoto Kwanza oyé oyé!
Mutoto Kwanza oyé oyé! Mutoto Kwanza oyé oyé!
Mutoto Kwanza oyé oyé! Mutoto Kwanza oyé oyé!
Mutoto Kwanza oyé oyé! Mutoto Kwanza oyé oyé!
Mutoto Kwanza oyé oyé! Mutoto Kwanza oyé oyé!
Mutoto Kwanza oyé oyé! Mutoto Kwanza oyé oyé!
Mutoto Kwanza oyé oyé! Mutoto Kwanza oyé oyé!
Mutoto Kwanza oyé oyé! Mutoto Kwanza oyé oyé!
Mutoto Kwanza oyé oyé! Mutoto Kwanza oyé oyé!
Mutoto Kwanza oyé oyé! Mutoto Kwanza oyé oyé!
Mutoto Kwanza oyé oyé! Mutoto Kwanza oyé oyé!
Mutoto Kwanza oyé oyé! Mutoto Kwanza oyé oyé!
Mutoto Kwanza oyé oyé! Mutoto Kwanza oyé oyé!
Mutoto Kwanza oyé oyé! Mutoto Kwanza oyé oyé!
Mutoto Kwanza oyé oyé! Mutoto Kwanza oyé oyé!
Mutoto Kwanza oyé oyé! Mutoto Kwanza oyé oyé!
Mutoto Kwanza oyé oyé! Mutoto Kwanza oyé oyé!
Mutoto Kwanza oyé oyé! Mutoto Kwanza oyé oyé!
Mutoto Kwanza oyé oyé! Mutoto Kwanza oyé oyé!
Mutoto Kwanza oyé oyé! Mutoto Kwanza oyé oyé!
Mutoto Kwanza oyé oyé! Mutoto Kwanza oyé oyé!

After listening, I asked him, "Can I use your cry in a song?" I knew that more people would hear this message in a song than in an interview or a speech, broadcast once and then forgotten. He looked at me, thought for a while, and then said, "As long as the song isn't sad, as long as it makes you feel like dancing, then it's all right with us."

Sometimes I feel I get most of my inspiration from the people I meet on my continent. From this first trip forward, my work as an ambassador and as an artist complemented each other. The work with UNICEF inspired my music and my music helped me recover from those trips. I could have said my music was enough for me, but that was no longer possible. I had already seen too much. And we shouldn't fool ourselves by thinking we're so virtuous because we're helping people. The truth is, we learn so much from everyone we meet. They help us too, sometimes even more than we help them. I've often noticed how the life of someone coming back from a trip to Africa has been changed for the better.

I returned from this trip with the little "Mutoto Kwanza" melody in my head. I was full of energy and ready to embrace the final part of the trilogy: Africa and the West Indies. I immersed myself in the music of the Antilles. It's incredible to see how much influence that small group of islands has had on the history of global music: reggae, dancehall, dub (the predecessor to rap), salsa, calypso, rumba, zouk, the beguine, the mazurka. All these styles differ enormously from each other, each having its own personality, but everyone knows them, whether they realize it or not. Harry Belafonte made them popular in the fifties and sixties and they're still being used today. They've become a part of each of us, like a heartbeat.

I travelled first to Jamaica searching for the spirit of Bob Marley. Jamaica is incredible. The moment you step out of the airport, reggae is playing. At first I thought it was just for the Reggae Sunsplash Festival, where I was going to sing, but it's like this all year long. People live their regular lives, but with music as a constant soundtrack. People talk fast and everyone knows everyone. Like Africans, they have a joy for life that transcends money.

When Bob Marley sang his "Redemption Song," he made African people understand the truth about slavery. In Montego Bay, singing at the Reggae Sunsplash Festival, I felt the ghost of Marcus Garvey, the man who had created the first pan-African consciousness.

Next, I traveled to Saint Lucia, Martinique, and then Cuba. What struck me every time I arrived on one of those islands was the rhythm of the people walking in the street. There has to be a connection between the gait of people and their music. It's hard to describe, but when people in the Antilles walk they have a different rhythm from American blacks, and somewhat different from that of African blacks. In North America walking is accentuated on the upbeat—it's like the sound of hip-hop—but in Africa, we walk on the beat.

In Havana we stayed on Calle 16 in the Vedado, the old quarter one block from the Malecón, the large esplanade that runs alongside the sea. We met some of the musicians from Buena Vista Social Club. They were playing *son*, a style of music that combines Spanish elements and African rhythms. The men were in their seventies and eighties, but the music made their age fade away.

Music there has the same role as it does in Africa. Concerts don't matter as much as the fact that people come together to play. A lot of their music is inspired by the Yoruba religion, and you can still feel its presence so many centuries later. The music of the Santéria, the religion brought from West Africa to Cuba by the slaves, with its three *batá* drums, just like the Yoruba use, is the rhythmic foundation of Cuban music. On the other hand, the dancers' costumes have lost a lot of their African origin and each Yoruba orisha has been given the name of a Catholic saint. This practice of syncretism, combining different beliefs, means that they still sometimes use the African name, but it's like every African god has been given an alter ego. Shango is Saint Jerome, Yemandja is Our Lady of Regla.

I loved the smell of the sea while I was on these islands. It's like the smell of Cotonou. But even though I grew up near the sea, being so completely surrounded by water bothers me a little. In Benin, the sea is so dangerous. You have what they call a *barre*, a threshold. If you go over it, you can't come back. Growing up, I lost many friends that way. When I'm surrounded by the sea, I feel that there is no escape. Benin touches the sea, but only in the south. To the north is desert. I need those two opposites to make me feel free. So I can escape from water and I can escape from land. On an island, wherever you turn, there is water.

OPPOSITE: Honoring Bob Marley's legacy during the concert organized in Ethiopia for the sixtieth anniversary of his birth.

I also had that vague feeling I used to have in Cotonou during the Communist regime, the sense of being constantly watched—a feeling that Jean, who has never lived under a dictatorship, couldn't understand. It's the paranoia that comes with the lack of freedom of speech. You don't know what it is if you haven't lived in such a place. People who've only ever lived in a free country don't realize what a privilege it is to be able to do whatever you want. Until the Communist regime arrived, I had no fear. I could go from one house to another, and could say what I wanted. Then, all of a sudden they arrived and our house—which used to be an open space—was restricted. It was strange to have this same feeling in Havana.

While we were there, the newspapers ran a story that Miriam Makeba was in Cuba to perform for the anniversary of Castro's revolution. Through the years, she had become one of my biggest supporters and my friend. A few years after opening for her at the Olympia music hall in

Onstage at the Africa Festival in Würtzburg. I was with my role model, Miriam Makeba, and singer Lokua Kanza.

Paris, I met her at the jazz festival in Basel, Switzerland. We were staying at the same hotel and I got a message that she was looking for me. I went to her room and we talked for hours. She asked me what I thought about this term "world music." "Don't get me started," I said.

"They always put labels on us," she said. "It's like some people were sitting in an office and they wanted to call it third world music, but then they realized that wasn't politically correct." Miriam believed that all music should be available to everyone, without a stigma.

That night was the beginning of Miriam becoming my musical mother. She began to teach me some of the things she had learned about performing. "Never wear a watch onstage," she said. "Even if you don't mean to, you may look at it. Your audience will think you're bored and wonder why the hell are you're there."

In 1996 I was in South Africa and Miriam and I performed together at a charity concert in a huge sports center in Johannesburg. We sang "Malaïka" in a packed stadium while the audience held their umbrellas up against a pouring rain. Miriam wore her usual traditional fine headband of color beads and walked in a slow, majestic way. That day, in her presence, I felt a sense of wonderment, awe. But I have to admit I was a little scared too. I wanted to do all I could possibly do to make the tone of our voices complementary, like those of a mother and her daughter, so we would sing in a perfect harmony.

Before the show, we were in Miriam's dressing room and Naïma was sitting on her lap. At some point, Miriam got angry, with good reason, about a problem. She was so intense. There existed in her a duality. She had a high, soft voice, but she wasn't afraid to show her anger. In it you saw the power she had. Naïma got a little scared, but a smile from Miriam instantly soothed her.

The next night, we went to her home in a suburb outside of the city. The house was modern with big windows and we could see it from afar, a lighted box in the distance. She cooked so much food for us and for her granddaughter and grandson. "Since my daughter died," she said to me, "I'm a walking dead woman. My grandchildren are the ones keeping me going." She'd also invited a bunch of young African artists. Miriam liked to be surrounded by young artists. She worried they would think things from the outside are better than what they know at home. She often

told them, "Our music will disappear unless you continue to mix the traditional with the new."

In Havana, we heard she was staying at the Hotel Nacional, the grand symbol of Cuba, but when we went to see her we were told she wasn't there. We searched every big hotel in the city, but had no luck. I decided to call her house in South Africa to ask her family how we could find her. It was so hard to make that phone call in Cuba. You had to try for hours. We had to use the old phone booths lined in a row in a hallway off the hotel lobby. Pushing open the door and stepping inside felt like traveling back in time. Again and again we dialed, but nothing happened. Finally, we got a line out and the phone rang. On the other end, Miriam was the one who answered! The whole story had just been a rumor, possibly part of the propaganda around the anniversary of the revolution.

We returned from our trip to Cuba to record *Oyaya*, the third part of the trilogy. We recorded it at Glenwood Place in Los Angeles with Steve Berlin, the producer of the band Los Lobos. With his goatee and glasses, he looked so serious, like a teacher. He scribbled in a little notebook as he listened to our demos. Steve told us the album could be very unique if we worked with a Latin arranger. He brought in Alberto Salas, a phenomenal pianist and arranger, who had worked on Carlos Santana's *Supernatural* album. The only problem was that he knew absolutely nothing about African music! Because he hadn't been exposed to it, the link there was broken. "I'm going to teach you," I told him.

We went to Amoeba Music, the gigantic record store on Sunset Boulevard where you can find everything. We bought him Youssou N'Dour's *Set*, Salif Keita's *Soro*, Fela Kuti's *Best of*, and Cesária Évora's *Miss Perfumado*. He listened to them and then made fantastic arrangements that combined Latin know-how with African roots. In order to come up with all the melodies he was weaving with my voice, he was inspired by the rhythmic phrases the drums created. He heard the subliminal song the percussion instruments were singing and transposed it to the guitars, the brass, and the piano. This was so inspiring because we thought maybe that was what happened when the slaves first used Western instruments to shape their music.

The casting of the musicians was extraordinary. The drummer came from Puerto Rico, the percussionist was a grandson of a very famous

Mixing African melodies with Latin rhythm can require some hard work. Here I am with some of the cast of the album *Oyaya*: Antonio Salas, Rene Camacho, Ramon Stagnaro, and Walter Rodriguez.

Cuban percussionist. Alberto's father was Cuban and his mother was from Costa Rica. The guitarist Ramon Stagnaro came from Peru, where a whole African tradition can be found. The guitarist Dominic James, who can play Congolese guitar like no one else, joined us too. In the fifties and sixties, Congolese music was heavily influenced by Latin music. People came and went during the making of the album. It was a ceaseless dialogue between Africa and America and America and Africa.

We also had Rene Camacho, Celia Cruz's bassist. Salsa is huge in West Africa. When I was growing up, Celia Cruz was so popular and people in Cotonou became amazing salsa dancers. It is a whole science. It's not just steps. The timing is very different from other dances; it's all in the upbeat. The bass always anticipates the beat. And it's not only the feet that are dancing, it's the whole body. When you go left, your body dances on the

right. When you go right, your body dances on the left. It's a smooth undulating movement. As a couple, you decide which foot to start on.

My mom and dad danced wonderful salsa. As they got older, they danced more slowly, but the groove was always there. They taught us how to dance it too. Most of my nieces and nephews have learned from my brothers at parties. Naïma says her aunts and uncles are crazy good salsa dancers. My brother Yves taught her and it made me so happy to see the patience he had with her.

In Paris, in the early nineties, I got to meet Celia Cruz. One night we had dinner plans at Le Meridien with the Radio Nova journalist Remi Culpa-Copoul. He knows everything about Latin and Brazilian music. He used to be a journalist for *Libération* and is a legend in the Paris music scene. He looks like the cliché of the Frenchman with the baguette and beret, so his taste in music doesn't match his outward appearance. When Remi said, "Celia's here," I said, "Forget the dinner. Let's go meet her." I had seen her live with Johnny Pacheco in Benin when I was sixteen or seventeen. It was a show I'll never forget. She was so flamboyant, like an orisha onstage.

I can't speak Spanish, but when I met Celia in person for the first time, I was so excited I started singing "*Quimbara quimbara quimbamba. . . .*" When Remi explained a little about who I am and what I do, she said, "You're *mi hermana negra* from the other side of the ocean." Then she asked me to come sing that song with her that night. Her husband was the conductor of the band and he was nervous because we did it without rehearsal, but the moment was wonderful. Celia used her voice like a conga drum. She was so rhythmic that she could carry the whole band on her shoulders and turn the groove on its head. It was intense—a double energy. And having her bassist play on *Oyaya* meant the world to me.

What I remember most from the first day of those recording sessions were the musicians arriving at the studio in Burbank around one p.m. and ordering huge amounts of Cuban food. Jean and I said to each other, "This isn't possible. They're eating too much. They'll be falling asleep and we'll never get any work done." But the food was their fuel and as soon as they finished their meal they began to play with tremendous energy.

The first song we recorded, "Djovami," was so complicated—full of breaks, harmonies, and solos—that it took us the entire day, but it launched

angélique kidjo

OYAYA!

angélique kidjo
CONGOLEO

TOP: The album _Oyaya. Oyaya_ means joy. **LEFT:** The single _Congoleo_ is about the journey drums took from Africa to the Caribbean.

the album. After that, everything was recorded very quickly. Not all musicians can read and write music, but Cubans can. It goes back to the nineteenth century when the Cuban Africans had access to classical training. In the Western world, in order for everyone to play the same thing, we have to have written music. In Africa, because we don't have written music, we learn the music from the time we're born. It becomes part of our memory. When I started to learn how to read music in Paris, my teacher said, "Stop right now. You have a memory people would kill to have." I stopped because it felt mechanical to me, and it got in the way of the emotion of the song.

While we were recording, Ziggy Marley was recording in the studio next door. He is so friendly and open-minded, so one day when we were talking I explained my project to him. I said, "You should listen to 'Mutoto Kwanza.' It's my homage to ska."

"Oh, really?" he asked. "Do you have Jamaicans recording that?"

"No, Cubans. It's Latin."

He scratched his head.

I had taken the cry of the children I met at the orphanage in Tanzania and arranged it to ska's frenetic rhythm. I had promised to write a song for them that made people get up and dance and also gave them courage to fight for what's right.

When Ziggy came to listen, the whole time he was looking at me as if he thought I was completely crazy. But then he said, "Well now, really, I didn't expect this at all. It's different, but it's fantastic."

With Ziggy giving his seal of approval, I felt we had really pulled it off.

That last session we did for *Oyaya* gave me the feeling of completion.

If you are talking about the Caribbean and South American music, Henri Salvador, the French singer of Guadeloupen descent, has to be in there. In France he was the first famous black musician apart from Josephine Baker. His career spans over fifty years. He went to Brazil in the fifties and they say he contributed to inventing the bossa nova. Working with Quincy Jones in the sixties, he brought Caribbean music to France. He is the symbol of those islands.

Henri Salvador's music came to me through the banjo of my father. It was the music he was listening to when he was in his thirties and he used to play all those songs for us. He especially loved to sing "Petite Fleur." It

was written by Sidney Bechet in 1952 and recorded by Salvador at the end of the decade.

With Henri, his voice is velvet. There is a connection between him and the microphone. It's like they were born together. It's as if his voice is caressing the capsules of those old vintage mics from the fifties that we still use in the studio today.

When we went to Paris to record "Le Monde Comme un Bébé" with Henri, another song inspired by my work with UNICEF, we had never met him before. Our music publisher, Warner/Chappell, had sent it to him. Jean and I had composed it in Yoruba and so the African version was the one he heard. He said he loved it, but he wanted French lyrics, so Pierre Grillet, a famous French songwriter, wrote them.

Salvador was eighty-six years old at the time but his album *Jardin D'Hiver* was number one on the French charts. He was of the same generation as

Singing at the NAACP Image Awards with Ziggy Marley in 2008.

In the studio with the late Henri Salvador.

Buena Vista Social Club and had the same phenomenal late success.

It was a rainy day in September and we were in the Studios Ferber in the twentieth arrondissement of Paris, working with Renaud Letang, the man behind Manu Chao's *Clandestino*. You had to take the stairs down to the studio. It's like a bunker filled with smoke. Down there you don't see the light of day. When Henri arrived with his wife, we were still setting up so he said, "Okay, when you're ready, wake me up." And just like that he took a little nap.

When we played him the traditional Beninese rhythm of the song, he said "That's exactly what mazurka is in the Islands." He began singing it with his mouth, like scatting, and they recorded it. On the song, you think it's a shaker but it's Henri Salvador's voice.

I'm not crazy about studios, but Henri loved them. When he started singing, I thought, *So that's how you do it.* In a matter of seconds, he created the mood of the song. He was in the light of the studio with the wood floors glowing golden under his feet. I was on the other side of the glass, listening. He came very close to the microphone and sang like he was whispering a lullaby to a newborn:

> *Ah, si tout était doux*
> *Si tout était beau*
> *Ta main*
> *j'aurais moins besoin . . .*
>
> *Imagine*
> *Le monde comme un bébé*
> *Caresser et beaucoup*
> *Pardonner*

Ah, if all was so soft
If all was divine
Your hand
I would need much less . . .

Imagine
The world as a baby
Give it much caress and
Forgiveness

When he came back to the control room he listened to my voice. Then he said, "In the studio, you have to breathe like this for people not to hear." He showed me how he exhaled through his mouth and inhaled through his nose at the same time. When he sang, you couldn't even feel when he was breathing. It is something I still use to this day.

A few years later he was gone, but I will always have that memory of him, that moment, when he taught me how to breathe.

CHAPTER NINE

batonga

In February 2005, I was traveling with UNICEF to the city of Addis Ababa, right in the heart of Ethiopia. I had gone to visit a program they had created for young girls in Ethiopia, called "Coffee Time." Every Saturday, teenage girls would meet in a youth center and serve tea or coffee to their mothers and grandmothers. They would use the occasion to break taboo and openly discuss some of the worst traditions that they have to suffer, like excision—the process of genital mutilation also known as female circumcision—and early marriage. It was so simple, but so effective. The women of the older generations came to understand the girls' concerns and the girls had become their own activists, helping one another. They

were extremely close and as soon as they heard anyone talk about a girl who was going to be taken out of school and subjected to excision, they would pressure the community to prevent it.

To see girls of fourteen or sixteen be so mature and responsible was magnificent. I was impressed by the self-assurance they had gained and the active role they were playing in their own lives and the life of their community. But it was also sad because at that age they should have been able to be out with their friends, being teenagers, enjoying life. Although they were only around Naïma's age, they seemed so grown up. They had to be.

Talking with these young girls renewed my courage, and reminded me of my own experience growing up. In the middle school of Gbégamé, there were three girls—Yolande, Mathilde, and me. Yolande was tall and strong and Mathilde was petite. Growing up with so many older brothers, I used to think I was the littlest person in the world, but Mathilde was tiny, even smaller than me. Yolande's mother was a midwife at the nursing school next to the general hospital, and I didn't live far from our school, so at noon each day the three of us would have lunch either at Yolande's parents' house or at mine.

We managed to get bicycles and went everywhere in town. For years, we were inseparable in school and out. They called us the three musketeers. Being a girl and going to school all the way through our senior year was unusual at the time, and the boys were constantly teasing us for it. Like the young Ethiopian girls, we had to band together. Finally, when we were tired of hearing the boys utter their stupidities, I asked my dad, "What are we going to do to make them stop bothering us?" He answered me using the philosophical tone he always enjoyed, "Be creative and use your brain. That is your ultimate weapon."

I said to the girls, "Let's invent a word the boys won't be able to understand." That's when I made up the word *batonga*, which for us meant "Give me a break. I'll do what I want. I can be who I want to be!"

As a UNICEF ambassador, I have recorded many public service announcements, messages for radio and television that encourage parents to register their daughters as well as their sons in school. Through the years, I realized that because of the Millennium Development Goals the UN had set in 2000, the focus was exclusively on primary education. In Africa, primary education is free, though you have to pay for uniforms

and books, but for high school you also have to pay tuition. For most families, the cost is prohibitive, and so the possibility doesn't really exist. If they can afford it, the priority is to educate boys. Once I understood this, I couldn't get it out of my mind. I wanted to continue supporting primary school education and the great strides that had been made in it, but I also wanted to help make a high school education available to girls.

The pressure to remove girls from school is so great after elementary school because by then they've reached an age when they can help at home, taking care of chores and housework. Secondary education also happens at the crucial age at which girls are generally married, so going to school helps prevent early marriage. A higher level of education for girls will change Africa because it will allow more women to run businesses, to understand good health practices for themselves and for their children. Perhaps most importantly, it will give them the confidence they need to raise a generation of boys with more respect for women. I know this could be a scary proposition to some men, but this is how we will escape the circle of poverty and oppression.

Often on my trips as an ambassador, mothers will come up to me and ask for help. They can't afford to provide for their children. This is heart-rending because you know the next day you'll be gone, off to a different town with a different agenda, and, as crucial as it is, your advocacy work won't have an immediate effect on their lives. I've always felt torn between the need to speak on subjects that would increase society's awareness of the problems that the women and their daughters face, and wanting to help them directly. The more I traveled the more I felt this frustration. How could I be an advocate and, at the same time, make a difference in the lives of the girls I meet?

In 2004, the great Kenyan environmental activist Wangari Maathai received the Nobel Peace Prize. She was the first African woman to win it. I learned from her life story that when she was a young woman she had been part of the Kennedy Airlift, a scholarship program that enabled her to go to the United States to attend college. I thought, if a scholarship had turned one young African girl into a Nobel laureate, it could happen again and again.

In a way, advocating on behalf of UNICEF didn't feel like enough for me. Even though it takes passion and conviction, the hard work of implementing

With some of the girls supported by the Batonga Foundation in Benin.

the program is done before you start the task you're given. Everything is prepared for you. I began to think I wanted to create a foundation, one I would design the mission for and develop from the get-go. But with my music career and constant touring, I knew I couldn't do it alone. I needed to find people who shared my passion and whose goal wasn't creating publicity.

In 2006, someone at the UN introduced me to Mary Louise Cohen and John Phillips, two lawyers from Washington, DC, with a noble and selfless concern for Africa. Mary Louise's son had studied in Ethiopia and when she visited him there, she embraced the beauty of the continent and its people. Once she got back she knew her very core had been changed. With her husband she adopted a teenage Ethiopian boy with cancer. And she and John, her business partner, devoted so much of their time and resources to finding ways to help make a difference in Africa. The day Jean and I met them in New York at a little office on West Twenty-

Reading with a Batonga girl.

Fifth Street, our own lives were changed. So many people in the entertainment world only think of themselves, this can easily turn you into a cynic, but meeting people who want to do good without being in the spotlight makes you feel alive again.

We created the Batonga Foundation to give girls access to a secondary education, so they can become leaders and change Africa. The solution to Africa's problems must be provided by Africans who've experienced them firsthand, especially the African women who are the continent's backbone.

While Batonga was being formed, I continued with my advocacy. In April of 2006, I made a trip to the Horn of Africa with UNICEF and Oxfam. We first went to Kenya because the northern part of the country had suffered five years of drought. The people who were most affected were the nomads from the Wajir district who follow the seasonal migration of

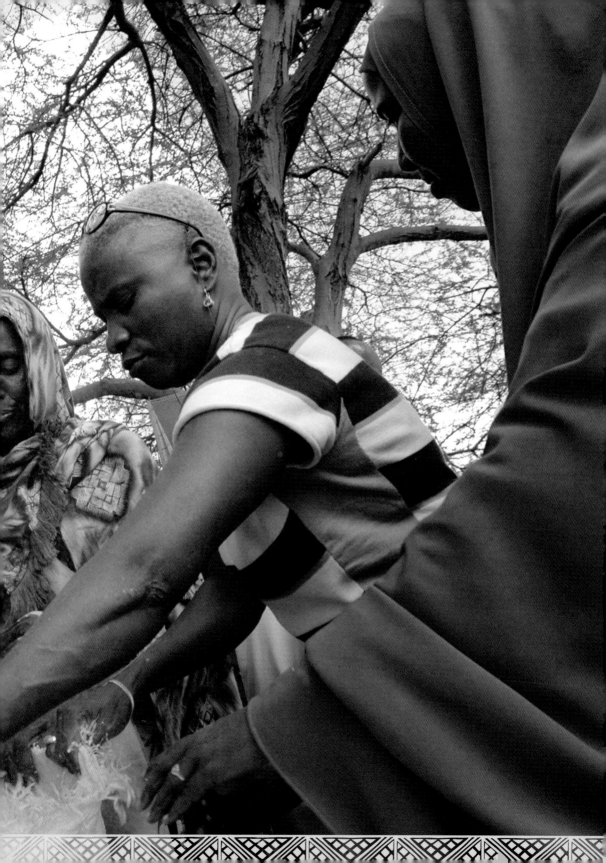

their livestock. Their livelihood is the herd. There is nothing else. The drought had been particularly violent that year, and when the rain finally came, it fell on the thousands of animal carcasses we passed along the way. The children were drinking toxic water from shallow wells contaminated by this runoff and by sewage from overflowing pit latrines. The carcasses had to be burned and the people had to be made aware of the harmfulness of the water and of the need to find a means for collecting clean rainwater.

UNICEF and Oxfam created mobile schools that followed the nomads so their children would be able to study. At a feeding center in the hospital in Kotode, I joined the health workers who were measuring out food for the families and weighing the children to evaluate the extent of their malnutrition. Chronic malnutrition experienced between birth and age two produces stunted growth. Young children who don't receive enough nutrients to grow at normal rates and aren't treated in time will be affected their entire lives, both physically and intellectually.

Almost one in four children are affected by stunting, but thanks to UNICEF advocacy, the rate is slowly dropping. The people who are part of the UNICEF and Oxfam communities understand that children must first and foremost be physically able to learn, and after that have access to education to improve their lives and the lives of future generations. It was inspiring for me to see these two organizations work together for the well-being of the people. They tried to help them in their emergency while at the same time building toward the future. Still, knowing change will take so much time is agonizing.

In Kenya I gave an interview about the conditions I was witnessing. This is how advocacy programs work. For governments to pay attention, for them to feel any pressure, there are interviews and a press conference on each trip. The interviewer and I watched severely malnourished babies we fed through tubes, and I could not hold my tears, even in front of her camera. She wanted to know my response, what I thought about what I was seeing, but in these moments it's hard to find words. I said, "I love my continent, more than I have any words to say. Every time I come here

PREVIOUS SPREAD: Visiting a feeding center in the village of Kotoda in 2006. Kotoda is in the Wajir district of Northern Kenya, which suffered a terrible drought.

I just want to cry. It's terrible. I don't know what to tell you, because there's too much pain."

We were working at the feeding center near the Somali border when a UNICEF staff member came to tell us that a village chief was waiting for us. He had come to bring me back to meet with some of the elders. I went with Dheepa Pandian. Originally from India with a heavy London accent, she is a tornado. She came to UNICEF from CNN and brought that culture of making things happen with her.

We soon found ourselves in a small village at the frontier, gathered in a hut behind someone's house. It provided some shade, but the sun still made its way through the woven palm fronds, spilling onto the sand under our feet. I was given a seat behind a little table. The men, each wearing a henna-dyed beard in the Muslim tradition, sat across from me. Dheepa was standing behind me, leaning against a cement wall at the edge of the yard. I knew she was nervous, that she wasn't sure how this was going to go. The elders began to talk to me about the education of the children in Somalia, and in their village. They told me that their country was in conflict, but they wanted to send their children to school. They valued education.

In Africa, respect for one's elders is sacred, and my parents taught me the importance of also having respect for people's traditions. But those that endanger the health of young girls—those that hurt women's bodies physically and symbolically—must be challenged. This conflict between tradition and modernity is felt all over the continent. The question is always how we can we find a third path—one where tradition is adapted to today's world without losing its identity.

I heard myself respond, saying "I want to help you establish an educational program, and I need you to help me help my sisters. You must promise me that excision will be done away with because mutilating girls is something I can neither accept nor support."

When I finished talking, the interpreter translated, and then there was silence. Who was I to teach them a moral lesson? A woman with short hair, without a veil in a country where most women are veiled, who knew so little about their culture and their traditions, and who had become socially privileged. What right did I have to speak to them in such a way?

Dheepa was shocked because I was speaking up to a group of men who were the same age as my parents, and because discussing female

Singing inside the General Assembly of the UN for the Raise Your Voice to End FGM concert in 2012.

genital mutilation is the ultimate taboo. But at that moment I was a UNICEF ambassador and an African woman, and I could not keep quiet about this while I had the chance to speak to these men face to face. It was essential for me to bring up this topic because if I wasn't going to do it, then who would? If you miss an opportunity like this, you regret it your entire life.

To my great surprise, the men agreed there was a very real problem. They may have been trying to deflect responsibility, but they said the cutting was done by women and they would have to work with them to stop it. Female genital mutilation is practiced as a rite of passage, and the women who perform it play an important role in their village. They hold positions of respect, and it's also a source of income for them. To stop it, a new rite has to be initiated to replace it, and new roles need to be created for these women. Instituting a ceremonial cutting helps to say that the tradition is respected. But awareness also needs to be raised to show that excision is nowhere in the Koran. It's not a Muslim practice.

It is hard for me to decide whether their response was really guided by a formal respect for my status as an ambassador and because they wanted my help, or whether they truly felt the world was changing and I was a messenger of that change. But I'll never forget the grave expression on their faces and the seriousness with which they promised me they'd change their custom. So far the violence has made it too dangerous for me to return. I'm hoping I will be able to go back soon. It was a conversation I wanted to continue.

In February 2012 the Italian Permanent Mission to the UN asked me to hold a concert inside the General Assembly building to help push a resolution condemning the practice of female genital mutilation and cutting (FGM/C). They felt that because I was a famous African woman, I was in a position to speak up. Many African ambassadors had been avoiding the topic. I don't know whether it is because of religious concerns or the shame of the matter, or because they're tired of being patronized by the West. But the Italian ambassador Cesare Maria Ragaglini and Stefano Mogini, one of his advisers, felt that a concert inside the General Assembly where I could freely talk about the subject would break the silence and provide an opportunity to have activists and UN agencies discuss means to end the practice in the presence of all the ambassadors who wouldn't want to miss the show.

At the end of the concert, it felt like a taboo had been broken by the joy of the event. People were dancing and singing in the aisles of the General Assembly. Still, that dome-shaped room, with its green marble and huge golden UN logo, had witnessed so much history. I worried that it would be just another concert and its purpose would be soon forgotten. Then, months later, in December of that year, we got the news that a resolution was passed and more than fifty African countries had finally agreed to sign it. I want to believe that the songs and speeches the night of my concert were instrumental in convincing the ambassadors to change their minds. Blending melody and message, music has special powers that politicians don't have.

Knowing that I felt that as an artist it was my responsibility to raise awareness when given the opportunity, the cultural services division of the French embassy asked me to sing during HIFA, Zimbabwe's Harare International Festival of the Arts. I accepted because I was eager to discover the country that Bob Marley had celebrated in 1980 at the time of its long-overdue independence: "Every man gotta right to decide his own destiny; and in this judgment there is no partiality," he sang.

But that same year, Robert Mugabe began his rule of Zimbabwe, first as prime minister and later as president. During this time, he had gone from being a liberator of his country to its merciless dictator.

My performance there in April 2006 was scheduled for almost exactly one year after Operation Murambatsvina, Shona for drive out rubbish, had begun. This large-scale movement of evictions and demolitions in urban areas was carried out without notice. More than seven hundred thousand people, most of them too poor to afford permanent housing, were affected. Many were rendered homeless at the start of the Zimbabwean winter. The government said it was an effort to rid cities of illegal housing, but the real goal was getting rid of Mugabe's political opposition, the urban poor.

Not long before my departure I received an e-mail from an anti-Mugabe activist who told me that if I were to perform in Zimbabwe, it would be seen as an act of support for Mugabe. Harare, the capital of Zimbabwe, was one of the hardest-hit cities and the activist urged me to either boycott HIFA or use my visit to speak out about the injustice in the country. I couldn't stop thinking about what she had written, so I discussed it with the people of Amnesty International. I had just worked

on *Instant Karma*, the John Lennon compilation benefitting Amnesty. Lynn Fredriksson, who was then their advocacy director for Africa, agreed that I could use the opportunity to speak out. She thought it could be done fairly subtly and still have a powerful effect. We all agreed it would be worth the risk and this advice strengthened my resolve to go to Zimbabwe.

Once there, I was in a country where although the infrastructures I saw from my taxi window seemed impressive—the roads were so clean and smooth—the people cannot even afford to feed themselves. Poverty can be evaluated by the outrageous inflation rate. To photocopy the set list of the concert at the hotel we were made to pay one hundred thousand Zimbabwean dollars in small banknotes.

The evening before the concert we held a press conference at the Crowne Plaza hotel with representatives of the French embassy in Zimbabwe. We were only supposed to talk about the festival, the music, the diversity of artists. Still, everyone was nervous. When the conference began someone came over to me and whispered that the CIO, President Mugabe's secret service, had just joined us, so we were careful to make sure we wouldn't create any controversy that would cancel the show.

Going onstage, I was like a warrior, I had a mission. I knew I had to make the Zimbabwean people understand how I felt. I knew that I had to say, *We know what is going on here—the president's abuse.* My voice would be with the ones who have no voice. The concert was in a little park behind the hotel, and with more than two thousand people in attendance it was jam-packed. The grass was burned brown by the sun and people were sitting up in the trees framing the park.

Jean was stressed out like crazy. In the dressing room, he told me to be

Talking to the audience during my concert in Harare.

careful. I said, "I'm not going to be careful. I'm mad as hell." He wouldn't stop me from singing–or from speaking–because he knew it was important, but you have to understand the paranoia of the country. The military is everywhere. Guns are everywhere. Everyone watches what they say. He looked at me for a long moment before saying, "Let's go for it."

I performed as if it were business as usual, until we were near the end. By now, "Afirika" had become something of an anthem, one I often sing with the audience, and it gives me a chance to go out into the crowd. Instead, I decided to use this moment to speak. As soon as I started talking, there was dead silence.

I looked out over the people and said, "We cannot always hold other countries responsible for our problems when, at times, it's our own leaders who are our executioners." Jean was in the wings, pacing back and forth, and now he stopped. We looked at each other and, even from onstage, I could see him holding his breath. I saw him thinking, *She's really doing it.*

"When a politician is at the head of a country, it is his duty to preserve and protect the people," I said, "not to take advantage of his position of power by torturing and abusing his population. This is untenable and unacceptable."

When I finished, the silence stretched on and on, like a long sustained note. Then, all at once, cheering rang out from everywhere. My guitarist started the syncopated introduction to "Afirika," and I moved to the steps in front of the stage and slowly danced down into the audience. The people surrounded me, forming a shield. I felt invincible. The crowd was so dense that it was hard to step anywhere. I saw the secret service moving behind the crowd. I couldn't tell if they were trying to get to me, but I knew they wouldn't make it through all those people. I was no longer afraid of anything. It was such an intense moment of communion–one that I will never forget. I saw tears in people's eyes. You can feel the pain of people in Zimbabwe, and this was a relief from the ceaseless tension they're forced to live with. People were clapping and screaming. It was like a cry of freedom.

Later that year, in November 2006, we traveled to Uganda. I was surprised by how beautiful it is there. I never expected it to be so green, so lush. It is called "the Pearl of Africa." Even after years of conflicts, you can still feel the infectious joy of the women. They came to welcome me

and held my hand and taught me their dance. It was unlike any I'd ever done in my life. You jump nonstop in a staccato rhythm. There I was in my jeans and UNICEF armband dancing with the women in their colorful dresses.

We went to the Lira district, in Northern Uganda, to visit the refugee camps of those who'd been displaced during the war with Joseph Kony's Lord's Resistance Army. Though the government had just agreed to a truce ending hostilities with the militia, a quick return to normal life was impossible. The devastation was too great. Some people returned to their homes, some remained in the refugee camps, but everyone was traumatized. We arrived in a camp that consisted of huts made of dried mud as far as the eye could see. It was then that I realized the scale of the conflict that had displaced so many. I went from hut to hut and tried to talk to as many people as possible.

BELOW: Speaking with a pregnant woman outside a health center at the Barr camp for people displaced by conflict in the northern Lira district in Uganda. • NEXT SPREAD: Surrounded by a group of children, I answered questions from the media at the Agweng camp for people displaced by conflict in the Lira district.

In Uganda there are very few teachers for the schools because most of them were killed during the conflict. Thousands and thousands of children were abducted to fight and kill for the LRA or forced into domestic and sexual slavery. You don't see everything these children have been through at first glance. I wondered how we ever got to this point. Our society is so developed, we have so much advanced technology. We are able to manage atoms, biology, communication, transportation, and construction, but we seem incapable of preserving the most basic human needs: the survival and education of our children.

UNICEF organized art workshops for these children and their drawings were unsettling. I met a child soldier and it was hard, very hard, to confront this boy's gaze. He didn't speak and he was always drawing people with guns in their hands. Just violence. I asked him to draw another story, and it was even more violent. These images still haunt me.

Next to this boy was a sixteen-year-old girl. This girl's entire family had been killed. She had managed to survive on her own before the militia found her and raped her repeatedly. She sat on the floor in front of me with her legs crossed. The way she was holding herself, it seemed like if death had taken her, she might have been happier. That's the sense I got, that her life had been crushed.

I was with a social worker and a psychologist and they told me how difficult it is to get the girls to talk. But how can you ask a girl of that age what happened to her? Even though she looks like a woman, she is still so young. She just looked at me like, *What can I tell you?*

I stayed with her for a long while, but I didn't ask her to speak. I knew exactly how she felt.

That evening in Uganda, after spending the afternoon in the camp, we were having a big meal with government representatives and UNICEF staff. Because UNICEF cannot get involved in the politics of the countries, the ambassadors serve as a conduit. I had to compose myself. I was there to take part in persuading the government to act, to help these children and protect them from further harm. Artists sometime have licenses that no one else does. We're able to deliver messages that aren't always politically correct.

After dinner, some of the children played music for us. The boy with the drawings came in and I watched him transform. He was singing with

the music, smiling. He came and took my hand and we danced together. I saw a flash of the boy he'd been and I was thankful that this world had not taken his childhood completely. The girl, though, would not come.

As difficult as this visit was, there would be another a few months later that would be even harder for me. In September 2007, I was invited by Mary Robinson, honorary president of Oxfam and the former president of Ireland, to join her on a trip with six other female activists to eastern Chad to meet the women living in the UN refugee camp for displaced persons from Darfur where tribal clashes have forced well over a million people from their homes. The group included Ngozi Okonjo-Iweala, who later became

Sitting down with the refugee women from Darfur and listening to their stories.

managing director of the World Bank; Jane Wales of the Global Philanthropy Forum; Bineta Diop, a powerful activist from Senegal and executive director of Femmes Africa Solidarité; Asha Hagi Elmi Amin, a member of the transitional parliament of Somalia; Dr. Herta Däubler-Gmelin, a German parliamentarian; and Musimbi Kanyoro, then the secretary general of the World YWCA (Young Women's Christian Association). Claire Lewis, a great voice from Oxfam, organized the delegation.

We went to the frontier of Sudan to talk with the women living in the camp. The horrors I learned about there hurt not only the woman I am, but also the mother I am, and the human being I am. We met twenty-three women, and each of their stories deeply affected me. It took weeks before I could sleep at night without being awakened by nightmares. One of the journalists accompanying us on the trip had brought her husband, and he came into the tent with us, but as soon as the first woman started talking he ran off. Just her story alone was too much for him. The woman had been kidnapped and raped, but she had managed to get away. When she made it back home, her husband said, "I don't want anything to do with you anymore" and then left, taking the children with him.

In World War II, it was tank against tank. But today, it's militias. Armed men they call the Janjaweed (Arabic for "armed horsemen") come to the house. They kill the husband and sons in front of the woman. At that moment she knows that to save her life and the lives of her daughters, she will do whatever they want. This is how rape has become a weapon. How can men find their own dignity again when they have raped a woman? To me it's as if they had violated their own mother, their daughter, or their sister. Why is it always the women who are made to suffer the most?

The camps in Chad aren't much safer than Sudanese villages because Janjaweed raids extend well into the frontier zone. When the women go to gather wood for cooking, they risk being attacked. But the camps provide these women with the opportunity to grow closer to each other and to take care of each other.

When they were in the village, they didn't believe much in educating their girls. They did what had been done for generations. But the women were offered education in the camps and began to learn how to read. It was the first time their daughters had ever gone to school. There were very few little boys because most of them had been killed.

These mothers had lost everything, but they saw the transformation of their children. They saw what could be. The women let us know that as soon as they were able to leave, the children would continue school because then their lives, at least, would be better. But in order for them to be able to go, a peace agreement would have to be reached between north and south Sudan. They asked us to campaign on their behalf so that this might happen.

Toward the end of our visit, one of the women charged us with a mission, and her words are engraved in my memory. She said, "When you're back in your countries and you talk about us, don't present us as victims but as strong women, as complete women, like you, fighting for our future. We don't want to be perceived as victims forever."

After our two days with these women, the delegation traveled to France to meet with the foreign minister and the Egyptian ambassador. In meetings like these, you feel angry and want to scream at our global complacency. Mary Robinson gave me lessons in diplomacy. You struggle with a boundary you can't cross, but you can't risk alienating these people either. She reminded me that anger will not bring a solution for these women. Instead, the frustration you feel should fuel your conviction. I know I must keep faith in the human spirit, and that I must remember the resilience of everyone I've met. I cannot forget how they've risen from ashes.

Mary Robinson and I have crossed paths many times. Here we are in Dakar, Senegal.

The emotions during these trips are always so intense, and I know I will be departing soon and leaving all these problems behind me. I always say to the UNICEF staff that my work is only the icing on the cake. They are the ones working there every day. Each time I leave, I

NEXT SPREAD: **The trip I made to the border of Chad and Darfur has affected me deeply.**

know I'm going back to Europe or to the United States. There, I'll realize how often people complain about trivial things. It's shocking to come back and deal with little problems that seem meaningless in comparison. But that, too, is life. We have to find ways to reconcile these two facets.

I still remember coming back from this trip. When I arrived at JFK I told the cab driver which way I wanted to go back to Brooklyn. After so many times, I know it by heart: the Van Wyck Expressway to North Conduit to Atlantic Ave, turn left onto Rockaway and then take Eastern Parkway. But he argued with me. He wanted to take another, longer route to increase the fare. I was tired and just wanted to get home, but you realize that this is his reality. And this is the reality that you live in, too.

Whenever I go back to my home continent, the strength of the people reminds me of the importance of life. They live under hard circumstances and are still able to laugh, to enjoy life to a certain extent. It's not like the Western world. Here, we live in fear of what we might lose. There, because of what is lost every day, you live in the moment. If I don't remember that, I can't help anyone. It's about honoring people's dignity; it's not about pity. Pity only brings you pain.

Back in Brooklyn, I started to dream of a new Africa, one that would spread its wings and change forever. The logo we had created for the Batonga Foundation is an image of two African maps, mirrored to form a butterfly. The metaphor inspired me to write the music for this song:

Djin, djin, djin
Abini n'djali
Djin, djin, djin
Abini n'djali
Djin, djin, djin
Abini ya dou ni ye
Abini ya dou ni ye

So now it's the time
Time for me to unwind
Take down the clock ticking on the wall
So I can free my mind

After the long exploration of the music of the diaspora, it was time to compose my next album, *Djin Djin*. My idea was to come back to my Beninese roots and share their beauty with artists from all corners of the world. Their presence would help me carry my message even further.

To help guide this effort, we asked Tony Visconti to produce the record. He had produced most of David Bowie's music, but he also recorded the Ghanaian band Osibisa in the seventies. He knows exactly how to capture the energy of African music: you create a moment of joy in the studio, and everybody plays together. I would record my vocal standing next to the drummer and although the sound would leak, we didn't care. I wanted to feel as if I was on a stage.

With Tony we assembled another great team of musicians. Joao Mota, who has played with me since *Logozo*, was there and also Habib Faye, the bass player from Youssou N'Dour's *Super Étoile*. I was also supported by Dominic James, Amp Fiddler, Puggie Bell, Benoit and Crespin from the Beninese Gangbé Brass Band, the horns from Antibalas, and Lionel Loueke, a young guitar player from Cotonou who had become Herbie Hancock's protégé. We rehearsed at a warehouse in Hell's Kitchen in New York and then moved to Electric Lady, Jimi Hendrix's studio in the West Village. The music was coming naturally, organically. I wanted to make it irresistible for the guest artists I was planning to invite.

The first one I called was Alicia Keys. I had met her in 2004 when Quincy Jones organized a concert in Rome at the Circus Maximus attended by everyone from Oprah to Angelina Jolie. I opened the concert with the Soweto Gospel Choir. When I saw that crowd—almost four hundred thousand people—it was the first time in my life that I had stage fright. When you're onstage under the lights, you can only see the faces of the people in the first couple of rows. After that, it's a moving, blurry mass. But I had never seen anything like this crowd. The people seemed to go on forever.

When I went back to my dressing room I passed Alicia in the hallway. We talked for a few minutes and she told me how much she enjoyed the performance. I didn't think I'd ever see her again, but a few months later I was in Glasgow doing a photo session for Oxfam's Make Trade Fair campaign. To criticize the dumping of subsidized produce from rich countries on African countries where the local farmers can't compete,

TOP LEFT: I recorded the album *Djin Djin* with the great producer Tony Visconti at Electric Lady in New York. • **TOP RIGHT:** Onstage with Josh Groban. Our musical worlds may be distant, but we made them meet in a beautiful way. • **MIDDLE:** Recording the album *Djin Djin* in New York with Romero Lubambo, Crespin Kpitiki, Benoit Avihoue, Habib Faye, and Amp Fiddler. • **BOTTOM:** Me and Peter Gabriel onstage for Mandela. Peter is one of the greatest supporters of African music.

Greg Williams photographed a series of musicians and actors covered in things like coffee, tomatoes, and milk. I was up to my ears in chicken feathers when I heard my cell phone ringing underneath the pile. It was Alicia calling to invite me to be a part of a concert on World Aids Day for her foundation, Keep a Child Alive. That's when we became friends.

In Alicia I sensed a passion for Africa that was devoid of any ambiguity or condescension. One day, while I was doing a tour in South Africa, I went with her while she visited her foundation's programs. We spent an afternoon with the grandmothers who've become like parents to their grandchildren because of the devastating effects of AIDS. Their stories were so painful that I reached a point where I couldn't handle it anymore and was on the verge of breaking down. I don't know how Alicia managed it, but she spent the entire afternoon taking it in, all while reassuring everyone.

The next day, during my concert in Johannesburg, I asked her to join us. Before the show, I asked her if she'd like to come down into the audience with me during "Afirika." Her bodyguards looked anxious, but she winked at me and said, "Don't worry, we'll do it." That really mattered to me. When she stepped off the stage, the crowd was so excited they couldn't believe their eyes. Alicia is part of a new generation of African Americans who are starting to be open to Africa.

When I sent her a few demos from *Djin Djin*, Alicia picked the title song right away. I remember the day she came to Electric Lady. It was a Friday. We'd prepared the tape, all the mics, set up a nice Indian rug and lit candles in the studio. Everyone was looking at their watches: 2:00, 2:15, 2:30. . . . Just when we wondered if she was coming, the phone rang. I could hear her smiling as she said, "Don't worry. I'll be there." She was just stuck in the traffic. When she arrived, she grabbed a yellow legal pad and had her lyrics written out in minutes. Done!

After this first guest, everything was easy: Carlos Santana joined Josh Groban on "Pearls." Josh's musical world seems so far from mine, but we both believe that music has no frontier. His heart is so big and so genuine. When he later invited me to open for his world tour, I knew how courageous this was. He was filling up stadiums and his fans had never heard African music before. After a couple of songs, they got it.

I met Joss Stone by accident upstairs at Electric Lady. She listened to my version of the Rolling Stones' "Gimme Shelter." She was so young she hadn't

ABOVE: A beautiful photo by Joshua Jordan for the album *Djin Djin*. ◦ OPPOSITE PAGE TOP: My notes. ◦ BOTTOM: Alicia's drafts of our song.

⑨ Djing, Djing

Djing, djing, djing ×2
Abini n'djali
Djing, djing, djing
∅ Abini ya dou ni yé ×2

Idées Couplet

Djing djing ~~nin agogo~~ lo dadjo
Agogo lo nin ayé wa
Djing, djing nin agogo ×2
N'kan l'okokan ninou ayéwa

Idées Pont

Igbadaun ni ayé
Madjé ki ayé è badjé o
Igbadou ni ayé
Awa omon ola o

Time takes us so many places
Fee the past to one future dreams
but the p.

Time goes so fast
from the past to the future we dream
but pres

Time goes so fast
So caught up in the past
~~wising~~ we so much of the future
So caught up in the future brings
we obet the present pass

So
~~bad~~ now is my time
time to ~~free my mind~~ ~~take me to~~ just unwinel
~~into alone~~ the clock ~~is telling~~ or the une
and so I can free my minel

Time goes so fast
So caught

life is about enjoyng every moment
grace its ~~fine~~ to ~~ag~~ me

yet heard the original, but when she sent me her tapes from Barbados a couple of weeks later her vocals had a fire that would have made Mick Jagger proud. Then Ziggy Marley joined on "Sedjedo." At last, with his sweet voice and lyrics, I could use the crazy *gogbahoun* rhythm of my village on a reggae song. This song would become one of my biggest successes in Benin. Amadou and Mariam, the blind couple from Mali, were coming through New York and they sang "C'est l'Amour," this is love, for me.

The most emotional moment came with Peter Gabriel. He is a true fan of the music of my continent. If you're an African artist, you know how important he is. I always see him by the side of a stage, and as he listens to an African artist he has that big smile across his face. He had agreed to sing on my song "Salala." In this song I am trying to express the inexplicable wonder I had experienced during the birth of my daughter. But we were getting close to the date of the mastering and nothing was coming. At the time we were mixing at Philip Glass's Looking Glass Studios in Noho when I took my courage in both hands and called Real World, Peter's studio in England. When I asked when he might be sending his work, he laughed and said, "You know that I have a reputation for taking a lot of time recording music, right?"

Once, in 2005 at the Africa Calling: Live 8 concert, Peter had introduced me onstage by saying "Angélique eats men for dinner," so he wasn't surprised when I responded, "No way, it has to be ready for Monday!" Sure enough, that Monday an e-mail came with a link to download a file. When Tony, Jean, and I listened the first time, his a cappella voice sent shivers down our spines:

> *O mama turn on the light in this place*
> *There's no smile like the smile on your face*
> *There's no joy like the joy of a soul coming in*

The album cover that Veronique and Paul, my old friends who had done the artwork of *Logozo*, designed expressed the album's message beautifully. Raising my arm, with the Batonga butterfly spreading its wings, I am looking up to a new Africa.

The following year was one of intense touring. At the end of it, my voice was so tired, I wasn't allowed to speak between shows. Then the news

came that *Djin Djin* was nominated for a Grammy. For the ceremony in Los Angeles, I was sent a few dresses to choose from, but because a singer's rib cage is developed from years of using your lungs, the only one that fit me was an empire-waist gown by Karl Lagerfeld. I got it the day before the show, so there wasn't time to hem it and I had to wear really high heels.

That night, Jean was on one side of me, and Kevin Morris and Jack Rovner, my managers, were on the other. I remember Jean kept turning his wedding ring around and around. This was my fourth nomination, so

The cover of the album *Djin Djin*. The title is the sound of the bell that will announce a new Africa.

I'd been through it before. Just before my category they announced the winner of the Grammy for Best Hawaiian Music. We watched as the forty musicians of *Treasures of Hawaiian Slack Key Guitar* all filed onstage. Jean said, "No, it's not possible. This will take forever."

Finally, they got to contemporary world music. When the presenter mispronounced *Djin Djin*, it took a few seconds for me to recognize the album title. When I realized I had won, even though I'd been in those heels for hours, I salsa danced my way across that stage. I remember holding my arms open and out, my gold and brown silk wrap fluttering around me.

After thanking Jean and Naïma for putting up with my craziness every day, and my management team and my label, I thanked the academy for recognizing that the music of this world comes from Africa. That we're all a part of Africa because humanity was born there. I said that from the time I started singing as a little girl, my mom and dad taught me always to follow my inspiration and never to compromise my music, but, above all, to give music to empower people all over the world. Music has no color, no language, no boundaries.

Backstage, when the photographers asked to take my picture, I had the sudden urge to balance the heavy Grammy trophy on my head, just as African women do to carry their load. It was my way of calling forth all of the women of my continent who had inspired me. I owed this moment to them. To their beauty, their resilience, and their strength.

OPPOSITE: I dedicated my Grammy to the women of Africa who carry their load on the head. They inspire me so much.

CHAPTER TEN

my father's voice

A few years ago, my mother told me about something that happened when I was a baby, just two months old. When she was pregnant with me, one of her cousins was getting married in Nigeria. The family really wanted my mother to be there, and so did she, so the bride set the wedding date for after I was born. At home, whatever the ceremony may be, whether it's a birth, a baptism, a wedding, you always need to make special clothes. You don't have to wear the same style of dress, but everyone has to wear the same printed fabric designed for the occasion. It's tradition. So my mother made her outfit and prepared the trip.

My father, on the other hand, wasn't all that eager for us to go. He said, "The baby is too small. She's too young for you to go to that wedding."

But my mother insisted. "They've waited just for my sake," she said. "I have to go." She wrapped me up in a swath of fabric and strapped me to her back as African mothers do and off we went. This is how my mother worked while caring for her children. We would feel her closeness, the rhythm as she pounded yams, and be lulled to sleep.

For the first forty-eight hours after we arrived in Lagos, everything was fine. And then, on the day of the wedding, I got sick. I had a fever. I wouldn't eat. I wouldn't drink. They took me to the doctor, but he didn't have an answer. My mother had told her family that my father didn't want me to go, and, finally, one of her great-aunts said to my mother, "You have to take this child back to her father. You'll miss the wedding, but it's better that you go back to Cotonou."

So she started the trip home in a panic. We rode sixty miles on a stretch of road along the Atlantic coast in a taxi packed with other people headed back to Cotonou. The whole time, I refused to nurse or take any water. I was moaning.

My father was a very elegant man. Here he is in the courtyard of our house in the sixties.

When my father arrived home from his work at the post office and he saw my mother with me, he knew something must be wrong. He jumped out of the car and came running toward us, all while asking one question after another. "Yvonne, what's going on? Why aren't you at the wedding? What happened?"

Before my mother can explain anything, I open my eyes and begin to babble. Suddenly, no more fever. There's nothing wrong with me.

I just needed to hear my father's voice.

To this day, if I don't have something of my father's with me, I feel sick. I keep a chain of his around my waist and I never remove it. It keeps him with me.

Before he passed away my father told me, "After I'm gone, just call on

In the courtyard of the family house in Cotonou with my brother Oscar, my mom, and my dad in 2004.

me and I will be there. It's only my body that is leaving." It comforts me when I think about that. Otherwise, I don't know how I would deal with his death. He was eighty-five when he suddenly got very sick. He was diagnosed with liver cancer, and, at first, we couldn't understand it because he never smoked or drank. But it was from his chronic malaria. He'd had it throughout his life.

When the sickness got bad, I had just finished touring the United States for *Djin Djin* after receiving my Grammy in Los Angeles. I was starting the European leg of the tour when Oscar and Paulette called to tell me, "He's waiting for you." I told everyone that if I didn't go, he would have to wait longer. It had only been a few weeks since his diagnosis and it didn't seem possible that this could be happening so soon. But Jean said, "No, no, you must go." Jean managed to find three days in between shows and he booked me a ticket from Paris to Cotonou.

When I got there, I could see that my father was not ready to die. He still had so much to say. He wanted to talk to us, but it was hard for him. That was so painful. You could see in his look that he hated to be powerless. I told him, "It's okay. Take your time."

Paulette and I stayed with him. He was dehydrated and I kept holding a cup of water to his lips so he would drink. As the hours slowly passed, I began to realize the gravity of the situation. My mom was in denial. She was in the kitchen, cooking, and she kept saying to me, "He's going to be fine." On his deathbed, my father told us to take care of our mother. He was worried she wouldn't be able to deal with it. That's why my father died in the arms of my sister. He said to her, "Stay with me. Don't let your mom stay with me."

When I left, I would not let myself believe I had seen my father for the last time, but ten days later, he passed away. That day, April 25, 2008, I was in Finland, playing at the Espoo Cultural Center just west of Helsinki. Jean called Manu, my tour manager, and said, "Please don't say anything to Angélique." He wanted to be the one to tell me. He felt it was his duty, and he was afraid of how I'd react. I remember this part happening in slow motion. Manu came to my room and handed me the phone. The first thing Jean said was, "You have to be courageous." And then he told me what happened.

My child and my husband were home in Brooklyn, alone without me. Naïma had a special relationship with my father. As a child, each time we returned to Cotonou, she would jump out of bed when she heard his voice. She'd run to sit on his lap, laughing and talking the whole time. My father would say, "Your daughter is as talkative as you." Jean only told me later that when Naïma heard the news, she couldn't stop crying. My child, who insists on going to school even when she's sick, would not go that day.

I was fortunate to have my cousin Evelyn there. She worked at a bank in London and every now and then she would come and see me on tour. Ten minutes after Jean called, Evelyn was in my hotel room. She found me on the floor crying, shaking,. She picked me up and said, "You can't do this. My uncle would not accept this."

Those first three hours were a blur. I was in another world. Evelyn walked me around and gave me water. She and my Manu didn't leave my side. I had a show that night, but I didn't think I could go on. I remembered my last conversation with my father. He asked me what a Grammy was and I explained it's like an Oscar, but for music instead of movies. "You've

OPPOSITE: I always receive so much love from my fans during a concert.

finally found a place where they recognize talent," he said. Then he said, "You came because you think I'm dying."

"No," I said, "I just want to take a little break from the tour."

He told me, "You have to promise not to cancel any show for me. Please promise. You were born to do this. It is a gift to be able to give joy and empower people."

I knew I had to keep my word. Manu and Evelyn helped me gather myself before the show. I barely put on any makeup. Evelyn had to help me get dressed. I thought maybe somehow my father had chosen where I was to be when he died. In a place that could help me. I've always loved Scandinavian countries because the women are empowered. Gender inequality is at its lowest level there. I told myself that I was singing in a country where women are strong, and that my father taught me to be strong.

When I walked onstage, I was there without being there. It was the first time I experienced being double. I was seeing myself walking in front of the spotlights. I thought, *Is it really me?* I couldn't feel my arms moving, my legs moving. It felt like the bones of my body were being set in place one by one.

When the concert started, I didn't hear the music. I just sang. It was coming from the place inside of me where the song lies waiting for me to perform it. That part of me was in charge. What kept me going was that every time I looked over at the musicians, they had big smiles on their faces. They were holding me up from the first song to the last. They'd all said we could cancel. They didn't know that my father had made me promise not to. In that moment, it felt like doing so would have been a betrayal.

It took so much out of me to do that show. It was the most painful thing I have ever done. It is not possible, not human, to be able to distance yourself from the heavy weight inside you, the pressure on your heart. To give a performance when you are grieving, it feels as if everything has been taken away from you because you are not yourself when you are out there, you are being someone else. It's something that you have to experience to understand. But somewhere there is a shred that is the link between you and that person and that is what keeps you going. Death is not the end of life, it's just another part of it. My mother always said that. Every child is born the same way. You bring nothing with you. You achieve everything

through your work on earth. The day you die, you leave it as your legacy. *All of us go down to the dust; yet even at the grave we make our song.*

The whole time I was thinking about my father. I said to him, *Wherever you are, you are doing this with me. You have to guide me through this.* And I know he was there that night because I could not have done it without him. At the end, during "Tumba," people from the audience came onstage to dance with me. It was such a comfort to have them around me. When I left the stage, everyone called for an encore, but I knew I would collapse. Still, they wouldn't stop asking, so I had to go back out. I was in tears and I said, "This is it. I'm sorry. I can't do it. I can't sing anymore because I just lost my father today." There was silence and then, after a moment, they all stood up for me. I felt so much love coming from them. Music had created a bond between us and that bond had the power to heal. This night will stay with me forever.

Afterward, I went back to Benin to help make arrangements for the funeral ceremony. At home, my brothers, sisters, and I gathered to prepare our father for burial. We each took a turn wrapping his

Mom and Dad dancing during a party at the house in Cotonou.

body in *aso oke*, hand-loomed cloth woven in many colors and patterns. This is a Yoruba funeral rite. The last layer is white, to symbolize becoming a child again. We were trying so hard to protect my mother that we didn't call her into the room before we closed the coffin. They had been married for sixty years. We knew it would not have been possible for her to say good-bye to him.

At the church, l'église Saint Jean-Baptiste, I wasn't prepared when the priest asked me to sing. It wasn't planned. I knew he meant well, but this is not a moment when you want to be singled out. My brothers, my sisters, we had all lost our father. All I wanted was to be with them, to carry our grief together. But I agreed. I sang "Okam Bale."

Okan balè o,okan balè o
Eminin kan ko lo wa l'ayé é
Omon dada l'émin
Mon nin èbi kpikpo
Mon mon gbogbo èbi témi l'ayé é

My heart is at peace
As I can feel the love
Of the whole family
So close to me

This song was written for my parents, and for my brothers and sisters. Knowing they will always love me for who I am, without judgment, gives me such strength. Knowing they will be there if I fall allows me to walk onto any stage. My wish, always, is to recreate for everyone the vibe and the life of our little house in Cotonou, to bring them to our world. At that moment in the church, I just wanted to get through the song, so I could return to my seat next to them. It was so hot. My throat was dry. I don't remember much else.

After I came home to Brooklyn, I had a dream where my father said to me, "Your crying and your pain are keeping me in limbo." He wanted me to tell my brothers and sisters that we had to let him go. He said he needed to prepare, so that he could continue to be there for us.

My father was a great listener. Whenever I called home to ask for his advice, he'd tell me to talk it through with him. When I'd finish my story, he would ask, "Why did you call me? Weren't you listening to yourself?" He sometimes put on a bit of a sententious tone, but he did it to make you laugh. "You have the solution already," he'd tell me. If I didn't see it, he would say, "Let's walk back." He made me find the solution, so I could learn and move on. I continue to try and approach my problems like this, and to try to help others to do it. When people come to a performance, they believe they're coming to listen to me, but what happens is that the music allows them to tap into themselves, to hear their own voices more clearly. This is the role my father played for me. For all of us.

At that time, Jean and I were listening to Bach's *Goldberg Variations*. There are periods when I listen to different music and I can't always explain

why. It fit my mood after my father's funeral. Everybody has a different way of dealing with trauma, and that was my way. In my pain, it was a link between home and my state of mind. When I listened to it I had the feeling I was floating, as if I wasn't really in direct contact with my soul. It was a way of distancing myself. Bach wrote that aria and here I am, centuries after, healing myself with it. Music is intemporal. It has no time. It stays forever.

I said to Jean, "Let's do something." I wrote down my father's words from my dream exactly. I took his words and printed them on the twenty-

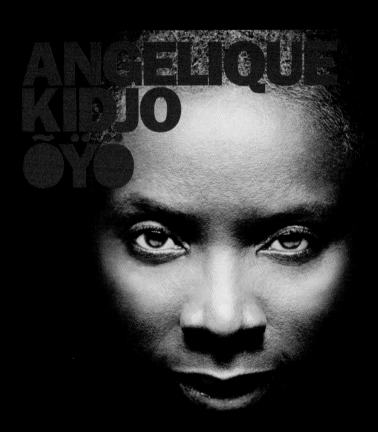

The album *Ōÿö*, a collection of songs from my childhood, dedicated to the memory of my father.

A publicity shot from *Ōÿö*.

fifth variation. The memory of my father's voice inspired me to record the album *Ōÿö*. In Yoruba, *öÿö* means beauty of arts, beauty of human spirit. My dad sang so beautifully and I had always said that one day we would record a duet together—but we never did. I thought I had more time. So this was a way to say good-bye to my father and to mourn and to really cry.

It was also my way of revisiting all those different kinds of music he was bringing to our home. He really opened our eyes to the music of Africa played by African descendants. James Brown, Curtis Mayfield, Aretha Franklin—all of those songs were turning in my head, like when the albums were spinning on that old record player in the living room back home. I can see all of my brothers and sisters hanging out under the *paillotte*, my parents in the kitchen, dancing. Santana's "Samba Pa Ti" is playing, my mother is in there cooking and he's reaching for her, saying, "Come on, let the food burn. This is our song." He is gone now, but the legacy of the music is there.

That year, 2008, a lot of things changed. As a girl, listening to those records, I was hopeful that one day we were going to see people of different backgrounds leading the world. The voice, the point of view of the West, would not be the only one heard. But I wasn't sure this change would happen in my lifetime. My father used to tell me, "Nothing is impossible." A few months after he passed away, the election of Barack Obama completely put that sentence in perspective for me.

The night he was elected, our daughter, Naïma, went to bed before the final results because she had school the next day, but she made us promise we would wake her up. When we did, she cried for an hour. "Mama, do you realize?" she kept saying. "Mama, do you realize the world is not a hopeless place?" She couldn't say anything else. As a child born to parents from different cultures, like she was and like Obama was, it showed her that skin color doesn't matter. We aren't really different from one another. Sorrow, suffering, and misery have no color, and no matter where we come from or what languages we speak, each of us must face up to our responsibilities, to our actions, and to our words. My father raised me to believe that, to keep believing that.

The next morning my dear friend Eve Ensler, the playwright who's all about empowering women, called and asked me to perform at the Peace

Ball on the night of the inauguration. When I sang at midnight at the Smithsonian National Postal Museum in Washington, DC, that venue, with its tall columns and marble floors, was nothing like the one in Benin where I appeared for the council of African presidents back in 1983. But for me it completed a full circle. It started with the president of Ghana telling me I had a responsibility to use my voice. After all these years of singing to bring understanding, compassion, I felt the world was moving, if slightly, in the right direction.

This day was a turning point: more than ever, it spurred my determination to help other African women and girls—and women around the world—fulfill their potential. I decided I would be unwavering in this. We have so much potential but the fear of how we will be perceived holds us back. I was so lucky to have the father I had. He put his three daughters through school when the whole neighborhood pressured him not to. I

At the Peace Ball on the night of Barack Obama's inauguration, with Joan Baez and my friend Eve Ensler.

want every African girl to have the same chance. I know the change won't come if the fathers in Africa–and elsewhere–don't realize a girl can achieve wonders if you give her wings to fly.

During my concerts, I always think that if my father was able to be the man he was, able to provide education for his ten children, there is no excuse for any other man not to try to do the same. He was not born from the moon. He was not perfect. But never at any moment in his life did he want us to do something other than what made us happy.

I remember him in his photo studio in the front of our house. He loved to capture moments with his camera, putting his Hasselblad on a tripod and standing tall behind it. He used to tell me he liked my profile, but as a young girl, I hated having to sit still and smile. I would say to him, "I want to play. I want to go," and bang my feet against the metal stool.

Behind the studio there was the dark room. I disliked the chemical smell, but I was always sneaking in there because with all the windows closed, it was the coolest place in the house. I liked assisting. I couldn't take pictures but I was good at the rest. I checked the timer and I loved seeing the image develop. I hung around during the portrait sittings just so later on I could watch the people appear on paper. Each time, I waited in the dark room, wondering if the picture would match what I'd seen. It was magic.

The process is like writing a song: it's you and your inspiration. It's a loneliness, but also very exciting. The result is always overwhelming. You think, *That was inside of me? Where did it come from?* For me, the inspiration is taking the picture and recording in the studio is developing it. In the end, you hope they match.

One photo my father took reveals the most decisive moment of my life: it's a picture of me from the night I left Benin and went into exile. Each time I look at it I am there again, reliving it: I am quiet, all day I am quiet, and as we prepare for the wedding, I run my hands up and down my dress, over and over again, trying to smooth out the wrinkles, to give my hands something to do, to contain my nerves, the fear, and sadness inside me.

We prepare ourselves and my things in advance. We have to be careful because everyone is watching. We attend my cousin's wedding in the afternoon, and I have to pretend everything is normal. In the evening, I

get ready as if I were going to the dinner. I bought this fancy white dress especially for that night, but I didn't realize it would be the only time I would wear it. I never saw it again.

As we leave, we close all the doors of the house. My father pulls the car into the garage and puts my suitcase in the trunk. When I was packing, my mother said, "You can't take the whole house with you. You're going to start a new life." But how do you pack for leaving forever? Inside are some winter clothes I made that will not be nearly warm enough, a few pieces of jewelry given to me by my grandmother that will eventually be stolen, and some photos in a little album.

Now my father turns to me and says, "We need to take one last picture." His voice was full, but even and calm as always.

Even in the heat, my hands go cold and sweaty. My heart pounds in my ears and I feel pain, like needles going down my back. I try to breathe it down, but it won't go away.

"You have to smile," my father says. I try to put on a good face, but what's going on behind my eyes is, *Am I really leaving all this behind?* If I stay, I may end up in jail. But if I go, what will be my fate? Will I disappear? One moment I think everything is going to be fine and the next moment I think, what if it all goes wrong?

I walk through the front door and wait for my father to bring the old white Citroën outside. I get in next to him on the passenger side. He's folded his tall, slender frame behind the wheel and his high cheekbones and fine features are outlined in the glimmer from the dashboard. As we drive slowly through the streets of Cotonou, people are out walking in all directions, making their way by the lighted store windows and the lamps of the vendors setting up for the night. We turn onto the Boulevard de la Marina and I open my window to let in the night air.

The smells of the city–tobacco, wood smoke, and hot palm oil for cooking–mix with the mineral smell of the ocean. With the sun down it's cooler, but only a little, and the wind is still warm on my face. In just a few hours, the fishermen will be back on the sand at the edge of the sea, preparing their nets for the day's work. By then, I will be landing in Paris. In my mind, these familiar images of home are already being replaced by the lights of Paris with its horizon of grey rooftops interrupted by the Eiffel Tower.

The night I left Benin.

We finally arrive, lucky not to have encountered any military road-blocks along the way. The airport is nearly deserted at this hour. The only people I see are Westerners, expatriates coming off the plane that will soon return to Paris. My father stops the car outside and leaves the engine running. It's better that he gets back to the party before anyone wonders where he is.

I am filled with that feeling of apprehension and hope so many immigrants must know. This is what carries me through the doors. One last look at my father and I know: there is no coming back.

epilogue

November 11, 2010

The night is falling early in New York at this time of year. People are lining up in the cold at the corner of Fifty-Seventh Street and Seventh Avenue. Looking downtown, you can see Times Square and its bright technicolor lights. A few people are still looking for tickets but a "SOLD OUT" banner crosses the white and red marquee: CARNEGIE HALL PRESENTS ANGÉLIQUE KIDJO AND SPECIAL GUESTS: THE SOUND OF THE DRUMS. You can see Times Square and its bright lights down on Seventh Avenue.

Inside, I am finishing my makeup in the master dressing room, and trying to keep my cool while friends are chatting all around me. There are black-and-white photos of Leonard Bernstein and Charles Munch on the wall, and on the Steinway, the beautiful flowers sent by Bono and the Edge.

I enter the glowing amber hall from the right singing Bella Bellow's "Sénié" a cappella. A gospel choir from Brooklyn joins in, walking slowly down the aisles. Behind me, my melting pot of musicians files onstage: Daniel, my drummer from New York, Magatte and Meia Noite,

Dancing with Omara Portuondo at Carnegie Hall in 2010.

percussionists from Senegal and Brazil; Romero on guitar is also from Brazil. Dominic is there with his African riffs. The pianist Thierry Vaton comes from the French West Indies and Alexis from Spain is on upright bass.

OPPOSITE: Singing "Afirika" with my audience.

Now I'm singing Miriam Makeba's "Lakutshoni Llanga." Always my role model, she played here exactly fifty years ago with Harry Belafonte. When I last saw her, she said to me, "My daughter, I can go now because you're here." Tonight I feel her standing at my side.

The music departs Africa for Cuba when Omara Portuondo, the great singer from Buena Vista Social Club, joins me on "Cachita," then on "Seyin Djro," and "Guantanamera." Like my mom, she has so much energy. She could sing forever. At the start of "Cold Sweat," my tribute to James Brown, the crowd gets on its feet. A few songs later, with Youssou N'Dour, we travel together to Jamaica for Bob Marley's "Redemption Song."

On this magical stage I am retracing the musical journey I have mapped through the years, following the steps of the slaves who left my country so long ago. Stomping her feet, the jazz singer Dianne Reeves enters the stage singing the negro spiritual "Canaan's Land." I join her on Aretha Franklin's "Baby I Love You." As if we are in a trance, our voices reach those high notes. During my Yoruba-inspired version of Curtis Mayfield's "Move On Up" everybody is dancing, and then I go down into the crowd for "Afirika." Even up in the balconies, people are singing with me! Our voices resonate under the arched ceiling. Tonight this place is my home.

Rules are strict at Carnegie Hall, and I don't know if they will let my audience join me onstage during "Tumba." Maybe the stage manager is taking a little nap? I'm not sure but the crowd suddenly rushes the bandstand and no one stops them! I see their smiling faces. People of every origin are following the crazy rhythm of the djembe solo: Americans from all the boroughs, Latinos and Haitians from Brooklyn, French people from the Upper East Side, and Africans from Little Senegal in Harlem. Naïma is here, getting down with me, while Jean watches everything from the wings.

Tonight, in our perfect little world, the spirit of love and understanding is rising.

It's a good start.

OPPOSITE TOP: Singing with the great Youssou N'Dour at Carnegie Hall. • MIDDLE: I always try to bring members of the audience on stage to dance with me, like we do in Benin. • BOTTOM LEFT: When you are onstage, you are one with the music. • BOTTOM RIGHT: At Carnegie Hall with Omara Portuando, Dianne Reeves, and audience members who came onstage to dance with us.

February 26, 2012

I am in the Nordeste region of Brazil for the opening of Carnival when I receive a message from Bono. In a couple of weeks, he is hosting an intimate dinner in Los Angeles with some of his friends who, like him, are passionate about the future of Africa. He would like me to be there.

When I arrive on March 4 at the Soho House restaurant on Sunset Boulevard in West Hollywood, I'm surprised to find a dining room full of people. There are no red carpets, no photographers, no TV crews, even though there must be thirty or forty of the most famous and glamorous people on the planet gathered together. We've been invited by Bono, George Clooney, and Bill Gates. I sit in front of Oprah Winfrey and Sean Penn, not far from Ellen DeGeneres, Ben Affleck, and Nicholas Kristof, the well-known journalist from the *New York Times*.

George Clooney opens the discussion and explains why we're here. He wanted to counter what he thinks is a general misconception about our reasons for raising funds for aid in Africa. It has even become the target of comedy. People are wondering why all these celebrities are involved in helping Africa. Are they doing it for their own publicity or are they sincere? People are asking, after all these years since the Live Aid concert in 1985, which raised millions to fight hunger in Africa, where are the results?

I have closely followed all the relief efforts, and I know that some of them have been very successful. I truly believe that music helped free Nelson Mandela. Johnny Clegg's song "Asimbonanga," which called for the release of Mandela, comes to mind, as does Peter Gabricl's "Biko" about anti-apartheid activist Steve Biko, who died while in police custody. Because so many artists wrote songs like these, it put real international pressure on South Africa to free Mandela and to end the apartheid.

Music has also lead to some amazing fundraisers. The 46664 concerts, which raised money for AIDS victims in Africa, are a good example of this. Musicians from all over the world have played at them. During one of these concerts, I went with Mandela to his former jail cell on Robben Island, off the coast of Cape Town. I entered the cell with Beyoncé and Peter Gabriel. It was so tiny, inversely proportional to the fame and aura of those artists whose voices worked to free him. I realized at that moment that the site of his humiliation and despair had become a place of pilgrimage.

In this beautiful restaurant, my mind also drifts to the time, in 1999, when I went to the New York offices of PolyGram Records to meet two high-ranking executives. Each wore a fancy pin on his lapel promoting debt relief in Africa. In those days, no one had heard about this yet, and talking about Africa was not in fashion. It was hard for me to wrap my mind around the fact that they were wearing these. I kept wondering, who put that issue on the map? Who made it "sexy" for them? They explained that Bono was launching this campaign, and they felt it was important to support it. It would become a tour de force, and a few years later after a lot of high profile campaigning, there was so much pressure on the G8 that a lot of African countries saw the burden of unjust debts lifted.

As the dinner progresses, some of the guests stand up and tell us about their experiences and their initiatives. An intense Sean Penn talks about the trials of Haiti. Matt Damon passionately explains his clean water project. Oprah announces the graduations of girls from her school in South Africa. There is also a speech by K'naan, the Somalian recording artist, explaining how painful and humiliating it can be for some African populations to always be on the receiving hand. It puts one's pride at risk. At one point Quincy Jones takes the floor and tells us what we need is more coordination between all these efforts. He explains that as an arranger he knows what it takes to make a powerful song. The flutes, the horns, the strings, they all have to be in their right place. All those beautiful parts interacting with one another makes the best song.

Before it is my turn to speak, I think about the women of my country. It is 9:00 p.m. here, so it must be 6:00 a.m. in West Africa. They are already up and going about their workload. I picture them and I look out at this room of beautiful people. There is so much goodwill to help Africa. I say, "Your great work will succeed when we have created a true human connection between all of us in the West and Africa. Most of the people we're trying to help are not familiar with the stars of the West. They don't even know that people so far away are trying to assist them. African people will have to be involved for a real change to be made in their lives."

This is not so hard to do and can be accomplished on a human level. If you know each other's culture through music and arts, you'll be able to call the person you're helping your friend. Only then will real change prevail.

recipes from my life

YASSA CHICKEN WITH LEMON AND SAFFRON JASMINE RICE

Serves 4 to 6 *Yassa chicken is a classic dish from West Africa and is very popular with guests who discover African food for the first time. My mom used to make it on special occasions. The way I personalize it is with my special Beninese marinade.*

BENINESE MARINADE
(makes 1 ¹/₃ cups*)
One 2.2 ounce bottle whole black peppercorns
¹/₃ cup peeled whole garlic cloves
¹/₂ cup peeled and coarsely chopped
   fresh ginger
²/₃ cup and 1 teaspoon water, divided
2 large white or yellow onions, halved,
   then cut into ¹/₄-inch slices
Juice of 10–12 lemons, about 2 cups

CHICKEN
2 pounds skinless boneless chicken breast,
   cut into 2-inch cubes
2 tablespoons instant chicken bouillon powder
2 cups water
2 teaspoons coarse salt
¹/₂ cup olive oil
2 cups low-sodium chicken stock
One whole green Scotch bonnet pepper
   or other chili pepper (optional)

SAFFRON JASMINE RICE
3 cups low-sodium chicken stock or water
Pinch saffron threads
¹/₂ teaspoon coarse salt
2 cups jasmine rice

PREPARE THE BENINESE MARINADE:
In a medium bowl, cover the peppercorns with cold water. Allow to soak overnight. Change water and then soak one more night.

Drain the peppercorns, put them in a blender with garlic, ginger, and 1 teaspoon water, and puree until smooth. Add ⅓ cup water and blend to form a smooth, moist paste. Add the remaining ⅓ cup water and continue to puree until the paste is very smooth and the peppercorns are barely visible.

Reserve a heaping tablespoon of the marinade for this recipe and refrigerate the rest in an airtight container for future use. It will keep for up to six months.

MARINATE THE ONIONS:
In a medium non-reactive bowl, combine onions and lemon juice, and cover. Make enough to able to be able to cover the chicken, so add more juice if necessary. Cover the bowl and refrigerate one hour.

MARINATE THE CHICKEN:
In a large bowl, combine the chicken with a heaping tablespoon of the marinade paste, chicken bouillon powder, 2 cups of water, and the salt. Stir well to coat the chicken. Cover with plastic wrap and refrigerate at least one hour or overnight.

PREPARE THE CHICKEN:
In a large Dutch oven or heavy-bottomed pot, heat olive oil until it is hot, but not smoking. Working in batches, place the chicken in the oil and brown it on all sides. Reduce heat to medium and return all the chicken to the pot. Add the onion-lemon juice mixture and chicken stock, and stir well to combine. Return the heat to high, and bring to a boil, then reduce it to medium, cover, and cook the chicken for 30 minutes.

Taste for seasoning and add the Scotch bonnet pepper if using. Reduce heat to low and continue cooking uncovered for 10 more minutes or until the chicken is cooked through. Remove the pepper before serving

While the chicken is cooking, prepare the saffron jasmine rice. In a large saucepan fitted with a lid, bring the chicken stock or water to a boil over high heat. Add saffron, salt, and rice and stir well. Return to a boil, then reduce the heat to low, cover, and cook 12–15 minutes or until liquid has been absorbed by the rice. Remove the pot from the heat and set aside, covered, for 5–10 minutes, to finish steaming the rice.

Fluff the rice with a fork and serve with the chicken.

MOYO WITH FISH AND PIRON

Serves 4 Moyo *is the name of a kind of cold salsa that is very popular in Benin. It can be eaten for lunch or dinner, or as a snack. It is something that anyone can make anywhere in the world and eat with anything. I often serve it with warm* piron, *which is a tasty tomato dough, and fish. The contrast between the cold salsa and the warm dough is delicious.*

FISH
4 cod fillets with skin, about 2 pounds
1 heaping teaspoon Beninese marinade
   (see recipe on page 246)
Coarse salt, to taste
1 tablespoon instant fish bouillon powder
⅓ cup water
1 tablespoon olive oil

MOYO SALSA *(yields 5 cups)*

1 medium red onion, cut into small, diced pieces
6 medium vine-ripened tomatoes, seeded and
   finely diced
Coarse salt and freshly ground black pepper,
   to taste
Juice of 2 lemons, about ½ cup
2 cups cold vegetable stock

PIRON

2 tablespoons olive oil
1 small red onion, thinly sliced
2 tablespoons tomato paste
1 Maggi vegetable bouillon cube
   (or ½ tablespoon instant vegetable
   bouillon powder)
1 cup tomato puree
½ teaspoon of brown sugar
2 cups cold water
1 cup *gari* flour (order online or purchase in
   African markets)

MARINATE THE FISH:

Place the cod fillets in a bowl and add Beninese marinade. Season to taste with salt, then add the fish bouillon and ⅓ cup water. With your hands, gently massage the marinade into the fish, and then add olive oil to coat it. Cover and refrigerate for at least 2 hours or overnight.

PREPARE THE MOYO SALSA:

Put the onion and tomatoes in an open airtight container. Season with salt and pepper, and stir to combine. Add the lemon juice and cold vegetable stock, and mix well. Taste and adjust the seasoning. Cover and refrigerate while you prepare the piron and finish the fish.

PREPARE THE PIRON:

Heat olive oil in a Dutch oven or heavy-bottomed pot over medium heat. Add the onion, and cook, stirring occasionally, until translucent. Stir

in the tomato paste. Then add the bouillon cube, crushing it with the back of a wooden spoon, and stir the mixture until the oil turns red. Stir in the pureed tomato and cook for 5 minutes. Taste for seasoning. If it is too acidic, add ½ teaspoon of brown sugar for balance. Keep heating for 5–7 minutes to cook the tomato. The sauce should not be too thick.

Add 2 cups cold water to the sauce, increase the heat to high, and bring it to a boil. Add more water if necessary to make the sauce a very thin broth. Slowly add the gari flour, stirring constantly with a wooden spoon to make sure there are no lumps. Reduce heat to medium-low and cook, stirring occasionally and pressing the mixture against the sides of the pan to achieve a smooth consistency. The piron is done cooking when the mixture is the consistency of smooth mashed potatoes, but sticky and beginning to pull away from the pot. This should take about 10 minutes.

Remove the pan from the heat. Sprinkle a bowl with water and transfer the piron to the bowl. With a wet hand, even out the top of the dough. Sprinkle a plate with water, cover the bowl with the plate, and invert the piron onto the plate. Keep the piron covered with the bowl until ready to serve.

GRILL THE FISH:

Heat a cast-iron grill pan over high heat and brush it with olive oil. Add the cod fillets skin side down and grill 5 minutes, then turn and cook 3 more minutes or until the fish is opaque and flaky.

Serve fish with the piron and moyo.

BEEF MAFFÉ / BEEF WITH PEANUT SAUCE AND YAM FUFU

Serves 4 to 6 *Maffé is one the most popular dishes in West Africa, particularly in Senegal, the Gambia, Mali, and the Ivory Coast. The dish has different names and different spellings depending on where you are, but it always includes a sauce thickened with peanuts.* Maffé *can be made with beef, lamb, chicken, or vegetables.* Fufu, *also very popular, is a thick paste made with starchy vegetables.*

BEEF
3 pounds of tender stewed beef, cut into
   1-inch cubes
1 tablespoon Beninese marinade
   (see recipe on page 246)
2 tablespoons (4 packages) Herb-ox®
   Sodium-Free Beef Bouillon
2 cups water
1 teaspoon coarse salt

PEANUT SAUCE
¹/₄ cup olive oil
1 large red onion, thinly sliced
2 tablespoons tomato paste
2 cups tomato puree
2 Maggi vegetable bouillon cubes
   (or 1 tablespoon instant vegetable
   bouillon powder)
1 raw sugar cube (or 1 teaspoon sugar)
1 cup smooth peanut butter
4 cups water

YAM FUFU
3 cups and 1 teaspoon of water
1 cup and two tablespoons powdered yam
   (available in African markets)

MARINATE THE MEAT:
In a large bowl, combine the beef, Beninese marinade, beef bouillon powder, and water. Stir well to combine the marinade and coat the beef. Cover and refrigerate for at least 2 hours or overnight.

COOK THE MEAT:
Place the beef in a large Dutch oven or heavy-bottomed pot. Add about two cups of water to cover, and bring to a boil over high heat. Boil 20 minutes. Transfer beef and water to a bowl and set aside.

MAKE THE SAUCE:
Wipe out the pot, then heat olive oil over medium heat. Add the onion

and sauté until translucent, about 10 minutes. Add the tomato paste, vegetable powder seasoning, and sugar cube. Stir in the pureed tomatoes and combine well. Cook partially covered and stirring occasionally for 20 minutes.

Return the beef with its water to the pot, add salt, stirring to combine, and cook 10 more minutes.

While the beef is cooking, combine peanut butter and warm water in a medium bowl. Mix together with your hands until it is smooth and all the water is incorporated. If it is too thick, add more water so it gets a sauce-like consistency.

Add the peanut sauce to the boiling beef stew, stirring well to incorporate it into the sauce. Reduce the heat to low and continue cooking, covered and stirring often for 10 minutes or until the meat is fork tender.

MAKE THE FUFU:
While the beef and peanut sauce cook, make the fufu. Bring 3 cups of water to a boil in a medium saucepan. Slowly add the powdered yam, stirring constantly with a wooden spoon and pressing the mixture against the sides of the pan to achieve a smooth consistency. The fufu is done cooking when the mixture is the consistency of smooth, but sticky whipped potatoes.

Place 1 teaspoon of water in a small bowl, and sprinkle a serving plate with water. Scoop out about ¾ cup of the fufu and place it in the bowl. With moist hands, begin rolling the fufu back and forth between your hands and the

bowl to form a ball. Transfer the fufu ball to the plate and repeat the process until you have used all the fufu. Cover with an inverted bowl until ready to serve.

Serve the beef with the fufu.

TROPICAL FRUIT SALAD WITH RHUBARB AND APPLE PIE

Serves 8 *I discovered rhubarb and Gala apples while living in France and combined the two to create this pie. A dear friend of mine has called it "haute couture" apple pie.*

RHUBARB AND APPLE PIE*
8 Gala apples
1 large rhubarb stalk
1 teaspoon liquid Stevia (or 2 teaspoons sugar)
1 teaspoon vanilla extract
⅓ cup water
PAM nonstick baking spray or one teaspoon unsalted butter, and flour for dusting
One store-bought pie dough for a 9-inch pie
2 heaping tablespoons dark brown sugar
1 teaspoon cinnamon

FRUIT SALAD *(makes 8 cups)*
½ teaspoon Stevia liquid (or 1 teaspoon sugar)
2 cups cubed pineapple, cut into ½-inch cubes
2 cups cubed papaya, cut into ½-inch cubes
2 cups cubed mango, cut into ½-inch cubes
One 20-ounce can of longan fruit, drained (see note below)
One 20-ounce can of jackfruit, drained and thinly sliced lengthwise (see note below)
2 cups Ceres® Medley of Fruits juice (or any blend of juices such as pear, guava, pineapple, papaya, mango, or passion fruit)

Note: Canned longan fruit and jackfruit can be found in Asian markets.

PREPARE THE RHUBARB APPLE SAUCE FOR THE PIE:

(Makes 2 ½ cups, more than you need for this recipe. The remaining rhubarb apple sauce can be refrigerated in an airtight container for up to one month.)

Core, peel, and cut 4 of the apples into 1-inch cubes. Place them in a medium saucepan. Clean, wash, and peel the rhubarb stalk. Cut it into 4 pieces and add them to the pot. Add the Stevia (or sugar), vanilla extract, and ⅓ cup of water. Cook over medium-high heat, stirring from time to time, or until the rhubarb dissolves and the apples are clear and soft, about 10–15 minutes. Remove pot from heat. Puree the fruit using an emersion blender or in batches in a food processor. Set aside to cool.

PREPARE THE APPLE PIE:

Preheat oven to 350°F (180°C) with a rack positioned in the lower third of the oven. Core, peel, and cut the 4 remaining apples into ¼-inch thick slices.

Spray a 9-inch pie pan with PAM nonstick baking spray or grease with one teaspoon of unsalted butter, then dust with flour. Line the pan with the pie dough, pressing evenly all around. Using the tines of a fork, prick the bottom and sides of the crust.

Spread ⅓ cup of the apple and rhubarb sauce evenly on top and up the sides of the crust. Begin by layering the slices of apple in an overlapping spiral pattern, working from the outer edge of the crust toward the center. Line the sides as well. Continue layering in this manner using all of the slices. Sprinkle the apples with dark brown sugar and cinnamon. Place the pie in the preheated oven and bake for 45 minutes or until the pie is bubbling around the edges and the crust is nicely browned.

PREPARE THE FRUIT SALAD:

Place the liquid Stevia (or 1 teaspoon sugar) in a large mixing bowl. Add the pineapple, papaya, mango, longan, jackfruit, and Ceres® fruit juice. Toss gently to combine. Cover with plastic wrap and refrigerate until ready to serve.

Slice the pie and serve with fruit salad on the side.

CRAB CURRY WITH SAFFRON JASMINE RICE

Serves 6 *We often ate crabs growing up in Benin, either in a gumbo or a crab-and-spinach stew, both very traditional dishes in West Africa. I learned this method of preparation from a South African friend of mine who is of Indian origin.*

SCOTCH BONNET PEPPER MIX*

20 Scotch bonnet peppers, stemmed and rinsed
1 medium red or sweet yellow onion, cut into
    large dices
1 tablespoon coarse salt
1/4 cup olive oil plus 2 tablespoons for topping
    the jar

CRAB

10 quarts water
3–4 tablespoons coarse salt
One dozen 6–7 1/2 inch live blue crabs,
    preferably female

CURRY

3 tablespoons olive oil
2 tablespoons tomato paste
Coarse salt, to taste
One 16 ounces box Pomi-brand strained
    tomatoes
1 raw sugar cube
1 heaping teaspoon whole cloves
1 heaping teaspoon coriander seeds
2 tablespoons ground turmeric
1 teaspoon pepper mix

SAFFRON JASMINE RICE

3 cups low-sodium chicken stock or water
Pinch saffron threads
1/2 teaspoon coarse salt
2 cups jasmine rice

PREPARE THE PEPPER MIX:

*(Makes about 2 cups, more than you need
for the recipe. The remaining mix can be
refrigerated in a jar topped with olive oil
and a tight-fitting lid.)*

Combine the Scotch bonnet pepper
and onion in a blender. Add salt and
puree until coarsely chopped. Add 1/4
cup olive oil and puree until combined,
scraping down the sides of the blender
as you go. The mixture should be
coarsely pureed. Transfer to an airtight
container and set aside. (Immerse the
blender jar in water for a week after
making the pepper mixture.)

PREPARE THE CRAB:

Combine 10 quarts of water and
3–4 tablespoons of salt in a very large
pot and bring to a boil. Add the crabs,
and boil for 12–15 minutes. Drain the
crabs and rinse under cold water.
When cool enough to handle, clean
the crabs and set aside.

MAKE THE CURRY:

Heat olive oil in a large Dutch oven or
heavy-bottomed pot over medium heat.
Add the tomato paste, 1 tablespoon of
salt, strained tomatoes, sugar cube,
cloves, coriander seeds, turmeric, and
1 teaspoon of the Scotch bonnet pepper
mix, stirring well to combine. Cook
10 minutes. Add the crabs and 1/2 cup
water. Reduce heat to medium and
cook, covered, stirring frequently,
for 25 minutes until the crabs absorb
the sauce.

Prepare the saffron rice while the crabs
are cooking. In a large saucepan fitted
with a lid, bring chicken stock or water
to a boil over high heat. Add saffron,
salt, and rice and stir well. Return to
boil, then reduce heat to low, cover,
and cook 12–15 minutes, or until liquid
has been absorbed by the rice. Remove
the pot from the heat and set aside,
covered for 5–10 minutes, to finish
steaming the rice.

Fluff rice with a fork and serve with the
crab curry.

BUYING AND CLEANING CRABS

Buy fresh, local, live crabs. They are available in warm water all months of the year. Reputable fish markets will often have live crabs, but call before you go. Once they arrive at the market, they are only good to be sold for a couple of days.

For this recipe, buy female crabs, also called *sooks*, because their egg roe adds a delicious element when added to the curry. Females can be easily identified by the orange color on the tips of their claws. Look for crabs that measure 6–7 ½ inches from point to point on their hard shell. This is the ideal size for the crab curry.

To clean the crabs after they have been boiled, first remove the claws from the body. Then, using the dull side of a knife, chop off the tips of the claws and crack the claws in several spots so when served, the shell comes off easily. Next, trim off the first two joints of each of the legs, leaving only the part that has meat in it. Slip your finger under the apron (this is a narrow and pointy plate in the male or a wide, triangular plate in the female), peel it back and discard. Then wedge your thumb under the top shell, pull it away from the body of the crab, and discard. Now clean the inside. Remove the feathery cones that line the inside of the body. These are the lungs and they are toxic, so be sure to get all pieces of them out. Reserve the eggs if the crabs are female, but scrape out the other gooey innards and discard. Finally, run the crab under cold water to rinse, and cut it in half.

acknowledgments

To my husband, Jean, and my daughter, Naïma, you are my inspiration!

I would like to thank my editor, Julia Abramoff, for her true passion and great tenacity. Rachel Wenrick, whose talent has been by my side even during the birth of her new child. Thank you Lynne Yeamans and Stephanie Stislow for a beautiful book. Melissa Vaughan, for helping me transcribe my African recipes into clear and detailed instructions. My managers, Jack Rovner and Kevin Morris, and their team, Summer Harty and Dexter Scott, for their never ending support. Bill Riley, my vocal coach, and Linda Caroll and Dr. Jean Abitbol for taking care of my vocal cords for so long. A special thanks also to Marta Schooler.

Archbishop Desmond Tutu, I can't thank you enough for your generosity and your heart. You are an inspiration for so many people in the world. Alicia Keys, your words have moved me so much, thank you!

I want to thank my whole family for being there for me since I was a little girl roaming the streets of Cotonou barefoot: Mom, Oscar, Paulette, Yves, Alfred, Mireille, Christian, Victor, Ernest. I hope we'll be able to gather in our courtyard soon. My family-in-law, Claudine, Yves, Georges, Maria, and all my nephews and nieces. All my friends, especially Véronique Mortaigne, Rémi Kolpa Kopoul, Bintou Simporé, Patrick Labesse, Karen Yee, Annie Ohayon, Evelyne Sodogandji, Roshnie Moonsammy, Jean-Claude, Janine and Groover, Virginie and Luc, Suzette, Véronique Kolasa, Paul Ritter, Romuald, Iman, and so many others around the globe.

A big thank you to all the great photographers who have contributed to this book, particularly Norman Jean Roy, Alfred Kidjo, Sophie Langlois, Tony Visconti, Pascal Signolet, Ueli Frey, Philippe Cibille, Xavier de Nauw, Michel Meyer, Bonnie Pietila, Bugs Steffen, Bill Akwa Bétotè, Banning Eyre, and Isabelle Rozenbaum. Thank you so much for your generosity. Georgine Dat at Vlsico, Antonio Pasagali, Patricia Escalda at Warner/Chappell, and Marie Jane Marcassiano, you've helped make this book very special!

To Chris Blackwell for his artistic support.

I want to salute my family at UNICEF, Fran, Dheepa, Marissa, Malene, and so many others who have traveled with me all over Africa. Big up to everyone at Oxfam International, and to Claire Lewis in

particular. Mary Louise and Bruce Cohen, John Philips and Stephanie Cate, your passion for the Batonga Foundation is amazing!

Acknowledgments to the late Miriam Makeba, Claude Nobs, Alain Guerini, Mamadou Konté, Timothy White, and Philippe Constantin, who believed in me.

So many musicians have given me much support through the years, just to cite a few: Carlos Santana, Peter Gabriel, Bono, Ziggy Marley, Josh Groban, Youssou N'Dour, Quincy Jones, Dave Matthews, Branford Marsalis, Dianne Reeves, Lizz Wright, John Legend, Steve Jordan, Christian McBride. Thank you for all the collaborations: I've learned so much from you.

Special thanks also go to Marjolijn de Jager for her amazing translation work and support. You have been instrumental in helping to create this book. I could not have done it without you.

PHOTOGRAPH CREDITS

VLISCO FABRICS

The patterns that open each chapter are from the fabrics of Vlisco. Since 1846, Vlisco has made authentic Dutch Wax fabrics through a production process derived from Batique techniques. As a result, each fabric has a unique story to tell.

To date, Vlisco has created more that 350,000 textile designs. The company is known for the influence it's had over the fashion landscape of West and Central Africa, and today their unique fabrics can be seen around the globe. For more information, visit their website, http://www.vlisco.com.